User's Guide and Reference

Microsoft® OLE Control
Developer's Kit

GW00500828

Microsoft Corporation

PUBLISHED BY
Microsoft Press
A Division of Microsoft Corporation
One Microsoft Way
Redmond, Washington 98052-6399

Library of Congress Cataloging-in-Publication Data
Microsoft OLE control developer's kit / Microsoft Corporation.
      p.   cm.
   Includes index.
   ISBN 1-55615-805-X
    1. C (Computer program language) 2. C++ (Computer program
language) 3. Microsoft Windows (Computer file) I. Microsoft
Corporation.
  QA76.73.C15M524   1994
  005.7'1262--dc20
                                94-30462
                                   CIP

Printed and bound in the United States of America.

1 2 3 4 5 6 7 8 9 QMQM 9 8 7 6 5 4

Distributed to the book trade in Canada by Macmillan of Canada, a division of Canada Publishing Corporation.

A CIP catalogue record for this book is available from the British Library.

Microsoft Press books are available through booksellers and distributors worldwide. For further information about international editions, contact your local Microsoft Corporation office. Or contact Microsoft Press International directly at fax (206) 936-7329.

Contents

Part 3   Class Library Reference: CDK Extensions

Part 4   Appendixes

About This Book

This book includes information to help you become familiar with the OLE Custom Control Development Kit (CDK) and to help you understand how to use the various development tools and new classes provided with the CDK. The book consists of four parts:

- The CDK Circle Sample Tutorial demonstrates various features of this product, including new concepts such as OLE event handling and OLE methods and properties.

- The CDK Programmer's Guide contains reference information on various features of an OLE control and many procedures for implementing features, such as event handling, adding methods and properties, and serializing the state of an OLE control.

- The CDK Extensions to the Class Library Reference contains an alphabetical listing of the classes available for building an OLE control.

- The Appendixes provide more detailed information on VBX Control Migration, Advanced Topics, Adding OLE Custom Controls to an Existing Project, and OLE Controls Architecture.

Document Conventions

This book uses the following typographic conventions:

Example	Description
STDIO.H	Uppercase letters indicate filenames, registers, and terms used at the operating-system command level
char, _setcolor, __far	Bold type indicates C and C++ keywords, operators, language-specific characters, and library routines. Within discussions of syntax, bold type indicates that the text must be entered exactly as shown.
	Many constants, functions, and keywords begin with either a single or double underscore. These are required as part of the name. For example, the compiler recognizes the **__cplusplus** manifest constant only when the leading double underscore is included.
expression	Words in italics indicate placeholders for information you must supply, such as a filename. Italic type is also used occasionally for emphasis in the text.
[[*option*]]	Items inside double square brackets are optional.

Example	Description
**#pragma pack {1	2}**	Braces and a vertical bar indicate a choice among two or more items. You must choose one of these items unless double square brackets (⟦ ⟧) surround the braces.
`#include <io.h>`	This font is used for examples, user input, program output, and error messages in text.
CL ⟦*option...*⟧ *file...*	Three dots (an ellipsis) following an item indicate that more items having the same form may appear.

`while()`
`{`
`.`
`.`
`.`
`}`
	A column or row of three dots tells you that part of an example program has been intentionally omitted.

CTRL+ENTER	Small capital letters are used to indicate the names of keys on the keyboard. When you see a plus sign (+) between two key names, you should hold down the first key while pressing the second. The carriage-return key, sometimes marked as a bent arrow on the keyboard, is called ENTER.
"argument"	Quotation marks enclose a new term the first time it is defined in text.
`"C string"`	Some C constructs, such as strings, require quotation marks. Quotation marks required by the language have the form " " and ' ' rather than " " and ' '.
Dynamic-Link Library (DLL)	The first time an acronym is used, it is usually spelled out.
Microsoft Specific →	Some features documented in this book have special usage constraints. A heading identifying the nature of the exception, followed by an arrow, marks the beginning of these exception features.
END Microsoft Specific	**END** followed by the exception heading marks the end of text about a feature which has a usage constraint.
▶ `CEnterDlg;`	The arrow adjacent to the code indicates that it has been altered from a previous example, usually because you are being instructed to edit it.

P A R T 1

CDK Circle Sample Tutorial

Introduction: Creating an OLE Custom Control

An "OLE custom control" is an Object Linking and Embedding (OLE) 2 object with an extended interface that lets it behave like a control for Windows.

In this tutorial you will use the tools included with the OLE Custom Control Development Kit (CDK) to create a simple OLE control called Circle. The Circle control demonstrates most of the features of an OLE control, such as properties, events, property pages, and data binding.

Note This tutorial assumes that you are already familiar with Microsoft Visual C++ and the basics of the Microsoft Foundation Class Library. If you are not, follow the Scribble tutorial in Chapter 2 of the *Class Library User's Guide* (if you are using Visual C++ 1.5) or Chapter 6 of *Introducing Visual C++* (if you are using Visual C++ 2.0) before you begin this tutorial. The Scribble tutorial introduces important class library concepts and techniques and teaches you how to use ClassWizard and the Visual C++ development environment.

The Tutorial Example: Circle

The Circle tutorial consists of several steps. The sample programs in CIRC1, CIRC2, and CIRC3 in \MSVC\CDK16\SAMPLES (\MSVC20\CDK32\SAMPLES for the 32-bit version of the CDK) contain a Visual C++ project file, complete source files, and other files for a version of the Circle control corresponding to progressive stages of the tutorial. Each directory contains everything needed to build a complete control. The CIRC1 sample shows Circle just after it has been created. The CIRC2 sample shows Circle after several properties and events have been added. The CIRC3 sample shows the completed Circle control. These samples are installed along with the CDK.

In successive chapters, you will learn how to:

- Create a skeleton OLE control.
- Test OLE controls in Test Container.
- Change the painting behavior of an OLE control.
- Add stock properties to an OLE control.
- Add various types of custom properties to an OLE control.
- Make an OLE control respond to mouse events.
- Add custom events to an OLE control.
- Use text and fonts in OLE controls.

- Implement OLE control property pages.
- Use simple data binding for control properties.

You can use the tutorial in two ways:

- Read the source files for each step along with the tutorial.
- Create files and enter code along with the tutorial. Lines of code you should enter are shown marked in the margin with a ▸ symbol. At the end of each step, build your program for that step and compare your source files with the samples.

Note that the sample source code in CIRC1, CIRC2, and CIRC3 is not exactly the same as the source code produced by the tutorial. In the tutorial, where strings, identifiers, or filenames contain the string "circ", CIRC1 uses "circ1", CIRC2 uses "circ2", and CIRC3 uses "circ3". The main control class in the tutorial is **CircCtrl**, but in the CIRC3 sample it is **Circ3Ctrl**. This naming difference permits each stage of the Circle control to be registered as a distinct OLE control. All three of the sample controls and the control you develop by following the tutorial can be used in Test Container at the same time. The sample controls behave the same way as the control produced by following the tutorial.

Other CDK Samples

The CIRC1, CIRC2, and CIRC3 samples are just a few of the samples included with the CDK. Other samples show how to use other features of the CDK:

- BUTTON - A control subclassed from a Windows button control. Demonstrates use of an in-place active menu, a stock property page, and the About box control option.
- CIRC1 - The Circle control just after it is created with ControlWizard.
- CIRC2 - The Circle control after several properties and events have been added.
- CIRC3 - The completed Circle control. Demonstrates OLE control basics, including control painting, stock and custom properties, stock and custom events, use of colors and fonts, the stock Font property page, the default property page, and versioning.
- LICENSED - A control which enforces use of a design time and run time license.
- LOCALIZE - A control with a localized user interface. Demonstrates use of separate type libraries and resource DLLs for localization.
- PAL - A control that displays the colors of a palette. Demonstrates read-only properties, persistent Get/Set properties, persistent parameterized properties, and picture properties.
- PUSH - A control subclassed from a Windows owner-drawn button control. Demonstrates stock properties, custom events, and picture holders.

- SPINDIAL - A control with the visual appearance of a spin-dial. Demonstrates property page data validation.
- TIME - A control which is invisible at runtime and fires a timer event at set intervals. Demonstrates notification functions and ambient properties.
- XLIST - A control, subclassed from a Windows list box, that displays text or bitmap items. Demonstrates methods, ambient properties, picture holders, and font holders.

CHAPTER 1

Creating the Circle Control

This chapter introduces the Circle sample tutorial, which uses the Circle control to explore the variety of features and functions provided by the Control Development Kit (CDK). Each chapter in this tutorial represents one step in the development cycle.

Note You can find the code produced by doing the code samples in this chapter in the CIRC1 sample source code directory.

The version of the Circle control developed in this chapter is designed to be simple. This tutorial describes the minimal requirements of a control and the default behaviors provided by the CDK.

In this chapter you will view a preview of the Circle control, and learn how to:

- Generate the Circle control template using ControlWizard.
- Modify the default control bitmap.
- Modifying the default About Circ control dialog box .
- Build the control.
- Register the control.
- Test the control using Test Container.

Preview of the Circle Control

Before you work through the steps for creating the Circle control, you may want to try out the completed control in Test Container. This will help you understand OLE controls and OLE control containers in general, and Circle in particular. The CIRC3 sample is an OLE control that is very similar to the completed Circle control.

Note The following procedures for building, registering, and testing the CIRC3 sample control assume that the Visual C++ development environment is running.

You'll begin by building the CIRC3 sample. An OLE control is built in much the same way as a typical dynamic-link library (DLL), but with an added step to build the OLE control's type library.

▶ **To build the CIRC3 version of the Circle control (16-bit version)**

1. Open the \MSVC\CDK16\SAMPLES\CIRC3\CIRC3.MAK project file.

2. Build the type library for CIRC3 by choosing Make TypeLib from the Tools menu.

   A message box appears, confirming that the Type Library was successfully generated. Choose OK to close the message box.

3. Build CIRC3.DLL by choosing Build CIRC3.DLL from the Project menu or by choosing the Build button on the toolbar.

▶ **To build the CIRC3 version of the Circle control (32-bit version)**

1. Open the \MSVC20\CDK32\SAMPLES\CIRC3\CIRC332.MAK project file.

2. Build CIRC3.DLL by choosing Build CIRC3.OCX from the Project menu or by choosing the Build button on the toolbar.

Next, register the CIRC3 control. OLE controls must be registered before they can be used.

▶ **To register the CIRC3 version of the Circle control**

1. Choose Register Control in the Tools menu.

   A message box appears, telling you that the control was successfully registered. Choose OK to close the message box.

Finally, insert a CIRC3 control into Test Container and experiment with it.

▶ **To insert the CIRC3 control into Test Container**

1. From the Tools menu, choose Test Container.

2. In Test Container, choose Insert OLE Control from the Edit menu.

   The Insert OLE Control dialog box appears.

3. Choose Circ3 Control in the Object Class list box and choose OK.

   A Circ3 control with a hashed border and resize handles is inserted into Test Container.

You can now experiment with CIRC3 to see how it works. Try any of the following:

- Click on the Test Container window outside of the control. The hashed border and resize handles disappear.
- Click on the control. The hashed border and resize handles reappear.
- Move the control around by clicking on the hashed border and dragging the control to a different place in the window.
- Change the size and shape of the control by clicking on any of the resize handles and dragging the control outline to a different shape.
- When you're done, close Test Container.

Following similar steps, the CIRC1 and CIRC2 samples can be built and Circ1 controls and Circ2 controls can be inserted into Test Container.

This is only an overview of OLE controls and Test Container. Each step above and many more details are explained in the tutorial.

Creating the Basic Control

The first step in developing an OLE custom control is to create the project using ControlWizard. A project is composed of a basic set of classes, resources, and definition files. You will use ControlWizard to create the first version of the Circle control. The control that is created by ControlWizard will draw itself as the outline of an ellipse. No properties, events, or methods are implemented in this step.

▶ **To create the Circle control**

1. From the Tools menu, choose ControlWizard.
2. In the Project Name text box, type `circ`.

    This specifies the name of the project.
3. Using the Directory list box, select an appropriate project path.
4. Choose the OK button.

    The New Control Information dialog box appears.
5. Choose the Create button.

    The New Control Information dialog box closes and the project is created and opened in the development environment.

ControlWizard creates all the necessary files to build the Circle control dynamic-link library (DLL). Of these files, three class templates are created:

Class	Files	Comments
CCircApp	CIRC.H CIRC.CPP	Implements the Main DLL source. Typically there will not be any need to modify this code.
CCircCtrl	CIRCCTL.H CIRCCTL.CPP	Implements the actual control functionality. Modify this class's code to implement control-specific behavior.
CCircPropPage	CIRCPPG.H CIRCPPG.CPP	Provides a template for the control's property page. Modify this class and its dialog template to implement a control-specific property page.

ControlWizard creates several other files that you will modify later in this chapter and in subsequent chapters:

File	Comments
CIRC.ODL	Textually defines the control's type information. This file is modified by ClassWizard when you add properties, events, or methods to the control. MKTYPLIB.EXE uses this file as input to generate the type library (CIRC.ODL) information that is ultimately added to the DLL as a resource.
CIRC.RC	Standard resource file. Contains a template for the control's property page.
CIRC.RC2	Contains user-defined resources that define a control's version information, include its type library information, and state that the control is self-registering.
CIRCCTL.BMP	The iconic representation of the control.
CIRC.ICO	The about box dialog icon.

ControlWizard also creates several other standard files: CIRC.CLW, CIRC.DEF, CIRC.MAK, CIRC.VCW, CIRC.WSP, CIRC332.DEF, CIRC332.MAK, MAKEFILE, README.TXT, RESOURCE.H, STDAFX.CPP, and STDAFX.H. Chapter 3, "Building an Elementary Control," in the *CDK Programmer's Guide* discusses files produced by ControlWizard in more detail.

Modifying the Control Bitmap

When ControlWizard created the Circle control classes, resources, and other files, it also generated a bitmap file called CIRCCTL.BMP. This bitmap provides an iconic representation of the control. Tools like Visual Basic can use this bitmap by loading it from the DLL and displaying it in a palette. The palette provides a pictorial representation of all the controls that are available to the user.

VBX controls require both an up (unselected) and down (selected) bitmap to be supplied with the control. This is not the case with OLE controls. Since only one bitmap is supplied with a control, it is up to the palette implementer to perform the appropriate processing to achieve a three-dimensional look when the control is selected and unselected in the palette.

For a user to select the Circle control from a palette of controls, the default control bitmap must be modified in order to give it some distinguishing features.

▶ **To modify the control bitmap (16-bit version)**

1. Load your project's .RC file into App Studio. If the project is open in the development environment and you start the resource editor by choosing App Studio from the Tools menu, the .RC file is loaded automatically.

2. Select Bitmap from the Type list box.

3. Select IDB_CIRC from the Resources list box.

4. Choose the Open button to edit the bitmap.

   The bitmap appears, as shown in Figure 1.1.

5. Modify the bitmap as you please, but you'll want to give it a look representative of a Circle control.

6. Choose Save from the File menu to save the changes to the bitmap.

7. Exit App Studio.

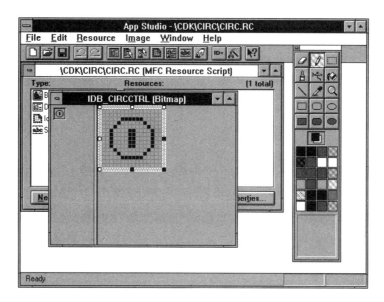

Figure 1.1   Editing the Circle Palette Bitmap with the Bitmap Editor

▶ **To modify the control bitmap (32-bit version)**

1. Open your project's .RC file by double-clicking on the .RC file icon in the Source File folder.

2. Double-click on the Bitmap folder to open it.

3. Double-click on the IDB_CIRC entry to start the resource editor on that bitmap.

4. Modify the bitmap as you please, but you'll want to give it a look representative of a Circle control.

5. Choose Save from the File menu to save the changes to the bitmap.

6. Close the bitmap editor window and the CIRC.RC window.

Modifying the About Circ Control Dialog Box

ControlWizard produced an About Circ Control dialog box template in the file CIRC.RC. ControlWizard also defined the AboutBox "method" for the Circle control. A method is a function in a control which can be called from outside the control. The About Circ Control dialog box is displayed when the control container calls the control's AboutBox method.

ControlWizard also created an icon file called CIRC.ICO. This icon is displayed in the About Circ Control dialog box. The About dialog box icon should be modified to individualize the control. It is modified using the icon editor in App Studio, in much the same way that the control bitmap was modified.

▶ **To modify the About dialog box icon (16-bit version)**

1. Load your project's .RC file into App Studio. If the project is open in the development environment and you start the resource editor by choosing App Studio from the Tools menu, the .RC file is loaded automatically.

2. Select Icon from the Type list box.

3. Select IDI_ABOUTDLL from the Resources list box.

4. Choose the Open button to edit the icon.

5. Edit the icon to your liking. Like the control bitmap, the icon should have a look representative of the Circle control.

6. Save the changes by choosing Save from the File menu.

7. Exit App Studio.

▶ **To modify the About dialog box icon (32-bit version)**

1. Open your project's .RC file by double-clicking on the .RC file icon in the Source File folder.

2. Double-click on the Icon folder to open it.

3. Double-click on the IDI_ABOUTDLL entry to start the resource editor on that icon.

4. Edit the icon to your liking. Like the control bitmap, the icon should have a look representative of the Circle control.

5. Choose Save from the File menu to save the changes to the icon.

6. Close the icon editor window and the CIRC.RC window.

Building the Control

Now that you have created all the necessary files to make the Circle control DLL and modified the control bitmap, you can build the control DLL.

▶ **To build the Circle control (16-bit version)**

1. From the Tools menu, choose Make TypeLib.

    A message box appears, confirming that the type library was successfully generated.

2. Choose the OK button to close the message box.

3. From the Project menu, choose Build CIRC.DLL.

▶ **To build the Circle control (32-bit version)**

▪ From the Project menu, choose Build CIRC.DLL.

The Circle control DLL is now built. For the 16-bit version, notice that the first step in building the DLL is to make the type library. This must be done because the standard MSVC project file does not support compiling the type library from a project's .ODL file. Whenever the project's .ODL file is modified, you must recompile the type library and force the build process to recompile the project resources. The .ODL file is modified by ClassWizard whenever you add, remove, or modify your control's properties, methods, and events. For the 32-bit version, type library compilation is automatically handled as part of the normal build process.

Registering the Control

Before you can use the control, it must be registered in the Registration Database.

▶ **To register the Circle control**

1. From the Tools menu, choose Register Control.

    A message box appears, indicating that the registration was successful.

2. Choose the OK button to close the message box.

When a control is registered, several items are added to the Registration Database:

- The text name of the control.
- The class name of the control.
- An indicator stating that the control conforms to the OLE control protocols.
- The path of the control DLL.
- The path and resource ID of the control palette bitmap.
- Whether the control can be inserted.
- The **IDispatch** IDs of the control's properties and events interfaces.

Controls built with the CDK are self-registering because there are two entry points, **DLLRegisterServer** and **DLLUnregisterServer**, in the Circle DLL that were automatically added when ControlWizard created the control's files. In the Circle control, these entry points are defined in the CIRC.CPP file. As their names imply, **DLLRegisterServer** and **DLLUnregisterServer** add and remove, respectively, the control's registration information from the Registration Database.

Testing the Control

When the Circle control DLL has been built and the control has been registered, you can use Test Container to see how it behaves.

▶ **To test the Circle control**

1. From the Tools menu, choose Test Container.
2. From the Edit menu, choose Insert OLE Control.

   The Insert OLE Control dialog box appears.
3. From the Control Class list box, select Circ Control.
4. Choose the OK button to close the Insert OLE Control dialog box and insert a control into Test Container.

   The Circle control will be displayed in the Test Container, as shown in Figure 1.2. Notice that the control is drawn as an ellipse within the bounding rectangle of the control.
5. Move the control within the container to observe how the control is redrawn. Resize the control to see how its ellipse is redrawn to the size of the bounding rectangle.
6. From the Edit menu, choose Invoke Methods.

   The Invoke Control Method dialog box appears.

   Notice that AboutBox is selected in the Name drop-down list box. This is the only method defined in the Circle control.

7. Choose the Invoke button.

   The About Circ Control dialog box appears. The icon you edited earlier is displayed in the dialog box.

8. Choose the OK button to close the About Circ Control dialog box.

9. Choose the Close button to close the Invoke Control Method dialog box.

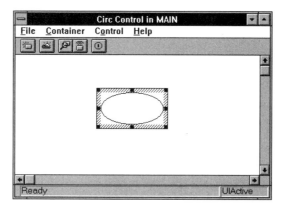

Figure 1.2   The Circle Control

Notice that the background color of the control is white. You'll modify the painting of the control in the next chapter.

At this point you have not defined any properties or events for the Circle control. From Test Container's View menu, choose Properties. Notice that there are no properties. From the View menu, choose Event Log. Click, move, and resize the control. You'll notice that no events are displayed. As the Circle control evolves, you will add a number of new properties and events.

C H A P T E R   2

Painting the Control

Now that the framework for the Circle control is in place, you can modify the control to do something more useful. In this chapter, you'll implement the specialized background painting behavior of the Circle control.

Note You can find the code produced by implementing the code samples in this chapter in the CIRC2 sample source code directory.

The control uses the container's ambient background color property as the default value for the background color of the control, and uses the stock background color property to maintain the value of the control's current background color. In addition, the OnDraw function in the CCircCtrl class will be modified to implement the proper behavior for painting the background color of the control when it is called on to do so.

In this chapter, you will learn how to:

- Use the BackColor stock property.
- Set the default background color value.
- Modify the default OnDraw function to implement new painting behavior.

Enabling the Background Color Property

The first step in implementing the new painting behavior is to add the background color property to the control. BackColor is a stock property, along with Caption, ForeColor, and Text.

▶ **To add the BackColor property**

1. From the Browse menu, choose ClassWizard. If you are using the 32-bit version of the CDK, choose ClassWizard from the Project menu.

2. Choose the OLE Automation tab.

3. From the Class Name drop-down list box, select CCircCtrl.

4. Choose the Add Property button.

   The Add Property dialog box appears.

5. From the External Name drop-down combo box, select `BackColor`.

6. Under Implementation, choose Stock.

7. Choose the OK button to close the Add Property dialog box.

   This returns you to the OLE Automation tab. Notice that the implementation of the BackColor property is listed as

   ```
   Implementation:
   Stock Property
   ```

8. Choose the OK button again to confirm your choices and close ClassWizard.

ClassWizard creates the appropriate code to add the BackColor property to the `CCircCtrl` class and adds the BackColor property to the type library file CIRC.ODL. The `CCircCtrl` class's dispatch map in CIRCCTL.CPP is modified by adding the **DISP_STDPROP_BACKCOLOR** macro:

```
BEGIN_DISPATCH_MAP(CCircCtrl, COleControl)
    //{{AFX_DISPATCH_MAP(CCircCtrl)
    DISP_STOCKPROP_BACKCOLOR()
    DISP_FUNCTION_ID(CCircCtrl, "AboutBox", DISPID_ABOUTBOX, AboutBox,
VT_EMPTY, VTS_NONE)
    //}}AFX_DISPATCH_MAP
END_DISPATCH_MAP()
```

The control's type library (CIRC.ODL file) is modified to add BackColor to its property section, as shown in the following code sample:

```
dispinterface _DCirc
{
    properties:
        // NOTE - ClassWizard will maintain property information here.
        //     Use extreme caution when editing this section.
        //{{AFX_ODL_PROP(CCircCtrl)
        [id(DISPID_BACKCOLOR), bindable, requestedit] OLE_COLOR
BackColor;
        //}}AFX_ODL_PROP
    methods:
        // NOTE - ClassWizard will maintain method information here.
        //     Use extreme caution when editing this section.
        //{{AFX_ODL_METHOD(CCircCtrl)
        [id(0)] void AboutBox();
        //}}AFX_ODL_METHOD

};
```

Because the BackColor property is of type **DISP_PROPERTY_EX**, its value can only be modified through its **Get** and **Set** methods.

The value of the BackColor property is maintained by the **COleControl** class. Note that the **SetBackColor** member function automatically calls the **OnBackColorChanged** member function after setting the BackColor value. This causes the control to be invalidated. Invalidating the control will ultimately cause the OnDraw function to be called, and the control will be redrawn using the new background color.

Setting the Default Background Color

Now that you have a place for the background color value of the Circle control to reside, the next step is to provide a default value for the background color. Normally, the background color of a control will be the same as the background color of the control's containers window, which can be obtained from the container's ambient properties.

The **COleControl** class implements a mechanism for obtaining the default values of stock properties. **COleControl::OnResetState** calls the function **COleControl::DoPropExchange**, which queries the container for its background color ambient property and sets the value of the control's BackColor property equal to this color.

Modifying the Draw Behavior

The control now implements the two prerequisites for providing the actual background color painting behavior. The final step is to modify the CCircCtrl::OnDraw function in CIRCCTL.CPP to implement the painting behavior.

As created by ControlWizard, the CCircCtrl::OnDraw function implements the basic Circle control drawing behavior:

```
void CCircCtrl::OnDraw(
          CDC* pdc, const CRect& rcBounds, const CRect& rcInvalid)
{
    // TODO: Replace the following code with your own drawing code.
    pdc->FillRect(rcBounds,
CBrush::FromHandle((HBRUSH)GetStockObject(WHITE_BRUSH)));
    pdc->Ellipse(rcBounds);

}
```

The default behavior of the `OnDraw` function is to draw an ellipse with a white background, which is exactly what was displayed from within Test Container earlier.

To modify `OnDraw` to use the background color value defined by the BackColor property of the control, remove the TODO comment line and the line on which `FillRect` is called and add the marked lines.

```
void CCircCtrl::OnDraw(
            CDC* pdc, const CRect& rcBounds, const CRect& rcInvalid)
{
►       CBrush* pOldBrush;
►       CBrush bkBrush(TranslateColor(GetBackColor()));
►       CPen* pOldPen;
►
►       // Paint the background using the BackColor property
►       pdc->FillRect(rcBounds, &bkBrush);
►
►       // Draw the ellipse using the BackColor property and a black pen
►       pOldBrush = pdc->SelectObject(&bkBrush);
►       pOldPen = (CPen*)pdc->SelectStockObject(BLACK_PEN);
        pdc->Ellipse(rcBounds);
►       pdc->SelectObject(pOldPen);
►       pdc->SelectObject(pOldBrush);
}
```

The code constructs a brush, called `bkBrush`, that uses the BackColor property color. Since a **COLORREF** value is expected for initializing the brush and the BackColor property value is an **OLE_COLOR** value, **TranslateColor** is called first. The bounding rectangle of the control is painted using **CDC::FillRect**, specifying `bkBrush` as the fill brush.

The ellipse is drawn within the bounding rectangle of the control using the **CDC::Ellipse** member function. Before the ellipse is drawn, the background color brush and the pen must be selected into the device context. This is done using **CDC::SelectObject**, as shown in the code. Now when the ellipse is drawn, it will be filled with the proper background color and will be drawn using a black pen. Finally, the old brush and pen are selected back into the device context, restoring the device context to the same state in which it entered the `OnDraw` function.

Rebuilding the Control

Now that the painting behavior is implemented, you need to rebuild the control. Since the BackColor property was added to the control, the type library must be updated first.

▶ **To update the type library (16-bit version only)**

1. From the Tools menu, choose Make TypeLib to update the Type Library.

   A message box appears, confirming that the type library was successfully generated.

2. Choose the OK button to close the message box.

▶ **To rebuild the control (16- and 32-bit versions)**

- From the Project menu, choose Build CIRC.DLL.

Testing the Control

Testing the new drawing behavior of the control is a simple matter of running Test Container and loading the control.

▶ **To test the control**

1. Use Control Panel to modify the Windows Background color of your system so that it is not white.

2. From the Tools menu, choose Test Container.

3. From the Edit menu, choose Insert OLE Control.

   The Insert OLE Control dialog box appears.

4. From the Control Class list box, select Circ Control.

5. Choose the OK button to close the Insert OLE Control dialog box and insert a control into Test Container.

The Circle control will be displayed in Test Container and painted using the same background color as Test Container's window. You can also modify the BackColor property value from the Properties dialog box in Test Container. To show the Properties dialog box, choose Properties from the View menu. For example, change the value of the BackColor property to 255. The Circle control will change its background color to red.

C H A P T E R   3

Adding a Custom Notification Property

The ability to define a custom set of properties, events, and methods for a control is one of the most powerful features of control writing. The previous chapter illustrated the use of a standard property. This chapter will illustrate how to add a new custom property to the Circle control.

Note You can find the code produced by implementing the code samples in this chapter in the CIRC2 sample source code directory.

In this chapter, you will:

- Learn the overview of properties in an OLE control.
- Define the CircleShape property's functionality.
- Add the CircleShape property to the control.
- Revise the control's draw behavior to reflect the value of the CircleShape property.

Overview of Properties in an OLE Control

Properties are typically used to represent an attribute or data of a control. For example, a Date control might define a DateValue property, which would provide access to the current date value displayed in the control; this type of property would represent control data. Additionally, the Date control may define a Format property, which allows the user to get and set the display format of the date; this type of property represents a control attribute.

The Control Development Kit (CDK) supports four different types of custom properties:

- **DISP_PROPERTY**
- **DISP_PROPERTY_NOTIFY**

- DISP_PROPERTY_EX
- DISP_PROPERTY_PARAM

DISP_PROPERTY and **DISP_PROPERTY_NOTIFY** custom properties are implemented using a member variable. **DISP_PROPERTY_NOTIFY** custom properties also have a notification function. **DISP_PROPERTY_EX** and **DISP_PROPERTY_PARAM** custom properties are implemented using a Get method and a Set method. **DISP_PROPERTY_PARAM** custom properties' Get and Set methods take an index parameter. The **DISP_PROPERTY_PARAM** custom property type is discussed in Appendix B, "Advanced Topics." The **DISP_PROPERTY_EX** and **DISP_PROPERTY** custom property types are used later in the tutorial.

This chapter demonstrates techniques for implementing a **DISP_PROPERTY_NOTIFY** custom property in the Circle control. You will add a property called CircleShape, which is an example of a **DISP_PROPERTY_NOTIFY** custom property. CircleShape is a Boolean property that causes the control to be displayed as a perfect circle, if set to **TRUE,** or causes the control to be displayed as an ellipse, if set to **FALSE.**

The CircleShape Property

This section discusses the functional aspects of the CircleShape property and the property's effect on the Circle control. In addition, you will devise a strategy for modifying the Circle control code in order to prepare for implementing the new behavior.

CircleShape Functional Specification

When the CircleShape property's value is set to **TRUE**, the Circle control will draw the largest possible perfect circle centered within the bounding rectangle of the control. When the CircleShape property is set to **FALSE**, the Circle control will draw an ellipse whose major and minor axes touch the bounding rectangle of the control. The initial value of the CircleShape property should be **TRUE**. Whenever the CircleShape property is changed, the Circle control should be redrawn to reflect the change.

Figure 3.1 shows the Circle control drawn as an ellipse. This is the desired effect when CircleShape is set to **FALSE**. Notice that the ellipse is drawn to the edges of the bounding rectangle. Currently, this is the standard drawing behavior of the Circle control, so there will be very little code to modify in order to implement the required drawing behavior when CircleShape is **FALSE**.

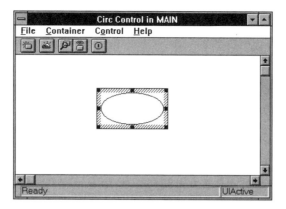

Figure 3.1   The CircleShape property is FALSE; therefore an ellipse is drawn.

When the CircleShape property is **TRUE**, the Circle control is required to draw
itself as a perfect circle. Figure 3.2 shows how the circle would be drawn within the
bounding rectangle of the control. To determine how to draw the circle, you simply
calculate the square region centered within the bounding rectangle of the control.

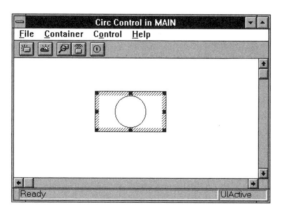

Figure 3.2   The CircleShape property is TRUE; therefore a circle is drawn.

Recall from the previous chapter that the `CCircCtrl::OnDraw` function used the
CDC::Ellipse function to draw the ellipse. This function can also be used to draw
the circle. By passing the calculated square region to the **Ellipse** function instead of
the bounding rectangle of the control, the **Ellipse** function will draw a perfect
circle.

Revising the Code

Now that the CircleShape property's functional specification is complete and the
basic logic is described, you can revise the code as follows:

- Add the CircleShape property to the control using ClassWizard.

- Set the default value of the CircleShape property when the control is created.
- Define the `GetDrawRect` member function in the `CCircCtrl` class. This function determines the drawing coordinates to use: if CircleShape is **FALSE**, use the entire bounding rectangle of the control; if CircleShape is **TRUE**, use the centered square region inside the bounding rectangle.
- Modify `CCircCtrl::OnDraw` to use the coordinates returned by the `CCircCtrl::GetDrawRect` member function when drawing the control.
- Modify the `CCircCtrl::OnCircleShapeChanged` member function to invalidate the control.

Notice that certain aspects of the strategy apply whenever you add any custom property. Adding the property using ClassWizard greatly simplifies the process by updating the appropriate class and .ODL files. It is always good practice to provide a default value for the new property. This can be done by adding initialization code for the property to the `DoPropExchange` member function in the control class.

Adding the CircleShape Property

The first step in implementing the CircleShape property's functionality is to add the CircleShape property to the control. Similar to adding a standard property, a custom property is also added using ClassWizard.

▶ **To add the CircleShape property**

1. From the Browse menu, choose ClassWizard. If you are using the 32-bit version of the CDK, choose ClassWizard from the Project menu.
2. Choose the OLE Automation tab.
3. From the Class Name drop-down list box, select `CCircCtrl`.
4. Choose the Add Property button.

   The Add Property dialog box appears.
5. In the edit control of the External Name drop-down combo box type `CircleShape`.
6. Under Implementation choose **Member Variable**.
7. Select **BOOL** from the Type drop-down list box.
8. Verify that the Notification Function edit control contains `OnCircleShapeChanged`.
9. Choose the OK button to close the Add Property dialog box.

   This returns you to the OLE Automation tab. Notice that the implementation of the CircleShape property is listed as:

   ```
   Implementation:
   BOOL m_circleShape;
   ```

```
void OnCircleShapeChanged();
```

10. Choose the OK button to confirm your choices and close ClassWizard.

ClassWizard creates the appropriate code to add the CircleShape property to the
CCircCtrl class and the CIRC.ODL file. When adding a
DISP_PROPERTY_NOTIFY property type, ClassWizard modifies the
CCircCtrl class's dispatch map by adding a **DISP_PROPERTY_NOTIFY**
macro entry for the property:

```
BEGIN_DISPATCH_MAP(CCircCtrl, COleControl)
    //{{AFX_DISPATCH_MAP(CCircCtrl)
    DISP_PROPERTY_NOTIFY(CCircCtrl, "CircleShape", m_circleShape,
OnCircleShapeChanged, VT_BOOL)
    DISP_STOCKPROP_BACKCOLOR()
    DISP_FUNCTION_ID(CCirc2Ctrl, "AboutBox", DISPID_ABOUTBOX, AboutBox,
VT_EMPTY, VTS_NONE)
    //}}AFX_DISPATCH_MAP
END_DISPATCH_MAP()
```

The **DISP_PROPERTY_NOTIFY** macro associates the CircleShape property
name with its corresponding CCircCtrl class member variable
(m_circleShape); the name of the CCircCtrl class notification function
(OnCircleShapeChanged), which is called whenever the value of CircleShape
property is changed, and the type (**VT_BOOL**) of the property.

ClassWizard also adds a declaration for the OnCircleShapeChanged
notification function in CIRCCTL.H and a function template in CIRCCTL.CPP:

```
void CCircCtrl::OnCircleShapeChanged()
{
    // TODO: Add notification handler code

    SetModifiedFlag();
}
```

You will modify OnCircleShapeChanged to invalidate the control later in this
chapter.

Setting the CircleShape Default Value

Since the Circle control uses the CircleShape property as a key to determine how to
draw itself, it is very important that the CircleShape property be initialized to a
specific value. This is easily accomplished by modifying the
CCircCtrl:DoPropExchange function in the file CIRCCTL.CPP:

```
void CCircCtrl::DoPropExchange(CPropExchange* pPX)
{
```

```
      ExchangeVersion(pPX, MAKELONG(_wVerMinor, _wVerMajor));
      COleControl::DoPropExchange(pPX);

►     PX_Bool(pPX, _T("CircleShape"), m_circleShape, TRUE);
}
```

The function specification states that the initialized state of CircleShape must be **TRUE**. This is accomplished by adding a call to the **PX_Bool** function in the DoPropExchange function, which sets the default value of the CircleShape property to **TRUE**. This forces the Circle control to be drawn initially as a perfect circle.

Notice that the property name string parameter to the **PX_Bool** function is first passed through the _T macro. This macro is used for compatibility between different string representations. For instance, UNICODE strings are available for the 32-bit version of the CDK and ANSI strings are available for the 16-bit version of the CDK. All literal strings in an OLE custom control project must be handled this way.

Any property initialized with a call to a **PX_** function in the DoPropExchange function is called a "persistent property." This is because the **PX_** functions do more than initialize a property when a control is created. The DoPropExchange function is called when a control is created, restored from a file or stream, or saved into a file or stream. It is the **PX_** functions which determine whether the value of a persistent property must change under any of these conditions. Whenever a persistent property is changed, a modified flag for persistent properties must be set to indicate that at least one persistent property must be updated. Setting the modified flag will be discussed later in this chapter in the Modifying the OnCircleShapeChanged Function section.

Drawing the Control

Now that the CircleShape property has been added to the CCircCtrl class and its initial value has been set in DoPropExchange, you can implement the new draw behavior. Several additions to the CCircCtrl class code will be made:

- Implementation of the GetDrawRect function, which will calculate the coordinates of the square region.
- Modification of the OnDraw function to call GetDrawRect.
- Modification of the OnCircleShapeChanged function to invalidate the control.

The GetDrawRect Function

The GetDrawRect function determines the coordinates of the bounding rectangle in which the ellipse should be drawn. If the CircleShape property is **TRUE**, GetDrawRect calculates the coordinates of the square region centered in the rectangle rc, which was passed to GetDrawRect. The coordinates of the square region are put back into rc. If CircleShape is **FALSE**, the function leaves rc untouched. Add the GetDrawRect function at the end of the file CIRCCTL.CPP:

```
void CCircCtrl::GetDrawRect(CRect* rc)
{
    if (m_circleShape)
    {
        int cx = rc->right - rc->left;
        int cy = rc->bottom - rc->top;

        if (cx > cy)
        {
            rc->left += (cx - cy) / 2;
            rc->right = rc->left + cy;
        }
        else
        {
            rc->top += (cy - cx) / 2;
            rc->bottom = rc->top + cx;
        }
    }
}
```

Declare the GetDrawRect as a protected member function in the file CIRCCTL.H. Placing the declaration immediately after the destructor is an easy way to do this:

```
class CCircCtrl : public COleControl
{
...
protected:
    ~CCircCtrl();
    void GetDrawRect(CRect* rc);
...
};
```

Modifying the OnDraw Function

The GetDrawRect function greatly simplifies the changes that need to be made to the OnDraw function. The modifications to OnDraw introduce a local **CRect** object, rc, whose value is initialized to the value of rcBounds. Before the ellipse is drawn, GetDrawRect is called. If the value of the CircleShape property is **TRUE**, GetDrawRect will adjust the coordinates in rc to be the square region centered within rcBounds.

```
void CCircCtrl::OnDraw(
            CDC* pdc, const CRect& rcBounds, const CRect& rcInvalid)
{
    CBrush* pOldBrush;
    CBrush bkBrush(TranslateColor(GetBackColor()));
    CPen* pOldPen;
```

```
►       CRect rc = rcBounds;

        // Paint the background using the BackColor property
        pdc->FillRect(rcBounds, &bkBrush);

        // Draw the ellipse using the BackColor property and a black pen
►       GetDrawRect(&rc);
        pOldBrush = pdc->SelectObject(&bkBrush);
        pOldPen = (CPen*)pdc->SelectStockObject(BLACK_PEN);
►       pdc->Ellipse(rc);
        pdc->SelectObject(pOldPen);
        pdc->SelectObject(pOldBrush);
    }
```

Modifying the OnCircleShapeChanged Function

Because CircleShape is a **DISP_PROPERTY_NOTIFY** property type,
ClassWizard created the required code to force a notification function to be called
if the CircleShape property's value changes. The default
OnCircleShapeChanged notification function, created by ClassWizard, does
nothing.

Recall that the CircleShape property is a persistent property since it is initialized by
calling the **PX_Bool** function in the CCircCtrl::DoPropExchange function.
The modified flag for persistent properties must be set by calling the
CCircCtrl::SetModifiedFlag function whenever the value of a persistent
property has changed. Since most properties are persistent, ClassWizard includes a
call to the CCircCtrl::SetModifiedFlag function in all notification functions.

If the value of the CircleShape property changes, the control must redraw itself to
ensure that it displays the right representation of the control, either a circle or an
ellipse. This is done by simply invalidating the control when the
OnCircleShapeChanged member function is called. The invalidation causes the
OnDraw member function to be called.

```
void CCircCtrl::OnCircleShapeChanged()
{
    SetModifiedFlag();
►
►       // force the control to redraw itself
►       InvalidateControl();
    }
```

Rebuilding the Control

Now that the CircleShape property is implemented, you need to rebuild the control.
Since the CIRC.ODL file was changed when the CircleShape property was added
to the control, the type library must be updated first.

▶ **To update the type library (16-bit version only)**

1. From the Tools menu, choose Make TypeLib to update the Type Library.

   A message box appears, confirming that the type library was successfully generated.

2. Choose the OK button to close the message box.

▶ **To rebuild the control (16- and 32-bit versions)**

1. From the Project menu, choose Build CIRC.DLL.

Testing the Control

The CircleShape property's functionality has now been fully implemented. The next step is to test the code using Test Container.

▶ **To test the CircleShape property**

1. Run Test Container.

2. From the Edit menu, choose Insert OLE Control.

   The Insert OLE Control dialog box appears.

3. From the Control Class list box, select Circ Control.

4. Choose the OK button to close the Insert OLE Control dialog box and insert a control into Test Container.

   The Circle control will be displayed in Test Container. Notice that the control is initially drawn as perfect circle. This is expected since you set the CircleShape property to **TRUE** in the DoPropExchange member function in the CCircCtrl class.

Next, change the value of the CircleShape property to cause the Circle control to redraw itself as an ellipse.

▶ **To change the CircleShape property**

1. From the View menu, choose Properties.

   The Properties dialog box appears.

2. Select CircleShape from the Property drop-down combo box.

   The Value edit control will display -1, which indicates a **TRUE** value. If the CircleShape property is not listed, the type library may not have been regenerated before the control was built last.

3. In the Value edit control, type 0 (zero). Zero indicates a **FALSE** value.

4. Choose the Apply button.

The Circle control is redrawn as an ellipse the size of the bounding rectangle of the control. It is immediately redrawn because changing the CircleShape property caused the `OnCircleShapeChanged` notification function to be called. The `OnCircleShapeChanged` function invalidated the control, causing the control to be redrawn.

CHAPTER 4

Adding a Custom Get/Set Property

The Control Development Kit (CDK) supports a property type that shields the property from direct access by the user. Access to the property can only be accomplished through a Get/Set method pair. By wrapping Get and Set methods around a property, you can shield the internal representation and implementation of the property from the user.

Note You can find the code produced by implementing the code samples in this chapter in the CIRC2 sample source code directory.

Forcing access to a property through methods can provide a great benefit. For example, a Set method can be coded to validate an input value before it is set the property's value, or a property can represent a computed value. When the computed property is accessed, its Get method can perform a computation and return the result as the property value.

In this chapter, you will implement a Get/Set property for the Circle control. The CircleOffset property will allow the circle to be offset from the center of the bounding rectangle of the control. Before the offset is modified, the Set method will make sure that the edge of the circle will stay within the bounding rectangle of the control. In the C++ language, Get and Set methods are implemented as member functions.

In this chapter you will:

- Define the CircleOffset property's functionality.
- Add the CircleOffset property to the control.
- Revise the control's draw behavior to reflect the value of the CircleOffset property.

The CircleOffset Property

This section discusses the functional aspects of the CircleOffset property and the property's effect on the behavior of the Circle control. You will also devise a strategy for modifying the Circle control's code in order to prepare for implementing the CircleOffset property's behavior.

CircleOffset Functional Specification

The CircleOffset property allows the user to offset the circle from the center of the control's bounding rectangle. The CircleOffset property has an effect only if the value of the CircleShape property is **TRUE**. When the CircleShape property is **FALSE**, the control is drawn as an ellipse the size of the bounding rectangle, so no movement would be possible. When CircleShape is **TRUE**, the circle can potentially be offset from center in either the x- or y- direction (Figure 4.1), depending on which has the greater extent.

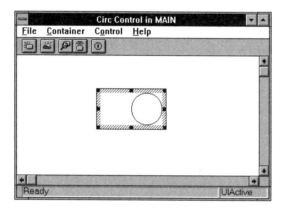

Figure 4.1   Circle offset 25 units from center

The circle can also be offset in the negative direction. For example, if a Circle control is drawn with a greater x-extent, a positive offset will cause the circle to move to the right and a negative offset will cause the circle to move to the left within the bounding rectangle. If the control is drawn with a greater y-extent as in Figure 4.2, a positive offset will move the circle toward the top and a negative offset will move the circle toward the bottom of the bounding rectangle.

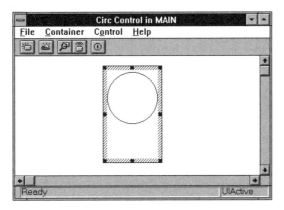

Figure 4.2   Circle control with a greater y-extent

The following rules apply to the behavior of CircleOffset:

- The control ignores any offset that would cause the circle to be placed outside the bounding rectangle of the control.
- If the control is resized, CircleOffset is set to 0.
- If the CircleShape property is set to **TRUE**, CircleOffset will be set to 0.

The control cannot allow the circle to be moved beyond the bounding rectangle of the control. Thus CircleOffset property's Set method must implement code that will validate the value of the offset passed to the Set method before setting the value of the CircleOffset property.

Revising the Code

The implementation of the CircleOffset property's functionality will be more complex than the implementation of the CircleShape property. Not only does the CircleOffset property affect the drawing behavior of the control, it also requires that the value of the CircleOffset property be reset to 0 when either the control is resized or the CircleShape property is set to **TRUE**. With this in mind and the basic logic understood, here are the code revisions that must be made:

- Add the CircleOffset property to the control using ClassWizard.
- Set the default value of the CircleOffset property to 0 when the control is created.
- Modify the CircleOffset property's Set method to perform offset validation.
- Modify the `CCircCtrl::GetDrawRect` member function to properly calculate the coordinates of the square region with regard to the current CircleOffset property value.

- Modify the `CCircCtrl::OnCircleShapeChanged` member function to reset the CircleOffset property value to 0 if the CircleShape property has been changed to **TRUE**.
- Add the `CCircCtrl::OnSize` notification function to reset the CircleOffset value to 0 when the size of the control is changed.

Adding the CircleOffset Property

The first step in implementing the CircleOffset functionality is to add the CircleOffset property to the control.

▶ **To add the CircleOffset property**

1. From the Browse menu, choose ClassWizard. If you are using the 32-bit version of the CDK, choose ClassWizard from the Project menu.

2. Choose the OLE Automation tab.

3. In the Class Name drop-down list box, select `CCircCtrl`.

4. Choose the Add Property button.

    The Add Property dialog box appears.

5. In the edit control of the External Name drop-down combo box, type `CircleOffset`.

6. Under Implementation choose **Get/Set Methods**.

    The Get Function and Set Function edit controls appears, replacing the Variable Name and Notification Function edit controls.

7. From the Type drop-down list box, select **short**.

8. Choose the OK button to close the Add Property dialog box.

    This returns you to the OLE Automation tab. Notice that the implementation of the CircleOffset property is listed as:

    ```
    Implementation:
    short GetCircleOffset();
    void SetCircleOffset(short nNewValue);
    ```

9. Choose the OK button to confirm your choices and close ClassWizard.

ClassWizard will create the appropriate code to add the CircleOffset property to the `CCircCtrl` class and the CIRC.ODL file. Since CircleOffset is a Get/Set property type, ClassWizard will modify the `CCircCtrl` class's dispatch map to include a **DISP_PROPERTY_EX** macro entry:

```
BEGIN_DISPATCH_MAP(CCircCtrl, COleControl)
    //{{AFX_DISPATCH_MAP(CCircCtrl)
    DISP_PROPERTY_NOTIFY(CCircCtrl, "CircleShape", m_circleShape,
OnCircleShapeChanged, VT_BOOL)
    DISP_PROPERTY_EX(CCircCtrl, "CircleOffset", GetCircleOffset,
SetCircleOffset, VT_I2)
    DISP_STOCKPROP_BACKCOLOR()
    DISP_FUNCTION_ID(CCircCtrl, "AboutBox", DISPID_ABOUTBOX, AboutBox,
VT_EMPTY, VTS_NONE)
    //}}AFX_DISPATCH_MAP
END_DISPATCH_MAP()
```

The **DISP_PROPERTY_EX** macro associates the CircleOffset property name with its corresponding CCircCtrl class's Get and Set methods, GetCircleOffset and SetCircleOffset. The type of the property value is also specified: in this case it is **VT_I2**, which corresponds to a **short**.

ClassWizard will also add a declaration in CIRCCTL.H for the GetCircleOffset and SetCircleOffset functions and add their function templates in CIRCCTL.CPP:

```
short CCircCtrl::GetCircleOffset()
{
    // TODO: Add your property handler here

    return 0;
}

void CCircCtrl::SetCircleOffset(short nNewValue)
{
    // TODO: Add your property handler here

    SetModifiedFlag();
}
```

You will modify the SetCircleOffset function to perform offset validation later in this chapter.

Since ClassWizard only creates the Get and Set functions, you must add a member variable to the CCircCtrl class to keep track of the actual value of the CircleOffset property. This is the variable that the Get and Set methods will query and modify. You can add this variable by modifying the declaration of the CCircCtrl class in the file CIRCCTL.H. Adding the member variable in the protected section just after the destructor is an easy way to do this:

```
class CCircCtrl : public COleControl
{
...
protected:
    ~CCircCtrl();
    void GetDrawRect(CRect* rc);
►   short m_circleOffset;
...
};
```

In addition, you must modify the Get method created by ClassWizard, GetCircleOffset in CIRCCTL.CPP, to return the value of this new variable (note that the TODO comment line can be removed):

```
short CCircCtrl::GetCircleOffset()
{
►   return m_circleOffset;
}
```

Setting the CircleOffset Default Value

Like previous properties, the CircleOffset property needs to be initialized to a default value when the control is created. In this case, setting CircleOffset to 0 would be logical. Add the following marked line to the DoPropExchange function in CIRCCTL.CPP:

```
void CCircCtrl::DoPropExchange(CPropExchange* pPX)
{
    ExchangeVersion(pPX, MAKELONG(_wVerMinor, _wVerMajor));
    COleControl::DoPropExchange(pPX);

    PX_Bool(pPX, _T("CircleShape"), m_circleShape, TRUE);
►   PX_Short(pPX, _T("CircleOffset"), m_circleOffset, 0);
}
```

The CircleOffset property is initialized by making a call to **PX_Short** in the CCircCtrl::DoPropExchange member function, passing 0 as the default value parameter (the last parameter in the function call). Now when the circle is first drawn, it will be centered in the bounding rectangle of the Circle control. As with all literal strings, the property name parameter must be passed through the **_T** macro.

Recall that properties initialized by calling a **PX_** function in a control's DoPropExchange function are persistent properties. This means that CircleOffset is a persistent property. Later steps in this chapter will set the modified flag for persistent properties whenever the value of the CircleOffset property changes.

Setting the CircleOffset Property

The reason that CircleOffset was defined as a Get/Set property was to provide an entry point where the offset can be validated when the user attempts to change its value. Two rules govern the offset validation:

- The CircleShape property must be **TRUE**.
- The new offset must not force the circle outside the control's bounding rectangle.

The Set function for Get/Set properties can be written to ignore requests to set the property value to the same value it currently has. Properties implemented using only member variables do not provide this ability. So there is another optional rule that governs validation of Get/Set properties in general:

- The new property value must be different than the old property value.

If any of the rules are not true, `SetCircleOffset` will simply ignore the request.

If the new offset is valid, the value of the CircleOffset property is updated. Since the CircleOffset property is persistent, the modified flag is set. Since CircleOffset affects the visual appearance of the control, the control is invalidated. Invalidating the control is the simplest approach to forcing the control to be redrawn.

Modify `SetCircleOffset` in CIRCCTL.CPP to validate the new value (note that the TODO comment line is removed and the `SetModifiedFlag` function call is now inside the `if` statement):

```
void CCircCtrl::SetCircleOffset(short nNewValue)
{
►       // Validate the specified offset value
►       if ((m_circleOffset != nNewValue) && m_circleShape &&
    InBounds(nNewValue))
►       {
►           m_circleOffset = nNewValue;
►           SetModifiedFlag();
►           InvalidateControl();
►       }
}
```

Notice that the function `SetCircleOffset` calls the `InBounds` member function. This function returns **TRUE** if the specified offset would not force the circle outside the bounding rectangle of the control.

► **To implement InBounds**

1. Add the following marked line to your CIRCCTL.H file:

```
class CCircCtrl : public COleControl
{
...
protected:
    ~CCircCtrl();
    void GetDrawRect(CRect* rc);
    short m_circleOffset;
►   BOOL InBounds(short nOffset);
...
};
```

2. Add the function implementation at the end of your CIRCCTL.CPP file:

```
►  BOOL CCircCtrl::InBounds(short nOffset)
►  {
►      CRect rc;
►      int diameter;
►      int length;
►
►      GetClientRect(rc);
►
►      int cx = rc.right - rc.left;
►      int cy = rc.bottom - rc.top;
►
►      if (cx > cy)
►      {
►          length = cx;
►          diameter = cy;
►      }
►      else
►      {
►          length = cy;
►          diameter = cx;
►      }
►      if (nOffset < 0)
►          nOffset = -nOffset;
►      return (diameter / 2 + nOffset) <= (length / 2);
►  }
```

Drawing the Control

The CircleOffset functionality does not require any major drawing modifications to be made. In fact the OnDraw function need not be changed at all. The only concern is that the coordinates of the square region returned by GetDrawRect are properly adjusted based on the current value of the CircleOffset property:

```
void CCircCtrl::GetDrawRect(CRect* rc)
{
    if (m_circleShape)
    {
        int cx = rc->right - rc->left;
        int cy = rc->bottom - rc->top;

        if (cx > cy)
        {
            rc->left += (cx - cy) / 2;
            rc->right = rc->left + cy;

            // offset circle in bounding rect
            rc->left += m_circleOffset;
            rc->right += m_circleOffset;
        }
        else
        {
            rc->top += (cy - cx) / 2;
            rc->bottom = rc->top + cx;

            // offset circle in bounding rect
            rc->bottom -= m_circleOffset;
            rc->top -= m_circleOffset;
        }
    }
}
```

The changes to the code for GetDrawRect are adjustments to the square region's left and right or top and bottom coordinates, depending on whether the x- or y-extent, respectively, is greater.

Modifying the OnCircleShapeChanged Function

The CircleOffset functional specification requires that the value of the CircleOffset property be reset to 0 when CircleShape is set to **TRUE**. Recall from the previous chapter that the OnCircleShapeChanged function will be called whenever the CircleShape property is modified, so it is. the appropriate place to handle this requirement:

```
void CCircCtrl::OnCircleShapeChanged()
{
    SetModifiedFlag();

    // force the control to redraw itself
    InvalidateControl();
```

```
▶        // reset the circle offset, if necessary
▶        if (m_circleShape)
▶            SetCircleOffset(0);
}
```

Setting the CircleOffset property to 0 under this condition will cause the circle to be centered whenever the CircleShape property is set back to **TRUE**. All actions related to the change to the CircleShape property are completed before the CircleOffset property is changed.

Adding the OnSize Function

The final requirement is to set CircleOffset to 0 whenever the size of the control changes. This can be done by adding a notification function to `CCircCtrl` that responds to a **WM_SIZE** message.

▶ **To add the OnSize function**

1. From the Browse menu, choose ClassWizard. If you are using the 32-bit version of the CDK, choose ClassWizard from the Project menu.

2. Choose the Message Maps tab.

3. From the Class Name drop-down list box, select `CCircCtrl`.

4. From the Object IDs list box, select `CCircCtrl`.

5. From the Messages list box, select **WM_SIZE**.

6. Choose the Add Function button.

   This returns you to the Message Maps tab. Notice this new handler is listed in the Member Functions list box as

   ```
   Member Functions
   OnSize                    ON_WM_SIZE
   ```

7. Choose the Edit Code button.

   ClassWizard will close and the cursor will be positioned at the code for the `OnSize` member function.

The `OnSize` member function will reset the CircleOffset property to 0 only if CircleShape is **TRUE**. This ensures that the circle will always stay within the bounding rectangle of the control no matter how the control is resized. Setting the CircleOffset property to 0 is the simplest approach to accomplishing this task.

```
void CCircCtrl::OnSize(UINT nType, int cx, int cy)
{
    COleControl::OnSize(nType, cx, cy);
```

```
►    // If circle shape is true, reset the offset when control size is
changed
►    if (m_circleShape)
►        SetCircleOffset(0);
}
```

Rebuilding the Control

Now that the CircleOffset property modifications are complete, rebuild the control. Since the CIRC.ODL file was changed when the CircleOffset property was added to the control, the type library must be updated first.

▶ **To update the type library (16-bit version only)**

1. From the Tools menu, choose Make TypeLib to update the Type Library.

   A message box appears, confirming that the type library was successfully generated.

2. Choose the OK button to close the message box.

▶ **To rebuild the control (16- and 32-bit versions)**

1. From the Project menu, choose Build CIRC.DLL.

Testing the Control

Now that the CircleOffset functionality has been implemented, you can test it using Test Container.

▶ **To test the CircleOffset property**

1. From the Tools Menu, choose Test Container.
2. From the Edit menu, select Insert OLE Object.

   The Insert OLE Control dialog box appears.

3. From the Control Class list box, select Circ Control.
4. Choose the OK button to close the Insert OLE Object dialog box and insert a control into Test Container.

The Circle control will be displayed in Test Container's window. Notice that the control is initially drawn as a perfect circle. The default bounding rectangle of the control is a rectangle whose x-extent is greater than its y-extent.

Next, change the value of CircleOffset to cause the circle to move from the center of the bounding rectangle:

▶   **To change the CircleOffset property**

1. From the View menu, choose Properties.

   The Properties dialog box appears.

2. From the Property drop-down combo box, select CircleOffset.

   The Value edit control will display a 0 (zero), which is the CircleOffset
   property's default value.

3. In the Value edit control, type 10.

   This indicates 10 units to the right of center. (If the y-extent of the control were
   larger, it would indicate 10 units to the top of center.)

4. Choose the Apply button.

   The Circle control will be redrawn and the circle will be offset from center by
   10 units.

Experiment with different values for the CircleOffset property: type a negative
number to force the circle to the left of center. Try a number larger than the width
or height of the control; for example, 2000. Notice that nothing happens. In the
Properties dialog box, the number in the Value edit control should revert to
CircleOffset's last valid value.

Now resize the control such that its y-extent is greater than its x-extent. Specify
positive and negative values for the CircleOffset property to see how the circle
moves above and below the center of the control's bounding rectangle.

C H A P T E R 5

Adding Special Effects

This chapter further evolves the functionality of the Circle control. A new behavior is introduced that will produce special effects in response to mouse events at run time.

Note You can find the code produced by implementing the code samples in this chapter in the CIRC2 sample source code directory.

When the left mouse button is clicked inside the circle, the control will briefly flash a different color. To implement this effect the control must respond to mouse events.

A new custom member variable property called FlashColor is introduced. The value of the FlashColor property will contain the color to flash when the left mouse button is clicked within the circle.

In this chapter, you will:

- Add the FlashColor property to the Circle control.
- Implement code to respond to mouse events.
- Implement code to perform hit testing.
- Add the `FlashColor` function.

Adding the FlashColor Property

The FlashColor property holds the color value that will be used to flash the circle. Windows represents a color as a 32-bit value, defined as a **COLORREF** type. The Control Development Kit (CDK) does not directly support the **COLORREF** type, but it does support an **OLE_COLOR** type that can hold the required information. Thus the FlashColor property is defined as an **OLE_COLOR** type.

The FlashColor property requires no special processing when its value is changed or accessed. This means that no Get/Set method pair or notification function is required. For that reason FlashColor can be defined as a simple member variable property.

▶ **To add the FlashColor property**

1. From the Browse menu, choose ClassWizard. If you are using the 32-bit version of the CDK, choose ClassWizard from the Project menu.

2. Choose the OLE Automation tab.

3. From the Class Name drop-down list box, select `CCircCtrl`.

4. Choose the Add Property button.

   The Add Property dialog box appears.

5. In the edit control of the External Name drop-down combo box, type `FlashColor`.

6. Under Implementation, choose Member Variable (it may already be selected).

7. From the Type drop-down list box, select **OLE_COLOR**.

8. Clear the Notification Function edit control.

9. Choose the OK button to close the Add Property dialog box.

   This returns you to the OLE Automation tab. Notice that the implementation of the FlashColor property is listed as

   ```
   Implementation
   OLE_COLOR m_flashColor;
   ```

10. Choose the OK button to confirm your choices and close ClassWizard.

ClassWizard will create the appropriate code to add the FlashColor property to the `CCircCtrl` class and the CIRC.ODL file. Since FlashColor is a member variable property type, ClassWizard will modify the `CCircCtrl` class's dispatch map in CIRCCTL.CPP to include a **DISP_PROPERTY** macro entry:

```
BEGIN_DISPATCH_MAP(CCircCtrl, COleControl)
    //{{AFX_DISPATCH_MAP(CCircCtrl)
    DISP_PROPERTY(CCircCtrl, "FlashColor", m_flashColor, VT_COLOR)
    DISP_PROPERTY_NOTIFY(CCircCtrl, "CircleShape", m_circleShape,
OnCircleShapeChanged, VT_BOOL)
    DISP_PROPERTY_EX(CCircCtrl, "CircleOffset", GetCircleOffset,
SetCircleOffset, VT_I2)
    DISP_STOCKPROP_BACKCOLOR()
    DISP_FUNCTION_ID(CCircCtrl, "AboutBox", DISPID_ABOUTBOX, AboutBox,
VT_EMPTY, VTS_NONE)
    //}}AFX_DISPATCH_MAP
END_DISPATCH_MAP()
```

The **DISP_PROPERTY** macro associates the FlashColor property name with its corresponding `CCircCtrl` class member variable and its type, **VT_COLOR**, which corresponds to an **OLE_COLOR** value.

Setting the Default FlashColor Value

You will now write the code that sets the default value of the FlashColor property. Choosing what the default value should be is relatively unimportant for the example; any arbitrary value will do as long as it's not the same as the background color.

Windows uses a 32-bit unsigned integer value to represent a color. The lowest three bytes specify red, green, and blue values, each with a range from 0 to 255. Therefore, the value 0x000000FF is red, 0x0000FF00 is green, and 0x00FF0000 is blue. To simplify things, the RGB macro will be used. Its three parameters consist of a red, green, and blue value, in that order.

The member function DoPropExchange will initialize the m_flashColor member variable to a value corresponding to the color red. Because the **PX_Long** function expects a reference to a long and m_flashColor is an unsigned long, m_flashColor is cast to a long reference. Add the following marked lines to the DoPropExchange function in CIRCCTL.CPP:

```
void CCircCtrl::DoPropExchange(CPropExchange* pPX)
{
    ExchangeVersion(pPX, MAKELONG(_wVerMinor, _wVerMajor));
    COleControl::DoPropExchange(pPX);

    PX_Bool(pPX, _T("CircleShape"), m_circleShape, TRUE);
    PX_Short(pPX, _T("CircleOffset"), m_circleOffset, 0);
►   PX_Long(pPX, _T("FlashColor"), (long &)m_flashColor, RGB(0xFF, 0x00,
0x00));
}
```

As with all literal strings, the property name string is passed through the **_T** macro before being passed as a parameter to the **PX_Long** function.

Responding to Mouse Events

To better understand how the FlashColor functionality can be implemented, you need to understand the behavior the control should have when the mouse is clicked while over the control. Specifically, when the left mouse button is pressed, the circle will be painted using the color stored as the value of the FlashColor property. When the left mouse button is released, the circle will be repainted using the color stored as the value of the BackColor property. Clicking on the circle will cause it to flash.

To implement the flash behavior, the control must have code that handles mouse events. The mouse events that must be handled map to the following Windows mouse messages:

Message	Response
WM_LBUTTONDOWN	The code responds by painting the circle with the color stored as the value of the FlashColor property.
WM_LBUTTONDBLCLK	The code responds by painting the circle with the color stored as the value of the FlashColor property.
WM_LBUTTONUP	The code responds by painting the circle with the color stored as the value of the BackColor property.

Notice that a **WM_LBUTTONDBLCLK** message will be handled in the same manner as a **WM_LBUTTONDOWN** message. This way, if the left mouse button is double-clicked in the circle, the desired flash effect will occur.

The next step is to use ClassWizard to add a message handler for each of the three mouse messages that you need to handle.

▶ **To add the message handlers**

1. From the Browse menu, choose ClassWizard. If you are using the 32-bit version of the CDK, choose ClassWizard from the Project menu.

2. Choose the Message Maps tab.

3. From the Class Name drop-down list box, select `CCircCtrl`.

4. From the Object IDs list box, select `CCircCtrl`.

   The list of message types appears in the Messages list box.

5. From the Messages list box, select **WM_LBUTTONDOWN**.

6. Choose the Add Function button.

   Notice this new handler is listed in the Member Functions list box as

   ```
   Member Functions
   OnLButtonDown      ON_WM_LBUTTONDOWN
   ```

7. From the Messages list box, select **WM_LBUTTONDBLCLK**.

8. Choose the Add Function button.

   Notice this new handler is listed in the Member Functions list box as

   ```
   Member Functions
   OnLButtonDblClk      ON_WM_LBUTTONDBLCLK
   ```

9. From the Messages list box, select **WM_LBUTTONUP**.

10. Choose the Add Function button.

    Notice this new handler is listed in the Member Functions list box as

    ```
    Member Functions
    OnLButtonUp     ON_WM_LBUTTONUP
    ```

11. Select the **OnLButtonDown...ON_WM_LBUTTONDOWN** entry in the Member Functions list box.

12. Choose the Edit Code button.

    ClassWizard will close and the cursor will be positioned at the `CCircCtrl:OnLButtonDown` function in CIRCCTL.CPP.

The following code shows the fully implemented mouse message handlers. Note that added lines are marked, other lines were inserted by ClassWizard, and the TODO comment lines inserted by ClassWizard have been removed.

```
void CCircCtrl::OnLButtonDown(UINT nFlags, CPoint point)
{
►    CDC* pdc;
►
►    // Flash the color of the control if within the ellipse.
►    if (InCircle(point))
►    {
►        pdc = GetDC();
►        FlashColor(pdc);
►        ReleaseDC(pdc);
►    }
►
     COleControl::OnLButtonDown(nFlags, point);
}

void CCircCtrl::OnLButtonDblClk(UINT nFlags, CPoint point)
{
►    CDC* pdc;
►
►    // Flash the color of the control if within the ellipse.
►    if (InCircle(point))
►    {
►        pdc = GetDC();
►        FlashColor(pdc);
►        ReleaseDC(pdc);
►    }
►
     COleControl::OnLButtonDblClk(nFlags, point);
}

void CCircCtrl::OnLButtonUp(UINT nFlags, CPoint point)
{
```

```
►        // Redraw the control.
►        if (InCircle(point))
►            InvalidateControl();
►
         COleControl::OnLButtonUp(nFlags, point);
     }
```

Both `OnLButtonDown` and `OnLButtonDblClk` implement the same code: the circle will be painted using the color stored as the value of the FlashColor property. The `OnLButtonUp` function performs its job by simply invalidating the control, causing the circle to be redrawn with the normal background color.

Notice that to implement the FlashColor property's behavior, two new functions, `InCircle` and `FlashColor`, have been introduced. These functions are described in the following sections.

Hit Testing

The rule governing the flash behavior of the Circle control is that the circle should only flash if the mouse is within the circular area of the control. To achieve this effect, you must implement what is called hit testing. This means that the coordinates of every mouse click within the control are checked to see if they are within the circle. Hit testing is implemented in the Circle control by the `InCircle` function. `InCircle` returns **TRUE** if the given point is within the area of the circle or ellipse.

► **To implement InCircle**

1. Add the following marked line to your CIRCCTL.H file:

```
class CCircCtrl : public COleControl
{
...
protected:
    ~CCircCtrl();
    void GetDrawRect(CRect* rc);
    short m_circleOffset;
    BOOL InBounds(short nOffset);
►   BOOL InCircle(CPoint& point);
    ...
};
```

2. Add the function implementation at the end of your CIRCCTL.CPP file:

```
BOOL CCircCtrl::InCircle(CPoint& point)
{
    CRect rc;
    GetClientRect(rc);
    GetDrawRect(&rc);

    // Determine radii
    double a = (rc.right - rc.left) / 2;
    double b = (rc.bottom - rc.top) / 2;

    // Determine x, y
    double x = point.x - (rc.left + rc.right) / 2;
    double y = point.y - (rc.top + rc.bottom) / 2;

    // Apply ellipse formula
    return ((x * x) / (a * a) + (y * y) / (b * b) <= 1);
}
```

The function works by calculating whether the point is within the boundary of an ellipse. The GetDrawRect function is called to make the necessary adjustments to the bounding rectangle if the value of the CircleShape property is **TRUE**.

The variables a and b are set to the horizontal and vertical radii of the ellipse. Based on the given point, the variables x and y are translated into the coordinates that are offsets from the center of the ellipse. The last line returns the Boolean result of the calculation, using the standard formula for an ellipse. Note that this calculation is also valid for a circle because a circle is simply a special case of an ellipse.

The mouse message handlers perform hit testing by passing the point coordinates that they receive as parameters to the InCircle member function. If InCircle returns **TRUE**, the circle will be painted appropriately.

The FlashColor Function

The FlashColor function paints the circle using the color value stored as the value of the FlashColor property. The code is similar to the code in the OnDraw function. The difference is that the FlashColor function paints the circle itself using only the value of the FlashColor property, rather than using the value of the BackColor property to fill the background of the ellipse.

▶ **To implement FlashColor**

1. Add the following marked line to your CIRCCTL.H file:

```
class CCircCtrl : public COleControl
{
...
protected:
    ~CCircCtrl();
    void GetDrawRect(CRect* rc);
    short m_circleOffset;
    BOOL InBounds(short nOffset);
    BOOL InCircle(CPoint& point);
    void FlashColor(CDC* pdc);
...
};
```

2. Add the function implementation at the end of your CIRCCTL.CPP file:

```
void CCircCtrl::FlashColor(CDC* pdc)
{
    CBrush* pOldBrush;
    CBrush flashBrush(TranslateColor(m_flashColor));
    CPen* pOldPen;
    CRect rc;

    GetClientRect(rc);
    GetDrawRect(&rc);
    pOldBrush = pdc->SelectObject(&flashBrush);
    pOldPen = (CPen*)pdc->SelectStockObject(BLACK_PEN);
    pdc->Ellipse(rc);
    pdc->SelectObject(pOldPen);
    pdc->SelectObject(pOldBrush);
}
```

The flashBrush variable constructs a solid brush using the value of the FlashColor property stored in m_flashBrush. Since m_flashBrush is an **OLE_COLOR** value, the TranslateColor function is called to convert it to a **COLORREF** value first. The code selects the brush into the device context pdc, making sure to retain the old brush value, in pOldBrush. A stock black pen is also selected into the device context. The old pen value is saved in pOldPen. The ellipse is then drawn with the black pen and filled in with the color specified by the value of the FlashColor property. Finally, the code selects the original pen and brush back into the device context pdc. The solid brush that was created when flashBrush was constructed will be deleted when the flashBrush destructor is called. This will occur when the FlashColor function returns and the flashBrush variable goes out of scope.

Rebuilding the Control

Now that the FlashColor property modifications are complete, you need to rebuild the control. Since the CIRC.ODL file was changed when the FlashColor property was added to the control, the type library must be updated first.

▶ **To update the type library (16-bit version only)**

1. From the Tools menu, choose Make TypeLib to update the Type Library.

   A message box appears, confirming that the type library was successfully generated.

2. Choose the OK button to close the message box.

▶ **To rebuild the control (16- and 32-bit versions)**

1. From the Project menu, choose Build CIRC.DLL.

Testing the FlashColor Property

Now that the FlashColor functionality has been implemented, you can test it using Test Container.

▶ **To test the FlashColor property**

1. Run Test Container by choosing Test Container from the Tools menu.

2. From the Edit menu, choose Insert OLE Control.

   The Insert OLE Control dialog box appears.

3. From the Control Class list box, select Circ Control.

4. Choose the OK button to close the Insert OLE Object dialog box and insert a control into Test Container.

The circle control will be displayed in Test Container's window. Move the mouse over the circle and click once. The circle will flash red, which is the default value to which the FlashColor property was initialized in the `CCircCtrl::DoPropExchange` member function.

▶ **To change the FlashColor property**

1. From the View menu, choose Properties.

   The Properties dialog box appears.

2. From the Property drop-down combo box, select FlashColor.

   The Value edit control will display 255, the default value of the FlashColor property.

3. In the Value edit control, type 0 (zero).

   0 corresponds to the color black.

4. Choose the Apply button.

5. Click on the circle to verify that it will flash black.

You can use these color values to test the control:

Color	Hex Value	Decimal Value
White	0x00FFFFFF	16777215
Black	0x00000000	0
Gray	0x00808080	8421504
Red	0x000000FF	255
Yellow	0x0000FFFF	65535
Green	0x0000FF00	65280
Cyan	0x00FFFF00	16776960
Blue	0x00FF0000	16711680
Magenta	0x00FF00FF	16711935

C H A P T E R   6

Adding Custom Events

This chapter illustrates how to add custom events to the Circle control. A custom event allows a control to represent an occurrence of a condition as an event. Firing a custom event allows the control to notify its container that an event has occurred. The control's container then has the option to act on the event or ignore it. Commonly an event is caused by user interaction, such as mouse or keyboard input, a Windows interaction, or a special condition occurring in the control itself.

Note   You can find the code produced by implementing the code samples in this chapter in the CIRC2 sample source code directory.

The ClickIn and ClickOut custom events will be added. The ClickIn event is fired when the user presses the left mouse button with the mouse pointer within the circle of the control. The ClickOut event is fired when the user clicks the left mouse button when the mouse pointer is positioned outside the circle.

In this chapter, you will:

- Add the ClickIn event to the control.
- Implement the code to fire the ClickIn event.
- Add the ClickOut event to the control.
- Implement the code to fire the ClickOut event.
- Test the operation of the new events.

Adding the ClickIn Event

Like properties, events are added to a control using ClassWizard. When you add a custom event, ClassWizard creates the appropriate code necessary to declare the event. Causing the event to be fired requires additional coding on the part of the control writer. A stock event such as KeyDown, however, will fire under predefined conditions.

Note When using ClassWizard, the .ODL, .H, .CPP, and .CLW files must have write permission.

An event can also define arguments that it can pass to the control's container when the event is fired. Event arguments can be added using ClassWizard. You will define two arguments for the ClickIn event: x and y. These arguments represent the x and y coordinates of the mouse position when the left mouse button is pressed.

▶ To add the ClickIn event

1. From the Browse menu, choose ClassWizard. If you are using the 32-bit version of the CDK, choose ClassWizard from the Project menu.

2. Choose the OLE Events tab.

3. From the Class Name drop-down list box, select `CCircCtrl`.

4. Choose the Add Event button.

    The Add Event dialog box appears.

5. In the edit control of the External Name drop-down combo box, type **ClickIn**.

6. Choose the Add button.

    The Add Event Parameter dialog box appears.

7. In the Name edit control, type x.

8. From the Type drop-down list box, select **OLE_XPOS_PIXELS**.

9. Choose the Add button to add the x parameter.

10. In the Name edit control, type y.

11. From the Type drop-down list box, select **OLE_YPOS_PIXELS**.

12. Choose the Add button to add the y parameter.

13. Choose the Close button to close the Add Event Parameter dialog box.

    This returns you to the Add Event dialog box. Notice that the x and y parameters of the ClickIn event are listed in the Parameter List list box as

    ```
    Name                     Type
    x                        OLE_XPOS_PIXELS
    y                        OLE_YPOS_PIXELS
    ```

14. Choose the OK button to close the Add Event dialog box.

    This returns you to the OLE Events tab. Notice that the implementation of the ClickIn event is listed as

    ```
    Implementation:
    void FireClickIn(OLE_XPOS_PIXELS x, OLE_YPOS_PIXELS y);
    ```

15. Choose the OK button to confirm your choices and close ClassWizard.

ClassWizard will create the appropriate code to add the ClickIn event, modifying the CCircCtrl class files and the CIRC.ODL file.

ClassWizard modifies the CCircCtrl class event map in CIRCCTL.CPP to add a macro entry for the ClickIn event:

```
BEGIN_EVENT_MAP(CCircCtrl, COleControl)
    //{{AFX_EVENT_MAP(CCircCtrl)
    EVENT_CUSTOM("ClickIn", FireClickIn, VTS_XPOS_PIXELS
VTS_YPOS_PIXELS)
    //}}AFX_EVENT_MAP
END_EVENT_MAP()
```

The macro **EVENT_CUSTOM** associates the ClickIn event name with FireClickIn, the function that actually fires the event, and with the type definitions for the x and y arguments that ClickIn uses.

An inline function is added to the CCircCtrl class declaration in CIRCCTL.H which, when called, causes the ClickIn event to be fired. The FireClickIn function simply calls the FireEvent function to do its work. Event functions like FireClickIn are added to provide a type-safe way of firing an event.

```
class CCircCtrl : public COleControl
{
    ...
    //{{AFX_EVENT(CCircCtrl)
    void FireClickIn(OLE_XPOS_PIXELS x, OLE_YPOS_PIXELS y)
        {FireEvent(eventidClickIn,EVENT_PARAM(VTS_XPOS_PIXELS
VTS_YPOS_PIXELS), x, y);}
    //}}AFX_EVENT
    ...
}
```

Firing the ClickIn Event

Now that the ClickIn event has been properly declared, it can be fired. The control itself determines when the custom event should be fired. In this example, the ClickIn event is to be fired when the user presses the left mouse button within the circle of the control.

The code which fires the ClickIn event should be triggered when a **WM_LBUTTONDOWN** message is received from Windows. The Circle control already has a message handler function defined for **WM_LBUTTONDOWN**— the OnLButtonDown function in CIRCCTL.CPP. Add the marked lines to change OnLButtonDown to fire the ClickIn event:

```
void CCircCtrl::OnLButtonDown(UINT nFlags, CPoint point)
{
    CDC* pdc;

    // Flash the color of the control if within the ellipse.
    if (InCircle(point))
    {
        pdc = GetDC();
        FlashColor(pdc);
        ReleaseDC(pdc);

        // Fire the ClickIn event
        FireClickIn(point.x, point.y);
    }

    COleControl::OnLButtonDown(nFlags, point);
}
```

Modifying `OnLButtonDown` to fire the event requires a call to the `FireClickIn` function. The call to `FireClickIn` is made only if the `InCircle` function returns **TRUE**, which means that the mouse pointer is within the circle.

Adding the ClickOut Event

When the left mouse button is pressed and the mouse pointer is outside the circle of the control, the ClickOut event should be fired. The ClickOut event is simpler than the ClickIn event in that it defines no arguments.

▶ **To add the ClickOut event**

1. From the Browse menu, choose ClassWizard. If you are using the 32-bit version of the CDK, choose ClassWizard from the Project menu.

2. Choose the OLE Events tab.

3. From the Class Name drop-down list box, select `CCircCtrl`.

4. Choose the Add Event button.

   The Add Event dialog box appears.

5. In the edit control of the External Name drop-down combo box, type `ClickOut`.

6. Choose the OK button to close the Add Event dialog box.

   This returns you to the OLE Events tab. Notice that the implementation of the ClickOut event is listed as

   ```
   Implementation:
   void FireClickOut();
   ```

7. Choose the OK button to confirm your choices and close ClassWizard.

As with the ClickIn event, ClassWizard creates the appropriate code to add the ClickOut event, modifying the files CIRC.ODL, CIRCCTL.H and CIRCCTL.CPP.

ClassWizard modifies the CCircCtrl class's event map in CIRCCTL.H to add a macro entry for the ClickOut event:

```
BEGIN_EVENT_MAP(CCircCtrl, COleControl)
    //{{AFX_EVENT_MAP(CCircCtrl)
    EVENT_CUSTOM("ClickIn", FireClickIn, VTS_XPOS_PIXELS
VTS_YPOS_PIXELS)
    EVENT_CUSTOM("ClickOut", FireClickOut, VTS_NONE)
    //}}AFX_EVENT_MAP
END_EVENT_MAP()
```

The macro **EVENT_CUSTOM** associates the ClickOut event name with the member function FireClickOut and with its argument type definition. The ClickOut argument type definition is set to **VTS_NONE**, which indicates that the ClickOut event passes no arguments.

An additional inline function is added to the CCircCtrl class declaration. The FireClickOut function provides a type-safe call to fire the event:

```
class CCircCtrl : public COleControl
{
    ...
    //{{AFX_EVENT(CCircCtrl)
    void FireClickIn(OLE_XPOS_PIXELS x, OLE_YPOS_PIXELS y)
        {FireEvent(eventidClickIn,EVENT_PARAM(VTS_XPOS_PIXELS
VTS_YPOS_PIXELS), x, y);}
    void FireClickOut()
        {FireEvent(eventidClickOut,EVENT_PARAM(VTS_NONE));}
    //}}AFX_EVENT
    ...
}
```

Firing the ClickOut Event

Firing the ClickOut event requires the existence of a condition opposite to the one that fires the ClickIn event. To accomplish this, you modify the OnLButtonDown function in CIRCCTL.CPP to call FireClickOut when the mouse pointer is not within the circle (that is, the InCircle function returns **FALSE**). The FireClickOut function will cause the event to be fired.

```
void CCircCtrl::OnLButtonDown(UINT nFlags, CPoint point)
{
    CDC*    pdc;

    // Flash the color of the control if within the ellipse.
    if (InCircle(point))
    {
        pdc = GetDC();
        FlashColor(pdc);
        ReleaseDC(pdc);

        // Fire the ClickIn event
        FireClickIn(point.x, point.y);
    }
    else
        // Fire the ClickOut event
        FireClickOut();

    COleControl::OnLButtonDown(nFlags, point);
}
```

Rebuilding the Control

Now that the ClickIn and ClickOut events have been added, you need to rebuild the control. Since the CIRC.ODL file was changed, the type library must be updated first.

▶ **To update the type library (16-bit version only)**

1. From the Tools menu, choose Make TypeLib to update the Type Library.

   A message box appears, confirming that the type library was successfully generated.

2. Choose the OK button to close the message box.

▶ **To rebuild the control (16- and 32-bit versions)**

1. From the Project menu, choose Build CIRC.DLL.

Testing the Events

Now that the ClickIn and ClickOut events have been defined and the code has been implemented to fire the events, you can use Test Container to verify that the events are indeed being fired.

▶ **To test the ClickIn and ClickOut events**

1. Run Test Container by choosing Test Container from the Tools menu.

2. From the Edit menu, choose Insert OLE Control.

The Insert OLE Control dialog box appears.

3. From the Control Class list box, select Circ Control.

4. Choose the OK button to close the Insert OLE Object dialog box and insert a control into Test Container.

5. From the View menu, choose Event Log.

    The Event Log dialog box appears.

The Event Log dialog displays events sent to Test Container as they occur.

▶   **To fire ClickIn and ClickOut events**

1. Position the mouse pointer within the circle and click the left mouse button.

    A ClickIn entry is added to the Event Log list box, and the x and y mouse coordinates are shown.

2. Position the mouse pointer outside the circle and click the left mouse button.

    A ClickOut entry is added to the Event Log. Notice that no arguments are shown because none were defined for this event.

C H A P T E R 7

Handling Text and Fonts

This chapter explores the text and font support in the Control Development Kit (CDK). Three stock properties will be added to implement a caption in the Circle control. These properties, Caption, Font, and ForeColor, allow you to draw text in the control using any font.

Note You can find the code produced by implementing the code samples in this chapter in the CIRC3 sample source code directory.

The Circle sample uses the stock Caption property to hold the text of the caption. The stock Font property holds the font that the Circle control uses to draw its caption. The caption text is drawn using the color stored as the value of the ForeColor property.

To obtain more information about stock properties, see Chapter 7 of the *CDK Programmer's Guide*, "Methods and Properties." Also see Chapter 10 of the *CDK Programmer's Guide*, "Using Fonts in Your Control," which contains additional information about fonts in the CDK.

In this chapter, you will:

- Add the stock Caption property.
- Add the stock Font property.
- Add the stock ForeColor property.
- Implement the caption drawing behavior.
- Add stock color and font property pages.
- Test the Caption drawing behavior.

Adding the Stock Caption Property

To add the stock Caption property, you will use ClassWizard. The same procedure used to add the stock Caption property from Chapter 7 of the *CDK Programmer's Guide*, "Methods and Properties," will be followed.

▶ **To add the stock Caption property**

1. From the Browse menu, choose ClassWizard. If you are using the 32-bit version of the CDK, choose ClassWizard from the Project menu.

2. Choose the OLE Automation tab.

3. In the Class Name drop-down list box, select `CCircCtrl`.

4. Choose the Add Property button.

   The Add Property dialog box appears.

5. From the External Name drop-down combo box, select Caption.

6. Under Implementation choose **Stock** (it may already be selected).

7. Choose the OK button to close the Add Property dialog box.

   This returns you to the OLE Automation tab. Notice that the implementation of the Caption property is listed as

   ```
   Implementation:
   Stock Property
   ```

8. Choose the OK button to confirm your choices and close ClassWizard.

ClassWizard creates the appropriate code to add the Caption property, modifying both the `CCircCtrl` class and the CIRC.ODL file.

ClassWizard modifies the `CCircCtrl` class dispatch map in CIRCCTL.CPP to add a macro entry for the Caption property:

```
BEGIN_DISPATCH_MAP(CCircCtrl, COleControl)
    //{{AFX_DISPATCH_MAP(CCircCtrl)
    DISP_PROPERTY(CCircCtrl, "FlashColor", m_flashColor, VT_COLOR)
    DISP_PROPERTY_NOTIFY(CCircCtrl, "CircleShape", m_circleShape,
OnCircleShapeChanged, VT_BOOL)
    DISP_PROPERTY_EX(CCircCtrl, "CircleOffset", GetCircleOffset,
SetCircleOffset, VT_I2)
    DISP_STOCKPROP_BACKCOLOR()
    DISP_STOCKPROP_CAPTION()
    DISP_FUNCTION_ID(CCircCtrl, "AboutBox", DISPID_ABOUTBOX, AboutBox,
VT_EMPTY, VTS_NONE)
    //}}AFX_DISPATCH_MAP
END_DISPATCH_MAP()
```

The macro **DISP_STOCKPROP_CAPTION** enables the stock Caption property in the Circle control. The Caption property is implemented as a Get/Set property. The Caption property is an alias for the stock Text property. The Get method, Set method, and notification function for the Caption property are the **GetText**, **SetText**, and **OnTextChanged** functions in the **COleControl** class.

The **OnTextChanged** function is invoked when the Caption property is modified through the **SetText** function. By default, **OnTextChanged** simply invalidates the control.

Stock property notification functions like **OnTextChanged** can be overridden in the descendant control class. For example, you may wish to provide a more optimal solution for redrawing the caption other than invalidating the control, which forces the whole control to repaint.

In addition to the **GetText** function, the Caption property can be accessed directly through the **InternalGetText** function of **COleControl**. **InternalGetText** is useful when the caption text is used in a read-only manner. The `CCircCtrl::OnDraw` function will be changed to use the **InternalGetText** function to draw the caption text.

Adding the Stock Font Property

The circle control will use the font information contained in the stock Font property to draw the caption text. The Font property is actually a pointer to a font object that is encapsulated by the **CFontHolder** class. The font object contains several properties of its own that describe the current font. These properties are accessible through the font object's **IDispatch** interface.

▶ **To add the stock Font property**

1. From the Browse menu, choose ClassWizard. If you are using the 32-bit version of the CDK, choose ClassWizard from the Project menu.

2. Choose the OLE Automation tab.

3. In the Class Name drop-down list box, select `CCircCtrl`.

4. Choose the Add Property button.

   The Add Property dialog box appears.

5. From the External Name drop-down combo box, select Font.

6. Under Implementation choose **Stock** (it may already be selected).

7. Choose the OK button to close the Add Property dialog box.

   This returns you to the OLE Automation tab. Notice that the implementation of the Font property is listed as

   ```
   Implementation:
   Stock Property
   ```

8. Choose the OK button to confirm your choices and close ClassWizard.

ClassWizard will create the appropriate code to add the Font property, modifying both the `CCircCtrl` class and the CIRC.ODL file.

ClassWizard modifies the `CCircCtrl` class dispatch map to add a
DISP_STOCKPROP_FONT macro entry for the Font property:

```
BEGIN_DISPATCH_MAP(CCircCtrl, COleControl)
    //{{AFX_DISPATCH_MAP(CCircCtrl)
    DISP_PROPERTY(CCircCtrl, "FlashColor", m_flashColor, VT_COLOR)
    DISP_PROPERTY_NOTIFY(CCircCtrl, "CircleShape", m_circleShape,
OnCircleShapeChanged, VT_BOOL)
    DISP_PROPERTY_EX(CCircCtrl, "CircleOffset", GetCircleOffset,
SetCircleOffset, VT_I2)
    DISP_STOCKPROP_BACKCOLOR()
    DISP_STOCKPROP_CAPTION()
    DISP_STOCKPROP_FONT()
    DISP_FUNCTION_ID(CCircCtrl, "AboutBox", DISPID_ABOUTBOX, AboutBox,
VT_EMPTY, VTS_NONE)
    //}}AFX_DISPATCH_MAP
END_DISPATCH_MAP()
```

Like the Caption property the Font property is implemented as a Get/Set property.
The Font property also supports a notification function called **OnFontChanged**,
which is defined in the **COleControl** class. This function by default simply
invalidates the control. **OnFontChanged** can be overridden in the control class to
provide a more optimal solution to reflecting the font change.

Adding the Stock ForeColor Property

The last property that you have to add is the stock ForeColor property. This
property contains the foreground color that the control will use to paint the caption
text. Like the stock BackColor property, the ForeColor property is also a Get/Set
property type.

▶ **To add the stock ForeColor property**

1. From the Browse menu, choose ClassWizard. If you are using the 32-bit version
   of the CDK, choose ClassWizard from the Project menu.

2. Choose the OLE Automation tab.

3. In the Class Name drop-down list box, select `CCircCtrl`.

4. Choose the Add Property button.

   The Add Property dialog box appears.

5. From the External Name drop-down combo box, select ForeColor.

6. Under Implementation choose **Stock** (it may already be selected).

7. Choose the OK button to close the Add Property dialog box.

   This returns you to the OLE Automation tab. Notice that the implementation of
   the ForeColor property is listed as

```
Implementation:
Stock Property
```

8. Choose the OK button to confirm your choices and close ClassWizard.

By now, you are an expert on adding properties. As with all the other stock properties that you have added, ClassWizard updates both the `CCircCtrl` class and the CIRC.ODL file.

Implementing the Caption Drawing

Now that all the necessary properties are in place, the caption drawing behavior can be implemented. To draw the caption text, you must modify the `CCircCtrl::OnDraw` function in CIRCCTL.CPP.

The drawing code changes require that the device context passed to the `OnDraw` function be modified to reflect the background and foreground colors stored as the values of the BackColor and ForeColor properties, respectively. The font contained in the Font property must also be selected into the device context before the caption text can be drawn. The **InternalGetText** function retrieves the caption text drawn using the **ExtTextOut** function.

▶ **To implement caption drawing in your control**

- Modify the `OnDraw` member function in CIRCCTL.CPP with the marked lines.

```
    void CCircCtrl::OnDraw(
            CDC* pdc, const CRect& rcBounds, const CRect& rcInvalid)
    {
        CBrush* pOldBrush;
        CBrush bkBrush(TranslateColor(GetBackColor()));
        CPen* pOldPen;
        CRect rc = rcBounds;
▶        CFont pOldFont;
▶        TEXTMETRIC tm;
▶        const CString& strCaption = InternalGetText();
▶
▶        // Set the ForeColor property color and transparent background
    mode into the device context
▶        pdc->SetTextColor(TranslateColor(GetForeColor()));
▶        pdc->SetBkMode(TRANSPARENT);

        // Paint the background using the BackColor property
        pdc->FillRect(rcBounds, &bkBrush);

        // Draw the ellipse
        GetDrawRect(&rc);
        pOldBrush = pdc->SelectObject(&bkBrush);
        pdc->Ellipse(rc);
```

```
▶        // Draw the caption using the stock Font and ForeColor properties
▶        pOldFont = SelectStockFont(pdc);
▶        pdc->GetTextMetrics(&tm);
▶        pdc->SetTextAlign(TA_CENTER | TA_TOP);
▶        pdc->ExtTextOut((rc.left + rc.right) / 2, (rc.top + rc.bottom -
   tm.tmHeight) / 2,
▶            ETO_CLIPPED, rc, strCaption, strCaption.GetLength(), NULL);
▶        pdc->SelectObject(pOldFont);
▶
        pdc->SelectObject(pOldPen);
        pdc->SelectObject(pOldBrush);
   }
```

The code changes above, indicated by the marked lines, start by declaring three new local variables. The pOldFont variable holds the old font from the device context. The tm variable holds text metric information about the font used to draw the text. The strCaption variable is the text to be drawn. It is initialized by calling the **InternalGetText** function to get the value of the Caption property. The **InternalGetText** function should be used instead of the **GetText** function whenever the returned text will not be modified, since the **GetText** function returns a copy of the caption text which must be freed.

```
CFont pOldFont;
TEXTMETRIC tm;
const CString& strCaption = InternalGetText();
```

The text color of the device context is set to the current value of the ForeColor property. The **OLE_COLOR** value returned by the **GetForeColor** function is translated by the **TranslateColor** function into a **COLORREF** value and is then passed as a parameter to the **SetTextColor** function to set the text color in the device context. **OLE_COLOR** values must be translated via the **TranslateColor** function whenever a **COLORREF** value is required.

```
pdc->SetTextColor(TranslateColor(GetForeColor()));
```

The background mode of the text is made transparent in the device context by calling the **SetBkMode** function.

```
pdc->SetBkMode(TRANSPARENT);
```

Calling the **SelectStockFont** function, defined in the **COleControl** base class, selects the current font stored as the value of the stock Font property into the device context. The font that used to be selected into the device context is kept in the **pOldFont** variable to be selected back into the device context later.

```
pOldfont = SelectStockFont(pdc);
```

The text metrics for the font in the device context are retrieved by calling the **GetTextMetrics** function. The text metrics will be used to center the text vertically. The text alignment of the device context is set using the **SetTextAlign** function so that text is centered horizontally. The text is drawn by calling the **ExtTextOut** function. The text is clipped to the bounding rectangle of the circle or ellipse (which may be different from the bounding rectangle of the control if the CircleShape property is true) and centered both horizontally and vertically. Note that any function affecting the device context passed to the **OnDraw** function must be among the subset of functions which are allowed for both metafile device contexts and standard device contexts. See Chapter 4 of the *CDK Programmer's Guide*, "Painting the Control," for more information.

```
pdc->GetTextMetrics(&tm);
pdc->SetTextAlign(TA_CENTER | TA_TOP);
pdc->ExtTextOut((rc.left + rc.right) / 2, (rc.top + rc.bottom -
tm.tmHeight) / 2,
        ETO_CLIPPED, rc, strCaption, strCaption.GetLength(), NULL);
```

The font that used to be selected in the device context is put back using the **SelectObject** function.

```
pdc->SelectObject(pOldFont);
```

Adding the Color and Font Property Pages

The CDK supports stock color and font property pages that can be easily implemented in a control by adding entries to a control's property page ID table. ClassWizard produced a property page ID table in CIRCCTL.CPP that looks like this:

```
BEGIN_PROPPAGEIDS(CCircCtrl, 1)
    PROPPAGEID(CCircPropPage::guid)
END_PROPPAGEIDS(CCircCtrl)
```

When editing the property page section, you must be careful to modify the page count number in the **BEGIN_PROPPAGEIDS** macro to reflect the actual number of property pages implemented by the control. In the case of the Circle control, the number will be 3 when the color and font property pages are added. The first property page is the default generated by ControlWizard, the second will be the color property page, and the third will be the font property page.

▶ **Change the ID count and add lines for the color and font property pages**

```
▶ BEGIN_PROPPAGEIDS(CCircCtrl, 3)
    PROPPAGEID(CCircPropPage::guid)
▶   PROPPAGEID(CLSID_CColorPropPage)
▶   PROPPAGEID(CLSID_CFontPropPage)
  END_PROPPAGEIDS(CCircCtrl)
```

The default property page is supplied so that properties can be viewed and edited. The CDK also provides a stock property page support for picture properties. See

Chapter 8 of the *CDK Programmer's Guide*, "Property Pages," for more information on property pages.

Rebuilding the Control

Now that font and color support and two stock property pages have been added, you need to rebuild the control. Since the CIRC.ODL file was changed, the type library must be updated first.

▶ **To update the type library (16-bit version only)**

1. From the Tools menu, choose Make TypeLib to update the Type Library.

   A message box appears, confirming that the type library was successfully generated.

2. Choose the OK button to close the message box.

▶ **To rebuild the control (16- and 32-bit versions)**

1. From the Project menu, choose Build CIRC.DLL.

Testing the Caption Property

The caption drawing behavior can now be tested using Test Container.

▶ **To test the caption property**

1. From the Tools menu, choose Test Container.
2. From the Edit menu, choose Insert OLE Control.

   The Insert OLE Control dialog box appears.

3. From the Control Class list box, select Circ Control.
4. Choose the OK button to close the Insert OLE Object dialog box and insert a control into Test Container.
5. From the View menu, choose Properties.

   The Properties dialog box appears.

6. From the Property drop-down combo box, select Caption..
7. In the Value edit control, type Hello.
8. Choose the Apply button.

The string "Hello" will be displayed in the circle. Now try typing some longer phrases for the caption. You will notice that the phrase will be clipped to the bounds of the circle.

The next test you can perform is to modify the color and font that the caption is being displayed in.

▶ **To modify the color and font properties**

1. From the Edit menu, choose Circ Control Object, then Properties.

   The Circ Control Properties dialog appears.

2. From the Circ Control Properties drop-down list box, select Fonts.

   You can now modify the different font properties as you please. Choose the Apply button whenever you wish to see your changes reflected in the control. Notice that the Property Name drop-down list box contains only one entry—the stock Font property that you added. If there were other custom font properties in the control, they would also be listed.

3. From the Circ Control Properties drop-down list box, select Colors.

   You can now modify the different color properties as you please. Choose the Apply button whenever you wish to see your changes reflected in the control. Notice that the Property Name drop-down list box contains three entries—the stock BackColor, stock ForeColor, and custom FlashColor properties

C H A P T E R   8

Modifying the Default
Property Page

This chapter illustrates how to work with the default property page. The default property page is essentially a dialog box to which various controls can be added. ControlWizard supplies the default property page when an OLE control project is first created.

Note The code produced by doing the code samples in this chapter can be found in the CIRC3 sample source code directory.

Property pages are the interface through which a control's properties may be viewed and/or edited at design time. The default property page is used to display and modify properties that are not handled by stock property pages, such as the stock font property page added to the Circle control in Chapter 7, "Handling Text and Fonts," or the stock color property page which is also provided by the CDK. See Chapter 8 "Property Pages" of the *CDK Programmer's Guide* for more information about custom and stock property pages.

The default property page will be modified so that it can be used to display and modify the Caption property.

In this chapter, you will:

- Add controls to the default property page.
- Link the controls to the Caption, CircleOffset, and CircleShape properties.
- Test the operation of the default property page.

Adding Controls to the Default Property Page

When the Circle control was created, ControlWizard included a default property page. The property pages are listed in the property page ID table in CIRCCTL.CPP:

```
BEGIN_PROPPAGEIDS(CCircCtrl, 3)
    PROPPAGEID(CCircPropPage::guid)
    PROPPAGEID(CLSID_CColorPropPage)
    PROPPAGEID(CLSID_CFontPropPage)
END_PROPPAGEIDS(CCircCtrl)
```

The first entry in the Property page ID table is the default (or general) property page. The second and third are the stock color and font property pages which were added in Chapter 7, "Handling Text and Fonts."

The default property page's dialog template is initially empty. Adding controls to the default property page dialog template is done using the dialog editor.

▶ **To add controls to the default property page(16-bit)**

1. Load your project's .RC file into App Studio. If the project is open in the development environment and you start the resource editor by choosing App Studio in the Tools menu, the .RC file is loaded automatically.

2. Choose Dialog from the Type list box.

3. Choose **IDD_PROPPAGE_CIRCCTRL** from the Resources list box.

4. Choose the Open button to edit the dialog.

5. Select the Static Text tool in the Control Palette and place a static text control in the dialog. Using the Property Window, change the static text control's Caption to "&Caption:".

6. Select the Edit box tool in the Control Palette and place an edit control next to the static text control in the dialog. Using the Property Window, change the edit control's ID to **IDC_CAPTION**.

7. Select the Static Text tool in the Control Palette and place another static text control in the dialog. Using the Property Window, change the static text control's Caption to "Circle&Offset:".

8. Select the Edit box tool in the Control Palette and place an edit control next to the static text control in the dialog. Using the Property Window, change the edit control's ID to **IDC_CIRCLEOFFSET**.

9. Select the Check box tool in the Control Palette and place a check box in the dialog. Using the Property Window, change the check box's ID to **IDC_CIRCLESHAPE**, change the chcck box's Caption to "Circle&Shape", and check the Left Text check box.

10. Arrange the controls to your liking.

11. Save the changes to the dialog and exit App Studio.

▶ **To add controls to the default property page(32-bit)**

1. Open the project's .RC file from the Source Files folder by double-clicking on the .RC file icon.

2.   Open the Dialog folder by double-clicking on the Dialog folder icon.

3.   Double-click on the **IDD_PROPPAGE_CIRCCTRL** entry under the Dialog folder to edit the dialog.

4.   Select the Static Text tool in the Control Palette and place a static text control in the dialog. Using the Property Window, change the static text control's Caption to "&Caption:".

5.   Select the Edit box tool in the Control Palette and place an edit control next to the static text control in the dialog. Using the Property Window, change the edit control's ID to **IDC_CAPTION**.

6.   Select the Static Text tool in the Control Palette and place another static text control in the dialog. Using the Property Window, change the static text control's Caption to "Circle&Offset:".

7.   Select the Edit box tool in the Control Palette and place an edit control next to the static text control in the dialog. Using the Property Window, change the edit control's ID to **IDC_CIRCLEOFFSET**.

8.   Select the Check box tool in the Control Palette and place a check box in the dialog. Using the Property Window, change the check box's ID to **IDC_CIRCLESHAPE**, change the check box's Caption to "Circle&Shape", and check the Left Text check box.

9.   Arrange the controls to your liking.

10. Save the changes to the dialog and close the dialog editor window and the CIRC.RC window.

Linking Controls with Properties

Now that the property page itself has controls for displaying and modifying properties, the controls need to be linked to the properties.

Links between controls in the property page and properties are established using ClassWizard.

▶   **To link the property page controls to properties**

1.   From the Browse menu, choose ClassWizard. If you are using the 32-bit version of the CDK, choose ClassWizard from the Project menu.

2.   Choose the Member Variables tab.

3.   In the Class Name drop-down list box, select `CCircPropPage`.

Notice that the control IDs are listed in the Control IDs list box as

```
Control IDs:              Type        Member
IDC_CAPTION
IDC_CIRCLEOFFSET
IDC_CIRCLESHAPE
```

4. Select IDC_CAPTION in the Control IDs list box.

5. Choose the Add Variable button.

   The Add Member Variable dialog box appears.

6. Type `caption` into the Member Variable Name edit control, after the m_ that is already there, so that the edit control contains `m_caption`.

7. Choose `Value` in the Category drop-down list box.

8. Choose `CString` in the Variable Type drop-down list box.

9. Choose `Caption` in the Optional OLE Property Name drop-down combo box.

10. Choose the OK button to close the Add Member Variable dialog box.

    This returns you to the Member Variable tab of ClassWizard. Notice that the control IDs are listed in the Control IDs list box as

    ```
    Control IDs:              Type      Member
    IDC_CAPTION               CString   m_caption
    IDC_CIRCLEOFFSET
    IDC_CIRCLESHAPE
    ```

11. Repeat steps 4 through 10 selecting IDC_CIRCLEOFFSET in the Control IDs list box, typing `circleOffset` into the Member Variable Name edit control so that the edit control contains `m_circleOffset`, choosing `int` in the Variable Type drop-down list box, and typing `CircleOffset` into the Optional OLE Property Name drop-down combo box.

    When you return to the Member Variable tab of ClassWizard, the control IDs should be listed in the Control IDs list box as

    ```
    Control IDs:              Type      Member
    IDC_CAPTION               CString   m_caption
    IDC_CIRCLEOFFSET          int       m_circleOffset
    IDC_CIRCLESHAPE
    ```

12. Repeat steps 4 through 10 selecting IDC_CIRCLESHAPE in the Control IDs list box, typing `circleShape` into the Member Variable Name edit control so that the edit control contains `m_circleShape`, choosing **BOOL** in the Variable Type drop-down list box, and typing `CircleShape` into the Optional OLE Property Name drop-down combo box.

    When you return to the Member Variable tab of ClassWizard, the control IDs should be listed in the Control IDs list box as

    ```
    Control IDs:              Type      Member
    IDC_CAPTION               CString   m_caption
    IDC_CIRCLEOFFSET          int       m_circleOffset
    IDC_CIRCLESHAPE           BOOL      m_circleShape
    ```

ClassWizard adds the member variables to the `CCircPropPage` class. ClassWizard also adds functions in the `CCircPropPage` class to initialize the member variables and handle the exchange of data between the dialog controls, the member variables, and the properties.

The `m_caption`, `m_circleOffset`, and `m_circleShape` member variables are declared in CIRCPPG.H:

```
class CCircPropPage : public CPropertyPageDialog
{
    ...
    //{{AFX_DATA(CCircPropPage)
    ...
    CString m_caption;
    int m_circleOffset;
    BOOL m_circleShape;
    //}}AFX_DATA
    ...
};
```

The member variables are initialized in the constructor for the `CCircPropPage` class, the `CCircPropPage` function in CIRCPPG.CPP:

```
CCircPropPage::CCircPropPage() :
    CPropertyPageDialog(AfxGetInstanceHandle(), IDD,
IDS_CIRCCTRL_PPG_CAPTION)
{
    //{{AFX_DATA_INIT(CCircPropPage)
    m_caption = _T("");
    m_circleOffset = 0;
    m_circleShape = FALSE;
    //}}AFX_DATA_INIT
}
```

Notice that strings assigned to member variables are first passed through the **_T** macro. This is the same macro used for string parameters to **PX_** functions in the **CCircCtrl::DoPropExchange** function. the **_T** macro is used to maintain compatibility between different string representations and must be used for all literal strings in an OLE custom control project.

Data transfer is handled by the **DDP_** and **DDX_** macros in the `DoDataExchange` function, in CIRCPPG.CPP:

```
void CCircPropPage::DoDataExchange(CDataExchange* pDX)
{
    //{{AFX_DATA_MAP(CCircPropPage)
    DDP_Text(pDX, IDC_CAPTION, m_caption, _T("Caption"));
    DDX_Text(pDX, IDC_CAPTION, m_caption);
    DDP_Text(pDX, IDC_CIRCLEOFFSET, m_circleOffset, _T("CircleOffset"));
    DDX_Text(pDX, IDC_CIRCLEOFFSET, m_circleOffset);
    DDP_Check(pDX, IDC_CIRCLESHAPE, m_circleShape, _T("CircleShape"));
    DDX_Check(pDX, IDC_CIRCLESHAPE, m_circleShape);
    //}}AFX_DATA_MAP
    DDP_PostProcessing(pDX);
}
```

The **DDX_** macros are the same macros used for normal MFC dialogs. They synchronize dialog controls with dialog member variables. The **DDP_**macros are used only in OLE custom control property pages. They synchronize property page dialog member variables with specific control properties. Translations between an edit control and a short value and between a check box and a **BOOL** value are automatic. As above with strings assigned to member variables, strings passed as parameters to **DDP_** macros are first passed through the **_T** macro.

The Circle control now has a general property page which can be used to display and modify the value of several of its properties. The IDC_CAPTION edit control, IDC_CIRCLEOFFSET edit control, and IDC_CIRCLESHAPE check box are linked through property page member variables to the Caption, CircleOffset, and CircleShape properties respectively. Between the general property page and the stock color and font property pages added earlier, all properties of the Circle control are now accessible through property pages.

The Circle control now has a general property page which can be used to display and modify the value of several of its properties..

Rebuilding the Control

Since changes have been made, you need to rebuild the control. This time the CIRC.ODL file was not changed, so the type library need not be updated first.

▶   **To rebuild the control**

- From the Project menu, choose Build CIRC.DLL.

Testing the Default Property Page

You can use Test Container to verify that the default property page now has controls which are linked to the Caption, CircleOffset, and CircleShape properties.

▶ **To test the default property page**

1. From the Tools menu, choose Test Container.

2. From the Edit menu, select Insert OLE Control.

   The Insert OLE Control dialog box appears.

3. From the Control Class list box, choose Circ Control.

4. Choose the OK button to close the Insert OLE Object dialog box and insert a control into Test Container.

5. From the Edit menu, choose Circ Control Object, then choose Properties.

   The Circ Control Properties dialog box appears.

6. From the Circ Control Properties drop-down list box, select General. The modified property page appears.

7. Change the Caption, CircleOffset, and CircleShape properties using the property page. Choose the Apply button whenever you wish to see your changes reflected in the control.

C H A P T E R   9

Simple Data Binding

One of the more powerful features of OLE custom controls is data binding, which is a notification mechanism that enables control properties to be linked through the container to a data source, such as a database field. In this chapter, a bound property will be added to the Circle control to illustrate simple data binding.

Note You can find the code produced by implementing the code samples in this chapter in the CIRC3 sample source code directory.

In this chapter you will:

- Define the Note custom Get/Set property.
- Make the Note property bindable.
- Notifying the control's container of changes.
- Learn how data binding works.
- Use Test Container to observe data binding notifications.

To clearly show the differences between a bindable and a non-bindable property, a normal Get/Set property will be implemented and changed into a bindable property in two separate steps.

Defining the Note Property

Initially, the Note property is a typical custom Get/Set property of type **BSTR**. After adding the property to the control, the `GetNote` and `SetNote` functions are completed, the property is made persistent and a control to edit its value is added to the property page.

▶ **To add a Get/Set property called Note**

1. From the Browse menu, choose ClassWizard. If you are using the 32-bit version of the CDK, choose ClassWizard from the Project menu.

2. Choose the OLE Automation tab.

3. In the Class Name drop-down list box, select `CCircCtrl`.

4. Choose the Add Property button.

   The Add Property dialog box appears.

5. In the edit control of the External Name drop-down combo box, type `Note`.

6. Under Implementation, choose Get/Set Methods.

7. From the Type drop-down list box, select **BSTR**.

8. Choose the OK button to close the Add Property dialog box.

   This returns you to the OLE Automation tab. Notice that the implementation of the Note property is listed as

   ```
   Implementation:

   BSTR GetNote();
   void SetNote(LPCSTR lpszNewValue);
   ```

9. Choose the OK button to confirm your choices and close ClassWizard.

ClassWizard adds the Note property to the Circle Control. As you've seen in earlier chapters, ClassWizard modifies CIRC.ODL, CIRCCTL.CPP, and CIRCCTL.H to define the Note property.

Completing the GetNote and SetNote Functions

To complete the `GetNote` and `SetNote` functions, add the `m_note` member variable to the `CCircCtrl` class to hold the value of the Note property. The `GetNote` and `SetNote` functions will be modified to use this member variable.

Note is a persistent property, so the `SetNote` function must call the `SetModifiedFlag` function to set the modified flag. A call to the `SetModifiedFlag` function is already included in the `SetNote` function produced by ClassWizard. Since the Note property will affect the visual appearance of the control, the `SetNote` function must also call the `InvalidateControl` function to cause the control to be redrawn.

▶ **To complete the GetNote and SetNote functions**

1. Add the following marked line to CIRCCTL.H:

   ```
   class CCircCtrl : public COleControl
   {
   ...
   ```

```
protected:
    ~CCircCtrl();
    void GetDrawRect(CRect* rc);
    short m_circleOffset;
    BOOL InBounds(short nOffset);
    BOOL InCircle(CPoint& point);
    void FlashColor(CDC* pdc);
▶   CString m_note;
...
};
```

2. Modify the GetNote and SetNote functions at the end of CIRCCTL.CPP to look like this:

```
BSTR CCircCtrl::GetNote()
{
▶   return m_note.AllocSysString();
}

void CCircCtrl::SetNote(LPCSTR lpszNewValue)
{
▶   if (m_note != lpszNewValue)
▶   {
▶       m_note = lpszNewValue;
▶       SetModifiedFlag();
▶       InvalidateControl();
▶   }
}
```

Making the Note Property Persistent

To manage the persistence of the Note property and initialize the Note property to a default value when the Circle control is created, add a call to a **PX_** function in the DoPropExchange function in CIRCCTL.CPP:

```
void CCircCtrl::DoPropExchange(CPropExchange* pPX)
{
    ExchangeVersion(pPX, MAKELONG(_wVerMinor, _wVerMajor));
    COleControl::DoPropExchange(pPX);

    PX_Bool(pPX, _T("CircleShape"), m_circleShape, TRUE);
    PX_Short(pPX, _T("CircleOffset"), m_circleOffset, 0);
    PX_Long(pPX, _T("FlashColor"), (long &)m_flashColor, RGB(0xFF, 0x00,
0x00));
▶   PX_String(pPX, _T("Note"), m_note, _T(""));
}
```

Since the Note property is of type BSTR, the **PX_String** function is used. The m_note member variable (which holds the Note property value), and a zero-length string (which is the default value for the Note property) are parameters to this function. As with all literal strings, the property name string and default value string are passed through the **_T** macro before being passed as parameters to the **PX_String** function.

Displaying the Note Property

To display the Note property, change the drawing behavior in the OnDraw function in CIRCCTL.CPP. The Note property is drawn in the upper-left corner of the control's bounding rectangle using the stock Font and ForeColor properties.

▶ **To change the OnDraw function to display the Note property**

- Change or add the following marked lines in the **OnDraw** function in CIRCCTL.CPP:

```
void CCircCtrl::OnDraw(
            CDC* pdc, const CRect& rcBounds, const CRect& rcInvalid)
{
    CBrush* pOldBrush;
    CBrush bkBrush(TranslateColor(GetBackColor()));
    CPen* pOldPen;
    CRect rc = rcBounds;
    CFont pOldFont;
    TEXTMETRIC tm;
    const CString& strCaption = InternalGetText();

    // Set the ForeColor property color and transparent background mode
into the device context
    pdc->SetTextColor(TranslateColor(GetForeColor()));
    pdc->SetBkMode(TRANSPARENT);

    // Paint the background using the BackColor property
    pdc->FillRect(rcBounds, &bkBrush);

    // Draw the ellipse using the BackColor property and a black pen
    GetDrawRect(&rc);
    pOldBrush = pdc->SelectObject(&bkBrush);
    pOldPen = (CPen*)pdc->SelectStockObject(BLACK_PEN);
    pdc->Ellipse(rc);
```

```
    // Draw the caption and note using the stock Font and ForeColor
properties
    pOldFont = SelectStockFont(pdc);
    pdc->GetTextMetrics(&tm);
    pdc->SetTextAlign(TA_CENTER | TA_TOP);
    pdc->ExtTextOut((rc.left + rc.right) / 2, (rc.top + rc.bottom -
tm.tmHeight) / 2,
        ETO_CLIPPED, rc, strCaption, strCaption.GetLength(), NULL);
    pdc->SetTextAlign(TA_LEFT | TA_TOP);
    pdc->ExtTextOut(rcBounds.left, rcBounds.top,
```

▶   ETO_CLIPPED, rcBounds, m_note, m_note.GetLength(), NULL);
```
        pdc->SelectObject(pOldFont);

        pdc->SelectObject(pOldPen);
        pdc->SelectObject(pOldBrush);
}
```

Adding the Note Property to the Default Property Page

The Note property should be added to the default property page to allow users of the Circle control to change the value of the Note property. This is done using the same technique used in Chapter 8, "Modifying the Default Property Page."

First, add an edit control to the default property page using the resource editor.

▶ **To add an edit control to the default property page(16-bit)**

1. Load your project's .RC file into the resource editor. If the project is open in the development environment and you start the resource editor, the .RC file should be loaded automatically.

2. Choose Dialog from the Type list box.

3. Choose **IDD_PROPPAGE_CIRCCTRL** from the Resources list box.

4. Choose the Open button to edit the dialog.

5. Select the Static Text tool in the Control Palette and place a static text control in the dialog. Using the Property Window, change the static text control's Caption to "&Note:".

6. Select the Edit box tool in the Control Palette and place an edit control next to the static text control in the dialog. Using the Property Window, change the edit control ID to **IDC_NOTE**.

7. Save the changes to the dialog and exit the resource editor.

▶ **To add an edit control to the default property page(32-bit)**

1. Open the project's .RC file from the Source Files folder by double-clicking on the .RC file icon.

2. Open the Dialog folder by double-clicking on the Dialog folder icon.

3. Double-click on the **IDD_PROPPAGE_CIRCCTRL** entry under the Dialog folder to edit the dialog.

4. Select the Static Text tool in the Control Palette and place a static text control in the dialog. Using the Property Window, change the static text control's Caption to "&Note:".

5. Select the Edit box tool in the Control Palette and place an edit control next to the static text control in the dialog. Using the Property Window, change the edit control ID to **IDC_NOTE**.

6. Save the changes to the dialog and exit the resource editor.

Link the Note property to the new edit control in the default property page using the Member Variables tab in ClassWizard.

▶ **To link the edit control with the Note property**

1. From the Browse menu, choose ClassWizard. If you are using the 32-bit version of the CDK, choose ClassWizard from the Project menu.

2. Choose the Member Variables tab.

3. In the Class Name drop down list box, select `CCircPropPage`.

    Notice that the control IDs are listed in the Control IDs list box as

    ```
    Control IDs:       Type       Member

    IDC_CAPTION        CString    m_caption
    IDC_CIRCLEOFFSET   int        m_circleOffset
    IDC_CIRCLESHAPE    BOOL       m_circleShape
    IDC_NOTE
    ```

4. Select IDC_NOTE in the Control IDs list box.

5. Choose the Add Variable button.

    The Add Member Variable dialog box will appear.

6. Type `note` into the Member Variable Name edit control, after the m_ that is already there, so that the edit control contains `m_note`.

7. Choose `Value` in the Category drop-down list box.

8. Choose `CString` in the Variable Type drop down list box.

9. Type `Note` into the Optional OLE Property Name drop down combo box.

10. Choose the OK button to confirm your choices and close the Add Member Variable dialog box.

    This returns you to the Member Variable tab of ClassWizard. Notice that the control IDs are listed in the Control IDs list box as

    ```
    Control IDs:       Type       Member

    IDC_CAPTION        CString    m_caption
    IDC_CIRCLEOFFSET   int        m_circleOffset
    IDC_CIRCLESHAPE    BOOL       m_circleShape
    IDC_NOTE           CString    m_note
    ```

11. Choose the OK button to confirm your choices and close ClassWizard.

ClassWizard adds the new `m_note` member variable to the `CCircPropPage` class. ClassWizard also modifies the `DoDataExchange` function in the `CCircPropPage` class.

The Note property is now fully implemented as a normal Get/Set property in the Circle control.

Making the Note Property Bindable

At this point, the Note property is a fully implemented, normal Get/Set property. The next step is to make the Note property a bindable property by using the OLE Automation tab in ClassWizard.

▶ **To make Note a bindable property**

1. From the Browse menu, choose ClassWizard. If you are using the 32-bit version of the CDK, choose ClassWizard from the Project menu.

2. Choose the OLE Automation tab.

3. In the Class Name drop down list box, select `CCircCtrl`.

4. In the Name list box, select `Note`.

5. Choose the Data Binding button.

   The Data Binding dialog box appears.

6. Check the Bindable Property check box.

   This specifies that this is a bindable property and that the container will be notified of all changes to this property.

   For more information on the other options in the Data Binding dialog box, see Chapter 11, "Using Data Binding in Your Control," in the *CDK Programmer's Guide*.

7. Choose the OK button to confirm the data binding settings and close the Data Binding dialog box.

8. Choose the OK button to confirm your choices and exit ClassWizard.

ClassWizard changes the Note property definition in the file CIRC.ODL so that the type library includes the information that the Note property is bindable.

Note that there is a difference between a bindable property and a bound property. Bindable refers to the fact that a property is available to be bound. A bindable property becomes a bound property at run time when the control is created and inserted in a container that responds to bound property notifications.

Notifying the Container of Changes

A control must notify the container when changes are made to a bound property. This notification is done by calling the `BoundPropertyChanged` function.

Since Note is a Get/Set property, all changes to the property are confined to the `SetNote` function. This is where `BoundPropertyChanged` is called.

▶ **To modify the SetNote function to notify the container about changes to the Note property**

- Add the following line to the `SetNote` function in CIRCCTL.CPP:

```
void CCircCtrl::SetNote(LPCSTR lpszNewValue)
{
    if (m_note != lpszNewValue)
    {
        m_note = lpszNewValue;
        SetModifiedFlag();
        InvalidateControl();
▶           BoundPropertyChanged(dispidNote);
    }
}
```

The call to `BoundPropertyChanged` is added after the `m_note` member variable is updated and all other actions involved in changing the Note property are completed.

The single parameter to `BoundPropertyChanged`, `dispidNote`, is the dispatch ID for the Note property. `dispidNote` is defined in an enumeration in CIRCCTL.H:

```
// Dispatch and event IDs
public:
    enum {
    //{{AFX_DISP_ID(CCircCtrl)
    ...
    dispidNote = 4L,
    ...
    //}}AFX_DISP_ID
    };
```

Rebuilding the Control

Now that a property with data binding support has been added, you need to rebuild the control. Since the CIRC.ODL file has changed, the type library must be updated first.

▶ **To update the type library (16-bit version only)**

1. From the Tools menu, choose Make TypeLib to update the Type Library.

   A message box appears, confirming that the type library was successfully generated.

2. Choose the OK button to close the message box.

▶ **To rebuild the control (16- and 32-bit versions)**

1. From the Project menu, choose Build CIRC.DLL.

How Data Binding Works

Whenever a bound property is changed, the control must notify the container by calling the **BoundPropertyChanged** function. This level of data binding is called "optimistic data binding" because the control assumes that changes can be made to the bound property. It is this form of data binding that is used for the Note property in the Circle control.

In pessimistic data binding, it is not assumed that changes can be made to a bound property. The control must first request permission from the container by calling the **BoundPropertyRequestEdit** function. If the **BoundPropertyRequestEdit** function returns TRUE, the control may change the bound property as it would for optimistic data binding. However, if the **BoundPropertyRequestEdit** function returns FALSE, the control must not change the bound property.

Test Container's Notification Log dialog box helps you test bound properties which use either optimistic or pessimistic data binding. Whenever the **BoundPropertyChanged** function is called, a notification is logged in the dialog box. You are also allowed to choose the response to each call to the **BoundPropertyRequestEdit** function. A different container might update a field in a database record whenever the **BoundPropertyChanged** function was called. It might also return false from a call to the **BoundPropertyRequestEdit** function if the field or record was in use.

Testing the Control

Since the Note property uses optimistic data binding, the Circle control assumes that all changes to the Note property are allowed. The `SetNote` function simply changes the Note property and notifies the container by calling the **BoundPropertyChanged** function. This notification is displayed in Test Container's Notification Log dialog box.

▶ **To test the data binding changes**

1. From the Tools menu, choose Test Container.
2. From the View menu, choose Notification Log.

   The Notification Log dialog box appears.

   The option buttons at the bottom of the Notification Log dialog box can be used to test control properties which use pessimistic data binding. Since the Note property uses optimistic data binding, they are not used here.

3. From the Edit menu, choose Insert OLE Control.

   The Insert OLE Control dialog box appears.

4. From the Control Class list box, select Circ Control.

5. Choose the OK button to close the Insert OLE Object dialog box and insert a control into Test Container.

   Notice that there is no notification in the Notification Log dialog box when a control is first created.

6. From the Edit Menu, choose Circ Control Object and then Properties.

   The Circ Control Properties dialog box appears.

7. Enter a new value for the Note property and choose the Apply button.

   The Note property is displayed in the upper left corner of the control.

   Information about the change to the Note property is also displayed in the Notification Log dialog box. The line in the Notification Log dialog box looks like this:

   ```
   00_Circ_Control: property 'Note' changed
   ```

   This kind of information is displayed in the Notification Log dialog box every time the **BoundPropertyChanged** function is called for a bound property. The line shows the control number, control type, and property name, and states that the property changed.

8. Change the Note property several more times and watch the Notification Log dialog. Close Test Container when you are done.

Using the **BoundPropertyChanged** function to notify the container of changes to bound properties provides the simplest level of data binding. For more information on data binding, see Chapter 11, "Using Data Binding in Your Control," in the *CDK Programmer's Guide*.

P A R T   2

CDK Programmer's Guide

Introduction: OLE CDK Programmer's Guide

This book contains reference material for the Microsoft Foundation OLE Control
Classes. The OLE control classes are part of the Microsoft Foundation Class
Library, a set of C++ classes that encapsulate the functionality of applications
written for the Microsoft Windows operating system.

Note This section assumes that you are familiar with the OLE 2 architecture and
that you will be using OLE 2 to directly implement an OLE custom control. It is not
required reading for developing controls using the Microsoft Foundation Class
Library extensions included in the CDK.

Chapters 1 through 3 introduce the general concepts of OLE controls and the
components of the CDK package.

Chapters 4 through 6 introduce the key concepts of an OLE control: painting,
events, methods, and properties. All examples are based on either the basic
framework created by ControlWizard or the Circle Sample tutorial.

Chapters 7 through 11 discuss advanced topics on OLE controls. These topics
include serialization, property pages, using fonts, and data binding.

C H A P T E R   1

Overview

The OLE Custom Control Developer's Kit (CDK) provides you with the tools for creating an Object Linking and Embedding OLE custom control dynamic link library (DLL). OLE custom controls incorporate the basic concepts of OLE and will be used by specialized OLE containers in future versions of Visual C++™, Visual Basic, and other products.

When you write an OLE control, you write the underlying code in C++. You also use components of the Microsoft Foundation Class Library (MFC), such as various classes, predefined macros, and global functions and variables.

In this chapter you will learn:

- What is the CDK
- What is installed
- What is an OLE control
- What you need to know to develop OLE controls

What Is the CDK?

The OLE Custom Control Development Kit (CDK) is a set of tools for developing OLE controls. These OLE controls are implemented with the help of several new MFC classes. The CDK makes it easy to develop new and powerful controls that take advantage of OLE 2 functionality, such as event firing, and the ability to expose a set of properties and methods to other OLE aware applications.

The CDK provides several tools that allow you to quickly build OLE controls and test them. These include ControlWizard, an extended version of ClassWizard, and Test Container.

During control development, you use ControlWizard to create the initial MFC source files for your project. To add functionality to your control, use the OLE automation and OLE Events features of ClassWizard. Finally, test your control in the Test Container.

The CDK contains the following major components:

- Microsoft ControlWizard
- Several new MFC classes dedicated to OLE control development
- Two extensions to ClassWizard, OLE Automation and OLE Events
- Sample source code
- Online documentation
- Help files
- Various tools

The CDK is designed as an add-on package for Visual C++. In order to use the CDK you need a copy of Visual C++, version 1.5 or 2.0.

What Is Installed

When you install the CDK, the following directories are created as subdirectories of the CDK's root (the root of the 16-bit version of the CDK is a directory named CDK16 under the Visual C++ 1.5 directory; the root of the 32-bit version of the CDK is a directory named CDK32 under the Visual C++ 2.0 directory):

\BIN

Contains the executables for ControlWizard, Test Container, and the Register Control tool. If the 16-bit version of the CDK is installed on a machine running Windows NT, this directory will also contain BLDTYPLB.BAT.

\HELP

Contains the online documentation and Help files for the CDK.

\INCLUDE

Contains the include files required to develop OLE controls.

\LIB

Contains the libraries required to develop OLE controls.

\SAMPLES

Contains a set of OLE control samples. Each subdirectory contains a sample that demonstrates various features of OLE controls.

\SRC

Contains the source code for specific OLE control classes in the class library.

In addition to these files, the appropriate OLE control run-time DLLs are installed in your \WINDOWS\SYSTEM or \WINNT\SYSTEM32 directory. Table 1.1 lists the different versions available.

Table 1.1   OLE Control Run-time DLL Versions

Library	Description
OC25.DLL	Release version: 16-bit OLE control
OC25D.DLL	Debug version: 16-bit OLE control
OC30.DLL	Release version: 32-bit OLE controls with ANSI/DBCS support
OC30D.DLL	Debug version: 32-bit OLE controls with ANSI/DBCS support
OC30U.DLL	Release version: 32-bit OLE controls with Unicode support
OC30UD.DLL	Debug version: 32-bit OLE controls with Unicode support

What Is an OLE Control

An OLE control is implemented as an OLE 2 compound document object with visual editing support. An OLE control has additional capabilities beyond those of ordinary OLE objects, such as the ability to fire events.

Most OLE 2 objects require a substantial amount of implementation effort. Fortunately, MFC provides you with most of the required implementation; you need only provide the details that are specific to your own control. As a developer of an OLE control, you determine:

- How your control is displayed and painted.
- The control's properties.

  These properties are made accessible to the control's user through the automation interface of the control. You determine what happens when these properties are changed. You can also design a user interface, called a property page, to allow your control's user to access control properties at run time.
- The control's events.

  You can assign arguments to these events and determine their names. You can also determine when an event should be fired.
- The control's methods.

  Methods are operations that can be called by the control's user. You define the arguments and return type for methods supported by the control.
- Which property states of your control need to be persistent.

When you write an OLE control, you produce an OLE control file, which is a dynamic link library with an .DLL extension. This file contains the entire implementation of your OLE control. When registered and loaded, the .DLL file defines one or more controls that can be accessed by the user. You can freely distribute the OLE controls you write to other developers and users.

Note If you are using the CDK with Visual C++ 2.0, the extension of your project will be .OCX.

What You Need to Know to Develop OLE Controls

Before you start learning about OLE controls you should be able to:

- Use Visual C++ and the Microsoft Foundation classes to write applications for the Windows operating system. You should be familiar with the fundamental concepts of Windows, including message handling, device contexts, and resources. A good source of information is *Inside Visual C++*, Microsoft Press, 1993.

- Program comfortably in the C++ programming language, including a knowledge of class derivation and overriding virtual functions. A good source of information is *C++ Primer*, Addison Wesley, 1991. This criterion is generally met if you have programmed MFC applications.

For further information about programming with MFC, see the Scribble tutorial found in *Class Library User's Guide*. This book is part of Microsoft Visual C++, version 1.5. For developers using the 32-bit version of the CDK, the Scribble tutorial is located in *Introducing Visual C++*.

C H A P T E R   2

Fundamental Concepts

Developing OLE custom controls is similar to developing an application for Windows using the Microsoft Foundation Class Library (MFC). In both cases, you handle Windows messages through a message map that automatically calls the proper function in your application. You also call member functions of MFC classes and Windows API functions.

However, developing an OLE control differs in some major ways. First, an OLE control is a Windows dynamic link library and is loaded in a special manner. Second, an OLE control is highly dependent on OLE 2's supporting architecture. Note that the full functionality of an OLE control is available only when used within an OLE container that is designed to be aware of OLE controls. This container, hereafter referred to as a control container, is able to operate your OLE control by using its properties and methods, and receive notifications from your OLE control in the form of events. Figure 2.1 demonstrates this interaction.

Figure 2.1   Interaction Between an OLE Control Container and an OLE Control

In this chapter you will learn:

- The basic components of an OLE control
- A high-level overview of controls and containers, and how they interact
- The process of control serialization
- How a control interacts with Windows itself (when active)

Basic Components of an OLE control

An OLE control is composed of several components that allow it to interact efficiently with a control container and with the user. The **COleControl** class, events, properties, and methods all combine to create an OLE control.

The COleControl Class

Every control object you develop with the CDK inherits a powerful set of features from its MFC base class, **COleControl**, such as customizable painting and serialization. This base class also provides your control object with the same functionality as an MFC window object, plus the ability to fire events.

Events

Because your control class derives from **COleControl**, it automatically inherits the capability to use a powerful new map that enables messages, referred to as events, to be sent to the control container when certain conditions are met. These events are used to notify the control container when something important happens in the control. You can also send additional valuable information about the event to your control container by attaching parameters to the event.

Properties and Methods

Another basic concept of OLE controls is the ability to expose a set of functions (called methods) and control properties (called an interface) to the user of the control. This interface allows the control container, or the control's user, to manipulate the control in various ways. The user is able to change the appearance of the control, change certain values of the control, or make requests of the control such as accessing a specific piece of data. This interface is determined by the control developer and is easily defined using ClassWizard.

Interaction Between Controls and OLE Control Containers

When a control is used within a control container, it is able to communicate efficiently using two mechanisms: by exposing properties and methods and by event firing. Figure 2.2 demonstrates how these two mechanisms are implemented.

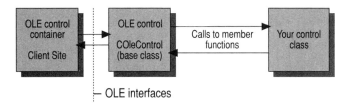

Figure 2.2   Communication Between an OLE Control Container and an OLE Control

All of a control's communication with the container is performed by the **COleControl** base class. To handle some of the container's requests, the base class will call member functions that you implement in your control's class. For example, all methods and some properties are handled in this way. Your control's class can also initiate communication with the container by calling member functions of **COleControl** base class. For example, events are fired in this manner.

Active and Inactive States of an OLE control

During execution, a control is always in one of two states: active or inactive. When inactive, the control has limited capabilities because it does not have an active window visible on the screen. This means that the control cannot respond to mouse clicks or keystrokes. However, the control container is still able to notify the control in certain cases, such as when a request for painting is made.

When a control becomes active, it is able to interact fully with the control container and the Windows system. Figure 2.3 demonstrates the paths of communication between the OLE control, the control container, and the operating system.

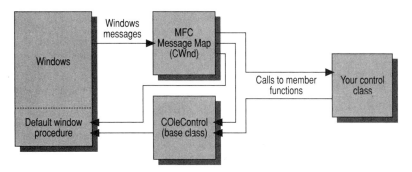

Figure 2.3   Windows Message Processing in an OLE Control (when active)

Serialization

The ability to serialize, sometimes referred to as persistence, allows the control to write the value of its properties to persistent storage. Controls can then be re-created by reading the object's state from the storage.

Please note that a control is not responsible for obtaining access to the storage medium. Rather, the control's container is responsible for providing the control with a storage medium to use at the appropriate times.

CHAPTER 3

Building an Elementary Control

This chapter describes the process of developing an OLE 2 control using ControlWizard and the development environment. You will create, build, and test a simple OLE 2 control, similar to the Circle sample control, found in the *CDK Circle Sample Tutorial.*

In this chapter you will learn how to:

- Use ControlWizard to create a project
- Understand the purpose of each class and file created by ControlWizard
- Build the control and test it using Test Container
- Use additional Control Development Kit (CDK) tools while developing your OLE control

Using ControlWizard

You use ControlWizard to create a set of starter files for an OLE 2 control. This set includes all the files necessary to build an OLE 2 control, including source and header files, resource files, a module-definition file, a project file, an object description language file, and so on. ControlWizard must be used first in order to generate a set of starter files that are compatible with ClassWizard. You can then use ClassWizard to define your control's events, properties, and methods, some of which have been previously implemented in the Microsoft Foundation Class library (MFC).

Building a project created by ControlWizard provides a large amount of built-in functionality. This includes code to draw the control, serialize data, and define dispatch, event, and message maps that you expand later in the development cycle.

The next section describes the various dialog boxes and options available in ControlWizard. The classes and files created are also described. Figure 3.1 shows ControlWizard.

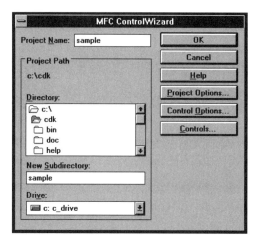

Figure 3.1   ControlWizard

Running ControlWizard

To open ControlWizard, choose the ControlWizard command from the Tools menu. After you specify the project's name, directory, options, and classes (described later in this section), choose OK to continue.

After you have confirmed your choices, ControlWizard displays a dialog box containing information about the DLL to be created, such as its name, the names of your control's classes, the names of the files that make up the project, and the features of your control. For more information, see the "ControlWizard-Created Files" section later in this chapter. Choose the Create button to create the project files.

When ControlWizard is finished, an OLE control project is created and automatically opened in the development environment.

Specifying the Project Name and Location

The OLE ControlWizard dialog box closely resembles AppWizard in that it allows you to specify a project name and choose the subdirectory name and root path where your project will be created. The project name is given a .MAK extension and appears in the complete path at the top of the Project Path group. The project name is also used to create class names and project filenames. This project name will also be used as the name of the DLL. This feature is useful for implementing naming conventions.

▶ **To select the project name and location**

1. From the Tools menu, choose ControlWizard.

2. In the Project Name box, type the name of your project.

The project name appears in the New Subdirectory box.

If you do not want the subdirectory to have the same name as your project, enter a different name or leave the New Subdirectory box blank. If the box is blank, a subdirectory will not be created and the project files will be located in the current directory path.

To select the drive and directory path for your project files, use the Directory and Drive boxes. These boxes work the same as similar controls in the Open File and Save As dialog boxes.

▶ **To select the drive and directory for your project's subdirectory**

1. In the Drive box, select the drive you want.

2. Select the directory path for your project's subdirectory by double-clicking the directory icons.

The drive and directory path you select are displayed at the top of the Project Path box.

Selecting Options

ControlWizard creates the basic skeleton of your control with many built-in features. ControlWizard also allows you to be very specific in what options your control will support in the initial build of your project. Specifying additional options is made easy by the Project Options button and the Control Options button.

To enable these additional options, choose either the Project Options or the Control Options button and then enable or disable the various options. Once you have chosen the options you want in your project, choose Close to close the Project Options or the Control Options dialog box.

Project Options

The following options are available in the Project Options dialog box:

Context-Sensitive Help
ControlWizard generates a set of help files that are used to provide context-sensitive help. Help support requires using the Help compiler, which is provided with Visual C++.

External Makefile
By default, ControlWizard creates a project file that is compatible with the environment (and NMAKE). Select this option if you want ControlWizard to create an NMAKE makefile that can only be directly edited. This means that the project cannot be edited while inside the development environment.

Generate Source Comments

    ControlWizard inserts comments in the source and header files that guide you in writing your control. The comments indicate where you need to add your own code. This option is enabled by default.

License Validation

    ControlWizard inserts several function calls and generates a separate .LIC file that supports licensing for your control. For more information on licensing, see Chapter 10, "Licensing Your Control."

Figure 3.2 shows the Project Options dialog box.

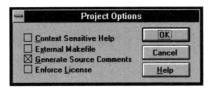

Figure 3.2   The Project Options Dialog Box

Control Options

This dialog box allows you to specify certain options for each control in your project. Use the Control box to choose the control whose options you wish to modify.

Activate when visible

    Indicates to the control container that your control prefers to be activated automatically when it is visible. The container is not required to support this request.

Show in Insert Object dialog

    Enabling this option, disabled by default, makes your control appear in the Insert Object dialog of every OLE container application. Since some OLE containers are not "control-aware," they may not provide a way to activate controls with the mouse. Therefore, this option also adds an "Edit" verb to your control's set of available verbs.

    If you initially create your control with this option disabled, and later decide to enable it, remember to also add an Edit verb in your control's message map. The Edit verb entry should look like this:

```
ON_OLEVERB(AFX_IDS_VERB_EDIT, OnEdit)
```

Invisible at runtime

    Allows your control to indicate to its container that it should be invisible when the container is operating in its "run time" mode. During the container's "design time," the control will be visible. Some containers may ignore the Invisible at runtime option. In such containers, your control will be visible at all times.

Simple Frame
> This option allows your control to behave as a simple frame. For more information, see "New MiscStatus Bits" in Appendix D and **COleControl::EnableSimpleFrame** in *Class Library Reference: CDK Extensions*.

About box
> Creates a standard About dialog box for your control.

Subclass Windows control
> Use this option to subclass common Windows controls, such as buttons, scroll bars, and edit controls.

Use VBX control as template
> Use this option to migrate an existing VBX control into a project framework. For more information regarding this procedure, see Appendix A, "VBX Control Migration."

Figure 3.3 shows the Control Options dialog box.

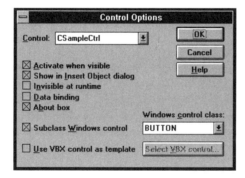

Figure 3.3   The Control Options Dialog Box

Controls

Figure 3.4 shows the Controls dialog box. ControlWizard names your control's classes and files by using the project name you specify in the Project Name box. The Controls dialog box allows you to modify various parts of these classes created by ControlWizard and add additional control classes to your project.

Use the Class box to select either the control class or the property page class. You can then modify various parts of that class, such as the Short name (base name of the class), the User Type name (the name exposed to the control's user), and the Programmatic ID (the ID of the OLE control class). The following discussion assumes that the project name is *PRJNAME*.

Note Modifying the short name of the control class or choosing a different class from the Class list box will automatically update the values of the edit boxes for various parts of a selected class.

C*Prjname*Ctrl

This is the main class of the control. You are able to change the values for class name, header file, and implementation file.

C*Prjname*PropPage

This is the property page for the control. The property page provides the user of the control with a way to view and modify its properties. You are able to change the values for the class name, header file, and implementation file.

Add Control

Click this button to add a new control class and property page class to your project. You must name the header and implementation files for each class. You can also change the default class names. If you already have a project that implements an OLE control and you would like to add other OLE controls, see Appendix C, "Adding an OLE Custom Control to an Existing Project."

Delete Control

Click this button to delete the selected control from your project. If the selected class is a control class or property page class, it will be deleted along with its associated property page class or control class.

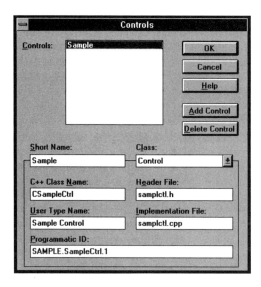

Figure 3.4   The Controls Dialog Box

ControlWizard-Created Files

ControlWizard always creates a basic list of files for every control. Additional files are created if context-sensitive help was checked in the Project Options dialog. This section first describes the core files every control must have and then describes additional files that implement other project options.

ControlWizard uses the project name you specified in the Project Name box to derive filenames and class names. In the following descriptions, where the full project name is used in the filename, *PRJNAME* is used as a placeholder for the name you specified. For some files, only the first five letters of your project name will be used as the base for the filename. In these cases, *PRJNA* will be used as a placeholder.

Note   The name substitutions indicated in these filenames might not apply if you have used the Classes dialog box to alter any of them.

Standard ControlWizard Files

This section describes the various files created by ControlWizard and categorizes them by function. ControlWizard also creates a file named README.TXT that describes each file in your project using the actual filename created by ControlWizard.

Project and Makefiles

PRJNAME.MAK

This is the project file used within the environment. It is also compatible with NMAKE, which is shipped with Visual C++. If you specified External Makefile, you will not be able to make modifications to the project options within the environment.

PRJNAME.CLW

This file is used by ClassWizard to add new classes and modify existing ones. It also contains information used to generate the event, dispatch, and message maps of your project.

PRJNAME.ODL

This file contains the Object Description Language source code for the control's type library. This file is used to generate a type library using the Make Type Library Tool. The generated library exposes your control's interface to other OLE automation clients. For more information on .ODL files and the Type Library Tool, see "Type Library Generator" in the "Additional CDK Tools" section later in this chapter.

Resource and Module-Definition Files

PRJNAME.RC, RESOURCE.H

This is the resource file for the project and its header file. The resource file contains a bitmap for use in a palette or toolbar, a dialog box used by the property page, and a default "About" dialog box.

*PRJNA*CTL.BMP

This file is used to represent your OLE 2 control in a toolbar or palette. This bitmap is included in the project's resource file.

PRJNAME.DEF

This is the module-definition file for the project. It provides the name and description of the control as well as the size of the run-time heap.

Control Source and Header Files

PRJNAME.H

This is the main include file for the OLE control DLL. It derives the `CPrjnameApp` class from **CWinApp** and declares an `InitInstance` member function.

PRJNAME.CPP

This file creates an instance of `CPrjNameApp`. The member function `CPrjNameApp::InitInstance` registers the control's object factory with OLE by calling **COleObjectFactory::RegisterAll** and makes a call to **AfxOLEControlInit**. In addition, the member function `CPrjNameApp::ExitInstance` is used to unload the control from memory with a call to **AfxOleControlTerm**.

This file also registers, and unregisters, your control in the Windows registration database by implementing the **DllRegisterServer** and **DllUnregisterServer** functions.

*PRJNA*CTL.H, *PRJNA*CTL.CPP

These files declare and implement the `CPrjnameCtrl` class. `CPrjnameCtrl` is derived from **COleControl**, and skeleton implementation of some member functions are defined that initialize, draw, and serialize (load and save) your control. Message, event, and dispatch maps are also defined.

*PRJNA*PPG.H, *PRJNA*PPG.CPP

These files declare and implement the `CPrjnamePropPage` class. `CPrjnamePropPage` is derived from **CPropertyPageDialog** and a skeleton member function, `DoDataExchange`, is provided to implement data exchange and validation.

Precompiled Header Files

STDAFX.H, STDAFX.CPP

These files are used to build a precompiled header (PCH) file named STDAFX.PCH and a precompiled types (PCT) file named STDAFX.OBJ.

Files Added By Options

Help support provides a number of files that implement context-sensitive help. These files are contained in the HLP subdirectory of the project.

Help Option

MAKEHELP.BAT

This batch file is used to create the help file *PRJNAME*.HLP for your OLE control.

PRJNAME.HPJ

This file is the Help Project file used by the Help compiler to create your OLE control's Help file.

CTRLCORE.RTF

This file contains the standard Help topics for the common properties, events, and methods supported by many OLE controls. You can edit this to add additional control-specific topics or remove existing ones.

*.BMP

These bitmaps are used by standard Help file topics for Microsoft Foundation Class Library standard commands.

Building the Control's Project

When a project is loaded into the development environment, you have two commands to help build your control. Choosing the Build command from the Project menu includes only those files in the build that have changed since the project was last built. Choosing the Rebuild All command from the Project menu forces all files to be included in the build.

By default, ControlWizard creates a project that can create a debug version of your control. This version contains information that can be used by the integrated debugger. The release version does not contain debugging information and, as a result, is much smaller and faster.

▶ **To select debug or release build options**

1. From the Options menu, choose Project.
2. Under Build Mode group, select either Debug or Release.
3. Choose OK to close the dialog.

Note If you are using the 32-bit version of the CDK, ignore the preceding steps and use the Target box, located in the Project Window, to select debug or release versions of your projects.

▶ **To build the project**

1. From the Tools menu, choose Make TypeLib. If you are using the 32-bit version of the CDK, this step is not required.

   For more information on making a type library, see "Type Library Generator" in the "Additional CDK Tools" section later in this chapter. Please note that when you add new events, properties, or methods you must choose the Make TypeLib command before rebuilding. This allows your interface to be properly updated.

2. From the Project menu, choose either Build *Targetname* (*Targetname* represents the name of the target file displayed on the menu).

   — Or —

   Choose the Build button on the toolbar.

▶ **To rebuild the project**

1. From the Tools menu, choose the Make TypeLib command. If you are using the 32-bit version of the CDK, this step is not required.

   For more information on making a type library, see "Type Library Generator" in the "Additional CDK Tools" section later in this chapter.

2. From the Project menu, choose either Rebuild All *Targetname* (*Targetname* represents the name of the target file displayed on the menu).

   — Or —

   Choose the Rebuild All button on the toolbar.

If you are using the 16-bit version of the CDK, you can find the control's DLL in the project directory. If you are using the 32-bit version of the CDK, the DLL is found in a subdirectory of the project named OBJ[D][U]32—if it's a debug build, it goes in a D variant, and Unicode builds go in a U variant. Because the control is implemented using a DLL you can easily use the development environment to test sections of your code and perform other diagnostics during runtime.

▶ **To test your control using the integrated debugger (16-bit version)**

1. Ensure that the DLL has been built as a debug version with symbolic debugging information.

2. Load your control's project.

3. From the Options menu, choose Debug.

4. In the Calling Program box, type the path of the Test Container executable.

   For a default installation, the path would be
   C:\MSVC\CDK16\BIN\TSTCON16.EXE.

5. Choose the OK button to close the Debug dialog box.

▶ **To test your control using the integrated debugger (32-bit version)**

1. Ensure that the DLL has been built as a debug version with symbolic debugging information.

2. Load your control's project.

3. From the Project menu, choose Settings.

   The Project Settings dialog box appears.

4. Select the Debug tab.

5. Type the name of the executable program which calls the DLL in your project in the Executable For Debug Session box.

   For a default installation, the path would be **C:\MSVC20\CDK32\BIN\TSTCON32.EXE**.

6. Type the name of any additional DLL (or DLLs) that you want to debug in the Additional DLLs box.

7. Choose OK.

   The information is now stored with your project.

After completing this procedure, the Test Container application automatically starts when you begin a debugging session of your control. Begin a debugging session by choosing the Go command from the Debug menu (or press F5).

When you first start debugging your control, a message box will appear stating that no debug information is available for the Test Container. You can safely ignore this by choosing the OK button. You can now step through your code, set breakpoints, or perform other debugging techniques.

Toolbar Bitmap Support

When you use ControlWizard to generate the framework for your control, a default bitmap is created as part of your project. Containers will take this image and place it on a button in a toolbox or toolbar (for example, Visual Basic's toolbox). When you have finished developing your control, you should modify this bitmap to accurately represent the purpose of your control. The resource editor provided with Visual C++ can be used to accomplish this task. For a detailed procedure that describes the necessary steps for modifying your bitmap, see Chapter 1 of the *CDK Circle Sample Tutorial*, "Modifying The Control Bitmap."

Note that unlike VBX, this bitmap shouldn't include borders, beveled edges, or margins around the edge. The bitmap should also have a light-gray background, which is the standard for toolbox bitmaps.

Additional CDK Tools

In addition to the ControlWizard, the CDK package provides several other tools that are useful when developing your OLE control. This section describes the following tools:

- Type Library Generator
- Register Control
- Unregister Control
- Test Container application

All these tools can be found on the Tools menu of Visual Workbench.

Type Library Generator

Because other applications will be using your control, type libraries are required for all OLE controls. To generate a Type Library, you need the .ODL file from your control's project and MKTYPLIB.EXE. If you used ControlWizard to generate the starter files for your control, the .ODL file was automatically generated along with the other project files. As you add properties, methods, and events to your control, ClassWizard updates this file with the new entries.

If you are using the 32-bit version of the CDK, this tool is not available. The generation of the type library and .ODL file is automatically handled by the project's makefile.

Note Whenever entries are added to or removed from the project's .ODL file, you must remake the type library. This ensures that changes to your control's interface are incorporated into the DLL.

▶ **To generate a type library for your control**

1. Load the desired control's project.
2. From the Tools menu, choose Make TypeLib.

   A message box appears when the library has been successfully generated or an error has occurred. If an error has occurred, first make sure that your project's .ODL file is in the project directory. Errors can also be caused by improper syntax if you have edited your .ODL file by hand.
3. Choose the OK button to close the message box.

Note If you are using an internal makefile, you should force your resources to be recompiled during the build operation. This can be done by deleting the .RES file.

Register Control

In order for other applications to insert your control into their containers, you must register it by adding information about your control to the Windows registration database, REG.DAT.

▶ **To register your control**

1. Load the control's project.

2. From the Tools menu, choose Register Control.

   A message box appears when your control has been successfully registered.

   When you choose the Register Control command, a tool named REGSVR.EXE loads your control's DLL into memory and calls its **DllRegisterServer** function, which adds information about the control, its type library, and its property page to the Windows registration database.

3. Choose the OK button to close the message box.

Unregister Control

▶ **To unregister your control**

1. Load the desired control's project.

2. From the Tools menu, choose the Unregister Control command.

   A message box appears when your control has been successfully unregistered.

   This command runs REGSVR.EXE /U, which calls the **DllUnregisterServer** function of your control's DLL.

3. Choose the OK button to close the message box.

Test Container Application

The Test Container tool provides an OLE Container in which you can test your control. Once you have successfully built the control, you can test its performance and functionality. For more information on the Test Container application, see the online help provided with Test Container.

▶ **To test your OLE control using the Test Container**

1. From the Tools menu, choose Test Container.

2. From the Edit menu of Test Container, choose Insert OLE Control... .

   Your control will be registered as "*PRJNAME* Control."

3. In the Insert OLE Control dialog box, select the desired control and choose OK. The control will then appear in the control container.

Note If your control is not listed in the Insert OLE Control dialog box, make sure you have registered it with the Register Control command from the Tools menu.

At this point you can test your control's properties or events.

▶ **To test properties**

1. From the Edit menu, choose PRJNAME Control Object and then the cascading Properties... menu item.

2. Modify the value of a property on the property page.

3. Choose the Apply button to apply the new value to the PRJNAME control.

   The property now contains the new value.

▶ **To test events**

1. From the View menu, choose Event Log.

2. Perform an action that causes the control to fire an event.

   The event will appear in the Event Log window.

After you have finished testing your control, close the Test Container by choosing the Exit command on the File menu, or double-click the system menu button.

Now that you are familiar with the skeleton code created by ControlWizard, later chapters discuss important topics that you can use to enhance the usability and performance of your OLE 2 control. Chapter 5 discusses stock and custom events. You will learn how events are implemented and how to add events using ClassWizard. Chapter 6 discusses stock and custom properties and methods. You will also learn how properties and methods are implemented using MFC and use ClassWizard to add custom and stock methods.

C H A P T E R   4

Painting the Control

When OLE 2 controls are initially displayed or redrawn, they follow a painting process similar to Microsoft Foundation Class Library (MFC) applications, except for one important distinction. OLE 2 controls, unlike older custom controls, can be in an active or inactive state.

An active control is represented in an OLE container by a child window. Like any other window, it is responsible for painting itself when it receives a **WM_PAINT** message. The control's base class, **COleControl**, normally handles this message in its **OnPaint** function. This default implementation calls the OnDraw function of your control.

A control that is not active is painted in a different fashion. When the control is inactive, its window is either invisible or nonexistent, so it does not receive a paint message. Instead, the control container directly calls the OnDraw function of your control. This differs from an active control's painting process in that the **OnPaint** member function is never called.

This chapter provides information on how to paint your own control, modify its existing default behavior, and other related information. This chapter uses as an example the control created using ControlWizard with default settings. For more information on creating a skeleton control application using ControlWizard, see Chapter 3, "Building An Elementary Control."

In this chapter you will learn:

- The overall process for painting your control and the code created by ControlWizard to support painting
- How to optimize the painting process
- How to paint your control using metafiles

The Painting Process of an OLE 2 Control

As discussed above, the process for updating an OLE 2 control differs slightly depending on the active state of the control. If the control is active, the **OnPaint** function of the control's base class is called, which simply calls your control's OnDraw member function. However, if the control is not active, the framework calls OnDraw directly. Because the framework calls the OnDraw member function in both cases, you will be adding the majority of your painting code in this member function.

The rectangle passed to the OnDraw member function contains the area occupied by your control. If the control is active, the upper-left corner is (0, 0) and the device context passed is for the child window that contains the control. If the control is not active, the upper-left coordinate is not necessarily (0, 0) and the device context passed is of the control container that contains the control.

The OnDraw member function handles the actual painting of the control. When a control is not active, the control container simply calls this member function, passing the device context of the control container and the coordinates of the rectangular area occupied by the control. The default implementation, shown below, simply paints the rectangular region with a white brush and fills in the ellipse with the current background color.

```
void CSampleCtrl::OnDraw( CDC* pdc, const CRect& rcBounds, const CRect&
rcInvalid )
{
    pdc->FillRect( rcBounds,
        CBrush::FromHandle((HBRUSH)GetStockObject(WHITE_BRUSH)));
    pdc->Ellipse( rcBounds );
}
```

Note When painting your control, you should not make assumptions about the state of the device context that is passed as the *pdc* parameter to your OnDraw function. Because the device context is occasionally supplied by the container application, it will not necessarily be initialized to the default state that a newly created device context would normally have. In particular, you should explicitly select whatever pens, brushes, colors, fonts, and other resources that your drawing code depends upon.

It is important that your modifications do not depend on the rectangle's upper-left point being equal to (0, 0). This assumption can cause unexplained drawing errors. It is also very important that you only draw inside the rectangle passed to OnDraw. Unexpected results can occur if you draw beyond the rectangle's area.

Optimizing Your Paint Code

Once your control is successfully redrawing itself, the next step usually involves optimizing the OnDraw function.

You will notice that the default process simply redraws the entire control area. This is sufficient for simple controls, but in most cases it would be faster if the control repainted only the portion that actually needed updating, instead of the entire control.

The OnDraw function provides an easy method of optimization by passing rcInvalid, which indicates the rectangular area that needs redrawing. This allows you to bypass unnecessary painting operations when only part of the control needs redrawing.

Painting Your Control Using Metafiles

In most cases the pdc parameter to the OnDraw function is a standard device context (DC). However, when printing images of your control or during a print preview session, the DC received for rendering is a special type called a metafile DC. Some container applications may also choose to render your control's image using a metafile DC when in design mode, such as Microsoft Access 2.0. Where a standard DC immediately handles requests sent to it, a metafile DC stores requests to be played back at a later time.

These requests can be made by the container through two interface functions: **IViewObject::Draw** and **IDataObject::GetData**. When these requests are made the MFC framework makes a call to **COleControl::**. Because this is a virtual member function, you can override this function in your control class if you need to do any special processing. The default behavior calls **::OnDraw** in your control.

There are several considerations for making sure your control can be drawn in both standard and metafile device contexts.

Because the default implementation of **OnDrawMetafile** calls your control's OnDraw function, you should use only member functions that are suitable for both a metafile and a standard device context unless you override **OnDrawMetafile**. The following lists the subset of **CDC** member functions that can be used in a metafile and standard device context. For more information on these functions, see the **CDC** class in the *Class Library Reference*.

Arc	Pie	SetMapMode
Chord	Polygon	SetMapperFlags
Ellipse	Polyline	SetPixel
Escape	PolyPolygon	SetPolyFillMode
BitBlt	RealizePalette	SetROP2
ExcludeClipRect	RestoreDC	SetStretchBltMode
ExtTextOut	RoundRect	SetTextColor
FloodFill	SaveDC	SetTextJustification
IntersectClipRect	ScaleViewportExt	SetViewportExt
LineTo	ScaleWindowExt	SetViewportOrg
MoveTo	SelectClipRgn	SetWindowExt
OffsetClipRgn	SelectObject	SetWindowOrg
OffsetViewportOrg	SelectPalette	StretchBlt
OffsetWindowOrg	SetBkColor	TextOut
PatBlt	SetBkMode	

In addition to the **CDC** member functions, there are several other functions that are compatible in a metafile DC. These include **CPalette::AnimatePalette**, **CFont::CreateFontIndirect**, and three member functions of **CBrush**: **CreateBrushIndirect**, **CreateDIBPatternBrush**, and **CreatePatternBrush**.

Another point to consider when using a metafile DC is that the coordinate system may not be measured in pixels. For this reason, all of your drawing code should be adjusted to fit in the rectangle passed to **OnDraw** in the *rcBounds* parameter. This will prevent accidental painting outside the control.

Once you have implemented metafile rendering for your control, use Test Container to test the metafile. The following procedure describes the steps required.

▶ **To test your control's metafile using Test Container**

1. From the Tools menu, choose Test Container.

2. From the Edit menu of Test Container, choose Insert OLE Control.

3. In the Insert OLE Control dialog box, select the desired control and choose OK.

   The control will appear in Test container.

4. From the Edit menu, choose Draw Metafile.

This causes a separate window to appear in which the metafile is displayed. You can change the size of this window to see how scaling affects your metafile. You can close this window at any time.

CHAPTER 5

Events

Events are an integral part of your OLE 2 control. They are used to notify the container that something important has happened to the control. Common examples include clicks on the control, data entry using the keyboard, and changes in the value of a control. When these actions occur, the control fires an event alerting the container that the action related to this event has occurred.

The Microsoft Foundation Class Library (MFC) provides two different kinds of events that your control can implement: stock and custom. Stock events are those that the **COleControl** class handles by default. For a complete list of stock events, see the "Adding Stock Events" section later in this chapter.

Custom events give the control the ability to notify the container when anything interesting happens. Some examples would be a change in the internal state of a control or receipt of a certain window message.

This chapter expands on this concept by introducing several key topics that are useful in understanding how MFC implements events for your OLE 2 control. These topics include:

- Overview of OLE 2 control events using MFC
- Adding custom events
- Adding stock events
- Stock events supported by the **COleControl** class

To further clarify the concept of events, follow this chapter to see how you use ClassWizard to add a custom ClickIn event and the stock KeyPress event to your control object. You should use the basic skeleton created by ControlWizard for these sections.

Overview of Events in an OLE 2 Control

Your control can fire events when certain actions have occurred. The relevant section of the framework consists of two parts. The first part is a mechanism, similar to the message map, called an event map. This map allows your OLE 2 control object to fire specific events, both custom and stock, by automatically firing the event with the correct number and types of parameters. The second part of the mechanism consists of the **COleControl** class. This class, derived from **CWnd**, contains member functions designed to fire events for common actions such as mouse clicking, data entered from the keyboard, and mouse button states. These events are called stock events.

For your control to properly fire events, your control class must have an event map. The main purpose of this mapping mechanism is to centralize information about the event. This also allows ClassWizard to easily access and manipulate your control's events, which is accomplished by the following macro, located in the header file of your control class declaration:

```
DECLARE_EVENT_MAP()
```

Once the event map has been declared, it needs to be defined in your control's implementation file. The following lines of code define the event map, allowing you to fire specific events from your control object:

```
BEGIN_EVENT_MAP(CSampleCtrl, COleControl)
//{{AFX_EVENT_MAP(CSampleCtrl)
...
END_EVENT_MAP()
//}}AFX_EVENT_MAP
```

If ControlWizard was used to create the project, it automatically added these lines. If ControlWizard was not used, you must add these lines manually.

Through new improvements to ClassWizard, implementing events for your control is easy and fast. ClassWizard allows you to add stock events supported by the **COleControl** class or custom events that you define. For each new event, ClassWizard will automatically add the proper entry to your control's event map. The following sections describe the process of adding custom and stock events to your control class using ClassWizard.

Note When an event is fired, there is a limit of 15 parameters that can be passed to the recipient. This limitation is due to the MFC implementation of the **IDispatch** interface.

Figure 5.1 shows the OLE Events tab of ClassWizard. You use this tab to add custom and stock events.

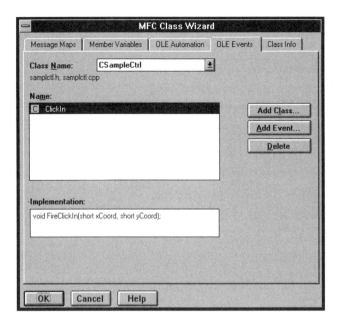

Figure 5.1   The OLE Events Tab

Adding Custom Events

Custom events differ from stock events in that they are not automatically fired by the **COleControl** class. A custom event is used to recognize a certain action, which you determine, as an event. The event map entries for custom events are always preceded by the **EVENT_CUSTOM** prefix. The following section implements a custom event called ClickIn, using the framework you created with ControlWizard.

Adding a Custom Event with ClassWizard

The following procedure demonstrates adding a specific custom event, ClickIn. This procedure can also be used to add other custom events you desire. Simply substitute your custom event name and its parameters for the ClickIn event name and parameters.

▶ **To add the ClickIn custom event using ClassWizard**

1. Load your control's project.

2. From the Browse menu, choose ClassWizard.

3. Choose the OLE Events dialog tab.

4. Choose the Add Event button.

5. In the External Name box, type ClickIn.

6. In the Internal Name box, type the name of the event's firing function. For this example, use the default value provided by ClassWizard (FireClickIn).

7. Choose the Add button.

8. In the Add Event Parameter dialog box, type **xCoord** for the name.

9. From the Type box, select **OLE_XPOS_PIXELS**.

10. Choose the OK button.

11. Add a second parameter by again choosing the Add button.

12. In the Add Event Parameter dialog box, type **yCoord** for the name.

13. From the Type box, select **OLE_YPOS_PIXELS**.

14. Choose Close to close the Add Event Parameter box.

15. Choose OK to close the Add Event box.

16. Choose OK again to confirm your choices and close ClassWizard.

Figure 5.2 shows the Add Event dialog box of ClassWizard.

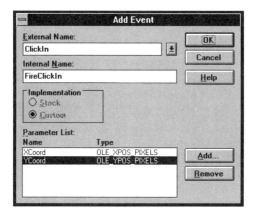

Figure 5.2   The Add Event Dialog Box

Changes Made by ClassWizard

When you add a custom event, ClassWizard makes changes to the .H, .CPP, and .ODL files of your control class.

The following line is added to the .H file of your control class:

```
void FireClickIn(OLE_XPOS_PIXELS XCoord, OLE_YPOS_PIXELS YCoord)
    {FireEvent(eventidClickIn,EVENT_PARAM(VTS_XPOS_PIXELS
VTS_YPOS_PIXELS), XCoord, YCoord);}
```

This code declares an inline function called `FireClickIn` that calls
COleControl::FireEvent with the ClickIn event and parameters you defined using
ClassWizard.

In addition, the following line is added to the event map of your control, located in
the .CPP file of your control class:

```
EVENT_CUSTOM("ClickIn", FireClickIn, VTS_XPOS_PIXELS  VTS_YPOS_PIXELS)
```

This code maps the event ClickIn to the inline function `FireClickIn`, passing the
parameters you defined using ClassWizard.

Finally, the following line is added to your control's .ODL file:

```
[id(1)] void ClickIn(OLE_XPOS_PIXELS XCoord, OLE_YPOS_PIXELS YCoord);
```

This line assigns the ClickIn event a specific ID number, taken from the event's
position in the event list of ClassWizard. This entry allows a container to anticipate
this event. For example, it might provide handler code to be executed when the
event is fired.

Calling FireClickIn

Now that you have added the ClickIn custom event using ClassWizard, you must
decide when this event is to be recognized. You do this by calling `FireClickIn`
when the appropriate action occurs. The following example uses the `InCircle`
function inside the **WM_LBUTTONDOWN** message handler to fire the ClickIn
event when a user clicks inside the control's circle.

▶ **To add a message handler with ClassWizard**

1. Load your control's project.
2. From the Browse menu, choose ClassWizard.
3. Choose the Message Maps dialog tab.
4. In the Object IDs box, select your control class name.
5. From the Messages box, select the message you would like to handle. For this
   example, select **WM_LBUTTONDOWN**.
6. Choose the Add Function button to add the handler function to your application.
7. Choose the Edit Code button to jump into your code at the location of your
   message handler, or the OK button to confirm your choice.

The following portion of code can be found in the **WM_LBUTTONDOWN**
handler of Chapter 5 of the *CDK Circle Sample Tutorial*. The `InCircle` function
will be called every time the left mouse button is clicked within the control window.
For more information on this function, see Chapter 5, "Hit Testing" in the *CDK
Circle Sample Tutorial*. If the point is inside the circle, the ClickIn event is fired:

```
void CSampleCtrl::OnLButtonDown(UINT nFlags, CPoint point)
{
    if (InCircle(point))
        FireClickIn(point.x, point.y);

    COleControl::OnLButtonDown(nFlags, point);
}
```

Note When message handlers for mouse button actions are created by ClassWizard, a call to the same message handler of the base class is automatically added. Do not remove this call. If your control uses any of the stock mouse messages, the message handlers in the base class must be called to ensure that mouse capture is handled properly.

For this example, the event is to be fired only when the click occurs inside a circular or elliptical region within the control. To determine this, you can place the InCircle function, taken from Chapter 5 of the *CDK Circle Sample Tutorial*, in your control's .CPP file:

```
BOOL CSampleCtrl::InCircle(CPoint& point)
{
    CRect rc;
    GetClientRect(rc);
    // Determine radii
    double a = (rc.right - rc.left) / 2;
    double b = (rc.bottom - rc.top) / 2;

    // Determine x, y
    double x = point.x - (rc.left + rc.right) / 2;
    double y = point.y - (rc.top + rc.bottom) / 2;

    // Apply ellipse formula
    return ((x * x) / (a * a) + (y * y) / (b * b) <= 1);
}
```

You will also need to add the following declaration of the InCircle function to your control's .H file:

```
BOOL InCircle( CPoint& point );
```

Adding Stock Events

Stock events differ from custom events in that they are automatically fired by the **COleControl** class. The **COleControl** class contains predefined member functions that are used to fire events resulting from common actions. Some common actions implemented by **COleControl** are single- and double-clicks on the control, keyboard events, and changes in the state of the mouse buttons. The event map entries for stock events are always preceded by the **EVENT_STOCK** prefix. The following section adds a stock event that fires whenever a key is pressed and your control is active, using the code created by ControlWizard.

Adding a Stock Event Using ClassWizard

Adding stock events requires less overhead than adding custom events because the firing of the actual event is handled automatically by the base class, **COleControl**. The following procedure demonstrates adding a specific stock event, KeyPress. This procedure can also be used to add other stock events you desire. Simply substitute the desired stock event name for KeyPress.

▶ **To add the KeyPress stock event using ClassWizard**

1. Load your control's project.

2. From the Browse menu, choose ClassWizard.

3. Choose the OLE Events dialog tab.

4. Choose the Add Event button.

5. From the External Name box, select KeyPress.

6. Choose OK.

7. Choose OK again to confirm your choices and exit ClassWizard.

Changes Made by ClassWizard

Because stock events are handled by the base class of your control, ClassWizard does not change your class declaration in any way; it simply adds the event to your event map and makes an entry in your .ODL file. The following line is added to your control's event map, located in the .CPP file of your control class:

```
EVENT_STOCK_KEYPRESS()
```

This code fires a KeyPress event whenever a **WM_CHAR** message is received and your control is active. This event can also be fired at other times by calling its firing function (`FireKeyPress` in this example).

The following line is added to your .ODL file:

```
[id(DISPID_KEYPRESS)] void KeyPress(short* KeyAscii);
```

This line assigns the KeyPress event a specific ID number, taken from the event's position in the event list of ClassWizard. This entry allows a container access to this event.

Stock Events Supported by ClassWizard

The **COleControl** class provides the eight stock events shown in Table 5.1. You can specify the events you want in your control from the OLE Events dialog page of ClassWizard.

Table 5.1   Stock Events

Event	Firing Function	Comments
Click	void **FireClick( )**	**EVENT_STOCK_CLICK( )**
		Fired when the control has captured the mouse, any **BUTTONUP** (left, middle, or right) message is received, and the button is released over the control. The stock MouseDown and MouseUp events occur before this event.
DblClick	void **FireDblClick( )**	**EVENT_STOCK_DBLCLICK( )**
		Similar to Click but fired when any **BUTTONDBLCLK** message is received.
Error	void **FireError(SCODE** *scode*, **LPCSTR** *lpszDescription*, **UINT** *nHelpID = 0*)	**EVENT_STOCK_ERROR( )**
		Fired when an error has occurred within your OLE control.
KeyDown	void **FireKeyDown(short** *nChar*, **short** *nShiftState*)	**EVENT_STOCK_KEYDOWN( )**
		Fired when a **WM_SYSKEYDOWN** or **WM_KEYDOWN** message is received.
KeyPress	void **FireKeyPress(short*** *pnChar*)	**EVENT_STOCK_KEYPRESS( )**
		Fired when a **WM_CHAR** message is received.
KeyUp	void **FireKeyUp(short** *nChar*, **short** *nShiftState*)	**EVENT_STOCK_KEYUP( )**
		Fired when a **WM_SYSKEYUP** or **WM_KEYUP** message is received.
MouseDown	void **FireMouseDown(short** *nButton*, **short** *nShiftState*, **float** *x*, **float** *y*)	**EVENT_STOCK_MOUSEDOWN( )**
		Fired if any **BUTTONDOWN** (left, middle, or right) is received. The mouse is captured immediately before this event is fired.
MouseMove	void **FireMouseMove(short** *nButton*, **short** *nShiftState*, **float** *x*, **float** *y*)	**EVENT_STOCK_MOUSEMOVE( )**
		Fired when a **WM_MOUSEMOVE** message is received.
MouseUp	void **FireMouseUp(short** *nButton*, **short** *nShiftState*, **float** *x*, **float** *y*)	**EVENT_STOCK_MOUSEUP( )**
		Fired if any **BUTTONUP** (left, middle, or right) is received. The mouse capture is released before this event is fired.

Custom Events with Stock Names

When you add a stock event to your control, it is fired when a certain action occurs. However, if you want to have an event with the same name as a stock event (such as Click) and you don't want it fired when the stock event would normally be fired, you can define a custom event with the same name. You can then fire the Click event at any time by calling its firing function.

This type of event is implemented in the same fashion as a custom event with the same name as a stock event. Note that it is not possible to have both a custom and a stock event of the same name. For example, you can implement either a custom Click event or a stock Click event, but not both.

▶   **To add a custom event that uses a stock event name**

1. Load your control's project.

2. From the Browse menu, choose the ClassWizard command.

3. Choose the OLE Events dialog tab.

4. Choose the Add Event button.

5. From the External Name box, select a stock event name. For this example, select Click.

6. Under the Implementation group, select Custom.

7. Choose OK.

8. Choose OK again to confirm your choices and exit ClassWizard.

CHAPTER 6

Methods and Properties

A control is able to fire events as a means of communication from an OLE custom control to its control container. A container can also communicate with a control by means of methods and properties. Methods and properties provide an exported interface for use by other applications, such as OLE Automation clients and OLE control containers. Methods and properties are quite similar in usage and purpose to the member functions and member variables of a C++ class, respectively. There are two types of both methods and properties your control can implement: stock and custom.

Similar to stock events, stock methods are those methods for which the **COleControl** class provides an implementation. For more information on this type of method, see the section "Adding a Stock Method" later in this chapter. Custom methods, defined by the developer, allow additional customization of the control. For more information, see the section "Adding Custom Methods" later in this chapter.

Stock properties are those properties for which the **COleControl** class provides an implementation. For a complete list of stock properties, see the section "Adding Stock Properties" later in this chapter. Custom properties, defined by the developer, are a powerful way to add specialized capabilities to your custom control. For more information see "Adding Custom Properties" later in this chapter.

Note Visual Basic custom (VBX) controls typically have properties such as Top, Left, Width, Height, Align, Tag, Name, Tab Index, Tab Stop, and Parent. Control containers are responsible for maintaining these aspects of each control. Therefore, OLE controls themselves should not support these properties.

This chapter discusses several topics essential to understanding and implementing properties and methods in your control. These topics include:

- Overview of OLE control methods
- Adding a custom method to a simple control
- Adding a stock method to a simple control

- Overview of OLE control properties
- Implementation choices available for custom properties
- Adding a custom property to a simple control
- Adding a stock property to a simple control
- Advanced implementation of properties and methods
- Available stock properties.
- Ambient properties

To further explain how methods and properties are implemented in your control, this chapter adds a custom method, called PointInControl, that allows the user to offset the control's circle. A stock Caption property and a custom property called CircleShape will also be added.

Figure 6.1 shows the OLE Automation tab of ClassWizard. You will use this tab to add your methods and properties.

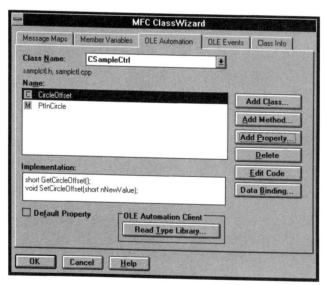

Figure 6.1   The OLE Automation Tab

Overview of Methods in an OLE Control

Methods are similar to C++ member functions in functionality and usage in that they are used to perform actions on the control.

The Microsoft Foundation Class Library (MFC) implements a mechanism that allows your control to support stock and custom methods. A part of this mechanism consists of another mechanism, similar to the message map, called a dispatch map.

It allows your OLE control object to support certain methods, both custom and stock, by automatically calling a member function with the correct number and type of parameters. The second part of the mechanism is the **COleControl** class. This class, derived from **CWnd**, contains member functions designed to support methods common to all OLE controls with less overhead than custom methods.

For your control to properly support various methods, your control class must declare a dispatch map. This is accomplished by the following line of code located in the .H file of your control class:

```
DECLARE_DISPATCH_MAP()
```

The main purpose of this mapping mechanism is to establish the relationship between the method names used by the external caller (such as the container) and the member functions of your control's class that implement the methods. Once the dispatch map has been declared, it needs to be defined in your control's .CPP file. The following lines of code define the dispatch map:

```
BEGIN_DISPATCH_MAP(CSampleCtrl, COleControl)
    //{{AFX_DISPATCH_MAP(CSampleCtrl)
    ...
    //}}AFX_DISPATCH_MAP
END_DISPATCH_MAP()
```

If ControlWizard was used to create the project, these lines were automatically added. If ControlWizard was not used, you must add these lines manually. The two comment lines allow ClassWizard to automatically insert macros into the dispatch map.

Note   The maximum number of parameters for a method is 15. This limitation is due to the MFC implementation of the **IDispatch** interface.

Adding Custom Methods

Custom methods differ from stock methods in that they are not automatically supported by **COleControl**. Furthermore, you must supply the implementation for each custom method you add to your control.

The user of a control is able to call a custom method at any time to perform control-specific actions. The dispatch map entry for custom methods is of the form **DISP_FUNCTION**. The custom method PtInCircle will be used as an example in the next section. This example uses the InCircle function from Chapter 5. For more information on this function, see the "Adding Custom Events" section in Chapter 5.

Adding a Custom Method With ClassWizard

The following procedure demonstrates adding the custom method PtInCircle to your control's skeleton code. Figure 6.2 shows the Add Method dialog box of ClassWizard. The method determines whether the coordinates passed to the control are inside or outside the circle. This same procedure can also be used to add other custom methods you desire. Simply substitute your custom method name and its parameters for the PtInCircle method name and parameters.

If you are using the 16-bit version of the CDK, the ClassWizard can be found on the Browse menu of the Visual C++ editor. If you are using the 32-bit version of the CDK, ClassWizard can be found on the Project menu of Visual C++.

▶   **To add the PtInCircle custom method using ClassWizard**

1. Load your control's project.
2. Open ClassWizard.
3. Choose the OLE Automation tab.
4. Choose the Add Method button.
5. In the External Name box, type **PtInCircle**.
6. In the Internal Name box, type **PtInCircle**.
7. From the Return Type box, select **BOOL** for the method's return type.
8. Choose the Add button.
9. In the Add Method Parameter dialog box, type **xCoord** for the name.
10. From the Type list box, select **short**.
11. Choose the Add button to add the parameter.
12. Repeat Steps 9-11 substituting **yCoord** for **xCoord**.
13. Choose the Close button to close the Add Method dialog box.
14. Choose the OK button to confirm your choices and close ClassWizard.

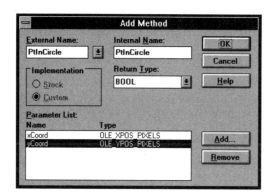

Figure 6.2   The Add Method Dialog Box

Changes Made by ClassWizard

When you add a custom method, ClassWizard makes some changes to the .H and the .CPP files of your control class. The following line is added to the dispatch map declaration in the .H file of your control class:

```
afx_msg BOOL PtinCircle(short xCoord, short yCoord);
```

This code declares a dispatch method handler called PtinCircle. This function can be called by the user of your control by using the external name PtInCircle.

In addition, the following line, which is located in the .CPP file of your control class, is added to the dispatch map of your control:

```
DISP_FUNCTION(CSampleCtrl, "PtInCircle", PtinCircle, VT_BOOL, VTS_I2
VTS_I2)
```

This macro maps the method PtInCircle to your handler function, PtinCircle, declares the return value to be **BOOL**, and declares two parameters of type **short** to be passed to PtinCircle.

Finally, the stub function CSampleCtrl::PtinCircle is added to the bottom of your .CPP file. In order for PtinCircle to function properly it needs to be modified as follows:

```
BOOL CSampleCtrl::PtinCircle(short xCoord, short yCoord)
{
    CPoint tmp(xCoord, yCoord);

    return InCircle(tmp);
}
```

Because ClassWizard was used to add this custom method, the entry for it was automatically added to the project's .ODL file.

Adding a Stock Method

A stock method differs from a custom method in that it is automatically supported by the **COleControl** class. For example, the **COleControl** class contains a predefined member function that is used to support the Refresh method for your control. The dispatch map entry for this stock method is **DISP_STOCKFUNC_REFRESH**. The following section adds the stock Refresh method to the control.

At this time the **COleControl** class supports two stock methods: DoClick and Refresh. The Refresh method can be invoked by the control's user to immediately update the control's appearance.

Method	Dispatch Map Entry	Comment
DoClick	DISP_STOCKPROP_DOCLICK( )	Fires a Click event.
Refresh	DISP_STOCKPROP_REFRESH	Immediately updates the control's appearance.

Adding a Stock Method Using ClassWizard

Adding a stock method is simple using ClassWizard. It requires less overhead than adding a custom method because the support of the method is automatically handled by the base class, **COleControl**. The following procedure demonstrates adding the stock Refresh method.

▶ **To add the stock Refresh method using ClassWizard**

1. Load your control's project.

2. Open ClassWizard.

3. Choose the OLE Automation tab.

4. Choose the Add Method button.

5. In the External Name box, select Refresh.

6. Choose the OK button.

7. Choose the OK button to confirm your choices and close ClassWizard.

Changes Made by ClassWizard

Because the stock Refresh method is supported by the base class of your control, ClassWizard does not change your class declaration in any way; it simply adds an entry for the method to your dispatch map. The following line is added to the dispatch map of your control located in the .CPP file of your control class:

```
DISP_STOCKFUNC_REFRESH( )
```

This code allows the user of your control to immediately update the appearance of the control.

Overview of Properties in an OLE Control

One of the most powerful features of OLE controls is the ability to implement custom properties. These properties help define the appearance and behavior of your control.

Properties, like methods, are supported by the same mechanism mentioned in the "Overview of Methods in an OLE Control" section earlier in this chapter. This mechanism consists of a dispatch map that handles properties and methods, together with existing member functions of the **COleControl** class. Similar to methods, the maximum number of parameters for a property is 15. This limitation is due to the MFC implementation of the **IDispatch** interface.

Note When using ClassWizard to add a stock property to your control, it is possible to change the implementation from stock to custom by choosing any option other than "Stock" in the "Implementation" option group. The resultant property implementation is then identical to a custom property implementation.

Adding Custom Properties

Custom properties differ from stock properties in that they are not automatically supported by the **COleControl** class. A custom property is used to expose a certain state or appearance of your control to a programmer using your control.

Custom properties come in four varieties of implementation: Member Variable, Member Variable with Notification, Get/Set Methods, and Parameterized.

- Member Variable Implementation

  This implementation represents the property's state as a member variable in your control class. Use the Member Variable implementation when it is not important to know when the value changes. Of the three types, this implementation creates the least amount of overhead for your control. The dispatch map entry for this implementation is **DISP_PROPERTY**. For a detailed example of this implementation, see Chapter 5, "Adding Special Effects," from the *CDK Circle Sample Tutorial*. The FlashColor property will be used in the example.

- Member Variable with Notification Implementation

  This implementation consists of a member variable as above, and a notification function created by ClassWizard. This notification function is automatically called after the property value changes. Use the Member Variable with Notification implementation when you need to be notified after the property value has changed. This implementation creates some overhead because it uses a function call. The dispatch map entry for this implementation is **DISP_PROPERTY_NOTIFY**. For a detailed example of this implementation, see Chapter 3, "Adding a Custom Notification Property," in *CDK Circle Sample Tutorial*. The CircleShape property will be used in the example.

- Get/Set Methods Implementation

  This implementation consists of a pair of member functions. The Get/Set Methods implementation automatically calls the Get member function when the user requests the current value of the property and the Set member function when the user requests that the property be changed. Use this implementation when you need to compute the value of a property during run time, validate a value passed by the user before changing the actual property, or implement a read-only or write-only property type. The dispatch map entry for this implementation is **DISP_PROPERTY_EX**. The CircleOffset property will be used in the following section to demonstrate this implementation.

- Parameterized Implementation

  Parameterized implementation is supported by ClassWizard. For more information on implementing this type, see "Implementing a Parameterized Property" in Appendix B.

Adding a Custom Property Using ClassWizard

The following procedure demonstrates adding a specific custom property, CircleOffset. This property will use the Get/Set Methods implementation. The procedure for adding custom properties with an implementation type other than Get/Set Methods is very similar.

This same procedure can also be used to add other custom properties you desire. Simply substitute your custom property name for the CircleOffset property name and parameters.

▶ **To add the CircleOffset custom property using ClassWizard**

1. Load your control's project.
2. Open ClassWizard.
3. Choose the OLE Automation tab.
4. Choose the Add Property button.
5. In the External Name box, type **CircleOffset**.
6. Under Implementation, select Get/Set Methods.
7. From the Type box, select short for the property's type.
8. Type unique names for your Get and Set Functions, or accept the default names.
9. Choose the OK button.
10. Choose the OK button to confirm your choices and close ClassWizard.

Figure 6.3 shows the Add Property dialog box of ClassWizard.

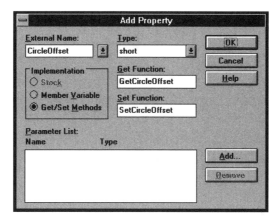

Figure 6.3   The Add Property Dialog Box

Changes Made by ClassWizard

When you add a custom property, ClassWizard makes changes to the .H and the .CPP files of your control class.

The following lines are added to the .H file of your control class:

```
afx_msg short GetCircleOffset( );
afx_msg void SetCircleOffset(short nNewValue);
```

This code declares two functions called GetCircleOffset and SetCircleOffset that are used to support your CircleOffset property.

In addition, the following line is added to the dispatch map of your control, located in the .CPP file of your control class:

```
DISP_PROPERTY_EX(CSampleCtrl,"CircleOffset", GetCircleOffset,
SetCircleOffset, VT_I2)
```

This code maps the property CircleOffset to your two handler functions.

Finally, the implementations of the GetCircleOffset and SetCircleOffset functions are added to the end of your .CPP file. In most cases, you will modify the Get function to simply return the value of the property. Your Set function will usually contain code that should be executed either before or after the property changes.

Note that ClassWizard automatically adds a call to the **COleControl** member function **SetModifiedFlag**. Calling this function marks the control as modified. If a control has been modified the new state will be saved when the control is destroyed. This function should be called whenever a property, saved as part of the control's persistent state, changes value.

In order for this method to be useful, you might want to declare a member variable of type **short** to hold the current offset of your circle. In your `SetCircleOffset` function you would simply set the member variable equal to the value passed. In your `GetDrawRect` function you would then add this member variable to the calculated rectangle dimensions to create the offset effect. For a detailed implementation of the CircleOffset property, see Chapter 4, "Adding Custom Properties," from the *CDK Circle Sample Tutorial*.

Note that this code example is the result of choosing the Get/Set Methods type of implementation. Other types of implementation are supported by slightly different code samples.

Adding Stock Properties

Stock properties differ from custom properties in that they are automatically supported by the **COleControl** class. The **COleControl** class contains predefined member functions that are used to support common properties for your control. Some common properties include the caption of your control and the foreground and background colors. The dispatch map entries for stock properties are always prefixed by **DISP_STOCKPROP**. The following section adds the stock Caption property to an OLE control.

Adding a Stock Property Using ClassWizard

Adding stock properties requires less overhead than adding custom properties because the support of the property is automatically handled by the base class, **COleControl**. The following procedure demonstrates adding a specific stock property, Caption. This same procedure can also be used to add other stock properties you desire. Simply substitute the desired stock property name for Caption.

▶ **To add the stock Caption property using ClassWizard**

1. Load your control's project.
2. Open ClassWizard.
3. Choose the OLE Automation tab.
4. Choose the Add Property button.
5. In the External Name box, select Caption.

   Note that in the Implementation group, Stock has been automatically selected.
6. Choose the OK button.
7. Choose the OK button to confirm your choices and close ClassWizard.

Changes Made by ClassWizard

Because stock properties are supported by the base class of your control, ClassWizard does not change your class declaration in any way; it simply adds the property to your dispatch map. The following line should have been added to the dispatch map of your control, located in the .CPP file of your control class:

```
DISP_STOCKPROP_CAPTION( )
```

This code allows the user to specify a caption for your control. To use the value of the stock property in your control, you can access a member variable of the **COleControl** base class. For more information on these member variables, see "Stock Properties Supported by ClassWizard" later in this chapter.

Advanced Implementation of Properties and Methods

The following two sections describe a process to implement read-only or write-only properties and the proper procedure to return an error code from a method or property.

Read-only and Write-only Properties

ClassWizard provides a quick and easy method to implement read-only or write-only properties for your control.

▶ **To implement a read-only or write-only property**

1. Load your control's project.

2. Open ClassWizard.

3. Choose the OLE Automation tab.

4. Choose the Add Property button.

5. In the External Name box, type the name of your property.

6. Under Implementation, select Get/Set Methods.

7. From the Type box, select the proper type for the property.

8. Clear the Set function name specified by ClassWizard if you want a read-only property. Clear the Get function name specified by ClassWizard if you want a write-only property.

9. Choose the OK button.

10. Choose the OK button to confirm your choices and close ClassWizard.

ClassWizard will insert the function **SetNotSupported** or **GetNotSupported** in the dispatch map entry in place of a normal Set or Get function.

If you want to change a property that already exists to be read-only or write-only, you can edit the dispatch map manually and remove the unnecessary Set or Get function from your class.

If you want a property to be conditionally read-only or write-only (for example, only when your control is operating in a particular mode), you can provide the Set or Get function, as normal, and call the **SetNotSupported** or **GetNotSupported** functions where appropriate. For example:

```
void CSampleCtrl::SetMyProperty( short propVal )
{
    if ( m_iReadOnlyMode )   //  some control-specific state
        SetNotSupported( );
    else
        m_ipropVal = propVal;   //  set property as normal
}
```

Returning Error Codes From a Method or Property

To indicate that an error has occurred within a property or method, you should use the **COleControl::ThrowError** function, which takes an **SCODE** (status code) as a parameter. You can use a predefined **SCODE** or define one of your own. For a list of predefined **SCODE**s and instructions on defining custom **SCODE**s, see "Handling Errors in Your OLE Control."

Helper functions exist for the most common predefined **SCODE**s, such as **COleControl::SetNotSupported**, **COleControl::GetNotSupported**, and **COleControl::SetNotPermitted**.

Note **ThrowError** is meant to be used only as a means of returning an error from within a property's Get or Set function or an automation Method. These are the only times that the appropriate exception handler will be present on the stack.

For more information on reporting exceptions in other areas of your code, see **COleControl::FireError** and "Handling Errors in Your OLE Control" in Appendix B.

Stock Properties Supported by ClassWizard

The **COleControl** class provides eight stock properties. You can specify the properties you want in your control in the OLE Automation dialog page of ClassWizard.

Property	Dispatch Map Entry	How to Access Value
BackColor	DISP_STOCKPROP_BACKCOLOR( )	Value accessible by calling **GetBackColor**.
BorderStyle	DISP_STOCKPROP_BORDERSTYLE( )	Value accessible as **m_sBorderStyle**.
Caption	DISP_STOCKPROP_CAPTION( )	Value accessible by calling **InternalGetText**.
Enabled	DISP_STOCKPROP_ENABLED( )	Value accessible as **m_bEnabled**.
Font	DISP_STOCKPROP_FONT	See "Using Fonts and Pictures in Your Control" for usage.
ForeColor	DISP_STOCKPROP_FORECOLOR( )	Value accessible by calling **GetForeColor**.
hWnd	DISP_STOCKPROP_HWND	Value accessible as **m_hWnd**.
Text	DISP_STOCKPROP_TEXT( )	Value accessible by calling **InternalGetText**. This property is the same as **Caption**, except for the property name.

Stock Properties and Notification

Most of the stock properties listed above have notification functions that you can override. For example, whenever the **BackColor** property is changed, the **OnBackColorChanged** function is called. The default implementation (in **COleControl**) calls **InvalidateControl**. Override this function if you want to take additional actions in response to this situation.

Color Properties

You can use the stock **ForeColor** and **BackColor** properties, or your own custom color properties, while painting your control. To use a color property while painting your control, call the **COleControl::TranslateColor** member function. The parameters of this function are the value of the color property and an optional palette handle. The return value is a **COLORREF** value that can be passed to GDI functions, such as **SetTextColor** and **CreateSolidBrush**.

The color values for the stock **ForeColor** and **BackColor** properties can be accessed by calling either the **GetForeColor** or **GetBackColor** function, respectively.

The following code sample demonstrates the usage of these two color properties when painting a control. The sample initializes two temporary **COLORREF** values with calls to **TranslateColor** using the **ForeColor** and **BackColor** properties. A temporary **CBrush** object is then initialized and used to paint the control's rectangle, and the text color is set using the **ForeColor** property:

```
        CBrush bkBrush(TranslateColor(GetBackColor()));
        COLORREF clrFore = TranslateColor(GetForeColor());
        pdc->FillRect( rcBounds, &bkbrush );
        pdc->SetTextColor( clrFore );
        pdc->DrawText( InternalGetText(), -1, rcBounds, DT_SINGLELINE |
DT_CENTER      | DT_VCENTER );
```

Ambient Properties

A control can obtain information about its container by accessing the container's "ambient properties." These properties expose visual characteristics such as the container's background color, the current font used by the container, and operational characteristics such as whether the container is currently in "user" mode or "designer" mode. A control can use ambient properties to tailor its appearance and behavior to the particular container in which it is embedded. However, a control should never assume that its container will support any particular ambient property. In fact, some containers may not support any ambient properties at all. In the absence of an ambient property, a control should assume a reasonable default value.

To access an ambient property, call **COleControl::GetAmbientProperty**. There are two versions of this member function: one that expects the ambient property name and one that expects the "dispatch ID" for the ambient property (the header file **oledisp.h** defines dispatch IDs for the standard set of ambient properties).

The parameters of the **GetAmbientProperty** function are the property name (or dispatch ID), a variant tag indicating the expected property type, and a pointer to memory where the value should be returned. The type of data to which this pointer refers will vary depending on the variant tag. The function returns **TRUE** if the container supports the property, **FALSE** otherwise.

The following sample code obtains the value of the ambient property called "UserMode." If the property is not supported by the container, a default value of **TRUE** is assumed:

```
        BOOL bUserMode;
        if( !GetAmbientProperty( DISPID_USERMODE, VT_BOOL, &bUserMode ) )
            bUserMode = TRUE;
```

For your convenience, **COleControl** supplies helper functions that access many of the commonly used ambient properties and return appropriate defaults when the properties are not available. These helper functions are as follows:

- **COLOR AmbientBackColor( );**
- **CString AmbientDisplayName( );**
- **LPFONTDISP AmbientFont( );**

Note Caller must call **Release( )** on the returned font.

- **COLOR AmbientForeColor( );**
- **LCID AmbientLocaleID( );**
- **CString AmbientScaleUnits( );**
- **short AmbientTextAlign( );**
- **BOOL AmbientUserMode( );**
- **BOOL AmbientUIDead( );**
- **BOOL AmbientDisplayHatching( );**
- **BOOL AmbientDisplayGrabHandles( );**

If the value of an ambient property is changed (through some action of the container), the **OnAmbientPropertyChanged** member function of the control will be called. Override this member function to handle such a notification. The parameter for **OnAmbientPropertyChanged** is the dispatch ID of the affected ambient property. The value of this dispatch ID may be **DISPID_UNKNOWN**, which indicates that one or more ambient properties have changed, but information about which properties were affected is unavailable.

C H A P T E R   7

Serializing Your Control

Serialization is the process of reading from or writing to a persistent storage medium, such as a disk file. The Microsoft Foundation Class Library (MFC) provides built-in support for serialization in the **CObject** class. Because the **COleControl** class is derived from **CObject**, your control can take advantage of serialization.

This ability is readily available to your OLE custom control by means of a specialized function called **COleControl::DoPropExchange**. This function, called during the loading and saving of your control object, will store all properties implemented with "member variable" or "member variable with notification" types.

The following sections cover the main issues related to serializing your control:

- Implementing `DoPropExchange` to properly serialize your control object
- Customizing the serialization process
- Implementing versioning support

Implementing the DoPropExchange Function

When you use ControlWizard to generate your control's project, several default handler functions are automatically added to your control class. One of these default handler functions is **DoPropExchange**. The default version of this function calls the **COleControl** version:

```
void CSampleCtrl::DoPropExchange( CPropExchange* pPX)
{
    COleControl::DoPropExchange(pPX);

    // TODO: Call PX_ functions for each persistent custom property.
}
```

If you want to make a certain property persistent, you must modify your DoPropExchange function. For example, the following function is taken from a control that has implemented the custom CircleShape property:

```
void CSampleCtrl::DoPropExchange(CPropExchange* pPX)
{
    COleControl::DoPropExchange(pPX);

    PX_Bool(pPX, "CircleShape", m_bCircleShape, TRUE);
}
```

The following table lists the eleven possible property exchange functions that you can use to serialize your properties:

Property Exchange Functions	Purpose
PX_Blob( )	Serializes a type Binary Large Object (BLOB) data property.
PX_Bool( )	Serializes a type Boolean property.
PX_Currency( )	Serializes a type **CY** (currency) property.
PX_Double( )	Serializes a type **double** property.
PX_Font( )	Serializes a font object property.
PX_Float( )	Serializes a type **float** property.
PX_IUnknown( )	Serializes a property of unknown type.
PX_Long( )	Serializes a type **long** property.
PX_Picture( )	Serializes a picture type property.
PX_Short( )	Serializes a type **short** property.
PX_String( )	Serializes a type **CString** property.

Customizing the Default Behavior of DoPropExchange

You will notice that the default implementation of this function makes a call to the base class. This is done to serialize the set of properties that are automatically supported by **COleControl**. Naturally, this uses more space than serializing only the custom properties of your control. If you would like to optimize your serializing code and the disk space needed to store your object, you can remove this call. This will allow your object to only serialize those properties you consider important. Any stock property states your control has implemented will not be serialized when saving or loading the control object unless you explicitly add **PX_** calls for them.

Implementing Versioning Support

Versioning enables a revised OLE control to add new or delete old persistent properties, while still being able to detect and load the persistent state created by an earlier version. A control's versioning is made available as part of the control's persistent data with a call to **COleControl::ExchangeVersion** in the control's `DoPropExchange` function. This call is automatically inserted if the OLE control was created using ControlWizard. It can be removed if versioning of your control is not desired. However, the cost is very small (4 bytes) for the added flexibility that versioning provides.

If your control was not created with ControlWizard, you can add a call to the **COleControl::ExchangeVersion** function by hand by simply inserting the following line at the very beginning of your `DoPropExchange` function (before the call to **COleControl::DoPropExchange**):

```
ExchangeVersion(pPX, MAKELONG(_wVerMinor, _wVerMajor));
```

You can use any **DWORD** you want as the version number. In a project generated by ControlWizard, **_wVerMinor** and **_wVerMajor** are used as the default. These are global constants defined in the implementation file of the main OLE custom control class. Within the remainder of your `DoPropExchange` function, you can call **CPropExchange::GetVersion** at any time to retrieve the version you are saving or retrieving.

For example, if version 2 of your control has additional properties that didn't exist in version 1, you might implement versioning as follows:

```
void CSampleCtrl::DoPropExchange(CPropExchange* pPX)
{
    ExchangeVersion(pPX, MAKELONG(_wVerMinor, _wVerMajor));
    COleControl::DoPropExchange(pPX);
    PX_Long(pPX, "ReleaseDate", m_releaseDate);
    if (pPX->GetVersion() >= MAKELONG(0, 2))
    {
        PX_Long(pPX, "OriginalDate", m_originalDate);
    }
    else
    {
        if (pPX->IsLoading())
            m_originalDate = 0;
    }
}
```

Version 1 of this sample control had only a "ReleaseDate" property. Version 2 added an "OriginalDate" property. If the control is instructed to load the persistent state from the old version, it simply initializes the member variable for the new property to a default value.

By default, a control will be requested to "convert" old data to the latest format. For example, if version 2 of a control loads data that was saved by version 1, it will write the version 2 format when it is saved again. If you want your control to save

data in the format last read, pass **FALSE** as a third parameter when calling
ExchangeVersion. This third parameter is optional and is **TRUE** by default.

C H A P T E R   8

Property Pages

An OLE custom control can have one or more "property pages." A property page provides a customized, graphical interface for viewing and editing the control's properties.

These property pages can be used in the following situations:

- When the control's "Properties" verb (**OLEIVERB_PROPERTIES**) is invoked, the control opens a modal property dialog box that contains the control's property pages.
- The container can display its own modeless dialog box that shows the property pages of the selected control.

In both cases, the standard interface of a property dialog is made up of an area for displaying the current property page, a device for switching between property pages, and a collection of buttons that perform the following tasks:

Button Title	Task
OK	Applies all changes on the current property page and closes the property dialog box.
Cancel	Ignores changes on the current property page and closes the property dialog box.
Apply	Applies all changes on the current property page.
Help	Displays help for the current property page.

This chapter expands on property pages with the following topics:

- Implementing the default property page for your control
- Adding more property pages
- Using stock property pages

Implementing the Default Property Page

If you use ControlWizard to create your control's project, a default property page class is provided for you. This property page class is derived from the **CPropertyPageDialog** class. Similar in design to a dialog box or form view, your property page will contain a set of controls, such as buttons, combination boxes, and other controls that are used to display current values the user can change when a property page is displayed. The first step in implementing your property page is to add controls to display your properties. For the following example, a simple control (created using ControlWizard) containing only the stock Caption property will be used.

Adding Controls to Your Property Page

▶ **To add controls to your property page (16-bit version)**

1. Load your project's .RC file, if it has not already been loaded.

2. Under the Type section of the MFC Resource Script dialog box, select Dialog.

3. Open the IDD_PROPPAGE_SAMPLE dialog box.

4. Choose the desired control on the Control Palette and insert it in the dialog box area.

   For this example, a text label "Caption :" and an edit box with an IDC_CAPTION identifier are sufficient.

5. Choose the Save button on the Toolbar to confirm your choices.

▶ **To add controls to your property page (32-bit version)**

1. Double-click the project's .RC file icon to load your project's resources.

2. Double-click the Dialog directory icon.

3. Open the IDD_PROPPAGE_SAMPLE dialog box.

4. Choose the desired control on the Control Palette and insert it in the dialog box area.

   For this example, a text label "Caption :" and an edit box with an IDC_CAPTION identifier are sufficient.

5. Choose the Save button on the Toolbar to confirm your choices.

Now that the interface has been modified, you need to link the edit box with the Caption property. This is done by editing the `CSampleCtrl::DoDataExchange` function.

Customizing the DoDataExchange Function

Your property page's `DoDataExchange` function allows you to establish links between property page values and the actual values of those properties in your control. To establish those links, you need to map the appropriate fields of the property page to their respective control properties.

These mappings are expressed in a manner similar to the **DDX_** functions used in normal MFC dialogs, with one exception. Instead of taking a reference to a member variable, the property page **DDP_** functions take the name of the relevant control property. The following line of code is a typical entry in the `DoDataExchange` function for a property page.

```
DDP_Text(pDX, IDC_CAPTION, m_caption, "Caption");
```

This function associates an edit box field (**IDC_CAPTION**) in the property page dialog with the Caption property of the control. For more information on establishing links between OLE control properties and property page controls, see Chapter 8, "Linking Controls with Properties," in the *CDK Circle Sample Tutorial*.

DDP_ functions are available for other dialog field types, such as check boxes, radio buttons, and list boxes. The following table lists the entire set of property page **DDP_** functions and their purposes:

Table 8.1   Property Page Functions

Function Name	Purpose
DDP_CBIndex	Use this function to link the selected string's index in a combo box with a control's property.
DDP_CBString	Use this function to link the selected string in a combo box with a control's property. The selected string can begin with the same letters as the property's value but need not match it fully.
DDP_CBStringExact	Use this function to link the selected string in a combo box with a control's property. The selected string and the property's string value must match exactly.
DDP_Check	Use this function to link a check box with a control property.
DDP_LBIndex	Use this function to link the selected string's index in a list box with a control's property.
DDP_LBString	Use this function to link the selected string in a list box with a control's property. The selected string can begin with the same letters as the property's value but need not match it fully.
DDP_LBStringExact	Use this function to link the selected string in a list box with a control's property. The selected string and the property's string value must match exactly.

Table 8.1   Property Page Functions (*continued*)

Function Name	Purpose
DDP_Radio	Use this function to link a radio button with a control property.
DDP_Text	Use this function to link text with a control property.

Adding Another Property Page

If you have more properties than you can reasonably fit on one property page, you can create additional property pages. It is strongly recommended that these new property pages follow the size standard for OLE control property pages.

The standard picture or color property pages measure 250x62 dialog units (DLUs). The standard font property page is 250x110 DLUs. The default property page created by ControlWizard uses the 250x62 DLU size, which also happens to correspond to the Visual C++ modeless property page size.

▶ **To create another property page (16-bit)**

1. Load your project's .RC file into App Studio.

   If the project is open in the development environment and you start the resource editor by choosing App Studio in the Tools menu, the .RC file is loaded automatically.

2. Choose Dialog from the Type list box.

3. Create a new dialog resource, named IID_PROPPAGE_NEWPAGE.

4. From the Dialog Properties list box, select **Styles**.

5. From the Style box, select **Child**.

6. From the Border box, select **None**.

   Make sure that the **Title bar** and **Visible** options are not checked.

   Save the project's .RC file.

7. Open ClassWizard.

8. In the Class Name box, type **CAddtlPropPage**.

9. Type in the names for your implementation and header files, or accept the default names.

10. From the Class Type box, select **COlePropertyPage**.

11. From the Dialog box, select **IDD_PROPPAGE_NEWPAGE**.

12. Choose Create Class to create the class.

13. Choose OK to close ClassWizard.

▶ **To create another property page (32-bit)**

1. Open the project's .RC file from the Source Files folder by double-clicking on the .RC file icon.

2. Open the Dialog folder by double-clicking on the Dialog folder icon.

3. Create a new dialog resource, named IID_PROPPAGE_NEWPAGE.

4. From the Dialog Properties dialog box, select the **Styles** tab.

5. From the Style box, select **Child**.

6. From the Border box, select **None**.

   Make sure that the **Title bar** and **Visible** options are not checked.

   Save the project's .RC file.

7. Open ClassWizard.

8. In the Class Name box, type **CAddtlPropPage**.

9. Type in the names for your implementation and header files, or accept the default names.

10. From the Class Type box, select **COlePropertyPage**.

11. From the Dialog box, select **IDD_PROPPAGE_NEWPAGE**.

12. Choose Create Class to create the class.

13. Choose OK to close ClassWizard.

To allow users of your control access to this new property page make the following changes to your control's property page IDs macro section (found in the control's implementation file):

```
▶   BEGIN_PROPPAGEIDS(CSampleCtrl, 2)
        PROPPAGEID(CMyPropPage::guid)
▶       PROPPAGEID(CAddtlPropPage::guid)
    ...
    END_PROPPAGEIDS(CSampleCtrl)
```

Note that the count of property pages increased from 1 to 2 in the **BEGIN_PROPPAGEIDS** macro.

You must also modify your control's .CPP file to include the .H file of the new property page class.

The next step involves creating two new resource string ID's that will provide a caption for the new property page and a dialog resource ID for the new property page constructor.

▶ **To add a string table entry (16-bit)**

1. Load your project's .RC file into App Studio.

If the project is open in the development environment and you start the resource editor by choosing App Studio in the Tools menu, the .RC file is loaded automatically.

2. Select String Table from the Type box.

3. Double-click the first entry in the Resources box.

4. Select an existing entry in the string table.

5. From the Resource menu, choose New String.

6. Enter a new string ID in the ID edit box.

   For this example, use IDS_SAMPLE_ADDPAGE for the new property page ID for the new property page caption.

7. Type a new string in the Caption box.

8. Repeat steps 6 and 7 using IDS_SAMPLE_ADDPPG_CAPTION for the ID.

▶   **To add a string table entry (32-bit)**

1. Open the project's .RC file from the Source Files folder by double-clicking on the .RC file icon.

2. Select an existing entry in the string table.

3. From the Resource menu, choose New String.

4. Enter a new string ID in the ID edit box.

   For this example, use IDS_SAMPLE_ADDPAGE for the new property page ID for the new property page caption.

5. Type a new string in the Caption box.

6. Repeat steps 4 and 5 using IDS_SAMPLE_ADDPPG_CAPTION for the ID.

In the .CPP file of your new property page class modify the `CAddtlPropPage::CAddtlPropPageFactory::UpdateRegistry` so that IDS_SAMPLE_ADDPAGE is passed by **AfxOleRegisterPropertyPageClass**, as in the following example:

```
BOOL CAddtlPropPage::CAddtlPropPageFactory::UpdateRegistry(BOOL
bRegister)
{
    if (bRegister)
        return AfxOleRegisterPropertyPageClass(AfxGetInstanceHandle(),
                    m_clsid, IDS_SAMPLE_ADDPAGE);
    else
        return AfxOleUnregisterClass(m_clsid, NULL);
}
```

In addition, modify the constructor of `CAddtlPropPage` so that IDS_SAMPLE_ADDPPG_CAPTION is passed to the **COlePropertyPage** constructor, as follows:

```
CAddtlPropPage::CAddtlPropPage() :
    COlePropertyPage(IDD, IDS_SAMPLE_ADDPPG_CAPTION)
{
    //{{AFX_DATA_INIT(CAddtlPropPage)
    // NOTE: ClassWizard will add member initialization here
    //    DO NOT EDIT what you see in these blocks of generated code !
    //}}AFX_DATA_INIT
}
```

After you have made the necessary modifications rebuild your project and test the new property page with Test Container.

Using Stock Property Pages

The CDK provides three stock property pages that you can use for your controls. These pages display a user interface for any font, picture, and color properties your control might have.

To incorporate these property pages into your control, just add their IDs to the code that initializes your control's array of property page IDs. The following sample code, located in the control's implementation file, initializes the array to contain all three stock property pages and the default property page:

```
BEGIN_PROPPAGEIDS( CSampleCtrl, 4 )
    PROPPAGEID( CMyPropPage::guid )
    PROPPAGEID( CLSID_CFontPropPage )
    PROPPAGEID( CLSID_CColorPropPage )
    PROPPAGEID( CLSID_CPicturePropPage )
...
END_PROPPAGEIDS(CSampleCtrl)
```

Note that the count of property pages increased to 4 in the **BEGIN_PROPPAGEIDS** macro.

After these modifications have been made, rebuild your project. Your control now has property pages for its font and color properties.

Note If the control stock property pages cannot be accessed, it may be because the run-time DLL has not been properly registered with the current operating system. This probably results from installing the CDK under a different operating system than the one currently running.

C H A P T E R   9

Using Fonts and Pictures in Your Control

Common property types, such as font or picture, are available to OLE controls and are used to customize the appearance of your control.

If your control displays text, you can allow the user of your control to change the appearance of the text by changing a font property. Font properties are implemented using a font object. Using the stock Font property page, the user may change the attributes of the font object, such as name, size, and style of the font. One example of using a font property in your control is using the stock Font property in conjunction with the stock Caption property to display the control's caption using a particular font.

The font object which implements the stock Font property is accessible through the **GetFont**, **SetFont**, and **InternalGetFont** functions defined in **COleControl**. The user of the control will access the font object via the GetFont and SetFont functions as with any other Get/Set property. When access to the font object is required from within a control, the **InternalGetFont** function should be used. For more information on using this property in your control, see the "Using the Stock Font Property" section later in this chapter.

A picture property allows the user to specify a picture to be displayed in your OLE control. Custom picture properties are implemented using a picture object. Using the stock Picture property page, the user can specify a bitmap, icon, or metafile to be displayed. For more information on implementing a custom picture property in your control, see the "Using Custom Picture Properties" section later in this chapter.

Topics in this chapter include:

- Using the stock Font property in your control
- Using custom font properties in your control
- Using custom picture properties

Using the Stock Font Property

As discussed in Chapter 6, ClassWizard makes adding stock properties easy. You simply choose the Font property, and ClassWizard automatically inserts the stock Font entry into your dispatch map.

If you are using the 16-bit version of the CDK, the ClassWizard can be found on the Browse menu of the Visual C++ editor. If you are using the 32-bit version of the CDK, ClassWizard can be found on the Project menu of Visual C++.

▶ **To add the stock Font property using ClassWizard**

1. Load your control's project.
2. Open ClassWizard.
3. Choose the OLE Automation tab.
4. Choose the Add Property button.
5. In the External Name box, select Font.
6. Choose the OK button.
7. Choose the OK button to confirm your choices and close ClassWizard.

The following line is added to the dispatch map of your control, located in the .CPP file of your control class:

```
DISP_STOCKPROP_FONT()
```

In addition, the following line is added to your control's .ODL file:

```
[id(DISPID_FONT), bindable] IFontDisp* Font;
```

The stock Caption property is an example of a text property that may be drawn using the stock Font property information. Adding the stock Caption property to your control is done by following almost exactly the same steps as were used for the stock Font property.

▶ **To add the stock Caption property using ClassWizard**

1. Load your control's project.
2. Open ClassWizard.
3. Choose the OLE Automation tab.
4. Choose the Add Property button.
5. In the External Name box, select Caption.
6. Choose the OK button.
7. Choose the OK button to confirm your choices and close ClassWizard.

The following line is added to the dispatch map of your control, located in the .CPP file of your control class:

```
DISP_STOCKPROP_CAPTION()
```

The default implementation of OnDraw uses the system font for any text displayed in the control. This means that you must modify the OnDraw code to make use of the new Font property. To reflect any changes made by the user, you must select the font object into the device context. You do this by making a call to the **SelectStockFont** member function, passing the device context of your control. The following OnDraw function has been modified to demonstrate the necessary code:

```
void CSampleCtrl::OnDraw( CDC* pdc, const CRect& rcBounds, const CRect&
rcInvalid)
{
    CFont* pOldFont;
    TEXTMETRIC tm;
     const CString& strCaption = InternalGetText();

    pOldFont = SelectStockFont( pdc );
    pdc->FillRect(rcBounds, CBrush::FromHandle(
       (HBRUSH )GetStockObject(WHITE_BRUSH)));
     pdc->Ellipse(rcBounds);
     pdc->GetTextMetrics(&tm);
     pdc->SetTextAlign(TA_CENTER | TA_TOP);
     pdc->ExtTextOut((rcBounds.left + rcBounds.right) / 2, (rcBounds.top
        + rcBounds.bottom - tm.tmHeight) / 2, ETO_CLIPPED, rcBounds,
        strCaption, strCaption.GetLength(), NULL);

    pdc->SelectObject(pOldFont);
}
```

Once this code has been inserted, the control will display any text within the control with characteristics from your control's stock Font property.

Using Custom Font Properties in Your Control

In addition to the stock Font property, your control can have custom Font properties. The process of adding a custom font property requires the completion of the following tasks, discussed in the following sections:

- Using ClassWizard to implement a custom Font property
- Processing standard font change notifications
- Implementing a New Font Notification Interface

Implementing a Custom Font Property

The process for implementing a custom font property consists of adding the property with ClassWizard and then making some modifications to the code. The following sections describe how to add the custom HeadingFont property.

Adding a Custom Font Property

▶ **To add a custom font property**

1. Load your control's project.

2. Open ClassWizard.

3. Choose the OLE Automation tab.

4. Choose the Add Property button.

5. In the External Name box, type a name for the property. For this example, use **HeadingFont**.

6. From the Implementation box, select Get/Set Methods.

7. From the Return Type box, select **LPFONTDISP** for the property's type.

8. Choose the OK button.

9. Choose the OK button to confirm your choices and close ClassWizard.

Modifications to the Control Code

Now that you have added the HeadingFont property you must make some changes to your control's header and implementation files to fully support the custom Font property. In your control's header file, add the following declaration of a protected member variable:

▶ `protected:`

▶ `CFontHolder* m_fontHeading;`

In your control's implementation file, do the following:

- Initialize m_fontHeading in the control's constructor.

▶
```
CSampleCtrl::CSampleCtrl( ) : m_fontHeading( &m_xFontNotification )
{
    // [...body of constructor...]
}
```

- Declare a static **FONTDESC** structure containing default attributes of the font.

▶ `static const FONTDESC _fontdescHeading =`
▶ `  { sizeof(FONTDESC), "MS Sans Serif", FONTSIZE( 12 ), FW_BOLD,`
▶ `    ANSI_CHARSET, FALSE, FALSE, FALSE };`

- In the control's `DoPropExchange` member function, add a call to the **PX_Font** function. This provides initialization and persistence for your custom font property.

```
void CSampleCtrl::DoPropExchange(CPropExchange* pPX)
{
    COleControl::DoPropExchange(pPX);

    // [...other PX_ function calls...]
►   PX_Font(pPX, _T("HeadingFont"), m_fontHeading,
    &_fontdescHeading);
}
```

- Finish implementing the control's `GetHeadingFont` member function.

```
LPFONTDISP CSampleCtrl::GetHeadingFont( )
{
►   return m_fontHeading.GetFontDispatch( );
}
```

- Finish implementing the control's `SetHeadingFont` member function.

```
void CSampleControl::SetHeadingFont( LPFONTDISP HeadingFont )
{
►   m_fontHeading.InitializeFont( &_fontdescHeading, newValue);
SetModifiedFlag( );
}
```

- Modify the control's `OnDraw` member function to define a variable to hold the previously selected font.

► `CFont* pOldHeadingFont;`

- Modify the control's `OnDraw` member function to select the custom font into the device context by adding the following line wherever the font is to be used.

► `pOldHeadingFont = SelectFontObject(pdc, m_fontHeading);`

- Modify the control's `OnDraw` member function to select the previous font back into the device context by adding the following line after the font has been used.

► `pdc->SelectObject(pOldHeadingFont);`

After the custom Font property has been implemented, the standard font property page should be implemented, allowing control users to change the current font of the control. To add the property page ID for the standard Font property page, insert the following line after the **BEGIN_PROPPAGEIDS** macro:

► `PROPPAGEID(CLSID_CFontPropPage)`

You must also increment the count parameter of your **BEGIN_PROPPAGEIDS** macro by one. The following line illustrates this:

▶ `BEGIN_PROPPAGEIDS(CSampleCtrl, 2)`

After these changes have been made, rebuild the entire project to incorporate the additional functionality.

Processing Font Notifications

In most cases your control needs to know when the characteristics of the font object have been modified by the user. Each font object is capable of providing notifications when it changes. It sends these notifications by calling a member function of the **IFontNotification** interface, implemented by the **COleControl** base class.

If your control uses the stock Font property, its notifications are handled by the **OnFontChanged** member function in the **COleControl** base class. When you add custom font properties, you can have them use the same implementation. In the example in the previous section, this was accomplished by passing **&m_xFontNotification** when initializing the **m_fontHeading** member variable.

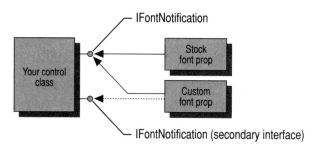

Figure 9.1   Implementing Multiple Font Object Interfaces

The solid lines in Figure 9.1 show that both font objects are using the same implementation of **IFontNotification**. This could cause problems if you wanted to distinguish which font actually changed.

One way to distinguish between your control's font object notifications is to create a separate implementation of the **IFontNotification** interface for each font object in your control. Using this technique allows you to optimize your drawing code by updating only the string, or strings, that use the recently modified font. The following sections demonstrate the steps necessary to implement another notification interface for a second font property. In the following discussion the second font property is assumed to be the `HeadingFont` property that was added in the previous section.

Implementing a New Font Notification Interface

To distinguish between the notifications of two or more fonts, a new notification interface must be implemented for each font used in your control. This interface is created by modifying your control's header and implementation files.

Additions to the Header File

In the control's header file, the following lines should be added to the class declaration:

```
protected:
BEGIN_INTERFACE_PART(HeadingFontNotify, IPropertyNotifySink)
INIT_INTERFACE_PART(CSampleCtrl, HeadingFontNotify)
        STDMETHOD(OnRequestEdit)(DISPID);
        STDMETHOD(OnChanged)(DISPID);
    END_INTERFACE_PART(HeadingFontNotify)
```

These lines of code create an implementation of the **IPropertyNotifySink** interface called HeadingFontNotify. This new interface contains a method called OnChanged.

Additions to the Implementation File

In the code that initializes the heading font (in the control's constructor), change &m_xFontNotification to &m_xHeadingFontNotify. Then add the following code:

```
▶  STDMETHODIMP_(ULONG) CSampleCtrl::XHeadingFontNotify::AddRef( )
▶  {
▶      METHOD_MANAGE_STATE(CSampleCtrl, HeadingFontNotify)
▶      return (ULONG)pThis->ExternalAddRef( );
▶  }
▶
▶  STDMETHODIMP_(ULONG) CSampleCtrl::XHeadingFontNotify::Release( )
▶  {
▶      METHOD_MANAGE_STATE(CSampleCtrl, HeadingFontNotify)
▶      return (ULONG)pThis->ExternalRelease( );
▶  }
▶
▶  STDMETHODIMP CSampleCtrl::XHeadingFontNotify::QueryInterface( REFIID
   iid, LPVOID FAR* ppvObj )
▶  {
▶      METHOD_MANAGE_STATE( CSampleCtrl, HeadingFontNotify )
▶      if( IsEqualIID( iid, IID_IUnknown ) ||
▶          IsEqualIID( iid, IPropertyNotifySink))
▶      {
▶        *ppvObj= this;
▶        AddRef( );
▶        return NOERROR;
```

```
    }
    return ResultFromScode(E_NOINTERFACE);
}

STDMETHODIMP CSampleCtrl::HeadingFontNotify::OnChanged(DISPID)
{
    METHOD_MANAGE_STATE( CSampleCtrl, HeadingFontNotify )
    pThis->InvalidateControl( );
    return NOERROR;
}

STDMETHODIMP CSampleCtrl::XHeadingFontNotify::OnRequestEdit(DISPID)
{
    return NOERROR;
}
```

The AddRef and Release methods in the **IPropertyNotifySink** interface keep track of the reference count for the OLE control object. When the control obtains access to interface pointer, the control calls AddRef to increment the reference count. When the control is finished with the pointer, it calls Release, in much the same way that one might call **GlobalFree** to free a global memory block. When the reference count for this interface goes to zero, the interface implementation can be freed. In this example, the QueryInterface function returns a pointer to a **IPropertyNotifySink** interface on a particular object. This function allows an OLE control to query an object to determine what interfaces it supports.

After these changes have been made to your project, you should rebuild the project and then test the interface using the Test Container application.

Using Custom Picture Properties

The CDK provides several components that you can use to display pictures (bitmaps, icons, and metafiles) within your control. These components include:

- The **CPictureHolder** class.
- Support for properties of type **LPPICTUREDISP**, implemented with Get/Set functions.
- A property page that manipulates a control's picture property or properties.

When you have completed the necessary steps, your control can display pictures chosen by the control's user. The user can change the displayed picture using a property page that shows the current picture and a Browse button that allows selection of a different picture.

Implementing a custom property of type Picture requires you to:

- Make several additions to your control's project, such as the standard Picture property page ID, a data member of type **CPictureHolder**, and a custom property of type **LPPICTUREDISP** with a Get/Set implementation.
- Modify several functions in your control's class.

Additions to Your Control Project

To add the property page ID for the standard Picture property page, insert the following line after the **BEGIN_PROPPAGEIDS** macro:

▶ `PROPPAGEID(CLSID_CPicturePropPage)`

You must also increment the count parameter of your **BEGIN_PROPPAGEIDS** macro by one. The following line illustrates this:

▶ `BEGIN_PROPPAGEIDS(CSampleCtrl, 2)`

To add the **CPictureHolder** data member to your control class, insert the following line under the protected section of your control class declaration:

▶ `CPictureHolder    m_pic;`

It is not necessary to name your data member `m_pic`; any name will suffice.

Next, you will need to add a picture property:

▶ **To add a custom picture property using ClassWizard**

1. Load your control's project.
2. Open ClassWizard.
3. Choose the OLE Automation tab.
4. Choose the Add Property button.
5. In the External Name box, type the property name. (For example purposes, `ControlPicture` is used in this procedure.)
6. Under Implementation, select Get/Set Methods.
7. From the Return Type box, select **LPPICTUREDISP** for the property type.
8. Type unique names for your Get and Set Functions or accept the default names. In this example, the default names, `GetControlPicture` and `SetControlPicture`, are used.
9. Choose the OK button to close the Add Property dialog box.
10. Choose the OK button to confirm your choices and close ClassWizard.

ClassWizard adds the following code between the dispatch map comments in your control's header file:

```
afx_msg LPPICTUREDISP GetControlPicture();
afx_msg void SetControlPicture(LPPICTUREDISP newValue);
```

In addition, the following code is added to the dispatch map in your control's implementation file:

```
DISP_PROPERTY_EX(CSampleCtrl, "ControlPicture", GetControlPicture,
SetControlPicture, VT_PICTURE)
```

ClassWizard also adds the following two stub functions in your control's implementation file:

```
LPPICTUREDISP CSampleCtrl::GetControlPicture()
{
    // TODO: Add your property handler here

    return NULL;
}

void CSampleCtrl::SetControlPicture(LPPICTUREDISP newValue)
{
    // TODO: Add your property handler here

    SetModifiedFlag();
}
```

Note   Your class and function names might differ from the example above.

Modifications to Your Control Project

Once the necessary additions have been made, you will need to modify several functions that affect the rendering of your OLE control. These functions, OnResetState, OnDraw, and the Get/Set functions of a custom picture property, are located in your control's implementation file. (Note that in this example the control class is called CSampleCtrl, the **CPictureHolder** data member is called m_pic, and the custom picture property is called ControlPicture.)

In your control's OnResetState function, add the following optional line after the call to the base class **OnResetState** function:

▶ m_pic.CreateEmpty();

This sets the control's picture to an empty picture.

In your control's OnDraw function, it is necessary only to make a call to **CPictureHolder::Render** to draw the picture properly. Modify your function so it resembles the following example:

```
void CSampleCtrl::OnDraw(
    CDC* pdc, const CRect& rcBounds, const CRect& rcInvalid)
{
► m_pic.Render(pdc, rcBounds, rcBounds);
}
```

In the Get function of your control's custom picture property, add the following line:

► `return m_pic.GetPictureDispatch();`

In the Set function of your control's custom Picture property, add the following lines:

► `m_pic.SetPictureDispatch(newValue);`
► `InvalidateControl();`

After you have completed the needed modifications, rebuild your project to incorporate the new functionality of the custom Picture property.

Note   Your class and function names might differ from the example above.

C H A P T E R   1 0

Licensing Your Control

An optional feature of OLE controls is the ability to support licensing, allowing you to determine who is able to use or distribute your control. Licensing your control involves some additional work on the part of ControlWizard. In addition to generating the default control framework, ControlWizard adds a small amount of licensing code to the declaration and implementation files of the control and creates a license file with a .LIC extension.

Licensing support allows you, as the control developer, to determine how other people will use the OLE control. You can provide the control's purchaser with the control and .LIC file, with the agreement that the purchaser may distribute the control, but not the .LIC file, with an application that uses the control. This prevents users of that application from writing new applications that use the control, without first licensing the control from you.

This chapter discusses the following topics:

- Overview of OLE control licensing
- Creating a licensed control
- Licensing support
- Customizing the licensing of an OLE control

Overview of OLE Control Licensing

In order to provide licensing support for OLE controls, the **COleObjectFactoryEx** class provides an implementation for several functions in the **IClassFactory2** interface: **IClassFactory2::RequestLicKey**, **IClassFactory2::GetLicInfo**, and **IClassFactory2::CreateInstanceLic**. Figure 10.1 demonstrates the process of verifying the licensing of an OLE control that will be used in the development of a container application. As mentioned previously, the developer of the container application must have the proper .LIC file present on the system to create an instance of the control.

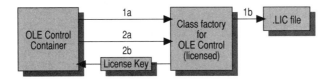

Figure 10.1   Verification of a Licensed OLE Control during Development

When the developer of the container application makes a request for an instance of the control, a call to **GetLicInfo** is made to verify that the control's .LIC file is present. If the control is licensed, an instance of the control can be created and placed in the container. After the developer has finished constructing the container application, another function call, this time to **RequestLicKey**, is made. This function returns a license key (a simple character string) to the container application. The returned key is then embedded into the application. The next process, shown in Figure 10.2, occurs when the end-user runs the container application.

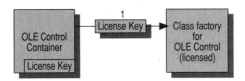

Figure 10.2   Verification of a Licensed OLE Control during Execution

When the application is started, an instance of the control usually needs to be created. The container accomplishes this by making a call to **CreateInstanceLic**, passing the embedded license key as a parameter. A string comparison is then made between the embedded license key and the control's own copy of the license key. If the match is successful, an instance of the control is created and the application continues to execute normally.

Two basic components combine to form the CDK's implementation of control licensing: (1) specific code in the control's implementation DLL related to licensing and (2) the license file. The code is composed of two (or possibly three) function calls and a character string, hereafter referred to as a license string, containing a copyright notice. The license file, generated by ControlWizard, is a text file with a copyright statement. It is named using the project name with an .LIC extension, for example SAMPLE.LIC. A control with licensing support must be accompanied by the license file if design-time usage is needed.

Creating a Licensed Control

When you use ControlWizard to create the framework for your control, it is easy to include support for licensing. When the License Validation option is selected,

ControlWizard adds code to the control class to support licensing. The code consists of functions for license verification using a key and a license file. These functions also can be modified to customize your control's licensing. For more information on license customization, see "Customizing the Licensing of an OLE Control" later in this chapter.

▶ **To add support for licensing with ControlWizard**

1. From the Tools menu, choose ControlWizard.

2. Specify the location of the new control project by selecting the drive and directory.

3. Choose the Project Options button.

4. Check the Enforce License check box.

5. Select any other options for your project.

6. Choose OK to close the Project Options dialog box.

7. Select other options for your control project.

8. Choose OK to confirm your project choices.

9. Choose OK to have ControlWizard generate the OLE control framework.

ControlWizard now generates an OLE control framework that includes basic licensing support. For a detailed explanation of the licensing code, see "Licensing Support" in the next section.

Licensing Support

When you use ControlWizard to add licensing support to your OLE control, code that declares and implements the licensing capability is added to the header and implementation files of your control. This code is composed of two member functions that override the default implementations in the **COleObjectFactoryEx** class. These functions perform the task of retrieving and verifying the license of a control. **VerifyUserLicense** is not generated by ControlWizard but can be overridden to customize the license key verification behavior. These member functions arc:

- **GetLicenseKey**

  Requests a unique key from the control's DLL. This key will be embedded in the container application and used later, in conjunction with **VerifyLicenseKey**, to create an instance of the control. This function is called by the framework as part of processing **IClassFactory2::RequestLicKey**.

- **VerifyLicenseKey**

  Verifies that the embedded key and the control's unique key are the same. This allows an instance of the control to be created for use by the container application. This function is called by the framework as part of processing

IClassFactory2::CreateInstanceLic. The default implementation simply performs a string comparison. This function can be overridden to provide customized verification of the license key. For more information, see "Customizing the Licensing of an OLE Control," later in this chapter.

- **VerifyUserLicense**

    Verifies that the control allows design-time usage by checking the system for the presence of the control's license file. This function is called by the framework as part of processing **IClassFactory2::GetLicInfo** and **IClassFactory::CreateInstanceLic**.

Header File Modifications

ControlWizard places the following code in your control's header file. In this example, two member functions of `CSampleCtrl` are declared, one that verifies the presence of the control's .LIC file and a second that retrieves the license key to be used in the application containing the control:

```
BEGIN_OLEFACTORY(CSampleCtrl)          // Class factory and guid
    virtual BOOL VerifyUserLicense();
    virtual BOOL GetLicenseKey(DWORD, BSTR FAR*);
END_OLEFACTORY(CSampleCtrl)
```

Implementation File Modifications

The following two statements, placed in your control's implementation file, declare the license filename and license string that will be used for the control:

```
static const char BASED_CODE _szLicFileName[] = "MY.LIC";
static const char BASED_CODE _szLicString[] =
    "Copyright (c) 1994 your_company_name";
```

Note The license string, **szLicString**, is generated by appending your company name (as entered during the CDK installation) to "Copyright (c) year." If you modify this string in any way, you must also modify the first line in the control's .LIC file or licensing will not function properly.

The following code, also placed in your control's implementation file, defines the control class' `VerifyUserLicense` and `GetLicenseKey` functions:

```
//////////////////////////////////////////////////////////////
// CSampleCtrl::CSampleCtrlFactory::VerifyUserLicense -
// Checks for existence of a user license

BOOL CSampleCtrl::CSampleCtrlFactory::VerifyUserLicense()
{
    return AfxVerifyLicFile(AfxGetInstanceHandle(), _szLicFileName,
            _szLicString);
}
```

```
///////////////////////////////////////////////
// CSampleCtrl::CSampleCtrlFactory::GetLicenseKey -
// Returns a runtime licensing key

BOOL CSampleCtrl::CSampleCtrlFactory::GetLicenseKey(DWORD dwReserved,
    BSTR FAR* pbstrKey)
{
 if (pbstrKey == NULL)
    return FALSE;

 *pbstrKey = SysAllocString(_szLicString);
 return (*pbstrKey != NULL);
}
```

Customizing the Licensing of an OLE Control

Because **VerifyUserLicense**, **GetLicenseKey**, and **VerifyLicenseKey** are
declared as virtual member functions of your control's factory class, you can
customize the licensing behavior of your control.

For example, you can provide several levels of licensing for your control by
overriding the **VerifyUserLicense** and/or **VerifyLicenseKey** member functions.
Inside this function you could adjust which properties and/or methods are exposed
to the user according to the license level you detected.

You can also add code to the **VerifyLicenseKey** function that provides a
customized method of informing the user that the creation of the control has failed.
For instance, in your **VerifyLicenseKey** member function you could display a
dialog box stating the reason why the control failed to initialize.

Another possible way to verify licensing would be to check the registration
database for a specific registry key instead of a call to **VerifyLicenseKey**.

CHAPTER 11

Using Data Binding in Your Control

One of the more powerful uses of OLE controls is "data binding." Data binding allows a property of your control to "bind" with a specific field in a database. When this control property is modified by the control's user, the control notifies the database that the value has changed and makes a request to have the record field updated. The database then notifies the control of the success or failure of the request. Data bound controls also have the ability to view several different records in a database by scrolling through the database using a row cursor object provided by the database.

This chapter explains the following topics:

- How data binding works
- Defining a bindable property
- Advanced data binding

How Data Binding Works

Data binding allows a database entry, such as a record field, to be linked to a property of an OLE control. This control is typically used in a form view and provides a visual interface to the current record state. Figure 11.1 shows a conceptual representation of this linkage. The OLE control is an edit box and its bound property is the "Text" property. This control is linked to a database entry, specifically the Name field of a record. When modifications are made to the control's Text property, these changes are communicated to the database.

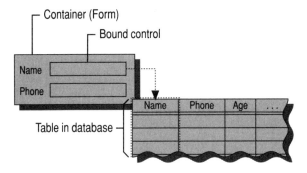

Figure 11.1   Conceptual Diagram of a Data Bound Control

When an OLE control property is bound, the developer must make sure that the control is able to send notifications to the database when the property changes. The notification is sent to an interface provided by the control's container, which processes it and returns the result to the container.

The **COleControl** class provides two member functions that make data binding an easy process to implement. The first function, **BoundPropertyRequestEdit** is used to request permission to change the property value. **BoundPropertyChanged**, the second function, is called after the property value has successfully been changed.

Defining a Bindable Property

If your control was created using ControlWizard, data binding is enabled automatically by a call to **EnableDataBinding**, found in your control's constructor. Once you have successfully compiled your OLE control, you can incorporate data binding using ClassWizard. ClassWizard allows you to choose which properties to make bindable and provides several options of binding.

Binding Option	Description
Sends OnRequestEdit	The property requests permission from the database before modifying the value.
Visible to the End User	The container displays the property in a property binding dialog.
Default Bindable Property	Makes the bindable property the default choice by the control's container.

The following sample demonstrates the procedure for adding a text property to an existing control that subclasses an edit box. This property can then be bound to a record field. Figure 11.2 shows the Data Binding dialog box you will be using.

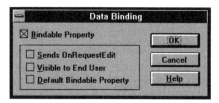

Figure 11.2   The Data Binding Dialog Box

▶ **To add a bound property using ClassWizard**

1. Load a control project to which you wish to add a data bound property.

2. Open ClassWizard.

3. Choose the OLE Automation tab.

4. Choose the Add Property button.

5. In the External Name box, type the external name of the property. For this example, use **RecordName**.

6. Under Implementation, select Get/Set Methods.

Note Data binding is not supported for properties implemented as member variables.

---

7. From the Return Type box, select the property's type. For this example, select **BSTR**.

8. Type unique names for your Get and Set Functions or accept the default names.

9. Choose the OK button to confirm your choices and close the Add Property dialog box.

10. Choose the Data Binding button.

11. Set the Bindable Property check box.

12. Set any other data binding options you desire.

    Choose the OK button to confirm your choices and close the Data Binding dialog box.

13. Choose the OK button to confirm your choices and close ClassWizard.

After completing this process you will have a property called `RecordName` that can be bound to a string-valued field in a database. The following code will be placed in your control's declaration file between the dispatch map comments:

```
afx_msg BSTR GetRecordName( );
afx_msg void SetRecordName( LPCTSTR lpszNewValue );
```

In addition, changes will be made to your control's implementation file. The following sample shows what would be added if you followed the above procedure:

```
BSTR CSampleCtrl::GetRecordName()
{
// TODO: Add your property handler here
CString s;
return s.AllocSysString();
}


void CSampleCtrl::SetRecordName(LPCTSTR lpszNewValue)
{
 SetModifiedFlag( );
}
```

In order to properly implement data binding you will have to modify the
`GetRecordName` and `SetRecordName` functions. For example, in the
`SetRecordName` function you would make a call to
BoundPropertyRequestEdit. If it was successful, you would then save the new
value and handle any other actions needed before notifying the container that the
property has changed. This notification would be done by making a call to
BoundPropertyChanged. The following code sample demonstrates this:

```
void CSampleCtrl::SetRecordName( LPCTSTR lpszNewValue )
{
 if( !BoundPropertyRequestEdit( dispidRecordName) )
    SetNotPermitted( );
//TODO: Actually set property value.
 BoundPropertyChanged( dispidRecordName);
 SetModifiedFlag( );

}
```

Advanced Data Binding

The default behavior of a data bound control requests changes to a record field,
which the container accesses by using an object referred to as a "row cursor". The
row cursor points to the "current record" in the database. In the default case, the
control is unable to navigate by itself in the database because it does not manipulate
the row cursor directly. Therefore, the OLE control has a limited capability with
regard to database manipulation.

However, the **COleControl** base class provides several functions that allow the
developer to implement more advanced features of data binding. For more
information, see the OLE Data Binding Functions listed in class COleControl in
Class Library Reference: CDK Extensions.

Class Library Reference: CDK Extensions

class CConnectionPoint : public CCmdTarget

The **CConnectionPoint** class defines a special type of interface used to communicate with other OLE objects, called a "connection point." Unlike normal OLE interfaces, which are used to implement and expose the functionality of an OLE control, a connection point implements an outgoing interface that is able to initiate actions on other objects, such as firing events and change notifications.

A connection consists of two parts: the object calling the interface, called the "source," and the object implementing the interface, called the "sink." By exposing a connection point, a source allows sinks to establish connections to itself. Through the connection point mechanism, a source object obtains a pointer to the sink's implementation of a set of member functions. For example, to fire an event implemented by the sink, the source can call the appropriate method of the sink's implementation.

By default, a **COleControl**-derived class implements two connection points: one for events and one for property change notifications. These connections are used, respectively, for event firing and for notifying a sink (for example, the control's container) when a property value has changed. Support is also provided for OLE controls to implements additional connection points. For each additional connection point implemented in your control class, you must declare a "connection part" that implements the connection point. If you implement one or more connection points, you also need to declare a single "connection map" in your control class.

The following example demonstrates a simple connection map and one connection point for the Sample OLE control, consisting of two fragments of code: the first portion declares the connection map and point, the second implements this map and point. The first fragment is inserted into the declaration of the control class, under the **protected** section:

```
// Connection point for ISample interface
BEGIN_CONNECTION_PART(CSampleCtrl, SampleConnPt)
    CONNECTION_IID(IID_ISampleSink)
END_CONNECTION_PART(SampleConnPt)

DECLARE_CONNECTION_MAP()
```

The **BEGIN_CONNECTION_PART** and **END_CONNECTION_PART** macros declare an embedded class, XSampleConnPt (derived from **CConnectionPoint**) that implements this particular connection point. If you want to override any **CConnectionPoint** member functions, or add member functions of your own, declare them between these two macros. For example, the **CONNECTION_IID** macro overrides the **CConnectionPoint::GetIID** member function when placed between these two macros.

The second code fragment is inserted into the implementation file (.CPP) of your control class. This code implements the connection map, which includes the additional connection point, `SampleConnPt`:

```
BEGIN_CONNECTION_MAP(CSampleCtrl, COleControl)
    CONNECTION_PART(CSampleCtrl, IID_ISampleSink, SampleConnPt)
END_CONNECTION_MAP()
```

Once these code fragments have been inserted, the Sample OLE control exposes a connection point for the **ISampleSink** interface.

Typically, connection points support "multicasting"; the ability to broadcast to multiple sinks connected to the same interface. The following code fragment demonstrates how to accomplish multicasting by iterating through each sink on a connection point:

```
void CSampleCtrl::CallSinkFunc()
{
    const CPtrArray* pConnections = m_xSampleConnPt.GetConnections();
    ASSERT(pConnections != NULL);

    int cConnections = pConnections->GetSize();
    ISampleSink* pSampleSink;
    for (int i = 0; i < cConnections; i++)
    {
        pSampleSink = (ISampleSink*)(pConnections->GetAt(i));
        ASSERT(pSampleSink != NULL);
        pSampleSink->SinkFunc();
    }
}
```

This example retrieves the current set of connections on the `SampleConnPt` connection point with a call to `CConnectionPoint::GetConnections`. It then iterates through the connections and calls `ISampleSink::SinkFunc` on every active connection.

#include <afxctl.h>

Class Members

Operations

GetConnections   Retrieves all connection points in a connection map.

Overridables

GetContainer	Retrieves the container of the control that owns the connection map.
GetIID	Retrieves the interface ID of a connection point.
GetMaxConnections	Retrieves the maximum number of connection points supported by a control.
OnAdvise	Called by the framework when establishing or breaking connections.

Member Functions

CConnectionPoint::GetConnections

const CPtrArray* GetConnections( );

Remarks   Call this function to retrieve all active connections for a connection point.

Return Value   A pointer to an array of active connections (sinks). Each pointer in this array can be safely converted to a pointer to the sink interface using a cast operator.

See Also   **CConnectionPoint::GetMaxConnections**

CConnectionPoint::GetContainer

virtual LPCONNECTIONPOINTCONTAINER GetContainer( ) = 0;

Remarks   Called by the framework to retrieve the **IConnectionPointContainer** for the connection point. This function is typically implemented by the **BEGIN_CONNECTION_PART** macro.

Return Value   If successful, a pointer to the container; otherwise **NULL**.

See Also   **BEGIN_CONNECTION_PART**

CConnectionPoint::GetIID

virtual REFIID GetIID( ) = 0;

Remarks   Called by the framework to retrieve the interface ID of a connection point.

Override this function to return the interface ID for this connection point.

Return Value   A reference to the connection point's interface ID.

See Also   **CONNECTION_IID**

CConnectionPoint::GetMaxConnections

virtual int GetMaxConnections( );

Remarks   Called by the framework to retrieve the maximum number of connections supported by the connection point. The default implementation returns -1, indicating no limit.

Override this function if you want to limit the number of sinks that may connect to your control.

Return Value   The maximum number of connections supported by the control, or -1 if no limit.

See Also   **CConnectionPoint::GetConnections**

CConnectionPoint::OnAdvise

virtual void OnAdvise(BOOL *bAdvise* **);**

bAdvise   **TRUE**, if a connection is being established; otherwise **FALSE**.

Remarks   Called by the framework when a connection is being established or broken. The default implementation does nothing.

Override this function if you want notification when sinks connect or disconnect with your connection point.

class CFontHolder

The **CFontHolder** class, which encapsulates the functionality of a Windows font object and the **IFont** interface, is used to implement the stock Font property.

Use this class to implement custom font properties for your control. For information on creating such properties, see Chapter 9, "Using Fonts and Pictures in Your Control," in the *CDK Programmer's Guide*.

#include <afxctl.h>

See Also   **CPropExchange**

Class Members

Data Members
m_pFont	A pointer to the **CFontHolder** object's **IFont** interface.

Construction/Destruction
CFontHolder	Constructs a **CFontHolder** object.

Operations
GetFontDispatch	Returns the font's **IDispatch** interface.
GetDisplayString	Retrieves the string displayed in a Visual Basic property sheet.
GetFontHandle	Returns a handle to a Windows font.
InitializeFont	Initializes a **CFontHolder** object.
ReleaseFont	Disconnects the **CFontHolder** object from the **IFont** and **IFontNotification** interfaces.
Select	Selects a font resource into a device context.
SetFont	Connects the **CFontHolder** object to an **IFont** interface.

Member Functions

CFontHolder::CFontHolder

CFontHolder(LPPROPERTYNOTIFYSINK *pNotify* **);**

pNotify   Pointer to the font's **IPropertyNotifySink** interface.

Remarks   Constructs a **CFontHolder** object. You must call **InitializeFont** to initialize the resulting object before using it.

See Also   **CFontHolder::InitializeFont**

CFontHolder::GetDisplayString

BOOL GetDisplayString(CString& *strValue* **);**

strValue   Reference to the **CString** that is to hold the display string.

Remarks   Retrieves a string that can be displayed in a container's property browser.

Return Value   Nonzero if the string is successfully retrieved; otherwise 0.

CFontHolder::GetFontDispatch

LPFONTDISP GetFontDispatch( );

Remarks   Call **InitializeFont** before calling **GetFontDispatch**.

Return Value   A pointer to the **CFontHolder** object's **IFontDisp** interface. Note that the function that calls **GetFontDispatch** must call **Release** on this interface pointer when done with it.

CFontHolder::GetFontHandle

HFONT GetFontHandle( );

HFONT GetFontHandle(long *cyLogical*, **long** *cyHimetric* **);**

cyLogical   Height, in logical units, of the rectangle in which the control is drawn.

cyHimetric   Height, in **MM_HIMETRIC** units, of the control.

Remarks   Call this function to get a handle to a Windows font.

The ratio of *cyLogical* and *cyHimetric* is used to calculate the proper display size, in logical units, for the font's point size expressed in **MM_HIMETRIC** units:

Display size = (*cyLogical* / *cyHimetric*) X font size

The version with no parameters returns a handle to a font sized correctly for the screen.

Return Value   A handle to the Font object; otherwise **NULL**.

CFontHolder::InitializeFont

void InitializeFont(const FONTDESC FAR* *pFontDesc* **= NULL,
LPDISPATCH** *pFontDispAmbient* **= NULL);**

pFontDesc   Pointer to a font description structure that specifies the font's characteristics.

pFontDispAmbient   Pointer to the container's ambient Font property.

Remarks   Initializes a **CFontHolder** object.

If *pFontDispAmbient* is not **NULL**, the **CFontHolder** object is connected to a clone of the **IFont** interface used by the container's ambient Font property.

If *pFontDispAmbient* is **NULL**, a new Font object is created either from the font description pointed to by *pFontDesc* or, if *pFontDesc* is **NULL**, from a default description.

Call this function after constructing a **CFontHolder** object.

See Also   **CFontHolder::CFontholder**

CFontHolder::ReleaseFont

void ReleaseFont( );

Remarks   This function disconnects the **CFontHolder** object from its **IFont** interface.

See Also   **CFontHolder::SetFont**

CFontHolder::Select

CFont* Select(CDC* *pDC*, **long** *cyLogical*, **long** *cyHimetric* **);**

pDC   Device context into which the font is selected.

cyLogical   Height, in logical units, of the rectangle in which the control is drawn.

cyHimetric   Height, in **MM_HIMETRIC** units, of the control.

Remarks   Call this function to select your control's font into the specified device context.

See **GetFontHandle** for a discussion of the *cyLogical* and *cyHimetric* parameters.

Return Value   A pointer to the font that is being replaced.

CFontHolder::SetFont

void SetFont(LPFONT *pNewFont* **);**

pNewFont   Pointer to the new **IFont** interface.

Remarks   Releases any existing font and connects the **CFontHolder** object to an **IFont** interface.

See Also   **CFontHolder::ReleaseFont**

Data Members

CFontHolder::m_pFont

Remarks   A pointer to the **CFontHolder** object's **IFont** interface.

See Also   **CFontHolder::SetFont**

class COleControl : public CWnd

The **COleControl** class is a powerful base class for developing OLE custom controls. Derived from **CWnd**, this class inherits all the functionality of a Windows window object plus additional functionality specific to OLE 2, such as event firing and the ability to support methods and properties.

OLE controls can be inserted into OLE 2 container applications and communicate with the container by using a two-way system of event firing and exposing methods and properties to the container. Note that standard OLE 2 containers only support the basic functionality of an OLE control. They are unable to support extended features of an OLE control. Event firing occurs when events are sent to the container as a result of certain actions taking place in the control. In turn, the container communicates with the control by using an exposed set of methods and properties analogous to the member functions and data members of a C++ class. This approach allows the developer to control the appearance of the control and notify the container when certain actions occur.

For more information on developing an OLE control framework using Control Wizard, see Chapter 3 of the *CDK Programmer's Guide*. For more information on adding functionality beyond the basic framework, see the *CDK Circle Sample Tutorial*.

#include <afxctl.h>

See Also **COlePropertyPage**, **CFontHolder**, **CPictureHolder**

Class Members

Construction/Destruction

COleControl	Creates a **COleControl** object.
RecreateControlWindow	Destroys and re-creates the control's window.

Initialization

InitializeIIDs	Informs the base class of the IIDs the control will use.
IsConvertingVBX	Allows specialized loading of an OLE control.
SetInitialSize	Sets the size of an OLE control when first displayed in a container.

Control Modification Functions

IsModified	Determines if the control state has changed.
SetModifiedFlag	Changes the modified state of a control.

Persistence

IsModified	Determines if the control state has changed.
ExchangeExtent	Serializes the control's width and height.
ExchangeStockProps	Serializes the control's stock properties.
ExchangeVersion	Serializes the control's version number.
SetModifiedFlag	Changes the modified state of a control.
WillAmbientsBeValidDuringLoad	Determines whether ambient properties will be available the next time the control is loaded.

Update/Painting Functions

DoSuperclassPaint	Redraws an OLE control that has been subclassed from a Windows control.
InvalidateControl	Invalidates an area of the displayed control, causing it to be redrawn.
SelectFontObject	Selects a custom font property into a device context.
SelectStockFont	Selects the stock Font property into a device context.
TranslateColor	Converts an **OLE_COLOR** value to a **COLORREF** value.

Dispatch Exceptions

GetNotSupported	Prevents access to a control's property value by the user.
SetNotPermitted	Indicates that an edit request has failed.
SetNotSupported	Prevents modification to a control's property value by the user.
ThrowError	Signals that an error has occurred in an OLE control.

Ambient Property Functions

AmbientBackColor	Returns the value of the ambient BackColor property.
AmbientDisplayName	Returns the name of the control as specified by the container.
AmbientForeColor	Returns the value of the ambient ForeColor property.
AmbientFont	Returns the value of the ambient Font property.
AmbientLocaleID	Returns the container's locale ID.
AmbientScaleUnits	Returns the type of units used by the container.
AmbientShowGrabHandles	Determines if grab handles should be displayed.
AmbientShowHatching	Determines if hatching should be displayed.
AmbientTextAlign	Returns the type of text alignment specified by the container.
AmbientUIDead	Determines if the control should respond to user-interface actions.
AmbientUserMode	Determines the mode of the container.
GetAmbientProperty	Returns the value of the specified ambient property.

Event Firing Functions

FireClick	Fires the stock Click event.
FireDblClick	Fires the stock DblClick event.
FireError	Fires the stock Error event.
FireEvent	Fires a custom event.
FireKeyDown	Fires the stock KeyDown event.
FireKeyPress	Fires the stock KeyPress event.
FireKeyUp	Fires the stock KeyUp event.
FireMouseDown	Fires the stock MouseDown event.
FireMouseMove	Fires the stock MouseMove event.
FireMouseUp	Fires the stock MouseUp event.

Stock Methods/Properties

DoClick	Implementation of the stock DoClick method.
Refresh	Forces a repaint of a control's appearance.
GetBackColor	Returns the value of the stock BackColor property.
SetBackColor	Sets the value of the stock BackColor property.
GetBorderStyle	Returns the value of the stock BorderStyle property.
SetBorderStyle	Sets the value of the stock BorderStyle property.
GetEnabled	Returns the value of the stock Enabled property.
SetEnabled	Sets the value of the stock Enabled property.
GetForeColor	Returns the value of the stock ForeColor property.
SetForeColor	Sets the value of the stock ForeColor property.
GetFont	Returns the value of the stock Font property.
InternalGetFont	Returns a **CFontHolder** object for the stock Font property.
SetFont	Sets the value of the stock Font property.
SelectStockFont	Selects the control's stock Font property into a device context.
GetHwnd	Returns the value of the stock hWnd property.
GetText	Returns the value of the stock Text or Caption property.
InternalGetText	Retrieves the stock Caption or Text property.
SetText	Sets the value of the stock Text or Caption property.

OLE Control Sizing Functions

GetControlSize   Returns the position and size of the OLE control.

SetControlSize   Sets the position and size of the OLE control.

GetRectInContainer   Returns the control's rectangle relative to its container.

SetRectInContainer   Sets the control's rectangle relative to its container.

OLE Data Binding Functions

BoundPropertyChanged   Notifies the container that a bound property has been changed.

BoundPropertyRequestEdit Requests permission to edit the property value.

Simple Frame Functions

EnableSimpleFrame   Enables simple frame support for a control.

OLE Control Site Functions

ControlInfoChanged   Call this function after the set of mnemonics handled by the control has changed.

GetExtendedControl   Retrieves a pointer to an extended control object belonging to the container.

LockInPlaceActive   Determines if your control can be deactivated by the container.

TransformCoords   Transforms coordinate values between a container and the control.

Modal Dialog Functions

PreModalDialog   Notifies the container that a modal dialog box is about to be displayed.

PostModalDialog   Notifies the container that a modal dialog box has been closed.

Overridables

DisplayError	Displays stock Error events to the control's user.
DoPropExchange	Serializes the properties of a **COleControl** object.
GetClassID	Retrieves the OLE class ID of the control.
GetMessageString	Provides status bar text for a menu item.
OnClick	Called to fire the stock Click event.
OnDoVerb	Called after a control verb has been executed.
OnDraw	Called when a control is requested to redraw itself.
OnDrawMetafile	Called by the container when a control is requested to redraw itself using a metafile device context.
OnEnumVerbs	Called by the container to enumerate a control's verbs.
OnEventAdvise	Called when event handlers are connected or disconnected from a control.
OnGetColorSet	Notifies the control that **IOleObject::GetColorSet** has been called.
OnKeyDownEvent	Called after the stock KeyDown event has been fired.
OnKeyPressEvent	Called after the stock KeyPress event has been fired.
OnKeyUpEvent	Called after the stock KeyUp event has been fired.
OnProperties	Called when the control's "Properties" verb has been invoked.
OnResetState	Resets a control's properties to the default values.

Change Notification Functions

OnBackColorChanged	Called when the stock BackColor property is changed.
OnBorderStyleChanged	Called when the stock BorderStyle property is changed.
OnEnabledChanged	Called when the stock Enabled property is changed.
OnFontChanged	Called when the stock Font property is changed.
OnForeColorChanged	Called when the stock ForeColor property is changed.
OnTextChanged	Called when the stock Text or Caption property is changed.

OLE Interface Notification Functions

OnAmbientPropertyChange	Called when an ambient property is changed.
OnFreezeEvents	Called when a control's events are frozen or unfrozen.
OnGetControlInfo	Provides mnemonic information to the container.
OnMnemonic	Called when a mnemonic key of the control has been pressed.
OnRenderData	Called by the framework to retrieve data in the specified format.
OnRenderFileData	Called by the framework to retrieve data from a file in the specified format.
OnRenderGlobalData	Called by the framework to retrieve data from global memory in the specified format.
OnSetClientSite	Notifies the control that **IOleControl::SetClientSite** has been called.
OnSetData	Replaces the control's data with another value.
OnSetExtent	Called after the control's extent has changed.
OnSetObjectRects	Called after the control's dimensions have been changed.

In-Place Activation Functions

OnGetInPlaceMenu	Requests the handle of the control's menu that will be merged with the container menu.
OnHideToolBars	Called by the container when the control is UI deactivated.
OnShowToolBars	Called when the control has been UI activated.

Property Browsing Functions

OnGetDisplayString	Called to obtain a string to represent a property value.
OnGetPredefinedStrings	Returns strings representing possible values for a property.
OnGetPredefinedValue	Returns the value corresponding to a predefined string.
OnMapPropertyToPage	Indicates which property page to use for editing a property.

Member Functions

COleControl::AmbientBackColor

OLE_COLOR AmbientBackColor( );

Remarks   The ambient BackColor property is available to all controls and is defined by the container. Note that the container is not required to support this property.

Return Value   The current value of the container's ambient BackColor property, if any. If the property is not supported, this function returns the system-defined Windows background color.

See Also   **COleControl::TranslateColor, COleControl::GetBackColor, COleControl::AmbientForeColor**

COleControl::AmbientDisplayName

CString AmbientDisplayName( );

Remarks   The name the container has assigned to the control can be used in error messages displayed to the user. Note that the container is not required to support this property.

Return Value   The name of the OLE control. The default is a zero length string.

COleControl::AmbientFont

LPFONTDISP AmbientFont( );

Remarks   The ambient Font property is available to all controls and is defined by the container. Note that the container is not required to support this property.

Return Value   A pointer to the container's ambient Font dispatch interface. The default value is **NULL**. If the return is not equal to **NULL**, you are responsible for releasing the font by calling its **Release** member function.

See Also   **COleControl::GetFont, COleControl::SetFont**

COleControl::AmbientForeColor

OLE_COLOR AmbientForeColor( );

Remarks   The ambient ForeColor property is available to all controls and is defined by the container. Note that the container is not required to support this property.

Return Value   The current value of the container's ambient ForeColor property, if any. If not supported, this function returns the system-defined Windows text color.

See Also   **COleControl::AmbientBackColor, COleControl::GetForeColor, COleControl::TranslateColor**

COleControl::AmbientLocaleID

LCID AmbientLocaleID( );

Remarks   The control can use the LocaleID to adapt its user interface for specific locales. Note that the container is not required to support this property.

Return Value   The value of the container's LocaleID property, if any. If this property is not supported, this function returns 0.

COleControl::AmbientScaleUnits

CString AmbientScaleUnits( );

Remarks   The container's ambient ScaleUnits property can be used to display positions or dimensions, labeled with the chosen unit, such as twips or centimeters. Note that the container is not required to support this property.

Return Value   A string containing the ambient ScaleUnits of the container. If this property is not supported, this function returns a zero-length string.

See Also   **COleControl::TransformCoords**

COleControl::AmbientShowGrabHandles

BOOL AmbientShowGrabHandles( );

Remarks   Call this function to determine whether the container allows the control to display grab handles for itself when active. Note that the container is not required to support this property.

Return Value   Nonzero if grab handles should be displayed; otherwise 0. If this property is not supported, this function returns nonzero.

See Also   **COleControl::AmbientShowHatching**

COleControl::AmbientShowHatching

BOOL AmbientShowHatching( );

Remarks   Call this function to determine whether the container allows the control to display itself with a hatched pattern when UI active. Note that the container is not required to support this property.

Return Value   Nonzero if the hatched pattern should be shown; otherwise 0. If this property is not supported, this function returns nonzero.

See Also   **COleControl::AmbientShowGrabHandles**

COleControl::AmbientTextAlign

short AmbientTextAlign( );

Remarks   Call this function to determine the ambient text alignment preferred by the control container. This property is available to all embedded controls and is defined by the container. Note that the container is not required to support this property.

Return Value   The status of the container's ambient TextAlign property. If this property is not supported, this function returns 0.

The following is a list of valid return values:

Return Value	Meaning
0	General alignment (numbers to the right, text to the left)
1	Left justify
2	Center
3	Right justify

COleControl::AmbientUIDead

BOOL AmbientUIDead( );

Remarks	Call this function to determine if the container wants the control to respond to user-interface actions. For example, a container might set this to **TRUE** in design mode.
Return Value	Nonzero if the control should respond to user-interface actions; otherwise 0. If this property is not supported, this function returns 0.
See Also	**COleControl::AmbientUserMode**

COleControl::AmbientUserMode

BOOL AmbientUserMode( );

Remarks	Call this function to determine if the container is in design mode or user mode. For example, a container might set this to **FALSE** in design mode.
Return Value	Nonzero if the container is in user mode; otherwise 0 (in design mode). If this property is not supported, this function returns 0.
See Also	**COleControl::AmbientUIDead**

COleControl::BoundPropertyChanged

void BoundPropertyChanged(DISPID *dispid* **);**

dispid   The dispatch ID of a bound property of the control.

Remarks	Call this function to signal that the bound property value has changed. This must be called every time the value of the property changes, even in cases where the change was not made through the property Set method. Be particularly aware of bound properties that are mapped to member variables. Any time such a member variable changes, **BoundPropertyChanged** must be called.
See Also	**COleControl::BoundPropertyRequestEdit**

COleControl::BoundPropertyRequestEdit

BOOL BoundPropertyRequestEdit(DISPID *dispid* **);**

dispid   The dispatch ID of a bound property of the control.

Remarks	Call this function to request permission from the **IPropChangeNotify** interface to change a bound property value provided by the control. If permission is denied, the control must not let the value of the property change. This can be done by ignoring or failing the action that attempted to change the property value.
Return Value	Nonzero if the change is permitted; otherwise 0. The default value is nonzero.
See Also	**COleControl::BoundPropertyChanged**

COleControl::COleControl

COleControl( );

Remarks   Constructs a **COleControl** object. This function is normally not called directly. Instead the OLE control is usually created by its class factory.

COleControl::ControlInfoChanged

void ControlInfoChanged( );

Remarks   Call this function when the set of mnemonics supported by the control has changed. Upon receiving this notification, the control's container obtains the new set of mnemonics by making a call to **IOleControl::GetControlInfo**. Note that the container is not required to respond to this notification.

COleControl::DisplayError

virtual void DisplayError(SCODE *scode***, LPCTSTR** *lpszDescription***, LPCTSTR** *lpszSource***, LPCTSTR** *lpszHelpFile***, UINT** *nHelpID* **);**

scode   The status code value to be reported. For a complete list of possible codes, see "Handling Errors in Your OLE Control" in Appendix B of the *CDK Programmer's Guide*.

lpszDescription   The description of the error being reported.

lpszSource   The name of the module generating the error (typically, the name of the OLE control module).

lpszHelpFile   The name of the help file containing a description of the error.

nHelpID   The Help Context ID of the error being reported.

Remarks   Called by the framework after the stock Error event has been handled (unless the event handler has suppressed the display of the error). The default behavior displays a message box containing the description of the error, contained in *lpszDescription*.

Override this function to customize how errors are displayed.

See Also   **COleControl::FireError**

COleControl::DoClick

void DoClick( );

Remarks   Call this function to simulate a mouse click action on the control. The overridable **COleControl::OnClick** member function will be called, and a stock Click event will be fired, if supported by the control.

This function is supported by the **COleControl** base class as a stock method, called DoClick. For more information, see Chapter 6, "Adding a Stock Method," in the *CDK Programmer's Guide*.

See Also   **COleControl::OnClick**

COleControl::DoPropExchange

virtual void DoPropExchange(CPropExchange* *pPX* **);**

pPX   A pointer to a **CPropExchange** object. The framework supplies this object to establish the context of the property exchange, including its direction.

Remarks   Called by the framework when loading or storing a control from a persistent storage representation, such as a stream or property set. This function normally makes calls to the **PX_** family of functions to load or store specific user-defined properties of an OLE control.

If Control Wizard has been used to create the OLE control project, the overridden version of this function will serialize the stock properties supported by **COleControl** with a call to the base class function, **COleControl::DoPropExchange**. As you add user-defined properties to your OLE control you will need to modify this function to serialize your new properties. For more information on serialization, see Chapter 7 of the *CDK Programmer's Guide*.

See Also   **PX_Bool**, **PX_Short**

COleControl::DoSuperclassPaint

void DoSuperclassPaint(CDC* *pDC***, const CRect&** *rcBounds* **);**

pDC   A pointer to the device context of the control container.

rcBounds   A pointer to the area in which the control is to be drawn.

Remarks   Call this function to properly handle the painting of a nonactive OLE control. This function should only be used if the OLE control subclasses a Windows control and should be called in the OnDraw function of your control.

For more information on this function and subclassing a Windows control, see Appendix B.

See Also   **COleControl::OnDraw**

COleControl::DrawContent

void DrawContent(CDC* *pDC***, CRect&** *rc* **);**

pDC   Pointer to the device context.

rc   Rectangular area to be drawn in.

Remarks   Called by the framework when the control's appearance needs to be updated. This function directly calls the overridable **OnDraw** function.

See Also   **COleControl::OnDraw**, **COleControl::DrawMetafile**, **COleControl::OnDrawMetafile**

COleControl::DrawMetafile

void DrawMetafile(CDC* *pDC***, CRect&** *rc***);**

pDC   Pointer to the metafile device context.

rc   Rectangular area to be drawn in.

Remarks   Called by the framework when the metafile device context is being used.

See Also   **COleControl::OnDraw**, **COleControl::DrawContent**, **COleControl::OnDrawMetafile**

COleControl::EnableSimpleFrame

void EnableSimpleFrame( );

Remarks   Call this function to enable the simple frame characteristic for an OLE control. This characteristic allows a control to support visual containment of other controls, but not true OLE 2 containment. An example would be a group box with several controls inside. These controls are not OLE contained, but they are in the same group box.

COleControl::ExchangeExtent

BOOL ExchangeExtent(CPropExchange* *pPX* **);**

pPX   A pointer to a **CPropExchange** object. The framework supplies this object to establish the context of the property exchange, including its direction.

Remarks   Call this function to serialize or initialize the state of the control's extent (its dimensions in **HIMETRIC** units). This function is normally called by the default implementation of **COleControl::DoPropExchange**.

Return Value   Nonzero if the function succeeded; zero otherwise.

See Also   **COleControl::DoPropExchange**

COleControl::ExchangeStockProps

void ExchangeStockProps(CPropExchange* *pPX* **);**

pPX   A pointer to a **CPropExchange** object. The framework supplies this object to establish the context of the property exchange, including its direction.

Remarks   Call this function to serialize or initialize the state of the control's stock properties. This function is normally called by the default implementation of **COleControl::DoPropExchange**.

See Also   **COleControl::DoPropExchange**

COleControl::ExchangeVersion

BOOL ExchangeVersion(CPropExchange* *pPX***, DWORD** *dwVersionDefault***, BOOL** *bConvert* **= TRUE);**

pPX   A pointer to a **CPropExchange** object. The framework supplies this object to establish the context of the property exchange, including its direction.

dwVersionDefault   The current version number of the control.

bConvert   Indicates whether persistent data should be converted to the latest format when saved, or maintained in the same format that was loaded.

Remarks   Call this function to serialize or initialize the state of a control's version information. Typically, this will be the first function called by a control's override of **COleControl::DoPropExchange**. When loading, this function reads the version number of the persistent data, and sets the version attribute of the **CPropExchange** object accordingly. When saving, this function writes the version number of the persistent data.

For more information on persistence and versioning, see Chapter 7, "Serializing Your Control" of the *CDK Programmer's Guide*.

Return Value   Nonzero of the function succeeded; zero otherwise.

See Also   **COleControl::DoPropExchange**

COleControl::FireClick

void FireClick( );

Remarks   Called by the framework when the mouse is clicked over an active control. If this event is defined as a custom event, you determine when the event is fired.

For automatic firing of a Click event to occur, the control's Event map must have a stock Click event defined.

See Also   COleControl::FireDblClick, COleControl::FireMouseDown,
                     COleControl::FireMouseUp

COleControl::FireDblClick

void FireDblClick( );

Remarks   Called by the framework when the mouse is double-clicked over an active control.
                     If this event is defined as a custom event, you determine when the event is fired.

                     For automatic firing of a DblClick event to occur, the control's Event map must
                     have a stock DblClick event defined.

See Also   COleControl::FireClick, COleControl::FireMouseDown,
                     COleControl::FireMouseUp

COleControl::FireError

void FireError(SCODE *scode***, LPCTSTR** *lpszDescription***,**
UINT *nHelpID* **= 0);**

                     scode   The status code value to be reported. For a complete list of possible codes,
                     see "Handling Errors in Your OLE Control" in Appendix B of the *CDK
                     Programmer's Guide*.

                     lpszDescription   The description of the error being reported.

                     nHelpID   The Help ID of the error being reported.

Remarks   Call this function to fire the stock Error event. This event provides a way of
                     signalling, at appropriate places in your code, that an error has occurred within your
                     control. Unlike other stock events, such as Click or MouseMove, Error is never
                     fired by the framework.

                     To report an error that occurs during a property get function, property set function,
                     or automation method, call **COleControl::ThrowError**.

See Also   COleControl::DisplayError

COleControl::FireEvent

void FireEvent(DISPID *dispid***, BYTE FAR*** *pbParams***, ...);**

                     dispid   The dispatch ID of the event to be fired.

                     pbParams   A descriptor for the event's parameter types.

Remarks   Call this function, with any number of optional arguments, to fire a user-defined
                     event from your control. Usually this function should not be called directly. Instead

you will call the event-firing functions generated by ClassWizard in the event map section of your control's class declaration.

COleControl::FireKeyDown

void FireKeyDown(USHORT* *pnChar***, short** *nShiftState* **);**

pnChar   Pointer to the virtual-key code value of the pressed key.

nShiftState   Contains a combination of the following flags:

- **SHIFT_MASK**   The SHIFT key was pressed during the action.
- **CTRL_MASK**   The CTRL key was pressed during the action.
- **ALT_MASK**   The ALT key was pressed during the action.

Remarks   Called by the framework when a key is pressed while the control is UI active. If this event is defined as a custom event, you determine when the event is fired.

For automatic firing of a KeyDown event to occur, the control's Event map must have a stock KeyDown event defined.

See Also   **COleControl::FireKeyUp, COleControl::FireKeyPress, COleControl::OnKeyPressEvent**

COleControl::FireKeyPress

void FireKeyPress(USHORT* *pnChar* **);**

pnChar   A pointer to the character value of the key pressed.

Remarks   Called by the framework when a key is pressed and released while the custom control is UI Active within the container. If this event is defined as a custom event, you determine when the event is fired.

The recipient of the event may modify *pnChar*, for example, convert all lowercase characters to uppercase. If you want to examine the modified character, override **OnKeyPressEvent**.

For automatic firing of a KeyPress event to occur, the control's Event map must have a stock KeyPress event defined.

See Also   **COleControl::OnKeyPressEvent, COleControl::FireKeyDown, COleControl::FireKeyUp**

COleControl::FireKeyUp

void FireKeyUp(USHORT* *pnChar***, short** *nShiftState* **);**

pnChar   Pointer to the virtual-key code value of the released key.

nShiftState   Contains a combination of the following flags:

- **SHIFT_MASK**   The SHIFT key was pressed during the action.
- **CTRL_MASK**   The CTRL key was pressed during the action.
- **ALT_MASK**   The ALT key was pressed during the action.

Remarks   Called by the framework when a key is released while the custom control is UI Active within the container. If this event is defined as a custom event, you determine when the event is fired.

For automatic firing of a KeyUp event to occur, the control's Event map must have a stock KeyUp event defined.

See Also   **COleControl::FireKeyDown, COleControl::FireKeyPress, COleControl::OnKeyUpEvent**

COleControl::FireMouseDown

void FireMouseDown(short *nButton***, short** *nShiftState***, OLE_XPOS_PIXELS** *x***, OLE_YPOS_PIXEL** *y* **);**

nButton   The numeric value of the mouse button pressed. It can contain one of the following values:

- **LEFT_BUTTON**   The left mouse button was pressed down.
- **MIDDLE_BUTTON**   The middle mouse button was pressed down.
- **RIGHT_BUTTON**   The right mouse button was pressed down.

nShiftState   Contains a combination of the following flags:

- **SHIFT_MASK**   The SHIFT key was pressed during the action.
- **CTRL_MASK**   The CTRL key was pressed during the action.
- **ALT_MASK**   The ALT key was pressed during the action.

x   The x-coordinate of the cursor when a mouse button was pressed down. The coordinate is relative to the upper-left corner of the control window.

y   The y-coordinate of the cursor when a mouse button was pressed down. The coordinate is relative to the upper-left corner of the control window.

Remarks   Called by the framework when a mouse button is pressed over an active custom control. If this event is defined as a custom event, you determine when the event is fired.

For automatic firing of a MouseDown event to occur, the control's Event map must have a stock MouseDown event defined.

See Also   COleControl::FireMouseUp, COleControl::FireMouseMove,
COleControl::FireClick

COleControl::FireMouseMove

void FireMouseMove(short *nButton***, short** *nShiftState***, OLE_XPOS_PIXELS**
*x***, OLE_YPOS_PIXELS** *y* **);**

nButton   The numeric value of the mouse buttons pressed. Contains a combination
of the following values:

- **LEFT_BUTTON**   The left mouse button was pressed down during the action.
- **MIDDLE_BUTTON**   The middle mouse button was pressed down during the action.
- **RIGHT_BUTTON**   The right mouse button was pressed down during the action.

nShiftState   Contains a combination of the following flags:

- **SHIFT_MASK**   The SHIFT key was pressed during the action.
- **CTRL_MASK**   The CTRL key was pressed during the action.
- **ALT_MASK**   The ALT key was pressed during the action.

x   The x-coordinate of the cursor. The coordinate is relative to the upper-left
corner of the control window.

y   The y-coordinate of the cursor. The coordinate is relative to the upper-left
corner of the control window.

Remarks   Called by the framework when the cursor is moved over an active custom control. If
this event is defined as a custom event, you determine when the event is fired.

For automatic firing of a MouseMove event to occur, the control's Event map must
have a stock MouseMove event defined.

COleControl::FireMouseUp

void FireMouseUp(short *nButton***, short** *nShiftState***, OLE_XPOS_PIXELS** *x***,**
OLE_YPOS_PIXELS *y* **);**

nButton   The numeric value of the mouse button released. It can have one of the
following values:

- **LEFT_BUTTON**   The left mouse button was released.
- **MIDDLE_BUTTON**   The middle mouse button was released.
- **RIGHT_BUTTON**   The right mouse button was released.

nShiftState   Contains a combination of the following flags:

- **SHIFT_MASK**   The SHIFT key was pressed during the action.
- **CTRL_MASK**   The CTRL key was pressed during the action.
- **ALT_MASK**   The ALT key was pressed during the action.

x   The x-coordinate of the cursor when a mouse button was released. The coordinate is relative to the upper-left corner of the control window.

y   The y-coordinate of a cursor when a mouse button was released. The coordinate is relative to the upper-left corner of the control window.

Remarks   Called by the framework when a mouse button is released over an active custom control. If this event is defined as a custom event, you determine when the event is fired.

For automatic firing of a MouseUp event to occur, the control's Event map must have a stock MouseUp event defined.

See Also   **COleControl::FireMouseDown**, **COleControl::FireClick**, **COleControl::FireDblClick**

COleControl::GetAmbientProperty

BOOL GetAmbientProperty(DISPID *dwDispid*, **VARTYPE** *vtProp*, **void*** *pvProp* **);**

dwDispid   The dispatch ID of the desired ambient property.

vtProp   A variant type tag that specifies the type of the value to be returned in *pvProp*.

pvProp   A pointer to the address of the variable that will receive the property value or return value. The actual type of this pointer must match the type specified by *vtProp*.

vtProp	Type of pvProp
VT_BOOL	BOOL*
VT_BSTR	CString*

vtProp	Type of pvProp
VT_I2	short*
VT_I4	long*
VT_R4	float*
VT_R8	double*
VT_CY	CY*
VT_COLOR	OLE_COLOR*
VT_DISPATCH	LPDISPATCH*
VT_FONT	LPFONTDISP*

Remarks   Call this function to get the value of an ambient property of the container. If you use **GetAmbientProperty** to retrieve the ambient DisplayName and ScaleUnits properties, set *vtProp* to **VT_BSTR** and *pvProp* to **CString***. If you are retrieving the ambient Font property, set *vtProp* to **VT_FONT** and *pvProp* to **LPFONTDISP***.

Note that functions have already been provided for common ambient properties, such as **AmbientBackColor** and **AmbientFont**.

Return Value   Nonzero if the ambient property is supported; otherwise 0.

See Also   **COleControl::AmbientForeColor, COleControl::AmbientScaleUnits, COleControl::AmbientShowGrabHandles**

COleControl::GetBackColor

OLE_COLOR GetBackColor( );

Remarks   This function implements the Get function of your control's stock BackColor property.

Return Value   The return value specifies the current background color as a **OLE_COLOR** value, if successful. This value can be translated to a **COLORREF** value with a call to **TranslateColor**.

See Also   **COleControl::AmbientBackColor, COleControl::TranslateColor, COleControl::SetBackColor, COleControl::GetForeColor**

COleControl::GetBorderStyle

short GetBorderStyle( );

Remarks   This function implements the Get function of your control's stock BorderStyle property.

Return Value   1 if the control has a normal border; 0 if the control has no border.

See Also   COleControl::SetBorderStyle, COleControl::OnBorderStyleChanged

COleControl::GetClassID

virtual HRESULT GetClassID(LPCLSID *pclsid* **) = 0;**

pclsid   Pointer to the location of the class ID.

Remarks   Called by the framework to retrieve the OLE class ID of the control. Usually implemented by the **IMPLEMENT_OLECREATE_EX** macro.

Return Value   Nonzero if the call was not successful; otherwise 0.

COleControl::GetControlSize

void GetControlSize(int* *pcx***, int*** *pcy* **);**

pcx   Specifies the width of the control in pixels.

pcy   Specifies the height of the control in pixels.

Remarks   Call this function to retrieve the size of the OLE control window.

Note that all coordinates for control windows are relative to the upper-left corner of the control.

See Also   COleControl::GetRectInContainer, COleControl::SetControlSize

COleControl::GetEnabled

BOOL GetEnabled( );

Remarks   This function implements the Get function of your control's stock Enabled property.

Return Value   Nonzero if the control is enabled; otherwise 0.

See Also   COleControl::SetEnabled, COleControl::OnEnabledChanged

COleControl::GetExtendedControl

LPDISPATCH GetExtendedControl( );

Remarks   Call this function to obtain a pointer to an object maintained by the container that represents the control with an extended set of properties. The function that calls this function is responsible for releasing the pointer when finished with the object. Note that the container is not required to support this object.

Return Value   A pointer to the container's extended control object. If there is no object available, the value is **NULL**.

This object may be manipulated through its **IDispatch** interface. You can also use **QueryInterface** to obtain other available interfaces provided by the object. However, the object is not required to support a specific set of interfaces. Note that relying on the specific features of a container's extended control object limits the portability of your control to other arbitrary containers.

COleControl::GetFont

LPFONTDISP GetFont( );

Remarks   This function implements the Get function of the stock Font property. Note that the caller must release the object when finished. Within the implementation of the control, use **InternalGetFont** to access the control's stock Font object. For more information on using fonts in your control, see Chapter 9 of the *CDK Programmer's Guide*.

Return Value   A pointer to the font dispatch interface of the control's stock Font property.

See Also   **COleControl::SetFont, COleControl::AmbientFont, COleControl::InternalGetFont**

COleControl::GetForeColor

OLE_COLOR GetForeColor( );

Remarks   This function implements the Get function of the stock ForeColor property.

Return Value   The return value specifies the current foreground color as a **OLE_COLOR** value, if successful. This value can be translated to a **COLORREF** value with a call to **TranslateColor**.

See Also   **COleControl::AmbientForeColor, COleControl::TranslateColor, COleControl::GetBackColor, COleControl::SetForeColor**

COleControl::GetHwnd

OLE_HANDLE GetHwnd( );

Remarks   This function implements the Get function of the stock hWnd property.

Return Value   The OLE control's window handle, if any; otherwise **NULL**.

COleControl::GetMessageString

virtual void GetMessageString(UINT *nID***, CString&** *rMessage* **) const;**

nID   A menu item ID.

rMessage   A reference to a **CString** object through which a string will be returned.

Remarks   Called by the framework to obtain a short string that describes the purpose of the menu item identified by *nID*. This can be used to obtain a message for display in a status bar while the menu item is highlighted. The default implementation attempts to load a string resource identified by *nID*.

COleControl::GetNotSupported

void GetNotSupported( );

Remarks   Call this function in place of the Get function of any property where retrieval of the property by the control's user is not supported. One example would be a property that is write-only in user mode.

See Also   **COleControl::SetNotSupported**

COleControl::GetRectInContainer

BOOL GetRectInContainer(LPRECT *lpRect*);

lpRect   A pointer to the rectangle structure into which the control's coordinates will be copied.

Remarks   Call this function to obtain the coordinates of the control's rectangle relative to the container, expressed in device units. The rectangle is only valid if the control is in-place active.

Return Value   Nonzero if the control is in-place active; otherwise 0.

See Also   **COleControl::SetRectInContainer**, **COleControl::GetControlSize**

COleControl::GetText

BSTR GetText( );

Remarks   This function implements the Get function of the stock Text or Caption property. Note that the caller of this function must call **SysFreeString** on the string returned in order to free the resource. Within the implementation of the control, use **InternalGetText** to access the control's stock Text or Caption property.

Return Value   The current value of the control text string or a zero-length string if no string is present.

Note   For more information on the **BSTR** data type, see Chapter 6, "Data Manipulation Functions," in *OLE 2 Programmers Reference*, *Volume 2*.

See Also   COleControl::InternalGetText, COleControl::SetText

COleControl::InitializeIIDs

void InitializeIIDs(const IID* *piidPrimary*, const IID* *piidEvents*);

piidPrimary   Pointer to the interface ID of the control's primary dispatch interface.

piidEvents   Pointer to the interface ID of the control's event interface.

Remarks   Call this function in the control's constructor to inform the base class of the interface IDs your control will be using.

COleControl::InternalGetFont

CFontHolder& InternalGetFont( );

Remarks   Call this function to access the stock Font property of your control

Return Value   A reference to a **CFontHolder** object that contains the stock Font object.

See Also   COleControl::GetFont, COleControl::SetFont

COleControl::InternalGetText

const CString& InternalGetText( );

Remarks   Call this function to access the stock Text or Caption property of your control.

Return Value   A reference to the control text string.

See Also   COleControl::GetText, COleControl::SetText

COleControl::InvalidateControl

void InvalidateControl(LPCRECT *lpRect* = NULL);

lpRect   A pointer to the region of the control to be invalidated.

Remarks   Call this function to force the control to redraw itself. If *lpRect* has a **NULL** value, the entire control will be redrawn. If *lpRect* is not **NULL**, this indicates the portion of the control's rectangle that is to be invalidated. In cases where the control has no window, or is currently not active, the rectangle is ignored, and a call is made to the client site's **IAdviseSink::OnViewChange** member function. Use this function instead of **CWnd::InvalidateRect** or **::InvalidateRect**.

See Also   COleControl::Refresh

COleControl::IsModified

BOOL IsModified( );

Remarks   Call this function to determine if the control's state has been modified. The state of a control is modified when a property changes value.

Return Value   Nonzero if the control's state has been modified since it was last saved; otherwise 0.

See Also   **COleControl::SetModifiedFlag**

COleControl::IsConvertingVBX

BOOL IsConvertingVBX( );

Remarks   When converting a form that uses VBX controls to one that uses OLE controls, special loading code for the OLE controls may be required. For example, if you are loading an instance of your OLE control, you might have a call to **PX_Font** in your **DoPropExchange**:

```
PX_Font(pPx, "Font", m_MyFont, pDefaultFont);
```

However, VBX controls did not have a Font object; each font property was saved individually. In this case, you would use **IsConvertingVBX** to distinguish between these two cases:

```
if (IsConvertingVBX()==FALSE)
    PX_Font(pPX, "Font", m_MyFont, pDefaultFont);
else
{
    PX_String(pPX, "FontName", tempString, DefaultName);
    m_MyFont->put_Name(tempString);
    PX_Bool(pPX, "FontUnderline", tempBool, DefaultValue);
    m_MyFont->put_Underline(tempBool);
...
}
```

Another case would be if your VBX control saved proprietary binary data (in its **VBM_SAVEPROPERTY** message handler), and your OLE control saves its binary data in a different format. If you want your OLE control to be backward-compatible with the VBX control, you could read both the old and new formats using the **IsConvertingVBX** function by distinguishing whether the VBX control or the OLE control was being loaded.

In your control's **DoPropExchange** function, you can check for this condition and if true, execute load code specific to this conversion (such as the previous examples). If the control is not being converted, you can execute normal load code. This ability is only applicable to controls being converted from VBX counterparts.

Return Value   Nonzero if the control is being converted; otherwise 0.

See Also   **COleControl::DoPropExchange**

COleControl::LockInPlaceActive

BOOL LockInPlaceActive(BOOL *bLock* **);**

bLock   **TRUE** if the in-place active state of the control is to be locked; **FALSE** if it is to be unlocked.

Remarks   Call this function to prevent the container from deactivating your control. Note that every locking of the control must be paired with an unlocking of the control when finished. You should only lock your control for short periods, such as while firing an event.

Return Value   Nonzero if the lock was successful; otherwise 0.

COleControl::OnAmbientPropertyChange

virtual void OnAmbientPropertyChange(DISPID *dispID* **);**

dispID   The dispatch ID of the ambient property that changed, or **DISPID_UNKNOWN** if multiple properties have changed.

Remarks   Called by the framework when an ambient property of the container has changed value.

See Also   **COleControl::GetAmbientProperty**

COleControl::OnBackColorChanged

virtual void OnBackColorChanged( );

Remarks   Called by the framework when the stock BackColor property value has changed.

Override this function if you want notification after this property changes. The default implementation calls **InvalidateControl**.

See Also   **COleControl::GetBackColor, COleControl::InvalidateControl**

COleControl::OnBorderStyleChanged

virtual void OnBorderStyleChanged( );

Remarks   Called by the framework when the stock BorderStyle property value has changed. The default implementation calls **InvalidateControl**.

Override this function if you want notification after this property changes.

See Also   COleControl::SetBorderStyle, COleControl::InvalidateControl

COleControl::OnClick

virtual void OnClick(USHORT *iButton* **);**

iButton   Index of a mouse button. Can have one of the following values:

- **LEFT_BUTTON**   The left mouse button was clicked.
- **MIDDLE_BUTTON**   The middle mouse button was clicked.
- **RIGHT_BUTTON**   The right mouse button was clicked.

Remarks   Called by the framework when a mouse button has been clicked or the DoClick stock method has been invoked. The default implementation calls **COleControl::FireClick**.

Override this member function to modify or extend the default handling.

See Also   COleControl::DoClick, COleControl::FireClick

COleControl::OnDoVerb

virtual BOOL OnDoVerb(LONG *iVerb*, **LPMSG** *lpMsg*, **HWND** *hWndParent*, **LPCRECT** *lpRect* **);**

iVerb   The index of the control verb to be invoked.

lpMsg   A pointer to the Windows message that caused the verb to be invoked.

hWndParent   The handle to the parent window of the control. If the execution of the verb creates a window (or windows), *hWndParent* should be used as the parent.

lpRect   A pointer to a **RECT** structure into which the coordinates of the control, relative to the container, will be copied.

Remarks   Called by the framework when the container calls the **IOleObject::DoVerb** member function. The default implementation uses the **ON_OLEVERB** and **ON_STDOLEVERB** message map entries to determine the proper function to invoke.

Override this function to change the default handling of verb.

Return Value   Nonzero if call was successful; otherwise 0.

See Also   ON_OLEVERB, ON_STDOLEVERB, COleControl::OnEnumVerbs

COleControl::OnDraw

virtual void OnDraw(CDC* *pDC*, **const CRect&** *rcBounds*, **const CRect&** *rcInvalid* **);**

pDC   The device context in which the drawing occurs.

rcBounds   The rectangular area of the control, including the border.

rcInvalid   The rectangular area of the control that is invalid.

Remarks   Called by the framework to draw the OLE control in the specified bounding rectangle using the specified device context.

OnDraw is typically called for screen display, passing a screen device context as *pDC*. The *rcBounds* parameter identifies the rectangle in the target device context (relative to its current mapping mode). The *rcInvalid* parameter is the actual rectangle that is invalid. In some cases this will be a smaller area than *rcBounds*.

See Also   **COleControl::OnDrawMetafile, COleControl::DrawContent, COleControl::DrawMetafile**

COleControl::OnDrawMetafile

virtual void OnDrawMetafile(CDC* *pDC*, **const CRect&** *rcBounds* **);**

pDC   The device context in which the drawing occurs.

rcBounds   The rectangular area of the control, including the border.

Remarks   Called by the framework to draw the OLE control in the specified bounding rectangle using the specified metafile device context. The default implementation calls the OnDraw function.

See Also   **COleControl::OnDraw, COleControl::DrawContent, COleControl::DrawMetafile**

COleControl::OnEnabledChanged

virtual void OnEnabledChanged( );

Remarks   Called by the framework when the stock Enabled property value has changed.

Override this function if you want notification after this property changes. The default implementation calls **InvalidateControl**.

See Also   **COleControl::SetEnabled, COleControl::GetEnabled**

COleControl::OnEnumVerbs

virtual BOOL OnEnumVerbs(LPENUMOLEVERB FAR* *ppenumOleVerb* **);**

ppenumOleVerb   A pointer to the **IEnumOLEVERB** object that enumerates the control's verbs.

Remarks   Called by the framework when the container calls the **IOleObject::EnumVerbs** member function. The default implementation enumerates the **ON_OLEVERB** entries in the message map.

Override this function to change the default way of enumerating verbs.

Return Value   Nonzero if verbs are available; otherwise 0.

See Also   **ON_OLEVERB, ON_STDOLEVERB**

COleControl::OnEventAdvise

virtual void OnEventAdvise(BOOL *bAdvise* **);**

bAdvise   **TRUE** indicates that an event handler has been connected to the control. **FALSE** indicates that an event handler has been disconnected from the control.

Remarks   Called by the framework when an event handler is connected to or disconnected from an OLE control.

COleControl::OnFontChanged

virtual void OnFontChanged( );

Remarks   Called by the framework when the stock Font property value has changed. The default implementation calls **COleControl::InvalidateControl**. If the control is subclassing a Windows control, the default implementation also sends a **WM_SETFONT** message to the control's window.

Override this function if you want notification after this property changes.

See Also   **COleControl::GetFont, COleControl::InternalGetFont, COleControl::InvalidateControl**

COleControl::OnForeColorChanged

virtual void OnForeColorChanged( );

Remarks   Called by the framework when the stock ForeColor property value has changed. The default implementation calls **InvalidateControl**.

Override this function if you want notification after this property changes.

See Also   **COleControl::SetForeColor, COleControl::InvalidateControl**

COleControl::OnFreezeEvents

virtual void OnFreezeEvents(BOOL *bFreeze* **);**

bFreeze   **TRUE** if the control's event handling is frozen; otherwise **FALSE**.

Remarks   Called by the framework after the container calls **IOleControl::FreezeEvents**. The default implementation does nothing.

Override this function if you want additional behavior when event handling is frozen or unfrozen.

COleControl::OnGetColorSet

virtual BOOL OnGetColorSet(DVTARGETDEVICE FAR* *ptd*, **HDC** *hicTargetDev*, **LPLOGPALETTE FAR*** *ppColorSet* **);**

ptd   Points to the target device for which the picture should be rendered. If this value is **NULL**, the picture should be rendered for a default target device, usually a display device.

hicTargetDev   Specifies the information context on the target device indicated by *ptd*. This parameter can be a device context, but is not necessarily. If *ptd* is **NULL**, *hicTargetDev* should also be **NULL**.

ppColorSet   A pointer to the location into which the set of colors that would be used should be copied. If the function does not return the color set, **NULL** is returned.

Remarks   Called by the framework when the container calls the **IOleObject::GetColorSet** member function. The container calls this function to obtain all the colors needed to draw the OLE control. The container can use the color sets obtained in conjunction with the colors it needs to set the overall color palette. The default implementation returns **FALSE**.

Override this function to do any special processing of this request.

Return Value   Nonzero if a valid color set is returned; otherwise 0.

COleControl::OnGetControlInfo

virtual void OnGetControlInfo(LPCONTROLINFO *pControlInfo* **);**

pControlInfo   Pointer to a CONTROLINFO structure to be filled in.

Remarks   Called by the framework when the control's container has requested information about the control. This information consists primarily of a description of the control's mnemonic keys. The default implementation fills *pControlInfo* with default information.

Override this function if your control needs to process mnemonic keys.

COleControl::OnGetDisplayString

virtual BOOL OnGetDisplayString(DISPID *dispid*, **CString&** *strValue* **);**

dispid   The dispatch ID of a property of the control.

strValue   A reference to a **CString** object through which a string will be returned.

Remarks   Called by the framework to obtain a string that represents the current value of the property identified by *dispid*.

Override this function if your control has a property whose value cannot be directly converted to a string and you want the property's value to be displayed in a container-supplied property browser.

Return Value   Nonzero if a string has been returned in *strValue;* otherwise 0.

See Also   **COleControl::OnMapPropertyToPage**

COleControl::OnGetInPlaceMenu

virtual HMENU OnGetInPlaceMenu( );

Remarks   Called by the framework when the control is UI activated to obtain the menu to be merged into the container's existing menu.

For more information on merging OLE resources, see the article "Menus and Resources" in *OLE 2 Classes*. If you are using the 32-bit version of the CDK this article is located in *Programming with the Microsoft Foundation Class Library*.

Return Value   The handle of the control's menu, or **NULL** if the control has none. The default implementation returns **NULL**.

COleControl::OnGetPredefinedStrings

virtual BOOL OnGetPredefinedStrings(DISPID *dispid*, **CStringArray*** *pStringArray*, **CDWordArray*** *pCookieArray* **);**

dispid   The dispatch ID of a property of the control.

pStringArray   A string array to be filled in with return values.

pCookieArray   A **DWORD** array to be filled in with return values.

Remarks Called by the framework to obtain a set of predefined strings representing the possible values for a property.

Override this function if your control has a property with a set of possible values that can be represented by strings. For each element added to *pStringArray*, you should add a corresponding "cookie" element to *pCookieArray*. These "cookie" values may later be passed by the framework to the **COleControl::OnGetPredefinedValue** function.

Return Value Nonzero if elements have been added to *pStringArray* and *pCookieArray*.

See Also **COleControl::OnGetPredefinedValue**, **COleControl::OnGetDisplayString**

COleControl::OnGetPredefinedValue

virtual BOOL OnGetPredefinedValue(DISPID *dispid*, **DWORD** *dwCookie*, **VARIANT FAR*** *lpvarOut* **);**

dispid   The dispatch ID of a property of the control.

dwCookie   A cookie value previously returned by an override of **COleControl::OnGetPredefinedStrings**

lpvarOut   Pointer to a **VARIANT** structure through which a property value will be returned.

Remarks Called by the framework to obtain the value corresponding to one of the predefined strings previously returned by an override of **COleControl::OnGetPredefinedStrings**.

Return Value Nonzero if a value has been returned in *lpvarOut*; otherwise 0.

See Also **COleControl::OnGetPredefinedStrings**, **COleControl::OnGetDisplayString**

COleControl::OnHideToolbars

virtual void OnHideToolbars( );

Remarks Called by the framework when the control is UI deactivated. The implementation should hide all toolbars displayed by **OnShowToolbars**.

See Also **COleControl::OnShowToolbars**

COleControl::OnKeyDownEvent

virtual void OnKeyDownEvent(USHORT *nChar*, **USHORT** *nShiftState* **);**

nChar   The virtual-key code value of the pressed key.

nShiftState   Contains a combination of the following flags:

- **SHIFT_MASK**   The SHIFT key was pressed during the action.
- **CTRL_MASK**   The CTRL key was pressed during the action.
- **ALT_MASK**   The ALT key was pressed during the action.

Remarks   Called by the framework after a stock KeyDown event has been processed.

Override this function if your control needs access to the key information after the event has been fired.

See Also   **COleControl::OnKeyUpEvent**, **COleControl::OnKeyPressEvent**

COleControl::OnKeyPressEvent

virtual void OnKeyPress(USHORT *nChar* **);**

nChar   Contains the virtual-key code value of the key pressed.

Remarks   Called by the framework after the stock KeyPress event has been fired. Note that the *nChar* value may have been modified by the container.

Override this function if you want notification after this event occurs.

See Also   **COleControl::FireKeyPress**

COleControl::OnKeyUpEvent

virtual void OnKeyUpEvent(USHORT *nChar*, **USHORT** *nShiftState* **);**

nChar   The virtual-key code value of the pressed key.

nShiftState   Contains a combination of the following flags:

- **SHIFT_MASK**   The SHIFT key was pressed during the action.
- **CTRL_MASK**   The CTRL key was pressed during the action.
- **ALT_MASK**   The ALT key was pressed during the action.

Remarks   Called by the framework after a stock KeyDown event has been processed.

Override this function if your control needs access to the key information after the event has been fired.

See Also   **COleControl::OnKeyDownEvent**, **COleControl::OnKeyPressEvent**

COleControl::OnMapPropertyToPage

virtual BOOL OnMapPropertyToPage(DISPID *dispid*, **LPCLSID** *lpclsid*, **BOOL*** *pbPageOptional* **);**

dispid   The dispatch ID of a property of the control.

lpclsid   Pointer to a **CLSID** structure through which a class ID will be returned.

pbPageOptional   Returns an indicator of whether use of the specified property page is optional.

Remarks   Called by the framework to obtain the class ID of a property page that implements editing of the specified property.

Override this function to provide a way to invoke your control's property pages from the container's property browser.

Return Value   Nonzero if a class ID has been returned in *lpclsid*; otherwise 0.

See Also   **COleControl::OnGetDisplayString**

COleControl::OnMnemonic

virtual void OnMnemonic(LPMSG *pMsg* **);**

pMsg   Pointer to the Windows message generated by a mnemonic key press.

Remarks   Called by the framework when the container has detected that a mnemonic key of the OLE control has been pressed.

COleControl::OnProperties

virtual BOOL OnProperties(LPMSG *lpMsg*, **HWND** *hWndParent*, **LPCRECT** *lpRect* **);**

lpMsg   A pointer to the Windows message that invoked the verb.

hWndParent   A handle to the parent window of the control.

lpRect   A pointer to the rectangle used by the control in the container.

Remarks   Called by the framework when the control's properties verb has been invoked by the container. The default implementation displays a modal property dialog box.

Return Value   An OLE result code. Therefore nonzero if the call is not successful; otherwise 0.

COleControl::OnRenderData

virtual BOOL OnRenderData(LPFORMATETC *lpFormatEtc*, **LPSTGMEDIUM** *lpStgMedium* **);**

lpFormatEtc   Points to the **FORMATETC** structure specifying the format in which information is requested.

lpStgMedium   Points to a **STGMEDIUM** structure in which the data is to be returned.

Remarks   Called by the framework to retrieve data in the specified format. The specified format is one previously placed in the control object using the **DelayRenderData** or **DelayRenderFileData** member functions for delayed rendering. The default implementation of this function calls **OnRenderFileData** or **OnRenderGlobalData**, respectively, if the supplied storage medium is either a file or memory. If the requested format is **CF_METAFILEPICT** or the persistent property set format, the default implementation renders the appropriate data and returns nonzero. Otherwise, it returns 0 and does nothing.

If *lpStgMedium->tymed* is **TYMED_NULL**, the **STGMEDIUM** should be allocated and filled as specified by *lpFormatEtc->tymed*. If not **TYMED_NULL**, the **STGMEDIUM** should be filled in place with the data.

Override this function to provide your data in the requested format and medium. Depending on your data, you may want to override one of the other versions of this function instead. If your data is small and fixed in size, override **OnRenderGlobalData**. If your data is in a file, or is of variable size, override **OnRenderFileData**.

For more information about the **FORMATETC**, see the *OLE 2 Programmer's Reference, Volume 1*.

Return Value   Nonzero if successful; otherwise 0.

See Also   **COleControl::OnRenderFileData**, **COleControl::OnRenderGlobalData**

COleControl::OnRenderFileData

virtual BOOL OnRenderFileData(LPFORMATETC *lpFormatEtc*, **CFile*** *pFile* **);**

lpFormatEtc   Points to the **FORMATETC** structure specifying the format in which information is requested.

pFile   Points to a **CFile** object in which the data is to be rendered.

Remarks   Called by the framework to retrieve data in the specified format when the storage medium is a file. The specified format is one previously placed in the control object using the **DelayRenderData** member function for delayed rendering. The default implementation of this function simply returns **FALSE**.

Override this function to provide your data in the requested format and medium. Depending on your data, you might want to override one of the other versions of this function instead. If you want to handle multiple storage mediums, override **OnRenderData**. If your data is in a file, or is of variable size, override **OnRenderFileData**.

For more information about the **FORMATETC**, see the *OLE 2 Programmer's Reference, Volume 1.*

Return Value   Nonzero if successful; otherwise 0.

See Also   **COleControl::OnRenderData, COleControl::OnRenderGlobalData**

COleControl::OnRenderGlobalData

virtual BOOL OnRenderFileData(LPFORMATETC *lpFormatEtc*, **HGLOBAL*** *phGlobal* **);**

lpFormatEtc   Points to the **FORMATETC** structure specifying the format in which information is requested.

phGlobal   Points to a handle to global memory in which the data is to be returned. If no memory has been allocated, this parameter can be **NULL**.

Remarks   Called by the framework to retrieve data in the specified format when the specified storage medium is global memory. The specified format is one previously placed in the control object using the **DelayRenderData** member function for delayed rendering. The default implementation of this function simply returns **FALSE**.

If *phGlobal* is **NULL**, then a new **HGLOBAL** should be allocated and returned in *phGlobal*. Otherwise, the **HGLOBAL** specified by *phGlobal* should be filled with the data. The amount of data placed in the **HGLOBAL** must not exceed the current size of the memory block. Also, the block cannot be reallocated to a larger size.

Override this function to provide your data in the requested format and medium. Depending on your data, you may want to override one of the other versions of this function instead. If you want to handle multiple storage mediums, override **OnRenderData**. If your data is in a file, or is of variable size, override **OnRenderFileData**.

Return Value   Nonzero if successful; otherwise 0.

See Also   **COleControl::OnRenderFileData, COleControl::OnRenderData**

COleControl::OnResetState

virtual void OnResetState( );

Remarks   Called by the framework when the control's properties should be set to their default values. The default implementation calls **DoPropExchange**, passing a **CPropExchange** object that causes properties to be set to their default values.

The control writer can insert initialization code for the OLE control in this overridable. This function is called when **IPersistStream::Load** or **IPersistStorage::Load** fails, or **IPersistStreamInit::InitNew or**

IPersistStorage::InitNew is called, without first calling either
IPersistStream::Load or **IPersistStorage::Load**.

See Also   **COleControl::OnSetClientSite**

COleControl::OnSetClientSite

virtual void OnSetClientSite( );

Remarks   Called by the framework when the container has called the control's
IOleControl::SetClientSite function.

Override this function to do any special processing of this function.

COleControl::OnSetData

virtual BOOL OnRenderFileData(LPFORMATETC *lpFormatEtc*,
LPSTGMEDIUM *lpStgMedium* **);**

lpFormatEtc   Pointer to a **FORMATETC** structure specifying the format of the
data.

lpStgMedium   Pointer to a **STGMEDIUM** structure in which the data resides.

Remarks   Called by the framework to replace the control's data with the specified data. If the
data is in the persistent property set format, the default implementation modifies the
control's state accordingly. Otherwise, the default implementation does nothing.
Override this function to replace the control's data with the specified data.

For more information about the **FORMATETC**, see the *OLE 2 Programmer's
Reference, Volume 1.*

Return Value   Nonzero if successful; otherwise 0.

See Also   **COleControl::DoPropExchange**

COleControl::OnSetExtent

virtual BOOL OnSetExtent(LPSIZEL *lpSizeL* **);**

lpSizeL   A pointer to the SIZEL structure that uses long integers to represent the
width and height of the control, expressed in **HIMETRIC** units.

Remarks   Called by the framework when the control's extent needs to be changed, as a result
of a call to **IOleObject::SetExtent**. The default implementation handles the
resizing of the control's extent. If the control is in-place active, a call to the
container's **OnPosRectChanged**.

Override this function to alter the default resizing of your control.

Return Value   Nonzero if the size change was accepted; otherwise 0.

COleControl::OnSetObjectRects

virtual BOOL OnSetObjectRects(LPCRECT *lpRectPos***, LPCRECT** *lpRectClip* **);**

lpRectPos   A pointer to a **RECT** structure indicating the control's new position and size relative to the container.

lpRectClip   A pointer to a **RECT** structure indicating a rectangular area to which the control is to be clipped.

Remarks   Called by the framework to implement a call to **IOleInPlaceObject::SetObjectRects**. The default implementation automatically handles the repositioning and resizing of the control window and returns **TRUE**.

Override this function to alter the default behavior of this function.

Return Value   Nonzero if the repositioning was accepted; otherwise 0.

COleControl::OnShowToolbars

virtual void OnShowToolbars( );

Remarks   Called by the framework when the control has been UI activated. The default implementation does nothing.

See Also   **COleControl::OnHideToolbars**

COleControl::OnTextChanged

virtual void OnTextChanged( );

Remarks   Called by the framework when the stock Caption or Text property value has changed. The default implementation calls **InvalidateControl**.

Override this function if you want notification after this property changes.

See Also   **COleControl::SetText, COleControl::InternalGetText, COleControl::InvalidateControl**

COleControl::PreModalDialog

void PreModalDialog( );

Remarks   Call this function prior to displaying any modal dialog box. You must call this function so that the container can disable all its top-level windows. After the modal dialog box has been displayed, you must then call **PostModalDialog**.

See Also   COleControl::PostModalDialog

COleControl::PostModalDialog

void PostModalDialog( );

Remarks   Call this function after displaying any modal dialog box. You must call this function so that the container can enable any top-level windows disabled by **PreModalDialog**. This function should be paired with a call to **PreModalDialog**.

See Also   COleControl::PreModalDialog

COleControl::RecreateControlWindow

void RecreateControlWindow( );

Remarks   Call this function to destroy and re-create the control's window. This may be necessary if you need to change the window's style bits.

COleControl::Refresh

void Refresh( );

Remarks   Call this function to force a repaint of the OLE control.

This function is supported by the **COleControl** base class as a stock method, called Refresh. This allows users of your OLE control to repaint the control at a specific time. For more information on this method, see Chapter 6, "Adding a Stock Method," in the *CDK Programmer's Guide.*

See Also   COleControl::InvalidateControl

COleControl::SelectFontObject

CFont* SelectFontObject(CDC* *pDC*, **CFontHolder&** *fontHolder* **);**

pDC   Pointer to a device context object.

fontHolder   Reference to the **CFontHolder** object representing the font to be selected.

Remarks   Call this function to select a font into a device context.

Return Value   A pointer to the previously selected font. When the caller has finished all drawing operations that use *fontHolder,* it should re-select the previously selected font by passing it as a parameter to **CDC::SelectObject**.

COleControl::SelectStockFont

virtual HFONT SelectStockFont(CDC* *pDC* **);**

pDC   The device context into which the font will be selected.

Remarks   Call this function to select the stock Font property into a device context.

Return Value   A handle to the previously selected font object. You should use **::SelectObject** to select this font back into the device context when you are finished.

See Also   **COleControl::GetFont**, **COleControl::SetFont**

COleControl::SetBackColor

void SetBackColor(OLE_COLOR *dwBackColor* **);**

dwBackColor   An **OLE_COLOR** value to be used for background drawing of your control.

Remarks   Call this function to set the stock BackColor property value of your control. For more information on using this property and other related properties, see Chapter 3 of the *CDK Circle Sample Tutorial* and Chapter 6 of the *CDK Programmer's Guide.*

See Also   **COleControl::SetForeColor, COleControl::GetBackColor, COleControl::OnBackColorChanged**

COleControl::SetBorderStyle

void SetBorderStyle(short *sBorderStyle* **);**

sBorderStyle   The new border style for the control; 0 indicates no border and 1 indicates a normal border.

Remarks   Call this function to set the stock BorderStyle property value of your control. The control window will then be re-created and **OnBorderStyleChanged** called.

See Also   **COleControl::GetBorderStyle, COleControl::OnBorderStyleChanged**

COleControl::SetControlSize

BOOL SetControlSize(int *cx,* **int** *cy* **);**

cx   Specifies the new width of the control in pixels.

cy   Specifies the new height of the control in pixels.

Remarks   Call this function to set the size of the OLE control window and notify the container that the control site is changing. This function should not be used in your control's constructor.

Note that all coordinates for control windows are relative to the upper-left corner of the control.

Return Value   Nonzero if the call was successful; otherwise 0.

See Also   **COleControl::GetControlSize, COleControl::GetRectInContainer**

COleControl::SetEnabled

void SetEnabled(BOOL *bEnabled* **);**

bEnabled   **TRUE** if the control is to be enabled; otherwise **FALSE**.

Remarks   Call this function to set the stock Enabled property value of your control. After setting this property, **OnEnabledChange** is called.

See Also   **COleControl::GetEnabled, COleControl::OnEnabledChanged**

COleControl::SetFont

void SetFont(LPFONTDISP *pFontDisp* **);**

pFontDisp   A pointer to a Font dispatch interface.

Remarks   Call this function to set the stock Font property of your control.

See Also   **COleControl::GetFont, COleControl::InternalGetText, COleControl::OnFontChanged**

COleControl::SetForeColor

void SetForeColor(OLE_COLOR *dwForeColor* **);**

dwForeColor   A **OLE_COLOR** value to be used for foreground drawing of your control.

Remarks   Call this function to set the stock ForeColor property value of your control. For more information on using this property and other related properties, see Chapter 3 of the *CDK Circle Sample Tutorial* and Chapter 6 of the *CDK Programmer's Guide*.

See Also   **COleControl::SetBackColor, COleControl::GetForeColor, COleControl::OnForeColorChanged**

COleControl::SetInitialDataFormats

virtual void SetInitialDataFormats( );

Remarks   Called by the framework to initialize the list of data formats supported by the control.

The default implementation specifies two formats: **CF_METAFILEPICT** and the persistent property set.

COleControl::SetInitialSize

void SetInitialSize(int *cx*, int *cy*);

cx   The initial width of the OLE control in pixels.

cy   The initial height of the OLE control in pixels.

Remarks   Call this function in your constructor to set the initial size of your control. The initial size is measured in device units, or pixels. It is recommended that this call be made in your control's constructor.

COleControl::SetModifiedFlag

void SetModifiedFlag(BOOL *bModified* = TRUE);

bModified   The new value for the control's modified flag. **TRUE** indicates that the control's state has been modified; **FALSE** indicates that the control's state has just been saved.

Remarks   Call this function whenever a change occurs that would affect your control's persistent state. For example, if the value of a persistent property changes, call this function with *bModified* **TRUE**.

See Also   **COleControl::IsModified**

COleControl::SetNotPermitted

void SetNotPermitted( );

Remarks   Call this function when **BoundPropertyRequestEdit** fails. This function throws an exception of type **COleDispScodeException** to indicate that the set operation was not permitted.

See Also   **COleControl::BoundPropertyRequestEdit**

COleControl::SetNotSupported

void SetNotSupported( );

Remarks

Call this function in place of the Set function of any property where modification of the property value by the control's user is not supported. One example would be a property that is read-only in user mode.

See Also

COleControl::GetNotSupported

COleControl::SetRectInContainer

BOOL SetRectInContainer(LPRECT *lpRect* **);**

lpRect   A pointer to a rectangle containing the control's new coordinates relative to the container.

Remarks

Call this function to set the coordinates of the control's rectangle relative to the container, expressed in device units. If the control is open, it is resized; otherwise the container's **OnPosRectChanged** function is called.

Return Value

Nonzero if the call was successful; otherwise 0.

See Also

COleControl::GetRectInContainer, **COleControl::GetControlSize**

COleControl::SetText

void SetText(LPCTSTR *pszText* **);**

pszText   A pointer to a character string.

Remarks

Call this function to set the value of your control's stock Caption or Text property.

Note that the stock Caption and Text properties are both mapped to the same value. This means that any changes made to either property will automatically change both properties. In general, a control should support either the stock Caption or Text property, but not both.

See Also

COleControl::GetText, **COleControl::InternalGetText**, **COleControl::OnTextChanged**

COleControl::ThrowError

void ThrowError(SCODE *sc*, **UINT** *nDescriptionID*, **UINT** *nHelpID* = **-1** **);**

void ThrowError(SCODE *sc*, **LPCTSTR** *pszDescription* = **NULL, UINT** *nHelpID* = **0** **);**

sc   The status code value to be reported. For a complete list of possible codes, see "Handling Errors in Your OLE Control" in Appendix B.

nDescriptionID   The string resource ID of the exception to be reported.

nHelpID   The help ID of the topic to be reported on.

pszDescription   A string containing an explanation of the exception to be reported.

Remarks   Call this function to signal the occurrence of an error in your control. This function should only be called from within a Get or Set function for an OLE property, or the implementation of an OLE automation method. If you need to signal errors that occur at other times, you should fire the stock Error event.

See Also   **COleControl::FireError**, **COleControl::DisplayError**

COleControl::TransformCoords

void TransformCoords(POINTL FAR* *lpptlHimetric*, **POINTF FAR*** *lpptfContainer*, **DWORD** *flags* **);**

lpptlHimetric   Pointer to a **POINTL** structure containing coordinates in **HIMETRIC** units.

lpptfContainer   Pointer to a **POINTF** structure containing coordinates in the containers unit size.

flags   A combination of the following values:

- **XFORMCOORDS_POSITION**   A position in the container.
- **XFORMCOORDS_SIZE**   A size in the container.
- **XFORMCOORDS_HIMETERICTOCONTAINER**   Transform **HIMETRIC** units to the container's units.
- **XFORMCOORDS_CONTAINERTOHIMETERIC**   Transform the container's units to **HIMETRIC** units.

Remarks   Call this function to transform coordinate values between **HIMETRIC** units and the container's native units.

The first two flags, **XFORMCOORDS_POSITION** and **XFORMCOORDS_POSITION** indicate whether the coordinates should be treated as a position or a size. The remaining two flags indicate the direction of transformation.

See Also   **COleControl::AmbientScaleUnits**

COleControl::TranslateColor

COLORREF TranslateColor(OLE_COLOR *clrColor*, **HPALETTE** *hpal* = **NULL** **);**

clrColor   A **OLE_COLOR** data type.

hpal   A handle to an optional palette; can be **NULL**.

Remarks   Call this function to convert a color value from the **OLE_COLOR** data type to the **COLORREF** data type. This function is useful to translate the stock ForeColor and BackColor properties to **COLORREF** types used by **CDC** member functions.

Return Value   An RGB (red, green, blue) color value that defines the solid color closest to the *clrColor* value that the device can represent.

See Also   **COleControl::GetForeColor**, **COleControl::GetBackColor**

COleControl::WillAmbientsBeValidDuringLoad

BOOL WillAmbientsBeValidDuringLoad( );

Remarks   Call this function to determine whether your control should use the values of ambient properties as default values, when it is subsequently loaded from its persistent state.

In some containers, your control may not have access to its ambient properties during the initial call to the override of **COleControl::DoPropExchange**. This is the case if the container calls **IPersistStreamInit::Load** or **IPersistStorage::Load** prior to calling **IOleObject::SetClientSite** (that is, if it does not honor the **OLEMISC_SETCLIENTSITEFIRST** status bit).

Return Value   Nonzero indicates that ambient properties will be valid; otherwise ambient properties will not be valid.

See Also   **COleControl::DoPropExchange**, **COleControl::GetAmbientProperty**

class COleControlModule : public CWinApp

The **COleControlModule** class is the base class from which you derive an OLE control module object. This class provides member functions for initializing your control module. Each OLE control module that uses the Microsoft Foundation classes can only contain one object derived from **COleControlModule**. This object is constructed when other C++ global objects are constructed. Declare your derived **COleControlModule** object at the global level.

For more information, see the **CWinApp** class in the *Class Library Reference*.

#include <afxctl.h>

See Also   **CWinApp**

class COleObjectFactoryEx : public COleObjectFactory

As its name implies, the **COleObjectFactoryEx** class extends the functionality of its base class, **COleObjectFactory**. The **COleObjectFactoryEx** class

- Enforces licensing by limiting use of the control to licensed developers at design time and to licensed applications at run time.
- Registers control object factories with the OLE system registry.

If you check the License Validation box on Control Wizard's Project Options dialog when you create your OLE control project, ControlWizard inserts the **BEGIN_OLEFACTORY** and **END_OLEFACTORY** macros in your control class declaration. These macros create a **COleObjectFactoryEx** object as an embedded member of your control class. ControlWizard also writes the functions **VerifyUserLicense** and **GetLicenseKey**. For more information, see Chapter 10, "**Licensing Your Control**," in the *CDK Programmer's Guide*.

#include <afxctl.h>

See Also   **COleObjectFactory**

Class Members

Construction/Destruction

COleObjectFactoryEx	Constructs a **COleObjectFactoryEx** object.

Operations

GetNextFactory	Gets the next object factory in the DLL.
UpdateRegistryAll	Registers all the DLL's object factories with the OLE system registry.
IsLicenseValid	Indicates whether the control is licensed for design-time use.

Overridables

UpdateRegistry	Registers this object factory with the OLE system registry.
VerifyUserLicense	Verifies that the control is licensed for design-time use.
GetLicenseKey	Requests a unique key from the control's DLL.
VerifyLicenseKey	Verifies that the key embedded in the control matches the key embedded in the container.

Member Functions

COleObjectFactoryEx::COleObjectFactoryEx

COleObjectFactoryEx(REFCLSID *clsid***, CRuntimeClass*** *pRuntimeClass***, BOOL** *bMultiInstance***, LPCTSTR** *lpszProgID* **);**

clsid   Reference to the OLE class ID this object factory represents.

pRuntimeClass   Pointer to the run-time class of the C++ objects this factory can create.

bMultiInstance   Indicates whether a single instance of the control object can support multiple instances of the control object. If **TRUE**, multiple instances of the control object are launched for each request to create an object.

lpszProgID   Pointer to a string containing a verbal control identifier, such as "Circ Control."

Remarks   Constructs a **COleObjectFactoryEx** object.

See Also   **COleObjectFactory**

COleObjectFactoryEx::GetLicenseKey

virtual BOOL GetLicenseKey(DWORD *dwReserved***, BSTR FAR*** *pbstrKey* **);**

dwReserved   Reserved for future use.

pbstrKey   Pointer to a **BSTR** that will store the license key.

Remarks   Requests a unique license key from the control's DLL and stores it in the **BSTR** pointed to by *pbstrKey*.

The default implementation of this function returns 0 and stores nothing in the **BSTR**. If you use ControlWizard to create your project, ControlWizard supplies an override that retrieves the control's license key.

Return Value	Nonzero if the license-key string is not **NULL**; otherwise 0.
See Also	**COleObjectFactoryEx::VerifyUserLicense**, **COleObjectFactoryEx::VerifyLicenseKey**

COleObjectFactoryEx::GetNextFactory

COleObjectFactory* GetNextFactory( );

Remarks	Returns a pointer to the next object factory in this DLL.
Return Value	A pointer to the next object factory, or **NULL** if no more factories remain.
See Also	**COleObjectFactoryEx::UpdateRegistry**

COleObjectFactoryEx::IsLicenseValid

BOOL IsLicenseValid( );

Remarks	This function calls **VerifyUserLicense** to determine whether the control is licensed for design-time use.
	Use **VerifyLicenseKey** to determine whether the control is licensed for run-time use.
Return Value	Nonzero if the design-time license is valid.
See Also	**COleObjectFactory::VerifyUserLicense**, **COleObjectFactory::VerifyLicenseKey**

COleObjectFactoryEx::UpdateRegistry

virtual void UpdateRegistry(BOOL *bRegister* **) = 0;**

bRegister   Determines whether the control class's object factory is to be registered.

Remarks	If *bRegister* is **TRUE**, this function registers the control class with the system registry. Otherwise, it unregisters the class.
	If you use ControlWizard to create your project, ControlWizard supplies an override to this pure virtual function.
See Also	**COleObjectFactoryEx::UpdateRegistryAll**

COleObjectFactoryEx::UpdateRegistryAll

static void PASCAL UpdateRegistryAll(BOOL *bRegister* **);**

bRegister   Determines whether the control classes' object factories are to be registered.

Remarks   Registers or unregisters object factories for all OLE controls in the current DLL.

See Also   **COleObjectFactoryEx::UpdateRegistry**

COleObjectFactoryEx::VerifyLicenseKey

virtual BOOL VerifyLicenseKey(BSTR *bstrKey* **);**

bstrKey   A **BSTR** storing the container's version of the license string.

Remarks   This function verifies that the container is licensed to use the OLE control. The default version calls **GetLicenseKey** to get a copy of the control's license string and compares it with the string in *bstrKey*. If the two strings match, the function returns a nonzero value; otherwise it returns 0.

You can override this function to provide customized verification of the license.

The function **VerifyUserLicense** verifies the design-time license.

Return Value   Nonzero if the run-time license is valid; otherwise 0.

See Also   **COleObjectFactoryEx::VerifyUserLicense**

COleObjectFactoryEx::VerifyUserLicense

virtual BOOL VerifyUserLicense( );

Remarks   Verifies the design-time license for the OLE control.

Return Value   Nonzero if the design-time license is valid; otherwise 0.

See Also   **COleObjectFactoryEx::VerifyLicenseKey**

class COlePropertyPage : public CDialog

The **COlePropertyPage** class is used to display the properties of a custom control in a graphical interface, similar to a dialog box. For instance, a property page may include an edit control that allows the user to view and modify the control's caption property.

Each custom or stock control property can have a dialog control that allows the control's user to view the current property value and modify that value if needed.

#include <afxctl.h>

See Also   **CDialog**

Class Members

Construction
COlePropertyPage	Constructs a **COlePropertyPage** object.

Operations
GetObjectArray	Returns the array of objects being edited by the property page.
SetModifiedFlag	Sets a flag indicating whether the user has modified the property page.
IsModified	Indicates whether the user has modified the property page.
GetPageSite	Returns a pointer to the property page's **IPropertyPageSite** interface.
SetDialogResource	Sets the property page's dialog resource.
SetPageName	Sets the property page's name (caption).
SetHelpInfo	Sets the property page's brief help text, the name of its help file, and its help context.
GetControlStatus	Indicates whether the user has modified the value in the control.
SetControlStatus	Sets a flag indicating whether the user has modified the value in the control.
IgnoreApply	Determines which controls do not enable the Apply button.

Overridables

OnHelp	Called by the framework when the user invokes help.
OnInitDialog	Called by the framework when the property page is initialized.
OnEditProperty	Called by the framework when the user edits a property.
OnSetPageSite	Called by the framework when the property frame provides the page's site.

Member Functions

COlePropertyPage::COlePropertyPage

COlePropertyPage(UINT *idDlg*, **UINT** *idCaption* **);**

idDlg   Resource ID of the dialog template.

idCaption   Resource ID of the property page's caption.

Remarks   When you implement a subclass of **COlePropertyPage**, your subclass's constructor should use the **COlePropertyPage** constructor to identify the dialog-template resource on which the property page is based and the string resource containing its caption.

COlePropertyPage::GetControlStatus

BOOL GetControlStatus(UINT *nID* **);**

nID   Resource ID of a property page control.

Remarks   Call this function to determine whether the user has modified the value of the property page control with the specified resource ID.

Return Value   **TRUE** if the control value has been modified; otherwise **FALSE**.

See Also   **COlePropertyPage::SetControlStatus**

COlePropertyPage::GetObjectArray

LPDISPATCH FAR* GetObjectArray(ULONG FAR* *pnObjects* **);**

pnObjects   Pointer to an unsigned long integer that will receive the number of objects being edited by the page.

Remarks   Each property page object maintains an array of pointers to the **IDispatch** interfaces of the objects being edited by the page. This function sets its *pnObjects* argument to the number of elements in that array and returns a pointer to the first element of the array.

Return Value   Pointer to an array of **IDispatch** pointers, which are used to access the properties of each control on the property page. The caller must not release these interface pointers.

COlePropertyPage::GetPageSite

LPPROPERTYPAGESITE GetPageSite( );

Remarks   Call this function to get a pointer to the property page's **IPropertyPageSite** interface.

Controls and containers cooperate so that users can browse and edit control properties. The control provides property pages, each of which is an OLE object that allows the user to edit a related set of properties. The container provides a property frame that displays the property pages. For each page, the property frame provides a page site, which supports the **IPropertyPageSite** interface.

Return Value   A pointer to the property page's **IPropertyPageSite** interface.

See Also   **COlePropertyPage::OnSetPageSite**

COlePropertyPage::IgnoreApply

void IgnoreApply(UINT *nID*);

nID   ID of the control to be ignored.

Remarks   The property page's Apply button is enabled only when values of property page controls have been changed. Use this function to specify controls that do not cause the Apply button to be enabled when their values change.

See Also   **COlePropertyPage::GetControlStatus**

COlePropertyPage::IsModified

BOOL IsModified( );

Remarks   Call this function to determine whether the user has changed any values on the property page.

Return Value   **TRUE** if the property page has been modified.

See Also   **COlePropertyPage::SetModifiedFlag**

COlePropertyPage::OnEditProperty

virtual BOOL OnEditProperty(DISPID *dispid* **);**

dispid   Dispatch ID of the property being edited.

Remarks   The framework calls this function when a specific property is to be edited. You can override it to set the focus to the appropriate control on the page. The default implementation does nothing and returns **FALSE**.

Return Value   The default implementation returns **FALSE**. Overrides of this function should return **TRUE**.

COlePropertyPage::OnHelp

virtual BOOL OnHelp(LPCTSTR *lpszHelpDir* **);**

lpszHelpDir   Directory containing the property page's help file.

Remarks   The framework calls this function when the user requests online help. Override it if your property page must perform any special action when the user accesses help. The default implementation does nothing and returns **FALSE**, which instructs the framework to call WinHelp.

Return Value   The default implementation returns **FALSE**.

COlePropertyPage::OnInitDialog

virtual BOOL OnInitDialog( );

Remarks   The framework calls this function when the property page's dialog is initialized. Override it if any special action is required when the dialog is initialized. The default implementation calls **CDialog::OnInitDialog** and returns **FALSE**.

Return Value   The default implementation returns **FALSE**.

See Also   **CDialog::OnInitDialog**

COlePropertyPage::OnSetPageSite

virtual void OnSetPageSite( );

Remarks   The framework calls this function when the property frame provides the property page's page site. The default implementation loads the page's caption and attempts to determine the page's size from the dialog resource. Override this function if your property page requires any further action; your override should call the base-class implementation.

See Also   **COlePropertyPage::GetPageSite**

COlePropertyPage::SetControlStatus

BOOL SetControlStatus(UINT *nID***, BOOL** *IsDirty* **);**

nID   Contains the ID of a property page control.

IsDirty   Specifies if a field of the property page has been modified. Set to **TRUE** if the field has been modified, **FALSE** if it has not been modified.

Remarks   Call this function to change the status of a property page control.

If the status of a property page control is dirty when the property page is closed or the Apply button is chosen, the control's property will be updated with the appropriate value.

Return Value   **TRUE**, if the specified control was set; otherwise **FALSE**.

See Also   **COlePropertyPage::GetControlStatus**

COlePropertyPage::SetDialogResource

void SetDialogResource(HGLOBAL *hDialog* **);**

hDialog   Handle to the property page's dialog resource.

Remarks   Call this function to set the property page's dialog resource.

COlePropertyPage::SetHelpInfo

void SetHelpInfo(LPCTSTR *lpszDocString***, LPCTSTR** *lpszHelpFile* **= NULL, DWORD** *dwHelpContext* **= 0);**

lpszDocString   A string containing brief help information for display in a status bar or other location.

lpszHelpFile   Name of the property page's help file.

dwHelpContext   Help context for the property page.

Remarks   Use this function to specify "tool tip" information, the help file name, and the help context for your property page.

COlePropertyPage::SetModifiedFlag

void SetModifiedFlag(BOOL *bModified* **= TRUE);**

bModified   Specifies the new value for the property page's modified flag.

Remarks   Use this function to indicate whether the user has modified the property page.

See Also   **COlePropertyPage::IsModified**

COlePropertyPage::SetPageName

void SetPageName(LPCTSTR *lpszPageName* **);**

lpszPageName   Pointer to a string containing the property page's name.

Remarks   Use this function to set the property page's name, which the property frame will typically display on the page's tab.

class CPictureHolder

The purpose of **CPictureHolder** class is implementation of a Picture property, which allows the user to display a picture in your control. With the stock Picture property, the developer can specify a bitmap, icon, or metafile for display.

For information on creating custom picture properties, see Chapter 9, "Using Fonts and Pictures in Your Control," in the *CDK Programmer's Guide*.

#include <afxctl.h>

See Also   **CFontHolder**

Class Members

Data Members

m_pPict	A pointer to a font object.

Construction/Destruction

CPictureHolder	Constructs a **CPictureHolder** object.
~CPictureHolder	Destroys a **CPictureHolder** object.

Operations

GetDisplayString	Retrieves the string displayed in a Visual Basic property sheet.
CreateEmpty	Creates an empty **CPictureHolder** object.
CreateFromBitmap	Creates a **CPictureHolder** object from a bitmap.
CreateFromMetafile	Creates a **CPictureHolder** object from a metafile.
CreateFromIcon	Creates a **CPictureHolder** object from an icon.
GetPictureDispatch	Returns the **CPictureHolder** object's **IDispatch** interface.
SetPictureDispatch	Sets the **CPictureHolder** object's **IDispatch** interface.
GetType	Tells whether the **CPictureHolder** object is a bitmap, a metafile, or an icon.
Render	Renders the picture.

Member Functions

CPictureHolder::CPictureHolder

CPictureHolder( );

Remarks   Constructs a **CPictureHolder** object.

See Also   **~CPictureHolder**

CPictureHolder::~CPictureHolder

CPictureHolder( );

Remarks   Destroys a **CPictureHolder** object.

See Also   **CPictureHolder**

CPictureHolder::CreateEmpty

BOOL CreateEmpty( );

Remarks   Creates an empty **CPictureHolder** object and connects it to an **IPicture** interface.

Return Value   Nonzero if the object is successfully created; otherwise 0.

See Also   **CPictureHolder::CreateFromBitmap**
        CPictureHolder::CreateFromIcon
        CPictureHolder::CreateFromMetafile

CPictureHolder::CreateFromBitmap

BOOL CreateFromBitmap(UINT *idResource* **);**

BOOL CreateFromBitmap(CBitmap* *pBitmap*, **CPalette*** *pPal* **= NULL,
BOOL** *bTransferOwnership* **= TRUE);**

BOOL CreateFromBitmap(HBITMAP *hbm*, **HPALETTE** *hpal* **= NULL);**

idResource   Resource ID of a bitmap resource.

pBitmap   Pointer to a **CBitmap** object.

pPal   Pointer to a **CPalette** object.

bTransferOwnership   Indicates whether the picture object will take ownership of the bitmap and palette objects.

hbm   Handle to the bitmap from which the **CPictureHolder** object is created.

hpal   Handle to the palette used for rendering the bitmap.

Remarks   Uses a bitmap to initialize the picture object in a **CPictureHolder**. If *bTransferOwnership* is **TRUE**, the caller should not use the bitmap or palette object in any way after this call returns. If *bTransferOwnership* is **FALSE**, the caller is responsible for ensuring that the bitmap and palette objects remain valid for the lifetime of the picture object.

Return Value   Nonzero if the object is successfully created; otherwise 0.

See Also   **CPictureHolder::CreateEmpty**
CPictureHolder::CreateFromIcon
CPictureHolder::CreateFromMetafile

CPictureHolder::CreateFromIcon

BOOL CreateFromIcon(UINT *idResource* **);**

BOOL CreateFromIcon(HICON *hIcon***, BOOL** *bTransferOwnership* **= FALSE);**

idResource   Resource ID of a bitmap resource.

hIcon   Handle to the icon from which the **CPictureHolder** object is created.

bTransferOwnership   Indicates whether the picture object will take ownership of the icon object.

Remarks   Uses an icon to initialize the picture object in a **CPictureHolder**. If *bTransferOwnership* is **TRUE**, the caller should not use the icon object in any way after this call returns. If *bTransferOwnership* is **FALSE**, the caller is responsible for ensuring that the icon object remains valid for the lifetime of the picture object.

Return Value   Nonzero if the object is successfully created; otherwise 0.

See Also   **CPictureHolder::CreateEmpty**
CPictureHolder::CreateFromBitmap
CPictureHolder::CreateFromMetafile

CPictureHolder::CreateFromMetafile

BOOL CreateFromMetafile(HMETAFILE *hmf***, int** *xExt***, int** *yExt***, BOOL** *bTransferOwnership* **= FALSE);**

hmf   Handle to the metafile used to create the **CPictureHolder** object.

xExt   X extent of the picture.

yExt   Y extent of the picture.

bTransferOwnership   Indicates whether the picture object will take ownership of the metafile object.

Remarks   Uses a metafile to initialize the picture object in a **CPictureHolder**. If *bTransferOwnership* is **TRUE**, the caller should not use the metafile object in any way after this call returns. If *bTransferOwnership* is **FALSE**, the caller is responsible for ensuring that the metafile object remains valid for the lifetime of the picture object.

Return Value   Nonzero, if the object is successfully created; otherwise 0.

See Also   **CPictureHolder::CreateEmpty**
CPictureHolder::CreateFromBitmap
CPictureHolder::CreateFromIcon

CPictureHolder::GetDisplayString

BOOL GetDisplayString(CString& *strValue* **);**

strValue   Reference to the **CString** that is to hold the display string.

Remarks   Retrieves the string that is displayed in Visual Basic's property page.

Return Value   Nonzero if the string is successfully retrieved; otherwise 0.

CPictureHolder::GetPictureDispatch

LPPICTUREDISP GetPictureDispatch( );

Remarks   This function returns a pointer to the **CPictureHolder** object's **IPictureDisp** interface. The caller must call **Release** on this pointer when finished with it.

Return Value   A pointer to the **CPictureHolder** object's **IPictureDisp** interface.

See Also   **CPictureHolder::SetPictureDispatch**

CPictureHolder::GetType

short GetType( );

Remarks   Indicates whether the picture is a bitmap, metafile, or icon.

Return Value   A value indicating the type of the picture. Possible values and their meanings are as follows:

Value	Meaning
PICTYPE_UNINITIALIZED	**CPictureHolder** object is uninitialized.
PICTYPE_NONE	**CPictureHolder** object is empty.

Value	Meaning
PICTYPE_BITMAP	Picture is a bitmap.
PICTYPE_METAFILE	Picture is a metafile.
PICTYPE_ICON	Picture is an icon.

CPictureHolder::Render

void Render(CDC* *pDC*, **const CRect&** *rcRender*,
const CRect& *rcWBounds* **);**

pDC   Pointer to the display context in which the picture is to be rendered.

rcRender   Rectangle in which the picture is to be rendered.

rcWBounds   A rectangle representing the bounding rectangle of the object rendering the picture. For a control, this rectangle is the *rcBounds* parameter passed to an override of **COleControl::OnDraw**.

Remarks   Renders the picture in the rectangle referenced by *rcRender*.

CPictureHolder::SetPictureDispatch

void SetPictureDisp(LPPICTUREDISP *pDisp* **);**

pDisp   Pointer to the new **IPictureDisp** interface.

Remarks   Connects the **CPictureHolder** object to a **IPictureDisp** interface.

Data Members

CPictureHolder::m_pPict

Remarks   A pointer to the **CPictureHolder** object's **IPicture** interface.

class CPropExchange

Establishes the context and direction of a property exchange.

The **CPropExchange** class and the classes derived from it, **CResetPropExchange** and **CArchivePropExchange**, support the implementation of persistence for your OLE controls. Persistence is the exchange of the control's state information, usually represented by its properties, between the control itself and a medium.

The framework constructs an object derived from **CPropExchange** when it is notified that an OLE control's properties are to be loaded from or stored to persistent storage.

The framework passes a pointer to this **CPropExchange** object to your control's DoPropExchange function. If you used ClassWizard to create the starter files for your control, your control's DoPropExchange function calls **DoPropExchange**. The base-class version exchanges the control's stock properties; you modify your derived class's version to exchange properties you have added to your control.

CPropExchange is the base class for **CArchivePropExchange**, which is used for serializing a control's properties, and **CResetPropExchange**, which is used for initializing properties. The **ExchangeProp** and **ExchangeFontProp** member functions of these classes override members of **CPropExchange** so that one **DoPropExchange** function can be used for storing properties to and loading them from different media.

#include <afxctl.h>

See Also   COleControl::DoPropExchange

Class Members

Operations

ExchangeFontProp	Exchanges a font property.
ExchangeProp	Exchanges properties of any built-in type.
ExchangeBlobProp	Exchanges a binary large object (**BLOB**) property.
ExchangePersistentProp	Exchanges a property between a control and a file.
ExchangeVersion	Exchanges the version number of an OLE control.
IsLoading	Indicates whether properties are being loaded into the control or saved from it.
GetVersion	Retrieves the version number of an OLE control.

Member Functions

CPropExchange::ExchangeBlobProp

virtual BOOL ExchangeBlobProp(LPCTSTR *pszPropName***, void**** *ppvBlob***, const void*** *pvBlobDefault* **= NULL) = 0;**

pszPropName   The name of the property being exchanged.

ppvBlob   Pointer to a variable pointing to where the property is stored (variable is typically a member of your class).

pvBlobDefault   Default value for the property.

Remarks   Serializes a property that stores Binary Large Object (**BLOB**) data.

The property's value is read from or written to, as appropriate, the variable referenced by *ppvBlob*. If *pvBlobDefault* is specified, it will be used as the property's default value. This value is used if, for any reason, the control's serialization fails.

The functions **CArchivePropExchange::ExchangeBlobProp**, **CResetPropExchange::ExchangeBlobProp**, and **CPropsetPropExchange::ExchangeBlobProp** override this pure virtual function.

Return Value   Nonzero if the exchange was successful; 0 if unsuccessful.

See Also   **COleControl::DoPropExchange, CPropExchange::ExchangeFontProp, CPropExchange::ExchangePersistentProp, CPropExchange::ExchangeProp**

CPropExchange::ExchangeFontProp

virtual BOOL ExchangeFontProp(LPCTSTR *pszPropName***, CFontHolder&** *font***, const FONTDESC FAR*** *pFontDesc***, LPFONTDISP** *pFontDispAmbient* **) = 0;**

pszPropName   The name of the property being exchanged.

font   A reference to a **CFontHolder** object that contains the font property.

pFontDesc   A pointer to a **FONTDESC** structure containing values for initializing the default state of the font property when *pFontDispAmbient* is **NULL**.

pFontDispAmbient   A pointer to the **IFontDisp** interface of a font to be used for initializing the default state of the font property.

Remarks   Exchanges a font property between a storage medium and the control.

If the font property is being loaded from the medium to the control, the font's characteristics are retrieved from the medium and the **CFontHolder** object referenced by *font* is initialized with them. If the font property is being stored, the characteristics in the font object are written to the medium.

The functions **CArchivePropExchange::ExchangeFontProp**, **CResetPropExchange::ExchangeFontProp**, and **CPropsetPropExchange::ExchangeFontProp** override this pure virtual function.

Return Value   Nonzero if the exchange was successful; 0 if unsuccessful.

See Also   **COleControl::DoPropExchange**, **CPropExchange::ExchangeBlobProp**, **CPropExchange::ExchangePersistentProp**, **CPropExchange::ExchangeProp**

CPropExchange::ExchangePersistentProp

virtual BOOL ExchangePersistentProp(LPCTSTR *pszPropName*, **LPUNKNOWN FAR*** *ppUnk*, **REFIID** *iid*, **LPUNKNOWN** *pUnkDefault*) = 0;

pszPropName   The name of the property being exchanged.

ppUnk   A pointer to a variable containing a pointer to the property's **IUnknown** interface (this variable is typically a member of your class).

iid   Interface ID of the interface on the property that the control will use.

pUnkDefault   Default value for the property.

Remarks   Exchanges a property between the control and a file.

If the property is being loaded from the file to the control, the property is created and initialized from the file. If the property is being stored, its value is written to the file.

The functions **CArchivePropExchange::ExchangePersistentProp**, **CResetPropExchange::ExchangePersistentProp**, and **CPropsetPropExchange::ExchangePersistentProp** override this pure virtual function.

Return Value   Nonzero if the exchange was successful; 0 if unsuccessful.

See Also   **COleControl::DoPropExchange**, **CPropExchange::ExchangeBlobProp**, **CPropExchange::ExchangeFontProp**, **CPropExchange::ExchangeProp**

CPropExchange::ExchangeProp

virtual BOOL ExchangeProp(LPCTSTR *pszPropName*, **VARTYPE** *vtProp*, **void*** *pvProp*, **const void*** *pvDefault* = **NULL**) = 0;

pszPropName   The name of the property being exchanged.

vtProp   A symbol specifying the type of the property being exchanged. Possible values are:

Symbol	Property Type
VT_I2	**short**
VT_I4	**long**
VT_BOOL	**BOOL**
VT_BSTR	**CString**
VT_CY	**CY**
VT_R4	**float**
VT_R8	**double**

pvProp   A pointer to the property's value.

pvDefault   Pointer to a default value for the property.

Remarks

Exchanges a property between a storage medium and the control.

If the property is being loaded from the medium to the control, the property's value is retrieved from the medium and stored in the object pointed to by *pvProp*. If the property is being stored to the medium, the value of the object pointed to by *pvProp* is written to the medium.

The functions **CArchivePropExchange::ExchangeProp, CResetPropExchange::ExchangeProp,** and **CPropsetPropExchange::ExchangeProp** override this pure virtual function.

Return Value

Nonzero if the exchange was successful; 0 if unsuccessful.

See Also

COleControl::DoPropExchange, CPropExchange::ExchangeBlobProp, CPropExchange::ExchangeFontProp, CPropExchange::ExchangePersistentProp

CPropExchange::ExchangeVersion

BOOL ExchangeVersion(DWORD& *dwVersionLoaded*, **DWORD** *dwVersionDefault*, **BOOL** *bConvert*);

dwVersionLoaded   Reference to a variable where the version number of the persistent data being loaded will be stored.

dwVersionDefault   The current version number of the control.

bConvert   Indicates whether to convert persistent data to the current version or keep it at the same version that was loaded.

Remarks

Called by the framework to handle persistence of a version number.

Return Value   Nonzero if the function succeeded; zero otherwise.

See Also   **COleControl::ExchangeVersion**

CPropExchange::GetVersion

DWORD GetVersion( );

Remarks   Call this function to retrieve the version number of the control.

Return Value   The version number of the control.

CPropExchange::IsLoading

BOOL IsLoading( );

Remarks   Call this function to determine whether properties are being loaded to the control or saved from it.

Return Value   **TRUE** if properties are being loaded; otherwise **FALSE**.

See Also   **COleControl::DoPropExchange**

Macros and Globals

The extensions to the Microsoft Foundation Class Library (MFC) that support OLE custom controls are divided into two major sections: 1) classes and 2) macros and globals. If a function or variable is not a member of a class, it is a global function or variable.

The OLE control macros and globals, which are designed to assist OLE control programmers, offer functionality in the following categories:

- Variant parameter type constants
- Type library access
- Property pages
- Event maps
- Connection maps
- Registering OLE controls
- Class factories and licensing
- Persistence of OLE controls

The first part of this section briefly discusses each of the categories and lists each global and macro in the category, along with a brief description of what it does. Following this is a complete alphabetical listing of all the global functions, global variables, and macros in the OLE custom control extension of the Microsoft Foundation Class Library.

Note All global functions start with the prefix "Afx." All global variables start with the prefix "afx." Macros do not start with any particular prefix, but they are all uppercase.

Variant Parameter Type Constants

This section lists new constants that indicate variant parameter types designed for use with the OLE Controls extension to the Microsoft Foundation Class Library.

The following is a list of class constants:

Variant Data Constants
- **VTS_COLOR**   A 32-bit integer used to represent a RGB color value.
- **VTS_FONT**   A pointer to the **IFontDisp** interface of an OLE font object.
- **VTS_HANDLE**   A Windows handle value.

- **VTS_PICTURE**   A pointer to the **IPictureDisp** interface of an OLE picture object.

- **VTS_OPTEXCLUSIVE**   A 16-bit value used for a control intended to be used in a group of controls, such as radio buttons. This type tells the container that if one control in a group has a **TRUE** value, all others must be **FALSE**.

- **VTS_TRISTATE**   A 16-bit signed integer used for properties that can have one of three possible values (checked, unchecked, gray), for example, a check box.

- **VTS_XPOS_HIMETRIC**   A 32-bit unsigned integer used to represent a position along the x-axis in **HIMETRIC** units.

- **VTS_YPOS_HIMETRIC**   A 32-bit unsigned integer used to represent a position along the y-axis in **HIMETRIC** units.

- **VTS_XPOS_PIXELS**   A 32-bit unsigned integer used to represent a position along the x-axis in pixels.

- **VTS_YPOS_PIXELS**   A 32-bit unsigned integer used to represent a position along the y-axis in pixels.

- **VTS_XSIZE_PIXELS**   A 32-bit unsigned integer used to represent the width of a screen object in pixels.

- **VTS_YSIZE_PIXELS**   A 32-bit unsigned integer used to represent the height of a screen object in pixels.

- **VTS_XSIZE_HIMETRIC**   A 32-bit unsigned integer used to represent the width of a screen object in **HIMETRIC** units.

- **VTS_YSIZE_HIMETRIC**   A 32-bit unsigned integer used to represent the height of a screen object in **HIMETRIC** units.

Note   Additional variant constants have been defined for all variant types, with the exception of **VTS_FONT** and **VTS_PICTURE**, that provide a pointer to the variant data constant. These constants are named using the **VTS_P***constantname* convention. For example, **VTS_PCOLOR** is a pointer to a **VTS_COLOR** constant.

Type Library Access

Type libraries expose the interfaces of an OLE control to other OLE-aware applications. Each OLE control must have a type library if one or more interfaces are to be exposed.

The following is a list of macros that allow an OLE control to provide access to its own type library:

Type Library Access

DECLARE_OLETYPELIB	Declares a **GetTypeLib** member function of an OLE control (must be used in the class declaration).
IMPLEMENT_OLETYPELIB	Implements a **GetTypeLib** member function of an OLE control (must be used in the class implementation).

Property Pages

Property pages display the current values of specific OLE control properties in a customizable, graphical interface for viewing and editing by supporting a data-mapping mechanism based on dialog data exchange (DDX).

This data-mapping mechanism maps property page controls to the individual properties of the OLE control. The value of the control property reflects the status or content of the property page control. The mapping between property page controls and properties is specified by **DDP_** function calls in the property page's DoDataExchange member function. The following is a list of **DDP_** functions that exchange data entered using the property page of your control:

Property Page Data Transfer

DDP_CBIndex	Use this function to link the selected string's index in a combo box with a control's property.
DDP_CBString	Use this function to link the selected string in a combo box with a control's property. The selected string can begin with the same letters as the property's value but need not match it fully.
DDP_CBStringExact	Use this function to link the selected string in a combo box with a control's property. The selected string and the property's string value must match exactly.
DDP_Check	Use this function to link a check box in the control's property page with a control's property.
DDP_LBIndex	Use this function to link the selected string's index in a list box with a control's property.
DDP_LBString	Use this function to link the selected string in a list box with a control's property. The selected string can begin with the same letters as the property's value but need not match it fully.
DDP_LBStringExact	Use this function to link the selected string in a list box with a control's property. The selected string and the property's string value must match exactly.

DDP_Radio	Use this function to link a radio button group in the control's property page with a control's property.
DDP_Text	Use this function to link a control in the control's property page with a control's property. This function handles several different types of properties, such as **double**, **short**, **BSTR**, and **long**.

For more information about the `DoDataExchange` function and property pages, see Chapter 8, "Implementing the Default Property Page," in the *CDK Programmer's Guide*.

The following is a list of macros used to create and manage property pages for an OLE control:

Property Pages

BEGIN_PROPPAGEIDS	Begins the list of property page ID's.
END_PROPPAGEIDS	Ends the list of property page ID's.
PROPPAGEID	Declares a property page of the control class.

Event Maps

Whenever a control wishes to notify its container that some action (determined by the control developer) has happened (such as a keystroke, mouse click, or a change to the control's state) it calls an event firing function. This function notifies the control container that some important action has occurred by firing the related event.

The Microsoft Foundation Class Library offers a programming model optimized for firing events. In this model, "event maps" are used to designate which functions fire which events for a particular control. Event maps contain one macro for each event. For example, an event map that fires a stock Click event might look like this:

```
BEGIN_EVENT_MAP(CSampleCtrl, COleControl)
    //{{AFX_EVENT_MAP(CSampleCtrl)
    EVENT_STOCK_CLICK( )
    //}}AFX_EVENT_MAP
END_EVENT_MAP()
```

The **EVENT_STOCK_CLICK** macro indicates that the control will fire a stock Click event every time it detects a mouse click. For a more detailed listing of other stock events, see Chapter 7, "Adding Stock Events," in the CDK *Programmer's Guide*. Macros are also available to indicate custom events.

Although event-map macros are important, you generally don't insert them directly. This is because ClassWizard automatically creates event-map entries in your source files when you use it to associate event firing functions with events. Any time you want to edit or add an event-map entry, you can use ClassWizard.

To support event maps, MFC provides the following macros.

Event Map Declaration and Demarcation

DECLARE_EVENT_MAP	Declares that an event map will be used in a class to map events to event firing functions (must be used in the class declaration).
BEGIN_EVENT_MAP	Begins the definition of an event map (must be used in the class implementation).
END_EVENT_MAP	Ends the definition of an event map (must be used in the class implementation).

Event Mapping Macros

EVENT_CUSTOM	Indicates which event firing function will fire the specified event.
EVENT_CUSTOM_ID	Indicates which event firing function will fire the specified event, with a designated dispatch ID.

Message Mapping Macros

ON_OLEVERB	Indicates a custom verb handled by the OLE control.
ON_STDOLEVERB	Overrides a standard verb mapping of the OLE control.

Connection Maps

OLE controls are able to expose interfaces to other applications. These interfaces only allow access from a container into that control. If an OLE control wants to access external interfaces of other OLE objects, a connection point must be established. This connection point allows a control outgoing access to external dispatch maps, such as event maps or notification functions.

The Microsoft Foundation Class Library offers a programming model that supports connection points. In this model, "connection maps" are used to designate interfaces (or connection points) for the OLE control. Connection maps contain one macro for each connection point. For more information on connection maps, see the **CConnectionPoint** class.

Typically, a control will support just two connection points: one for events and one for property notifications. These are implemented by the **COleControl** base class and require no additional work by the control writer. Any additional connection points you wish to implement in your class must be added by hand. To support connection maps and points, MFC provides the following macros.

Connection Map Declaration and Demarcation

BEGIN_CONNECTION_PART	Declares an embedded class that implements an additional connection point (must be used in the class declaration).
END_CONNECTION_PART	Ends the declaration of a connection point (must be used in the class declaration).
CONNECTION_IID	Specifies the interface ID of the control's connection point.
DECLARE_CONNECTION_MAP	Declares that a connection map will be used in a class (must be used in the class declaration).
BEGIN_CONNECTION_MAP	Begins the definition of a connection map (must be used in the class implementation).
END_CONNECTION_MAP	Ends the definition of a connection map (must be used in the class implementation).
CONNECTION_PART	Specifies a connection point in the control's connection map.

The following functions assist a sink in establishing and disconnecting a connection using connection points:

Initialization/Termination of Connection Points

AfxConnectionAdvise	Establishes a connection between a source and a sink.
AfxConnectionUnadvise	Breaks a connection between a source and a sink.

Registering OLE Controls

OLE controls, like other OLE server objects, can be accessed by other OLE-aware applications. This is achieved by registering the control's type library and class.

The following functions allow you to add and remove the control's class, property pages, and type library in the Windows registration database:

Registering OLE Controls

AfxOleRegisterControlClass	Adds the control's class to the registration database.
AfxOleRegisterPropertyPageClass	Adds a control property page to the registration database.
AfxOleRegisterTypeLib	Adds the control's type library to the registration database.
AfxOleUnregisterClass	Removes a control class or a property page class from the registration database.
AfxOleUnregisterTypeLib	Removes the control's type library from the registration database.

AfxOleRegisterTypeLib is typically called in a control DLL's implementation of `DllRegisterServer`. Similarly, **AfxOleUnregisterTypeLib** is called by `DllUnregisterServer`. **AfxOleRegisterControlClass**, **AfxOleRegisterPropertyPageClass**, and **AfxOleUnregisterClass** are typically called by the `UpdateRegistry` member function of a control's class factory or property page.

Class Factories and Licensing

To create an instance of your OLE control, a container application calls a member function of the control's class factory. Because your control is an actual OLE 2 object, the class factory is responsible for creating instances of your control. Every OLE control class must have a class factory.

Another important feature of OLE controls is their ability to enforce a license. ControlWizard allows you to incorporate licensing during the creation of your control project. For more information on control licensing, see Chapter 10, "Licensing Your Control," in the CDK *Programmer's Guide*.

The following table lists several functions used to declare and implement your control's class factory and for licensing of your control.

Class Factories and Licensing

DECLARE_OLECREATE_EX	Declares the class factory for an OLE control or property page.
IMPLEMENT_OLECREATE_EX	Implements the control's GetClassID function and declares an instance of the class factory.
BEGIN_OLEFACTORY	Begins the declaration of any licensing functions.
END_OLEFACTORY	Ends the declaration of any licensing functions.
AfxVerifyLicFile	Verifies whether a control is licensed for use on a particular computer.

Persistence of OLE Controls

One capability of OLE controls is property persistence (or serialization), which allows the OLE control to read or write property values to and from a file or stream. A container application can use serialization to store a control's property values even after the application has destroyed the control. The property values of the OLE control can then be read from the file or stream when a new instance of the control is created at a later time.

Persistence of OLE Controls

PX_Blob	Exchanges a control property that stores Binary Large Object (**BLOB**) data.
PX_Bool	Exchanges a control property of type **BOOL**.
PX_Currency	Exchanges a control property of type **CY**.
PX_Double	Exchanges a control property of type **double**.
PX_Font	Exchanges a font property of a control.
PX_Float	Exchanges a control property of type **float**.
PX_IUnknown	Exchanges a control property of undefined type.
PX_Long	Exchanges a control property of type **long**.
PX_Picture	Exchanges a picture property of a control.
PX_Short	Exchanges a control property of type **short**.
PX_String	Exchanges a character string control property.

In addition, the **AfxOleTypeMatchGuid** global function is provided to test for a match between a **TYPEDESC** and a given **GUID**.

Macros, Global Functions, and Global Variables

AfxConnectionAdvise

BOOL AFXAPI AfxConnectionAdvise(LPUNKNOWN *pUnkSrc*, **REFIID** *iid*, **LPUNKNOWN** *pUnkSink*, **BOOL** *bRefCount*, **DWORD FAR*** *pdwCookie* **);**

pUnkSrc   A pointer to the object that calls the interface.

pUnkSink   A pointer to the object that implements the interface.

iid   The interface ID of the connection.

bRefCount   **TRUE** indicates that creating the connection should cause the reference count of *pUnkSink* to be incremented. **FALSE** indicates that the reference count should not be incremented.

pdwCookie   A pointer to a **DWORD** where a connection identifier is returned. This value should be passed as the *dwCookie* parameter to **AfxConnectionUnadvise** when disconnecting the connection.

Remarks   Call this function to establish a connection between a source, specified by *pUnkSrc*, and a sink, specified by *pUnkSink*.

Return Value   Nonzero if a connection was established; otherwise 0.

See Also   **AfxConnectionUnadvise**

AfxConnectionUnadvise

BOOL AFXAPI AfxConnectionUnadvise(LPUNKNOWN *pUnkSrc*, **REFIID** *iid*, **LPUNKNOWN** *pUnkSink*, **BOOL** *bRefCount*, **DWORD** *dwCookie* **);**

pUnkSrc   A pointer to the object that calls the interface.

pUnkSink   A pointer to the object that implements the interface.

iid   The interface ID of the connection point interface.

bRefCount   **TRUE** indicates that disconnecting the connection should cause the reference count of *pUnkSink* to be decremented. **FALSE** indicates that the reference count should not be decremented.

dwCookie   The connection identifier returned by **AfxConnectionAdvise**.

Remarks   Call this function to disconnect a connection between a source, specified by *pUnkSrc*, and a sink, specified by *pUnkSink*.

Return Value   Nonzero if a connection was disconnected; otherwise 0.

See Also   **AfxConnectionAdvise**

AfxOleRegisterControlClass

BOOL AfxOleRegisterControlClass(HINSTANCE *hInstance*, **REFCLSID** *clsid*, **LPCTSTR** *pszProgID*, **UINT** *idTypeName*, **UINT** *idBitmap*, **BOOL** *bInsertable*, **DWORD** *dwMiscStatus*, **REFGUID** *tlid*, **WORD** *wVerMajor*, **WORD** *wVerMinor* **);**

hInstance   The instance handle of the module associated with the control class.

clsid   The unique class ID of the control.

pszProgID   The unique program ID of the control.

idTypeName   The resource ID of the string that contains a user-readable type name for the control.

idBitmap   The resource ID of the bitmap used to represent the OLE control in a toolbar or palette.

bInsertable   Allows the control to be inserted from a container's Insert Object dialog box if set to **TRUE**; **FALSE** prevents the control from being inserted.

dwMiscStatus   Contains one or more status flags. For more information on the following flags, see **IOleObject::GetMiscStatus** in the *OLE 2 Programmer's Reference, Volume 1*, and Appendix D, "New MiscStatus Bits."

- **OLEMISC_RECOMPOSEONRESIZE**
- **OLEMISC_ONLYICONIC**
- **OLEMISC_INSERTNOTREPLACE**
- **OLEMISC_STATIC**
- **OLEMISC_CANTLINKINSIDE**
- **OLEMISC_CANLINKBYOLE1**
- **OLEMISC_ISLINKOBJECT**
- **OLEMISC_INSIDEOUT**
- **OLEMISC_ACTIVATEWHENVISABLE**
- **OLEMISC_RENDERINGISDEVICEINDEPENDENT**
- **OLEMISC_INVISIBLEATRUNTIME**
- **OLEMISC_ALWAYSRUN**
- **OLEMISC_ACTSLIKEBUTTON**

- **OLEMISC_ACTSLIKELABEL**
- **OLEMISC_NOUIACTIVATE**
- **OLEMISC_ALIGNABLE**
- **OLEMISC_IMEMODE**
- **OLEMISC_SIMPLEFRAME**
- **OLEMISC_SETCLIENTSITEFIRST**

tlid   The unique ID of the control class.

wVerMajor   The major version number of the control class.

wVerMinor   The minor version number of the control class.

Remarks   Registers the control class with the Windows registration database and allows the control to be used by containers that are OLE-control aware. This function updates the registry with the control's name and location on the system.

Return Value   Nonzero if the control class was registered; otherwise 0.

See Also   **AfxOleRegisterPropertyPageClass**, **AfxOleRegisterTypeLib**, **AfxOleUnregisterClass**, **AfxOleUnregisterTypeLib**

AfxOleRegisterPropertyPageClass

BOOL AFXAPI AfxOleRegisterPropertyPageClass(HINSTANCE *hInstance*, **REFCLSID** *clsid*, **UINT** *idTypeName* **);**

hInstance   The instance handle of the module associated with the property page class.

clsid   The unique class ID of the property page.

idTypeName   The resource ID of the string that contains a user-readable name for the property page.

Remarks   Registers the property page class with the Windows registration database and allows the property page to be used by other containers that are OLE-control aware. This function updates the registry with the property page name and its location on the system.

Return Value   Nonzero if the control class was registered; otherwise 0.

See Also   **AfxOleRegisterControlClass**, **AfxOleRegisterTypeLib**

AfxOleRegisterTypeLib

BOOL AfxOleRegisterTypeLib(HINSTANCE *hInstance*, **REFGUID** *tlid*, **LPCTSTR** *pszFileName* = **NULL, LPCTSTR** *pszHelpDir* = **NULL);**

hInstance   The instance handle of the application associated with the type library.

tlid   The unique ID of the type library.

pszFileName   Points to the optional filename of a localized type library (.TLB) file for the control.

pszHelpDir   The name of the directory where the help file for the type library may be found. If **NULL**, the help file is assumed to be in the same directory as the type library itself.

Remarks   Registers the type library with the Windows registration database and allows the type library to be used by other containers that are OLE-control aware. This function updates the registry with the type library name and its location on the system.

Return Value   Nonzero if the type library was registered; otherwise 0.

See Also   **AfxOleUnregisterTypeLib, AfxOleRegisterControlClass, AfxOleUnregisterClass**

AfxOleTypeMatchGuid

BOOL AfxOleTypeMatchGuid(LPTYPEINFO *pTypeInfo*, **TYPEDESC FAR*** *pTypeDesc*, **REFGUID** *guidType*, **ULONG** *cIndirectionLevels* **);**

pTypeInfo   Pointer to the type info object from which *pTypeDesc* was obtained.

pTypeDesc   Pointer to a **TYPEDESC** structure.

guidType   The unique ID of the type.

cIndirectionLevels   The number of indirection levels.

Remarks   Call this function to determine whether a type descriptor (obtained from the type info) describes the type indicated by *guidType* with the given number of levels of indirection.

Return Value   Nonzero if the match was successful; otherwise 0.

Example   To check whether `typedesc` refers to a pointer to a **IFontDisp**:

```
AfxOleTypeMatchGuid( ptypeinfo, &typedesc, IID_IFontDisp, 1);
```

where `IID_IFontDisp` refers to the type and the number of indirection levels is 1 (because the sample is checking for a simple pointer).

AfxOleUnregisterClass

BOOL AFXAPI AfxOleUnregisterClass(REFCLSID *clsID*, **LPCSTR** *pszProgID* **);**

clsID   The unique class ID of the control or property page.

pszProgID   The unique program ID of the control or property page.

Remarks   Removes the control or property page class entry from the Windows registration database.

Return Value   Nonzero if the control or property page class was successfully unregistered; otherwise 0.

See Also   **AfxOleRegisterPropertyPageClass**, **AfxOleRegisterControlClass**, **AfxOleRegisterTypeLib**

AfxOleUnregisterTypeLib

BOOL AFXAPI AfxOleUnregisterTypeLib(REFGUID *tlID* **);**

tlID   The unique ID of the type library.

Remarks   Call this function to remove the type library entry from the Windows registration database.

Return Value   Nonzero if the type library was successfully unregistered; otherwise 0.

See Also   **AfxOleUnregisterClass**, **AfxOleRegisterTypeLib**

AfxVerifyLicFile

BOOL AFXAPI AfxVerifyLicFile(HINSTANCE *hInstance*, **LPCTSTR** *pszLicFileName*, **LPCTCSTR** *pszLicFileContents*, **UINT** *cch* = **-1** **);**

hInstance   The instance handle of the DLL associated with the licensed control.

pszLicFileName   Points to a null-terminated character string containing the license filename.

pszLicFileContents   Points to a byte sequence that must match the sequence found at the beginning of the license file.

cch   Number of characters in *pbLicFileContents*.

Remarks   Call this function to verify that the license file named by *pszLicFileName* is valid for the OLE control. If *cch* is -1, this function uses:

```
_tcslen(pszLicFileContents)
```

Return Value   Nonzero if the license file exists and begins with the character sequence in *pszLicFileContents*; otherwise 0.

See Also   **COleObjectFactoryEx::VerifyUserLicense**

BEGIN_CONNECTION_MAP

BEGIN_CONNECTION_MAP(*theClass***,** *theBase* **)**

theClass   Specifies the name of the control class whose connection map this is.

theBase   Specifies the name of the base class of *theClass*.

Remarks   Each **COleControl**-derived class in your program can provide a connection map to specify connection points that your control will support. In the implementation (.CPP) file that defines the member functions for your class, start the connection map with the **BEGIN_CONNECTION_MAP** macro, then add macro entries for each of your connection points using the **CONNECTION_PART** macro. Finally, complete the connection map with the **END_CONNECTION_MAP** macro.

See Also   **BEGIN_CONNECTION_PART**, **DECLARE_CONNECTION_MAP**

BEGIN_CONNECTION_PART

BEGIN_CONNECTION_PART(*theClass***,** *localClass* **)**

theClass   Specifies the name of the control class whose connection point this is.

localClass   Specifies the name of the local class that implements the connection point.

Remarks   Use the **BEGIN_CONNECTION_PART** macro to begin the definition of additional connection points beyond the event and property notification connection points.

In the declaration (.H) file that defines the member functions for your class, start the connection point with the **BEGIN_CONNECTION_PART** macro, then add the **CONNECTION_IID** macro and any other member functions you wish to implement and complete the connection point map with the **END_CONNECTION_PART** macro.

See Also   **BEGIN_CONNECTION_MAP**, **DECLARE_CONNECTION_MAP**

BEGIN_EVENT_MAP

BEGIN_EVENT_MAP(*theClass***,** *baseClass* **)**

theClass   Specifies the name of the control class whose event map this is.

baseClass   Specifies the name of the base class of *theClass*.

Remarks   Use the **BEGIN_EVENT_MAP** macro to begin the definition of your event map.

In the implementation (.CPP) file that defines the member functions for your class, start the event map with the **BEGIN_EVENT_MAP** macro, then add macro entries for each of your events and complete the event map with the **END_EVENT_MAP** macro.

For more information on event maps and the **BEGIN_EVENT_MAP** macro, see Chapter 5, "Events," in the CDK *Programmer's Guide*.

See Also   **DECLARE_EVENT_MAP**, **END_EVENT_MAP**

BEGIN_OLEFACTORY

BEGIN_OLEFACTORY(*class_name*)

class_name   Specifies the name of the control class whose class factory this is.

Remarks   In the header file of your control class, use the **BEGIN_OLEFACTORY** macro to begin the declaration of your class factory. Declarations of class factory licensing functions should begin immediately after **BEGIN_OLEFACTORY**.

See Also   **END_OLEFACTORY, DECLARE_OLECREATE_EX**

BEGIN_PROPPAGEIDS

BEGIN_PROPPAGEIDS(*class_name*, *count*)

class_name   The name of the control class for which property pages are being specified.

count   The number of property pages used by the control class.

Remarks   Use the **BEGIN_PROPPAGEIDS** macro to begin the definition of your control's list of property page IDs.

In the implementation (.CPP) file that defines the member functions for your class, start the property page list with the **BEGIN_PROPPAGEIDS** macro, then add macro entries for each of your property pages and complete the property page list with the **END_PROPPAGEIDS** macro.

For more information on property pages, see Chapter 8, "Property Pages," in the CDK *Programmer's Guide*.

See Also   **END_PROPPAGEIDS, DECLARE_PROPPAGEIDS, PROPPAGEID**

CONNECTION_IID

CONNECTION_IID(*iid*)

iid   The interface ID of the interface called by the connection point.

Remarks   Use the **CONNECTION_IID** macro between the **BEGIN_CONNECTION_PART** and **END_CONNECTION_PART** macros to define an interface ID for a connection point supported by your OLE control.

The *iid* argument is an interface ID used to identify the interface that the connection point will call on its connected sinks. For example:

```
CONNECTION_IID(IID_ISinkInterface)
```

specifies a connection point that calls the ISinkInterface interface.

See Also   **BEGIN_CONNECTION_PART, DECLARE_CONNECTION_MAP**

CONNECTION_PART

CONNECTION_PART(*theClass*, *iid*, *localClass* **)**

theClass   Specifies the name of the control class whose connection point this is.

iid   The interface ID of the interface called by the the connection point.

localClass   Specifies the name of the local class that implements the connection point.

Remarks   Use the **CONNECTION_PART** macro to map a connection point for your OLE control to a specific interface ID.

For example:

```
BEGIN_CONNECTION_MAP(CSampleCtrl, COleControl)
    CONNECTION_PART(CSampleCtrl, IID_ISinkInterface, MyConnPt)
END_CONNECTION_MAP()
```

implements a connection map, with a connection point, that calls the IID_ISinkInterface interface.

See Also   **BEGIN_CONNECTION_PART, DECLARE_CONNECTION_MAP, BEGIN_CONNECTION_MAP, CONNECTION_IID**

DDP_CBIndex

void AFXAPI DDP_CBIndex(CDataExchange* *pDX*, **int** *id*, **int&** *member*, **LPCTSTR** *pszPropName* **);**

pDX   Pointer to a **CDataExchange** object. The framework supplies this object to establish the context of the data exchange, including its direction.

id   The resource ID of the combo box control associated with the control property specified by *pszPropName*.

member   The member variable associated with the property page control specified by *id* and the property specified by *pszPropName*.

pszPropName   The property name of the control property to be exchanged with the combo box control specified by *id*.

Remarks   Call this function in your property page's `DoDataExchange` function to synchronize the value of an integer property with the index of the current selection in a combo box on the property page. This function should be called before the corresponding **DDX_CBIndex** function call.

See Also   **DDP_CBString**, **DDP_Text**, **COleControl::DoPropExchange**

DDP_CBString

void AFXAPI DDP_CBString(CDataExchange* *pDX***, int** *id***, CString&** *member***, LPCTSTR** *pszPropName* **);**

pDX   Pointer to a **CDataExchange** object. The framework supplies this object to establish the context of the data exchange, including its direction.

id   The resource ID of the combo box control associated with the control property specified by *pszPropName*.

member   The member variable associated with the property page control specified by *id* and the property specified by *pszPropName*.

pszPropName   The property name of the control property to be exchanged with the combo box string specified by *id*.

Remarks   Call this function in your property page's `DoDataExchange` function to synchronize the value of a string property with the current selection in a combo box on the property page. This function should be called before the corresponding **DDX_CBString** function call.

See Also   **DDP_CBStringExact**, **DDP_CBIndex**, **COleControl::DoPropExchange**

DDP_CBStringExact

void AFXAPI DDP_CBStringExact(CDataExchange* *pDX***, int** *id***, CString&** *member***, LPCTSTR** *pszPropName* **);**

pDX   Pointer to a **CDataExchange** object. The framework supplies this object to establish the context of the data exchange, including its direction.

id   The resource ID of the combo box control associated with the control property specified by *pszPropName*.

member   The member variable associated with the property page control specified by *id* and the property specified by *pszPropName*.

pszPropName   The property name of the control property to be exchanged with the combo box string specified by *id*.

Remarks   Call this function in your property page's `DoDataExchange` function to synchronize the value of a string property with the current selection in a combo box on the property page. This function should be called before the corresponding **DDX_CBStringExact** function call.

See Also   **DDP_CBString, DDP_CBIndex, COleControl::DoPropExchange**

DDP_Check

void AFXAPI DDP_Check(CDataExchange**pDX***, int** *id***, int &***member***, LPCSTR** *pszPropName* **);**

pDX   Pointer to a **CDataExchange** object. The framework supplies this object to establish the context of the data exchange, including its direction.

id   The resource ID of the check box control associated with the control property specified by *pszPropName*.

member   The member variable associated with the property page control specified by *id* and the property specified by *pszPropName*.

pszPropName   The property name of the control property to be exchanged with the check box control specified by *id*.

Remarks   Call this function in your property page's `DoDataExchange` function to synchronize the value of the property with the associated property page check box control. This function should be called before the corresponding **DDX_Check** function call.

See Also   **DDP_Radio, DDP_Text, COleControl::DoPropExchange**

DDP_LBIndex

void AFXAPI DDP_LBIndex(CDataExchange* *pDX***, int** *id***, int&** *member***, LPCTSTR** *pszPropName* **);**

pDX   Pointer to a **CDataExchange** object. The framework supplies this object to establish the context of the data exchange, including its direction.

id   The resource ID of the list box control associated with the control property specified by *pszPropName*.

member   The member variable associated with the property page control specified by *id* and the property specified by *pszPropName*.

pszPropName   The property name of the control property to be exchanged with the list box string specified by *id*.

Remarks   Call this function in your property page's `DoDataExchange` function to synchronize the value of an integer property with the index of the current selection in a list box on the property page. This function should be called before the corresponding **DDX_LBIndex** function call.

See Also   **DDP_LBString, DDP_CBIndex, COleControl::DoPropExchange**

DDP_LBString

void **AFXAPI DDP_LBString(CDataExchange*** *pDX***, int** *id***, CString&** *member***, LPCTSTR** *pszPropName* **);**

pDX   Pointer to a **CDataExchange** object. The framework supplies this object to establish the context of the data exchange, including its direction.

id   The resource ID of the list box control associated with the control property specified by *pszPropName*.

member   The member variable associated with the property page control specified by *id* and the property specified by *pszPropName*.

pszPropName   The property name of the control property to be exchanged with the list box string specified by *id*.

Remarks   Call this function in your property page's `DoDataExchange` function to synchronize the value of a string property with the current selection in a list box on the property page. This function should be called before the corresponding **DDX_LBString** function call.

See Also   **DDP_LBStringExact, DDP_LBIndex, COleControl::DoPropExchange**

DDP_LBStringExact

void **AFXAPI DDP_LBStringExact(CDataExchange*** *pDX***, int** *id***, CString&** *member***, LPCTSTR** *pszPropName* **);**

pDX   Pointer to a **CDataExchange** object. The framework supplies this object to establish the context of the data exchange, including its direction.

id   The resource ID of the list box control associated with the control property specified by *pszPropName*.

member   The member variable associated with the property page control specified by *id* and the property specified by *pszPropName*.

pszPropName   The property name of the control property to be exchanged with the list box string specified by *id*.

Remarks   Call this function in your property page's `DoDataExchange` function to synchronize the value of a string property with the current selection in a list box on the property page. This function should be called before the corresponding **DDX_LBStringExact** function call.

See Also   **DDP_LBString**, **DDP_LBIndex**, **COleControl::DoPropExchange**

DDP_Radio

void AFXAPI DDP_Radio(CDataExchange**pDX***, int** *id***, int &***member***, LPCTSTR** *pszPropName* **);**

pDX   Pointer to a **CDataExchange** object. The framework supplies this object to establish the context of the data exchange, including its direction.

id   The resource ID of the radio button control associated with the control property specified by *pszPropName*.

member   The member variable associated with the property page control specified by *id* and the property specified by *pszPropName*.

pszPropName   The property name of the control property to be exchanged with the radio button control specified by *id*.

Remarks   Call this function in your control's `DoPropExchange` function to synchronize the value of the property with the associated property page radio button control. This function should be called before the corresponding **DDX_Radio** function call.

See Also   **DDP_Check**, **DDP_Text**, **COleControl::DoPropExchange**

DDP_Text

void AFXAPI DDP_Text(CDataExchange**pDX***, int** *id***, BYTE &***member***, LPCTSTR** *pszPropName* **);**

void AFXAPI DDP_Text(CDataExchange**pDX***, int** *id***, int &***member***, LPCTSTR** *pszPropName* **);**

void AFXAPI DDP_Text(CDataExchange**pDX***, int** *id***, UINT &***member***, LPCTSTR** *pszPropName* **);**

void AFXAPI DDP_Text(CDataExchange**pDX***, int** *id***, long &***member***, LPCTSTR** *pszPropName* **);**

void AFXAPI DDP_Text(CDataExchange**pDX***, int** *id***, DWORD &***member***, LPCTSTR** *pszPropName* **);**

void AFXAPI DDP_Text(CDataExchange**pDX***, int** *id***, float &***member***, LPCTSTR** *pszPropName* **);**

void AFXAPI DDP_Text(CDataExchange*_pDX_, int _id_, double &_member_, LPCTSTR _pszPropName_);

void AFXAPI DDP_Text(CDataExchange*_pDX_, int _id_, CString &_member_, LPCTSTR _pszPropName_);

pDX   Pointer to a **CDataExchange** object. The framework supplies this object to establish the context of the data exchange, including its direction.

_id_   The resource ID of the control associated with the control property specified by _pszPropName_.

member   The member variable associated with the property page control specified by _id_ and the property specified by _pszPropName_.

pszPropName   The property name of the control property to be exchanged with the control specified by _id_.

Remarks   Call this function in your control's DoDataExchange function to synchronize the value of the property with the associated property page control. This function should be called before the corresponding **DDX_Text** function call.

See Also   **DDP_Check, DDP_Radio, COleControl::DoPropExchange**

DECLARE_CONNECTION_MAP

DECLARE_CONNECTION_MAP( )

Remarks   Each **COleControl**-derived class in your program can provide a connection map to specify additional connection points that your control supports.

If your control supports additional points, use the **DECLARE_CONNECTION_MAP** macro at the end of your class declaration. Then, in the .CPP file that defines the member functions for the class, use the **BEGIN_CONNECTION_MAP** macro, **CONNECTION_PART** macros for each of the control's connection points, and the **END_CONNECTION_MAP** macro to declare the end of the connection map.

See Also   **BEGIN_CONNECTION_PART, BEGIN_CONNECTION_MAP, CONNECTION_IID**

DECLARE_EVENT_MAP

DECLARE_EVENT_MAP( )

Remarks   Each **COleControl**-derived class in your program can provide an event map to specify the events your control will fire. Use the **DECLARE_EVENT_MAP** macro at the end of your class declaration. Then, in the .CPP file that defines the member functions for the class, use the **BEGIN_EVENT_MAP** macro, macro entries for each of the control's events and the **END_EVENT_MAP** macro to declare the end of the event list.

For more information on event maps, see Chapter 5, "Events," in the CDK *Programmer's Guide*.

See Also   **BEGIN_EVENT_MAP, END_EVENT_MAP, EVENT_CUSTOM, EVENT_CUSTOM_ID**

DECLARE_OLECREATE_EX

DECLARE_OLECREATE_EX(*class_name* **)**

class_name   The name of the control class.

Remarks   Declares a class factory and the **GetClassID** member function of your control class. Use this macro in the control class header file for a control that does not support licensing.

Note that this macro serves the same purpose as the following code sample:

```
BEGIN_OLEFACTORY(CSampleCtrl)
END_OLEFACTORY(CSampleCtrl)
```

See Also   **BEGIN_OLEFACTORY, END_OLEFACTORY**

DECLARE_OLETYPELIB

DECLARE_OLETYPELIB(*class_name* **)**

class_name   The name of the control class related to the type library.

Remarks   Declares the **GetTypeLib** member function of your control class. Use this macro in the control class header file.

See Also   **IMPLEMENT_OLETYPELIB**

DECLARE_PROPPAGEIDS

DECLARE_PROPPAGEIDS(*class_name* **)**

class_name   The name of the control class that owns the property pages.

Remarks   An OLE control can provide a list of property pages to display its properties. Use the **DECLARE_PROPPAGEIDS** macro at the end of your class declaration. Then, in the .CPP file that defines the member functions for the class, use the **BEGIN_PROPPAGEIDS** macro, macro entries for each of your control's property pages, and the **END_PROPPAGEIDS** macro to declare the end of the property page list.

For more information on property pages, see Chapter 8, "Property Pages," in the CDK *Programmer's Guide*.

See Also   **BEGIN_PROPPAGEIDS, END_PROPPAGEIDS**

END_CONNECTION_MAP

END_CONNECTION_MAP( )

Remarks   Use the **END_CONNECTION_MAP** macro to end the definition of your connection map.

See Also   **BEGIN_CONNECTION_MAP, DECLARE_CONNECTION_MAP**

END_CONNECTION_PART

END_CONNECTION_PART(*localClass* **)**

localClass   Specifies the name of the local class that implements the connection point.

Remarks   Use the **END_CONNECTION_PART** macro to end the declaration of your connection point.

See Also   **BEGIN_CONNECTION_PART, DECLARE_CONNECTION_MAP**

END_EVENT_MAP

END_EVENT_MAP( )

Remarks   Use the **END_EVENT_MAP** macro to end the definition of your event map.

See Also   **DECLARE_EVENT_MAP, BEGIN_EVENT_MAP**

END_OLEFACTORY

END_OLEFACTORY(*class_name* **)**

class_name   The name of the control class whose class factory this is.

Remarks   Use the **END_OLEFACTORY** macro to end the declaration of your control's class factory.

See Also   **BEGIN_OLEFACTORY, DECLARE_OLECREATE_EX**

END_PROPPAGEIDS

END_PROPPAGEIDS(*class_name* **)**

class_name   The name of the control class that owns the property page.

Remarks   Use the **END_PROPPAGEIDS** macro to end the definition of your property page ID list.

See Also   **DECLARE_PROPPAGEIDS**, **BEGIN_PROPPAGEIDS**

EVENT_CUSTOM

EVENT_CUSTOM(*pszName*, *pfnFire*, *vtsParams* **)**

pszName   The name of the event.

pfnFire   The name of the event firing function.

vtsParams   A space-separated list of one or more constants specifying the function's parameter list.

Remarks   Use the **EVENT_CUSTOM** macro to define an event-map entry for a custom event.

The *vtsParams* parameter is a space-separated list of values from the **VTS_** constants. One or more of these values separated by spaces (not commas) specifies the function's parameter list. For example:

```
VTS_COLOR VTS_FONT
```

specifies a list containing a short integer followed by a **BOOL**.

The **VTS_** constants and their meanings are as follows:

Symbol	Parameter Type
VTS_COLOR	**OLE_COLOR**
VTS_FONT	**IFontDispatch***

Symbol	Parameter Type
VTS_HANDLE	HANDLE
VTS_OPTEXCLUSIVE	OLE_OPTEXCLUSIVE
VTS_PICTURE	IPictureDisp*
VTS_TRISTATE	OLE_TRISTATE
VTS_XPOS_PIXELS	OLE_XPOS_PIXELS
VTS_YPOS_PIXELS	OLE_YPOS_PIXELS
VTS_XSIZE_PIXELS	OLE_XSIZE_PIXELS
VTS_YSIZE_PIXELS	OLE_YSIZE_PIXELS
VTS_XPOS_HIMETRIC	OLE_XPOS_HIMETRIC
VTS_YPOS_HIMETRIC	OLE_YPOS_HIMETRIC
VTS_XSIZE_HIMETRIC	OLE_XSIZE_HIMETRIC
VTS_YSIZE_HIMETRIC	OLE_YSIZE_HIMETRIC

See Also   **EVENT_CUSTOM_ID, DECLARE_EVENT_MAP**

EVENT_CUSTOM_ID

EVENT_CUSTOM_ID(*pszName*, *dispid*, *pfnFire*, *vtsParams* **)**

pszName   The name of the event.

dispid   The dispatch ID used by the control when firing the event.

pfnFire   The name of the event firing function.

vtsParams   A variable list of parameters passed to the control container when the event is fired.

Remarks   Use the **EVENT_CUSTOM_ID** macro to define an event firing function for a custom event belonging to the dispatch ID specified by *dispid*.

The *vtsParams* argument is a space-separated list of values from the **VTS_** constants. One or more of these values separated by spaces (not commas) specifies the function's parameter list. For example:

```
VTS_COLOR VTS_FONT
```

specifies a list containing a short integer followed by a **BOOL**.

For a list of the **VTS_** constants, see **EVENT_CUSTOM**.

See Also   **EVENT_CUSTOM**

IMPLEMENT_OLECREATE_EX

IMPLEMENT_OLECREATE_EX(*class_name*, *external_name*, *l*, *w1*, *w2*, *b1*, *b2*, *b3*, *b4*, *b5*, *b6*, *b7*, *b8*)

class_name   The name of the control property page class.

external_name   The object name exposed to applications.

l, *w1*, *w2*, *b1*, *b2*, *b3*, *b4*, *b5*, *b6*, *b7*, *b8*   Components of the class's **CLSID**.

Remarks   Implements your control's property page class factory and the **GetClassID** member function of your control class. This macro must appear in the implementation file for any control class that uses the **DECLARE_OLECREATE_EX** macro or the **BEGIN_OLEFACTORY** and **END_OLEFACTORY** macros. The external name is the identifier of the OLE control that is exposed to other applications. Containers use this name to request an object of this control class.

See Also   **DECLARE_OLECREATE_EX**, **BEGIN_OLEFACTORY**, **END_OLEFACTORY**

IMPLEMENT_OLETYPELIB

IMPLEMENT_OLETYPELIB(*class_name*, *tlid*, *wVerMajor*, *wVerMinor*)

class_name   The name of the control class related to the type library.

tlid   The ID number of the type library.

wVerMajor   The type library major version number.

wVerMinor   The type library minor version number.

Remarks   Implements the control's **GetTypeLib** member function. This macro must appear in the implementation file for any control class that uses the **DECLARE_OLETYPELIB** macro.

See Also   **DECLARE_OLETYPELIB**

ON_OLEVERB

ON_OLEVERB(*idsVerbName*, *memberFxn*)

idsVerbName   The string resource ID of the verb's name.

memberFxn   The function called by the framework when the verb is invoked.

Remarks   This macro defines a message map entry that maps a custom verb to a specific member function of your control.

The resource editor can be used to create custom verb names that are added to your string table.

The function prototype for *memberFxn* is

BOOL memberFxn(LPMSG *lpMsg*, **HWND** *hWndParent*, **LPCRECT** *lpRect* **);**

The values of the *lpMsg*, *hWndParent*, and *lpRect* parameters are taken from the corresponding parameters of the **IOleObject::DoVerb** member function.

See Also   **ON_STDOLEVERB**

ON_STDOLEVERB

ON_STDOLEVERB(*iVerb*, *memberFxn* **)**

iVerb   The standard verb index for the verb being overridden.

memberFxn   The function called by the framework when the verb is invoked.

Remarks   Use this macro to override the default behavior of a standard verb.

The standard verb index is of the form **OLEIVERB_**, followed by an action. **OLEIVERB_SHOW**, **OLEIVERB_HIDE,** and **OLEIVERB_UIACTIVATE** are some examples of standard verbs.

See **ON_OLEVERB** for a description of the function prototype to be used as the *memberFxn* parameter.

See Also   **ON_OLEVERB**

PROPPAGEID

PROPPAGEID(*clsid* **)**

clsid   The unique class ID of a property page.

Remarks   Use this macro to add a property page for use by your OLE control. All **PROPPAGEID** macros must be placed between the **BEGIN_PROPPAGEIDS** and **END_PROPPAGEIDS** macros in your control's implementation file.

See Also   **BEGIN_PROPPAGEIDS**, **END_PROPPAGEIDS**

PX_Blob

BOOL PX_Blob(CPropExchange* *pPX*, **LPCTSTR** *pszPropName*, **void*&** *pvBlob*, **void*** *pvBlobDefault* = **NULL** **);**

pPX   Pointer to the **CPropertyExchange** object (typically passed as a parameter to **DoPropExchange**).

pszPropName   The name of the property being exchanged.

pvBlob   Reference to the variable where the property is stored (typically a member variable of your class).

pvBlobDefault   Default value for the property.

Remarks

Call this function within your control's `DoPropExchange` member function to serialize or initialize a property that stores Binary Large Object (**BLOB**) data. The property's value will be read from or written to the variable referenced by *pvBlob*, as appropriate. This variable should be initialized to **NULL** before initially calling **PX_Blob** for the first time (typically, this can be done in the control's constructor). If *pvBlobDefault* is specified, it will be used as the property's default value. This value is used if, for any reason, the control's initialization or serialization process fails.

Note that **PX_Blob** will allocate memory, using the **new** operator, when loading **BLOB**-type properties. Therefore, the destructor of your control should call **delete** on any **BLOB**-type property pointers to free up any memory allocated to your control.

Return Value

Nonzero if the exchange was successful; 0 if unsuccessful.

See Also

COleControl::DoPropExchange

PX_Bool

BOOL PX_Bool(CPropExchange* *pPX*, **LPCTSTR** *pszPropName*, **BOOL&** *bValue*);

BOOL PX_Bool(CPropExchange* *pPX*, **LPCTSTR** *pszPropName*, **BOOL&** *bValue*, **BOOL** *bDefault*);

pPX   Pointer to the **CPropertyExchange** object (typically passed as a parameter to **DoPropExchange**).

pszPropName   The name of the property being exchanged.

bValue   Reference to the variable where the property is stored (typically a member variable of your class).

bDefault   Default value for the property.

Remarks

Call this function within your control's `DoPropExchange` member function to serialize or initialize a property of type **BOOL**. The property's value will be read from or written to the variable referenced by *bValue*, as appropriate. If *bDefault* is specified, it will be used as the property's default value. This value is used if, for any reason, the control's serialization process fails.

Return Value   Nonzero if the exchange was successful; 0 if unsuccessful.

See Also   **COleControl::DoPropExchange**

PX_Currency

BOOL PX_Currency(CPropExchange* *pPX*, **LPCTSTR** *pszPropName*, **CY&** *cyValue*);

BOOL PX_Currency(CPropExchange* *pPX*, **LPCTSTR** *pszPropName*, **CY&** *cyValue*, **CY** *cyDefault*);

pPX   Pointer to the **CPropertyExchange** object (typically passed as a parameter to **DoPropExchange**).

pszPropName   The name of the property being exchanged.

cyValue   Reference to the variable where the property is stored (typically a member variable of your class).

cyDefault   Default value for the property.

Remarks   Call this function within your control's DoPropExchange member function to serialize or initialize a property of type currency. The property's value will be read from or written to the variable referenced by *cyValue*, as appropriate. If *cyDefault* is specified, it will be used as the property's default value. This value is used if, for any reason, the control's serialization process fails.

Return Value   Nonzero if the exchange was successful; 0 if unsuccessful.

See Also   **COleControl::DoPropExchange**

PX_Double

BOOL PX_Double(CPropExchange* *pPX*, **LPCTSTR** *pszPropName*, **double&** *doubleValue*);

BOOL PX_Double(CPropExchange* *pPX*, **LPCTSTR** *pszPropName*, **double&** *doubleValue*, **double** *doubleDefault*);

pPX   Pointer to the **CPropertyExchange** object (typically passed as a parameter to **DoPropExchange**).

pszPropName   The name of the property being exchanged.

doubleValue   Reference to the variable where the property is stored (typically a member variable of your class).

doubleDefault   Default value for the property.

Remarks   Call this function within your control's `DoPropExchange` member function to serialize or initialize a property of type **double**. The property's value is read from or written to the variable referenced by *doubleValue*, as appropriate. If *doubleDefault* is specified, it will be used as the property's default value. This value is used if, for any reason, the control's serialization process fails.

Return Value   Nonzero if the exchange was successful; 0 if unsuccessful.

See Also   **COleControl::DoPropExchange, PX_Float, PX_Short**

PX_Float

BOOL PX_Float(CPropExchange* *pPX*, **LPCTSTR** *pszPropName*, **float&** *floatValue* **);**

BOOL PX_Double(CPropExchange* *pPX*, **LPCTSTR** *pszPropName*, **float&** *floatValue*, **double** *floatDefault* **);**

pPX   Pointer to the **CPropertyExchange** object (typically passed as a parameter to **DoPropExchange**).

pszPropName   The name of the property being exchanged.

floatValue   Reference to the variable where the property is stored (typically a member variable of your class).

floatDefault   Default value for the property.

Remarks   Call this function within your control's `DoPropExchange` member function to serialize or initialize a property of type **float**. The property's value is read from or written to the variable referenced by *floatValue*, as appropriate. If *floatDefault* is specified, it will be used as the property's default value. This value is used if, for any reason, the control's serialization process fails.

Return Value   Nonzero if the exchange was successful; 0 if unsuccessful.

See Also   **COleControl::DoPropExchange, PX_Double, PX_String**

PX_Font

BOOL PX_Font(CPropExchange* *pPX*, **LPCTSTR** *pszPropName*, **CFontHolder&** *font*, **const FONTDESC FAR*** *pFontDesc* = **NULL**, **LPFONTDISP** *pFontDispAmbient* = **NULL** **);**

pPX   Pointer to the **CPropertyExchange** object (typically passed as a parameter to **DoPropExchange**).

pszPropName   The name of the property being exchanged.

font A reference to a **CFontHolder** object that contains the font property.

pFontDesc A pointer to a **FONTDESC** structure containing the values to use in intializing the default state of the font property, in the case where *pFontDispAmbient* is **NULL**.

pFontDispAmbient A pointer to the **IFontDisp** interface of a font to use in initializing the default state of the font property.

Remarks

Call this function within your control's `DoPropExchange` member function to serialize or initialize a property of type font. The property's value is read from or written to *font*, a **CFontHolder** reference, when appropriate. If *pFontDesc* and *pFontDispAmbient* are specified, they are used for initializing the property's default value, when needed. These values are used if, for any reason, the control's serialization process fails. Typically, you pass **NULL** for *pFontDesc* and the ambient value returned by **COleControl::AmbientFont()** for *pFontDispAmbient*. Note that the font object returned by **COleControl::AmbientFont** must be released by a call to the **IFontDisp::Release** member function.

Return Value

Nonzero if the exchange was successful; 0 if unsuccessful.

See Also

COleControl::DoPropExchange, **COleControl::AmbientFont**

PX_IUnknown

BOOL PX_IUnknown(CPropExchange* *pPX*, **LPCTSTR** *pszPropName*, **LPUNKNOWN&** *pUnk*, **REFIID** *iid*, **LPUNKNOWN** *pUnkDefault* = **NULL**);

pPX Pointer to the **CPropertyExchange** object (typically passed as a parameter to **DoPropExchange**).

pszPropName The name of the property being exchanged.

pUnk Reference to a variable containing the interface of the object that represents the value of the property.

iid An interface ID indicating which interface of the property object is used by the control.

pUnkDefault Default value for the property.

Remarks

Call this function within your control's `DoPropExchange` member function to serialize or initialize a property represented by an object having an **IUnknown**-derived interface. The property's value is read from or written to the variable referenced by *pUnk*, as appropriate. If *pUnkDefault* is specified, it will be used as the property's default value. This value is used if, for any reason, the control's serialization process fails.

Return Value

Nonzero if the exchange was successful; 0 if unsuccessful.

COleControl::DoPropExchange

PX_Long

BOOL PX_Long(CPropExchange* *pPX*, LPCTSTR *pszPropName*, **long&** *lValue*);

BOOL PX_Long(CPropExchange* *pPX*, LPCTSTR *pszPropName*, **long&** *lValue*, **long** *lDefault*);

pPX   Pointer to the **CPropertyExchange** object (typically passed as a parameter to **DoPropExchange**).

pszPropName   The name of the property being exchanged.

lValue   Reference to the variable where the property is stored (typically a member variable of your class).

lDefault   Default value for the property.

Remarks   Call this function within your control's DoPropExchange member function to serialize or initialize a property of type **long**. The property's value is read from or written to the variable referenced by *lValue*, as appropriate. If *lDefault* is specified, it will be used as the property's default value. This value is used if, for any reason, the control's serialization process fails.

Return Value   Nonzero if the exchange was successful; 0 if unsuccessful.

See Also   **COleControl::DoPropExchange**

PX_Picture

BOOL PX_Picture(CPropExchange* *pPX*, LPCTSTR *pszPropName*, **CPictureHolder&** *pict*);

BOOL PX_Picture(CPropExchange* *pPX*, LPCTSTR *pszPropName*, **CPictureHolder&** *pict*, **CPictureHolder&** *pictDefault*);

pPX   Pointer to the **CPropertyExchange** object (typically passed as a parameter to **DoPropExchange**).

pszPropName   The name of the property being exchanged.

pict   Reference to the variable where the property is stored (typically a member variable of your class).

pictDefault   Default value for the property.

Remarks   Call this function within your control's DoPropExchange member function to serialize or initialize a picture property of your control. The property's value is read from or written to the variable referenced by *pict*, as appropriate. If *pictDefault* is specified, it will be used as the property's default value. This value is used if, for any reason, the control's serialization process fails.

Return Value   Nonzero if the exchange was successful; 0 if unsuccessful.

See Also   **COleControl::DoPropExchange**

PX_Short

BOOL PX_Short(CPropExchange* *pPX***, LPCTSTR** *pszPropName***, short&** *sValue* **);**

BOOL PX_Short(CPropExchange* *pPX***, LPCTSTR** *pszPropName***, short&** *sValue***, short** *sDefault***);**

pPX   Pointer to the **CPropertyExchange** object (typically passed as a parameter to **DoPropExchange**).

pszPropName   The name of the property being exchanged.

sValue   Reference to the variable where the property is stored (typically a member variable of your class).

sDefault   Default value for the property.

Remarks   Call this function within your control's `DoPropExchange` member function to serialize or initialize a property of type **short**. The property's value is read from or written to the variable referenced by *sValue*, as appropriate. If *sDefault* is specified, it will be used as the property's default value. This value is used if, for any reason, the control's serialization process fails.

Return Value   Nonzero if the exchange was successful; 0 if unsuccessful.

See Also   **COleControl::DoPropExchange**

PX_String

BOOL PX_String(CPropExchange* *pPX***, LPCTSTR** *pszPropName***, CString&** *strValue* **);**

BOOL PX_String(CPropExchange* *pPX***, LPCSTR** *pszPropName***, CString&** *strValue***, CString** *strDefault* **);**

pPX   Pointer to the **CPropertyExchange** object (typically passed as a parameter to **DoPropExchange**).

pszPropName   The name of the property being exchanged.

strValue   Reference to the variable where the property is stored (typically a member variable of your class).

strDefault   Default value for the property.

Remarks   Call this function within your control's `DoPropExchange` member function to serialize or initialize a character string property. The property's value is read from or written to the variable referenced by *strValue*, as appropriate. If *strDefault* is specified, it will be used as the property's default value. This value is used if, for any reason, the control's serialization process fails.

Return Value   Nonzero if the exchange was successful; 0 if unsuccessful.

See Also   **COleControl::DoPropExchange**

P A R T   4

Appendixes

A P P E N D I X   A

VBX Control Migration

For developers with existing VBX controls, the CDK provides a way to convert existing VBX controls to the OLE 2 Custom Control format using the VBX template tool, found in ControlWizard. The VBX template tool helps you migrate your VBX custom control to an OLE control. The template tool uses model information in the .VBX file and creates a Visual C++ project file, as well as source code files for creating the OLE control. These files can be compiled and linked to produce a working skeleton for the OLE control.

Once this skeleton is built and tested, the next step is to take code from your VBX source files and place it in the appropriate areas of the generated OLE source files. The transplanted code will probably require some degree of modification to work in the new source code files.

This appendix explains:

- Preparing your .VBX source code files for conversion.
- Using the VBX template tool.
- What gets converted.
- Building and testing the skeleton of your OLE control.

Preparing the VBX Custom Control

In order for the VBX template tool to properly translate the VBX control, you must expose the VBX control's model information to the template builder. If your VBX source code does not already define the function **VBGetModelInfo**, you must define the function and rebuild your VBX before you can use the template tool. This function should be defined as an exported function.

Before creating the **VBGetModelInfo** function, you must first define a **MODELINFO** structure containing a specific Visual Basic version number, and a **NULL**-terminated array of **MODEL** structures. The CIRC3 custom control sample defines the **MODELINFO** structure as follows:

```
LPMODEL modellistCircle[] =
    {
    &modelCircle,
    NULL
    };
```

Note Remember to NULL-terminate the array of model pointers.

```
MODELINFO modelinfoCircle =
    {
    VB_VERSION,          // VB version being used
    modellistCircle      // MODEL list
    };
```

Note If your .VBX file provides different models to support earlier versions, you should create similar **MODELINFO** structures to point to those models. The CIRC3 custom control, for example, also defines ModelinfoCircle_VB1 and ModelinfoCircle_VB2 structures.

Once you have defined the **MODELINFO** structure(s), you can define the **VBGetModelInfo** function in your source code. The CIRC3 custom control sample defines the function:

```
LPMODELINFO FAR PASCAL _export VBGetModelInfo
(
    USHORT usVersion
)
{
    if (usVersion <= VB100_VERSION)
        return &modelinfoCircle_Vb1;

    if (usVersion <= VB200_VERSION)
        return &modelinfoCircle_Vb2;
    else
        return &modelinfoCircle;
}
```

Running the VBX Template Tool

After your VBX control has been built with the **VBGetModelInfo** function, as described above, you are ready to run the VBX template tool on it. Figure A.1 shows the dialog box.

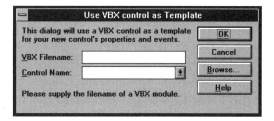

Figure A.1   The Use VBX control as Template dialog box

▶ **To run the VBX template tool**

1. Open the ControlWizard dialog box by choosing ControlWizard from the Tools menu.

2. When the MFC ControlWizard dialog box appears, change to the desired drive and directory and enter a project name. ControlWizard will automatically create a new subdirectory with the same name as the project.

3. Choose the Control Options button. When the Control Options dialog box appears, choose the Use VBX Control as Template check box.

4. Choose the Select VBX Control button.

5. When the Use VBX Control as Template dialog box appears, type the .VBX file name, including the drive and directory path. Alternatively, you can use the Browse button to locate and select your .VBX file. All control names defined in the .VBX file are displayed in the control name drop down list. Select the desired control name from the drop down list.

Note If you select a .VBX file that does not properly export the model information (as described above), Visual C++ may crash at this point.

---

6. Choose OK twice to close the Use VBX Control as Template dialog box and the Control Options dialog box. Choose OK on the MFC ControlWizard dialog box to prepare to create the template.

7. When the New Control Information dialog appears, a summary of the generated files are displayed. Choose the Create button to create all the files for the OLE control.

8. When the template tool is finished, your project directory should contain the following files (these files assume CIRC3.VBX was used as the project name):

   - CIRC3.CLW
   - CIRC3.CPP
   - CIRC332.DEF
   - CIRC3.DEF
   - CIRC3.H

- CIRC3.ICO
- CIRC3.MAK
- CIRC332.MAK
- MAKEFILE
- CIRC3.ODL
- CIRC3.RC
- CIRC3.RC2
- CIRC3CTL.BMP
- CIRC3CTL.CPP
- CIRC3CTL.H
- CIRC3PPG.CPP
- CIRC3PPG.H
- README.TXT
- RESOURCE.H
- STDAFX.CPP
- STDAFX.H

In addition, a sub-directory for the Type library file is created. If you are using the 16-bit version of the CDK, it is called TLB16. If you are using the 32-bit version of the CDK, it is called OBJDU.

The README.TXT file contains a summary description of each file created by the VBX template tool. These files are all that is required to build a complete working skeleton of the new OLE control.

What Gets Converted

The template generated by the VBX template tool is similar to the "blank" template that is generated when you use ControlWizard to create a new control, with the following differences:

Custom Properties and Events

Custom properties and events in your VBX are provided in the template as stub functions. In order to make these properties and events functional, you need to port the implementation code from your VBX source files into the appropriate files in the new control template. These places are indicated by comments of the following type in the template's source code files:

```
// TODO: Initialize your control's instance data here.
```

Stock Properties and Events

Most of the standard properties and events in your .VBX will be converted to fully implemented stock properties and events in the template's source code.

Stock properties supported by the current version of the tool include:

- BorderStyle
- Enabled
- Font
- Caption
- Text
- ForeColor
- BackColor
- hWnd

Stock events supported by the current version of the tool include:

- Click
- DblClick
- KeyDown
- KeyPress
- KeyUp
- MouseDown
- MouseMove
- MouseUp

Note A number properties not mentioned above, that were formerly "standard" in the .VBX Control model, are automatically supported by OLE as standard "extender" properties (e.g., Left, Top, Height, Width); therefore, these properties are not needed in an OLE control, and are not converted by the VBX template tool.

Currently Unimplemented Properties and Events

Some stock properties of the VBX model are not supported:

- DragIcon
- DragMode
- MouseCursor
- MousePointer

Some stock events of the VBX model are not supported:

- DragDrop
- DragOver
- LinkOpen
- LinkClose
- LinkError
- LinkNotify

Building and Testing the OLE Control Skeleton

After ControlWizard generates a basic framework for your VBX control you should build and test the control to familiarize yourself with the behavior of an OLE control. The following sections describe this process and demonstrate how to test your new OLE control using Test Container.

Creating the Type Library for the OLE Control

Before you can compile and link the control template, you must create a type library. This will be based on the information contained in the Object Description Library (.ODL) file created by the porting tool.

Note If you are using the 32-bit version of the CDK, the type library is automatically generated by the control's makefile.

▶ **To create the type library**

1. Load the project make file that you generated by running the VBX template tool.
2. From the Tools menu, choose Make TypeLib. MKTYPLIB.EXE creates a type library based on the .ODL file in the project. After MKTYPLIB.EXE runs successfully, the resulting *.TLB file is automatically added to your project. The information in this .TLB file will be built into your .DLL as a resource.

Compiling, Linking, and Registering the OLE Control Skeleton

After creating the Type Library, you can build the skeleton control by choosing Build from the Visual C++ Project menu.

When the project has built successfully, you must register the new control before you can test it. Choose Register Control from the Tools menu. A message box appears, indicating that the control was successfully registered.

Testing the OLE Control Skeleton

Once compiled and linked, you can immediately test the functionality of the new control skeleton using the Test Container.

▶ **To test your new OLE control skeleton**

1. From the Tools menu, choose the Test Container command.

2. From the Edit menu of Test Container, choose the Insert OLE Control... command.

3. In the Insert OLE Control dialog box, select the desired control and choose OK. The control will then appear in the control container.

Note If your control is not listed in the Insert OLE Control dialog box, make sure you have registered it with the Register Control command from the Tools menu.

At this point you can test your control's properties or events.

▶ **To test properties**

1. From the Edit menu, choose the Circ3 Control Object command.

   For this example, the CIRC3 sample was converted.

2. Modify the value of a property on the property page.

3. Click the Apply button to apply the new value to the Circ3 control

   The property now contains the new value.

▶ **To test events**

1. From the View menu, choose the Event Log command.

2. Perform an action that causes the control to fire an event.

   The event will appear in the Event Log window.

After you have finished testing your control, close the Test Container by choosing the Close command on the File menu, or double-click the system menu button.

Where To Go From Here

When you are satisfied that the skeleton control is working properly, the next step is to port the implementation of your OLE control's custom properties and events from your VBX source code to the new control's source code files. To do this, use ClassWizard and the implementation guidelines in the OLE Custom Control Developer's Kit documentation. Remember to back up your files frequently and test each new block of code as you go, using the Test Container.

APPENDIX B

Advanced Topics

This appendix describes how to:

- Subclass a Windows control using the Control Development Kit (CDK).
- Implement a parameterized property.
- Implement localization support for your OLE control.
- Handle errors in your OLE control

Subclassing a Windows Control

Subclassing an existing Windows control is a quick way to develop an OLE custom control. Because you are subclassing, the abilities of the existing control, such as painting and responding to mouse clicks, are handled by the control's window procedure. The BUTTON sample, found in the SAMPLES directory, is an example of subclassing a Windows control.

To properly subclass a Windows control, you must complete the following tasks:

- Override two member functions of **COleControl**, called **GetSuperWndProcAddr** and **PreCreateWindow**.
- Modify your OnDraw member function.
- Handle any OCM messages reflected to your control.

Note Much of this work is done for you by ControlWizard, if you select the Subclass Windows Control option in the Control Options dialog box.

Overriding PreCreateWindow and GetSuperWndProcAddr

To override **PreCreateWindow** and **GetSuperWndProcAddr**, add the following lines of code to the **protected** section of your control's class declaration:

```
BOOL PreCreateWindow( CREATESTRUCT& cs );
WNDPROC* GetSuperWndProcAddr( );
```

In your control's implementation file, add the following lines of code that implement the two overridden functions:

```
▶ BOOL CSampleCtrl::PreCreateWindow( CREATESTRUCT& cs )
▶ {
▶     cs.lpszClass = _T("BUTTON");
▶     return COleControl::PreCreateWindow(cs);
▶ }
▶ WNDPROC* CSampleCtrl::GetSuperWndProcAddr( )
▶ {
▶     static WNDPROC NEAR pfnSuper;
▶     return &pfnSuper;
▶ }
```

Notice that the Windows button control is specified in **PreCreateWindow**. However, any of the standard Windows controls can be subclassed.

When subclassing a Windows control, you may want to specify particular window style (WS_) or extended window style (WS_EX_) flags to be used in creating the control's window. You can set values for these parameters in the **PreCreateWindow** member function, by modifying the **cs.style** and **cs.dwExStyle** structure fields. Modifications to these fields should be made using an "or" operation, to preserve the default flags that are set by the **COleControl** base class. For example, if your control is subclassing the BUTTON control and you want the control to appear as a check box, insert the following line of code into the implementation of CSampleCtrl::PreCreateWindow, just before the return statement:

```
cs.style |= BS_CHECKBOX;
```

This operation will add the **BS_CHECKBOX** style flag, while leaving the default style flag (**WS_CHILD**) of the **COleControl** base class intact.

Modifying the OnDraw Member Function

The OnDraw member function for your subclassed control should just contain a call to the **DoSuperclassPaint** member function, as in the following example:

```
void CSampleCtrl::OnDraw( CDC* pdc, const CRect& rcBounds,
    const CRect& rcInvalid )
{
 DoSuperclassPaint( pdc, rcBounds );
}
```

The **DoSuperclassPaint** member function, implemented by **COleControl**, uses the window procedure of the Windows control to cause the control to be drawn in the specified device context, within the bounding rectangle. This enables the control to be visible even when it is not active.

Note The **DoSuperclassPaint** member function will only work with those control types that allow a device context to be passed as the **wParam** of a **WM_PAINT** message, such as **SCROLLBAR** and **BUTTON**. For controls that do not support this behavior, you will have to write the code to display the control in the inactive state.

Handling Reflected Window Messages

Windows controls typically send certain window messages to their parent window. Some of these messages, such as **WM_COMMAND**, provide notification of an action by the user. Others, such as **WM_CTLCOLOR**, are used to obtain information from the parent window. For an OLE control, this kind of communication with the parent window is usually accomplished by other means. Notifications are communicated by firing events, and information about the control container is obtained by accessing the container's ambient properties. Because these communication techniques exist, OLE control containers are not expected to process any window messages sent by the control.

To prevent the container from receiving the window messages sent by a Windows control to its parent window, the **COleControl** base class causes an extra window to be created, to serve as the control's parent. Note that this extra window is only created for an OLE control that subclasses a Windows control. This window, called the "reflector" window, intercepts certain window messages and sends similar messages back to the control itself. The control, in its window procedure, can then process these reflected messages by doing something appropriate for an OLE control (for example, firing an event). The following table shows the messages that are intercepted, and the corresponding messages that the reflector window sends:

Message Sent By Control	Message Reflected To Control
WM_COMMAND	OCM_COMMAND
WM_CTLCOLOR	OCM_CTLCOLOR
WM_DRAWITEM	OCM_DRAWITEM
WM_MEASUREITEM	OCM_MEASUREITEM
WM_DELETEITEM	OCM_DELETEITEM
WM_VKEYTOITEM	OCM_VKEYTOITEM
WM_CHARTOITEM	OCM_CHARTOITEM
WM_COMPAREITEM	OCM_COMPAREITEM
WM_HSCROLL	OCM_HSCROLL
WM_VSCROLL	OCM_VSCROLL
WM_PARENTNOTIFY	OCM_PARENTNOTIFY

An OLE control container may choose to perform message reflection itself, eliminating the need for **COleControl** to create the reflector window and reducing the run-time overhead for a subclassed Windows control. **COleControl** can detect whether the container supports this capability by checking for a "MessageReflect" ambient property with a value of **TRUE**.

To handle a reflected window message, you need to add an entry to your control's message map, and implement a handler function. Because the reflected messages are not part of the standard set of messages defined by Windows, there is no support provided by ClassWizard for adding such message handlers. However, it is not difficult to add a handler manually.

▶ **To add a message handler for a reflected window message**

1. In the .H file of your control's class, declare a handler function. The function should have a return type of **LRESULT** and two parameters, with types **WPARAM** and **LPARAM**, respectively. For example:

```
LRESULT OnOcmCommand( WPARAM wParam, LPARAM lParam );
```

2. In the .CPP file of your control's class, add an **ON_MESSAGE** entry to the message map. The parameters of this entry should be the message identifier and the name of the handler function. For example:

```
ON_MESSAGE( OCM_COMMAND, OnOcmCommand )
```

3. Also in the .CPP file, implement the OnOcmCommand member function to process the reflected message. The wParam and lParam parameters are the same as those of the original window message.

For an example of how reflected messages are processed, refer to the BUTTON sample. It provides an OnOcmCommand handler that detects the **BN_CLICKED** notification code and responds by firing a Click event.

Implementing a Parameterized Property

A parameterized property (sometimes called an property array) is a way of exposing a homogeneous collection of values as a single property of your control. For example, one can expose an array or a dictionary as a property. In Visual Basic, such a property would be accessed using array notation:

```
x = obj.ArrayProp(2, 3)      ' gets element of 2D array
obj.ArrayProp(2, 3) = 7      ' sets element of 2D array
```

You can easily implement a parameterized property using the OLE Automation tab of ClassWizard. ClassWizard implements the property by adding a pair of Get/Set functions that allow the control's user to access the property using the above notation or in the standard fashion. Figure B.1 shows the Add Method Parameter dialog box.

Similar to methods and properties, parameterized properties also have a limit to the number of parameters allowed. In this case, parameterized properties have a limit of 14 parameters (the remaining parameter stores the property value).

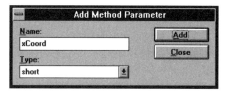

Figure B.1   The Add Method Parameter dialog box

The following procedure demonstrates adding a parameterized property, called Array that can be accessed as a two-dimensional array of integers.

▶ **To add a parameterized property using ClassWizard**

1. Load your control's project.

2. From the Browse menu, choose ClassWizard.

   Note If you are using the 32-bit version of the CDK, ClassWizard is found on the Project menu.

3. Choose the OLE Automation tab.

4. Choose the Add Property button.

5. In the External Name box, type **Array**.

6. Under Implementation, select Get/Set Methods.

7. From the Type box, select **short** for the property's type.

8. Type unique names for your Get and Set Functions or accept the default names.

9. Choose the Add button.

10. In the Add Property Parameter dialog box, type **row** for the name.

11. From the Type list box, select **short**.

12. Choose the Add button.

13. Repeat Steps 10-12 substituting **column** for **row**.

14. Choose the Close button.

15. Choose the OK button to confirm your choices and close ClassWizard.

Changes Made by ClassWizard

When you add any custom property, ClassWizard makes changes to the .H and the .CPP files of your control class.

The following lines are added to the .H file of your control class:

```
afx_msg short GetArray(short row, short column);
afx_msg void SetArray(short row, short column, short nNewValue);
```

This code declares two functions called `GetArray` and `SetArray` that are used to support the parameterized property. Note that the Get and Set functions allow the user to request a specific row and column when accessing the property.

In addition, the following lines are added to the dispatch map of your control, located in the .CPP file of your control class:

```
DISP_PROPERTY_PARAM(CSampleCtrl, "Array", GetArray, SetArray, VT_I2,
    VTS_I2 VTS_I2)
```

Finally, the implementations of the `GetArray` and `SetArray` functions are added to the end of your .CPP file. In most cases, you will modify the Get function to simply return the value of the property. Your Set function will usually contain code that should be executed either before or after the property changes.

In order for this method to be useful you could declare a two-dimensional array member variable of type **short** to store values for the parameterized property. You could then modify your Get function to return the value stored at the proper row and column, as indicated by the parameters and modify your Set function to update the value referenced by the row and column parameters.

Implementing Localization Support

In order for your OLE control to adapt easily to an international market you will need to address the issue of localization. The Windows operating system has the ability to support several languages in addition to the default English, such as German, French, and Swedish. This can present problems for your control when its interface is in English only.

In general, OLE controls should always base their locale on the ambient LocaleID property. Specifically, there are three strategies:

- Load resources, always on demand, based on the current value of the ambient LocaleID property.

- Load resources when the first control is instanced, based on the ambient LocaleID property, and use this locale (resources) for all other instances.

    Note This will not work correctly in some cases, if future instances have different locales.

- Use the **OnAmbientChanged** notification function to load the proper resources dynamically.

Note This will work for the control, but the run-time DLL will not dynamically update its own resources when the ambient LocaleID property changes.

The run-time DLL's for OLE controls also follow certain rules, regarding localization. The 16-bit run-time DLL will use the first ambient LocaleID property it sees from the container to determine the locale for its resources. Note that this will not work correctly in cases where a later container has a different ambient LocaleID property. The 32-bit run-time DLL will use the thread locale to determine the locale for its resources.

The following procedures describe two kinds of localizing you may want to give your control. The first strategy localizes your control's programmability interface (names of properties, methods, and events). The second strategy localizes your control's user interface by using the container's ambient LocaleID property. For a demonstration of control localization, see the LOCALIZE sample in the SAMPLES directory.

Localizing Your Control's Programmability Interface

When implementing the localization of your control's programmability interface (the interface used by programmers writing applications that use your control), you need to create a modified version of the control's .ODL file. Separate .ODL files should be created for each language you intend to support. This is the only place where you will need to localize the property names of your control. It is recommended that you include the locale ID as an attribute at the type library level.

For example, if you want to provide a type library with French localized property names, copy your SAMPLE.ODL file to SAMPLEFR.ODL. Add a locale identifier attribute to the file, like the following:

```
[ uuid(xxxxxxxx-xxxx-xxxx-xxxx-xxxxxxxxxxxx), version(1.0), lcid(0x040c)
]
library Sample
{
```

The locale identifier for French is 0x040c. Change the property names in SAMPLEFR.ODL to their French equivalents, and then use MKTYPLIB.EXE to produce the French type library, SAMPLEFR.TLB.

To create multiple localized type libraries you can add a special command to the Tools menu that allows you to create a type library with any .ODL file found in the current project directory. When creating a localized type library there are three possible scenarios:

- Developing a 16-bit control under Windows 3.1 or later.
- Developing a 16-bit control under Windows NT.
- Developing a 32-bit control.

If you are developing a 16-bit control under Windows 3.1 (or Windows for Workgroups 3.11), use the following procedure to add a command to the Tools menu that creates a type library from a .ODL file.

▶ **To add a new type library command to the Tools menu**

1. From the Options menu, choose Tools.

   The Tools dialog box appears.

2. Choose Add to open the Add Tool dialog box.

3. Use the Directories list box to go to the C:\MSVC\BIN directory.

4. Select MKTYPLIB.EXE from the list of filenames and choose OK.

5. Enter the following line in the Arguments edit box:

   ```
   /cpp_cmd C:\MSVC\BIN\cl /W0 /I C:\MSVC\CDK16\INCLUDE /nologo
   $Filename
   ```

   For this example. Visual C++ was installed in C:\MSVC and the CDK was installed in C:\MSVC. Modify these two paths if you have installed Visual C++, or the CDK, in a different location.

6. Type Localize TypeLib in the Menu Text edit box.

7. Choose OK to close the Tools dialog box.

To build a type library from a localized .ODL file located in the current project directory, open the .ODL file in Visual C++ and make sure it has the current focus. Then choose Localize TypeLib from the Tools menu. The resultant type library can be found in the current project directory.

If you are developing a 16-bit control under NT or Chicago, use the following procedure to add a command to the Tools menu that creates a type library from a .ODL file. Because projects built under NT or Chicago store 16-bit type libraries in the TLB16 subdirectory, you must move any .ODL.

▶ **To add a new type library command to the Tools menu**

1. From the Options menu, choose Tools.

   The Tools dialog box appears.

2. Choose Add to open the Add Tool dialog box.

3. Use the Directories list box to go to the C:\MSVC\CDK16\BIN directory.

4. Select BLDTYPLB.BAT from the list of filenames and choose OK.

5. Enter the following line in the Arguments edit box:

   ```
   $FileName C:\MSVC\BIN  $ProjDir /IC:\MSVC\CDK16\INCLUDE
   ```

For this example. Visual C++ was installed in C:\MSVC and the CDK was installed in C:\CDK16. Modify these two paths if you have installed Visual C++, or the CDK, in a different location.

6. Choose OK to close the Tools dialog box.

To build a type library from a localized .ODL file located in the current project directory, open the .ODL file in Visual C++ and make sure it has the current focus. Then choose Localize TypeLib from the Tools menu. The resultant type library can be found in the \TLB16 subdirectory of the current project.

Because projects built under NT or Chicago store 16-bit type libraries in the \TLB16 subdirectory of the project, you must move these localized type libraries to the project directory before they can be registered.

If you are localizing a 32-bit OLE control you can simply add any localized .ODL files to the project and they will be built automatically.

▶ **To add an .ODL file to your OLE control project**

1. From the Project menu, choose Files.

   The Project Files dialog box appears.

2. If necessary, select the drive and directory to view.

3. Add files with the following methods:

   - Single file: Select the .ODL file in the File Name list and choose Add.
   - Single file: Double-click the .ODL file in the File Name list.

Close the Project Files dialog box when you have added all necessary .ODL files. Because the files have been added to the project they will be built, along with the rest of the project, when necessary. The localized type libraries can be found in the current OLE control project directory.

Within your code, the internal property names (usually in English) are always used and are never localized. This includes the control's dispatch map, the property exchange functions, and your property page data exchange code.

Only one .TLB file may be bound into the resources of your .OCX file. This will usually be the version with the standardized (typically, English) names. To ship a localized version of your control you need to ship the .DLL (which has already been bound to the canonical .TLB version) and the .TLB for the appropriate locale. This means that only the .OCX is needed for English versions, since the correct .TLB has already been bound to it. For other locales, the localized type library also must be shipped with the .OCX.

To ensure that clients of your control can find the localized type library, you'll need to register your locale-specific .TLB file(s) under the TypeLib section of the registry. An optional parameter of the **AfxOleRegisterTypeLib** function is provided for this purpose. The following example will register a French type library for the OLE control:

```
STDAPI DllRegisterServer(void)
{
    AFX_MANAGE_STATE(_afxModuleAddrThis);

    if (!AfxOleRegisterTypeLib(AfxGetInstanceHandle(), _tlid))
        return ResultFromScode(SELFREG_E_TYPELIB);
    AfxOleRegisterTypeLib(AfxGetInstanceHandle(), _tlid,
        _T("samplefr.tlb"))
    if (!COleObjectFactoryEx::UpdateRegistryAll(TRUE))
        return ResultFromScode(SELFREG_E_CLASS);

    return NOERROR;
}
```

When your control is registered, the **AfxOleRegisterTypeLib** function will automatically look for the specified .TLB file in the same directory as the control itself, and register it in the Windows registration database. If the .TLB file isn't found, the function has no effect.

Localizing Your Control's User Interface

To localize the user interface of your control, you can place all the user-visible resources of your control (such as property pages and error messages) into language-specific resource DLLs. You then can make use of the container's ambient LocaleID property to select the appropriate DLL for the user's locale.

The following code example demonstrates one approach to locate and load the resource DLL for a specific locale. This member function, called GetLocalizedResourceHandle for this example, can be a member function of your OLE control class:

```
HINSTANCE CSampleCtrl::GetLocalizedResourceHandle(LCID lcid)
{
    LPCTSTR lpszResDll;
    HINSTANCE hResHandle = NULL;
    LANGID lang = LANGIDFROMLCID(lcid);
    switch (PRIMARYLANGID(lang))
    {
    case LANG_ENGLISH:
        lpszResDll = "myctlen.dll";
        break;

    case LANG_FRENCH:
        lpszResDll = "myctlfr.dll";
        break;

    case LANG_GERMAN:
```

```
            lpszResDll = "myctlde.dll";
            break;

        case 0:
        default:
            lpszResDll = NULL;
        }

        if (lpszResDll != NULL)
            hResHandle = LoadLibrary(lpszResDll);
    #ifndef _WIN32
        if(hResHandle <= HINSTANCE_ERROR)
            hResHandle = NULL;
    #endif

        return hResHandle;
}
```

Note that the sublanguage ID could be checked in each case of the switch statement, to provide more specialized localization if desired (for example, local dialects of German). For a demonstration of this function, see the `GetResourceHandle` function in the LOCALIZE sample.

When your control first loads itself into a container you can make a call to **COleControl::AmbientLocaleID** to retrieve the locale ID. You can then pass the returned locale ID value to your `GetLocalizedResourceHandle` function, which loads the proper resource library. Pass the resulting handle, if any, to **AfxSetResourceHandle**:

```
m_hResDll = GetLocalizedResourceHandle( AmbientLocaleID() );
if (m_hResDll != NULL)
    AfxSetResourceHandle(m_hResDll);
```

You should place the code sample above into a member function of your control, such as an override of **COleControl::OnSetClientSite**. In addition, m_hResDLL should be a member variable of your control class.

You can use similar logic for localizing the control's property page. To localize the property page, use code similar to the following sample code in your property page's implementation file (in an override of **COlePropertyPage::OnSetPageSite**):

```
LPPROPERTYPAGESITE pSite;
LCID lcid = 0;
LANGID lang;
if((pSite = GetPageSite()) != NULL)
    pSite->GetLocaleID(&lcid);
HINSTANCE hResource = GetLocalizedResourceHandle(lcid);
HINSTANCE hResourceSave = NULL;
```

```
if (hResource != NULL)
{
    hResourceSave = AfxGetResourceHandle();
    AfxSetResourceHandle(hResource);
}

// Load dialog template and caption string.
COlePropertyPage::OnSetPageSite( );

if (hResource != NULL)
    AfxSetResourceHandle(hResourceSave);
```

Handling Errors in Your OLE Control

When error conditions arise in your control, you may need to report the error to the control's container. There are two methods for reporting errors, depending on the situation in which the error occurs. If the error occurs within a property's Get or Set function, or within the implementation of an OLE Automation method, your control should call **COleControl::ThrowError**. If the error occurs at any other time, your control should instead call **COleControl::FireError**, which fires a stock Error event.

To indicate what kind of error has occurred, your control needs to pass an error code to the **ThrowError** or **FireError** member functions. An error code is an OLE status code, which is a 32-bit value. Whenever possible, you should choose an error code from the standard set of codes defined in the OLECTL.H header file. The following table summarizes these standard codes.

Table B.1   OLE Control Error Codes

Error Code	Description
CTL_E_ILLEGALFUNCTIONCALL	Illegal function call
CTL_E_OVERFLOW	Overflow
CTL_E_OUTOFMEMORY	Out of memory
CTL_E_DIVISIONBYZERO	Division by zero
CTL_E_OUTOFSTRINGSPACE	Out of string space
CTL_E_OUTOFSTACKSPACE	Out of stack space
CTL_E_BADFILENAMEORNUMBER	Bad file name or number
CTL_E_FILENOTFOUND	File not found
CTL_E_BADFILEMODE	Bad file mode
CTL_E_FILEALREADYOPEN	File already open
CTL_E_DEVICEIOERROR	Device I/O error
CTL_E_FILEALREADYEXISTS	File already exists

Table B.1   OLE Control Error Codes (*continued*)

Error Code	Description
CTL_E_BADRECORDLENGTH	Bad record length
CTL_E_DISKFULL	Disk full
CTL_E_BADRECORDNUMBER	Bad record number
CTL_E_BADFILENAME	Bad file name
CTL_E_TOOMANYFILES	Too many files
CTL_E_DEVICEUNAVAILABLE	Device unavailable
CTL_E_PERMISSIONDENIED	Permission denied
CTL_E_DISKNOTREADY	Disk not ready
CTL_E_PATHFILEACCESSERROR	Path/file access error
CTL_E_PATHNOTFOUND	Path not found
CTL_E_INVALIDPATTERNSTRING	Invalid pattern string
CTL_E_INVALIDUSEOFNULL	Invalid use of NULL
CTL_E_INVALIDFILEFORMAT	Invalid file format
CTL_E_INVALIDPROPERTYVALUE	Invalid property value
CTL_E_INVALIDPROPERTYARRAYINDEX	Invalid property array index
CTL_E_SETNOTSUPPORTEDATRUNTIME	Set not supported at runtime
CTL_E_SETNOTSUPPORTED	Set not supported (read-only property)
CTL_E_NEEDPROPERTYARRAYINDEX	Need property array index
CTL_E_SETNOTPERMITTED	Set not permitted
CTL_E_GETNOTSUPPORTEDATRUNTIME	Get not supported at runtime
CTL_E_GETNOTSUPPORTED	Get not supported (write-only property)
CTL_E_PROPERTYNOTFOUND	Property not found
CTL_E_INVALIDCLIPBOARDFORMAT	Invalid clipboard format
CTL_E_INVALIDPICTURE	Invalid picture
CTL_E_PRINTERERROR	Printer error
CTL_E_CANTSAVEFILETOTEMP	Can't save file to TEMP
CTL_E_SEARCHTEXTNOTFOUND	Search text not found
CTL_E_REPLACEMENTSTOOLONG	Replacements too long

If necessary, you can use the **CUSTOM_CTL_SCODE** macro to define a custom error code for a condition that isn't covered by one of the standard codes. The parameter for this macro should be an integer between 1000 and 32767, inclusive. For example:

```
#define MYCTL_E_SPECIALERROR CUSTOM_CTL_SCODE(1000)
```

If you are creating an OLE control that is intended to replace an existing VBX control, you should define your OLE control's error codes with the same numeric values as those that the VBX control uses to ensure that the error codes are compatible.

Adding an OLE Custom Control to an Existing Project

This appendix provides a step-by-step procedure for combining two existing OLE custom controls into one project. For clarity, the first control project is named *Proj1* and the second is named *Proj2*.

You should use a separate directory to combine the two controls. This protects the original code from becoming corrupted and creates a project that includes the *Proj1* and *Proj2* controls in a separate directory referred to as COMBINED. It is also recommended that you use Visual Workbench for modifying and saving project files.

To successfully add an OLE control to another project you must take the following steps:

- Collect all relevant .H, .CPP, .PPG, and resource files together.
- Combine both .ODL files into one .ODL file.
- Modify the *PROJ2*.MAK makefile.
- Combine the resources of both controls.
- Build the resultant project.

Collecting Implementation Files

The *Proj1* and *Proj2* directories both contain files that you can simply copy to the COMBINED directory with no changes. These files deal mainly with initializing the DLL and basic implementation of the control classes. You should copy the following files into the COMBINED directory:

- STDAFX.H, STDAFX.CPP
- *PROJ2*.RC, RESOURCE.H
- *PROJ2*.RC2
- *PROJ2*.H, *PROJ2*.CPP
- *PROJ1*CTL.H, *PROJ1*CTL.CPP

- *PROJ1*PPG.H, *PROJ1*PPG.CPP
- *PROJ2*CTL.H, *PROJ2*CTL.CPP
- *PROJ2*PPG.H, *PROJ2*PPG.CPP
- *PROJ2*.DEF or *PROJ232*.DEF
- MAKEFILE

There are also two other files, used as templates, that must be copied to the COMBINED directory:

- *PROJ2*.MAK or *PROJ232*.MAK

  In a following section, this makefile will be modified to include the necessary files from *PROJ1*.

- *PROJ2*.ODL

  This file will eventually contain both OLE control interfaces.

Merging the .ODL Files

Because there are two controls in the project, you will have to merge *PROJ1*.ODL into *PROJ2*.ODL. Because the .ODL file contains definitions for interfaces you need, copy only those interfaces unique to *Proj1* and insert them into the *PROJ2*.ODL file.

▶ **To merge PROJ1.ODL with PROJ2.ODL**

1. Copy the marked lines in the following PROJ1.ODL file:

```
//
// Type Library for Proj1.DLL
//
    #include <otldisp.h>
    [ uuid(A7A91CE8-B974-101A-8077-00AA00339DC7), version(1.0),
      helpstring("PROJ1 OLE Custom Control module") ]
    library Proj1
    {
    importlib("stdole.tlb");
    importlib("stdtype.tlb");

▶        [ uuid(A7A91CE6-B974-101A-8077-00AA00339DC7),
▶          helpstring("Dispatch interface for PROJ1 Control") ]
▶        dispinterface IProj1Ctrl
▶        {
▶            properties:
▶                //{{AFX_ODL_PROP(CProj1Ctrl)
▶                //}}AFX_ODL_PROP
▶
▶            methods:
```

```
►      //{{AFX_ODL_METHOD(CProj1Ctrl)
►      //}}AFX_ODL_METHOD
►
►   };
►
►   [ uuid(A7A91CE7-B974-101A-8077-00AA00339DC7),
►     helpstring("Event interface for PROJ1 Control") ]
►   dispinterface IProj1CtrlEvents
►   {
►       properties:
►           //  Event interface has no properties
►
►       methods:
►           //{{AFX_ODL_EVENT(CProj1Ctrl)
►           //}}AFX_ODL_EVENT
►   };
};
```

2. Paste the code that you copied above into *PROJ2*.ODL, just prior to the last closing brace.

Note If you are using the 16-bit version of the CDK, you must create a TLB16 subdirectory under the COMBINED project directory.

Modifying the Proj2 Makefile

Now that you have moved the needed files from *Proj1* to the COMBINED directory you need to incorporate them into the *Proj2* makefile.

Note If *PROJ2*.MAK is an external makefile you will need to edit it directly to add the new files from *Proj1*.

► **To incorporate Proj1 files into the Proj2 makefile (16-bit version)**

1. Load the *Proj2* project, from the COMBINED directory, into Visual Workbench.

2. From the Project menu, choose the Edit command.

3. From the Project menu, choose Edit.

4. From the File Name box, select *PROJ1*CTL.CPP.

5. Choose the Add button.

6. Repeat Steps 3 and 4 for *PROJ1*PPG.CPP.

7. Choose Close to save changes made to the makefile and to close the Edit - *PROJ1* dialog box.

▶ **To incorporate Proj1 files into the Proj2 makefile (32-bit version)**

1. Load the *Proj2* project, from the COMBINED directory.

2. From the Project menu, choose the Files... command.

3. From the File Name box, select *PROJ1*CTL.CPP.

5. Choose the Add button.

6. Repeat Steps 3 and 4 for *PROJ1*PPG.CPP.

7. Choose Close to save changes made to the makefile and to close the Edit - *PROJ1* dialog box.

Combining the Resources of Both Controls

The last modification required before building the project is to add the resources from *PROJ1*.RC to *PROJ2*.RC. This is made easy because you can drag and drop resources from one project into another.

▶ **To add resources from Proj1 to Proj2 (16-bit)**

1. Load the *Proj2* project, from the COMBINED directory, into Visual Workbench.

2. Open App Studio.

3. Open *PROJ1*.RC in the PROJ1 directory. Notice that *PROJ2*.RC has already been opened.

4. Drag and drop any resources from *Proj1* that you want to include into *Proj2*. Be sure to hold down the CTRL key so the resources are copied and not moved. For an example, see "Adding Help to Scribble" in Chapter 10 of the *Class Library User's Guide*. The same process applies to situations in which you decide to add an AppWizard feature after you have created your project.

5. After you have added your resources, save your changes by choosing the Save toolbar button or closing App Studio.

▶ **To add resources from Proj1 to Proj2 (32-bit)**

1. Load the *Proj2* project, from the COMBINED directory.

2. Double-click the .RC file icon to open *PROJ2*'s resources.

3. Drag and drop any resources from *Proj1* that you want to include into *Proj2*. Be sure to hold down the CTRL key so the resources are copied and not moved. For an example, see "Adding Context-Sensitive Help" in Chapter 15 of *Introducing Visual C++*. The same process applies to situations in which you decide to add an AppWizard feature after you have created your project.

4. After you have added your resources, save your changes by choosing the Save toolbar button.

Building the New Project

After completing the preceding steps, you can now build the new project as you would any OLE control project. Once the project has been successfully built, register the controls. You can now test your OLE control DLL using Test Container or other container applications.

Please note that the .CLW file for *Proj2* needs to be rebuilt so that any new classes will be integrated.

▶ **To rebuild your .CLW file (16-bit)**

1. Delete PROJ2.CLW.

2. Load the *Proj2* project, from the COMBINED directory, into Visual Workbench.

3. Open App Studio.

4. Choose the ClassWizard button on the App Studio toolbar.

   A dialog box will appear, stating that your project's .CLW file does not exist.

5. Choose OK.

6. Choose OK again to rebuild the .CLW file.

ClassWizard will now open with all classes from *Proj2* already loaded and accessible.

▶ **To rebuild your .CLW file (32-bit)**

1. Delete PROJ2.CLW.

2. Load the *Proj2* project, from the COMBINED directory.

3. Double-click the .RC file icon to open the control's resources.

4. Choose the ClassWizard button on the App Studio toolbar.

   A dialog box will appear, stating that your project's .CLW file does not exist.

5. Choose OK.

6. Choose OK again to rebuild the .CLW file.

ClassWizard will now open with all classes from *Proj2* already loaded and accessible.

A P P E N D I X   D

OLE Controls Architecture

OLE custom controls comprise a set of extensions that turn OLE 2 containers and objects into more powerful "control containers" and "controls." These extensions use standard compound document interfaces and new interfaces that can be accessed by control containers and controls. A control container implements a "site" object for each contained object or control. The interfaces, control-specific or not, are on the same site object. The **QueryInterface** function of any interface can access the other interfaces on that object, with a few minor exceptions.

To support OLE controls fully, a control container must be a full embedding container—linking support is not necessary—that also supports in-place activation. In the same manner, a control must be an embeddable object implemented in an in-process server dynamic link library (DLL) that also supports in-place activation as an inside-out object. Controls must also be self-registering (that is, they export the new function **DllRegisterServer**).

In this chapter the following topics are discussed:

- Events and connection points
- Standards for events, properties, and methods for OLE custom controls
- New interfaces for controls
- Standard types
- Installation and registration
- Licensing
- Versioning
- Property browsing

Extended Controls

In the OLE compound document model, an embedded object is responsible for its content area, but the placement of the object within its containing document is controlled by the container. In effect, the container "owns" the embedded object's position. This is necessary since different containers—Word and Excel, for example—have different positioning models. Word positions embedded objects as if they were characters, while Excel positions them relative to cell positions.

A container normally models per-control container-specific information as properties. For example, a form-like container might implement Top and Left properties for each control, and have those container-implemented properties appear as peers of the properties implemented directly by the control. Or the container might express a Visible property on each and every control, or express the Z order for a control with a property, and so on. For a more complete set of examples, see the "Standard Types" section.

The container implements these properties for each control by creating another object that is parallel to, but separate from, the site object created for that control. This third object (the "extended control") implements the properties the container adds to each control. The extended control object is also responsible for delegating the control's properties to the container, so that the container can dispense pointers to the extended control object in lieu of the control.

The container can add appropriate properties to the extended control object. In addition, containers can implement methods on the extended control object; these methods appear as siblings to methods implemented by the control itself.

Object Identity with Extended Controls

Containers normally attempt to aggregate the extended control object with the control when creating the control, so that the extended control object acts as an invisible controller for the control. This makes the boundary between the control's native properties and methods and those added by the container seamless, for both early- and late-bound access. That is, a user of the control can use **IDispatch** to get at properties provided by either the control or the extended control; the extended control implements **IDispatch** and delegates unimplemented properties to the actual control. Or, the user can use **QueryInterface** for either the control's primary interface or the extended control's primary interface for direct early-bound access to properties and methods.

This aggregation is likely to succeed for controls, since control development kits are expected to produce in-process servers that can be aggregated. If the aggregation fails, the container will only be able to provide late-bound access to the control's properties and methods.

Assuming aggregation succeeds, the container assigns pointers to the aggregated control and the extended control object when enumerating its contents. If aggregation fails, the container assigns pointers to the controls when enumerating objects from an OLE compound document (CD) interface (**IOleContainer**) as well as pointers to the corresponding extended control objects in its language integration code.

Properties and Methods

In addition to supporting the compound document interfaces, controls also follow the OLE Automation guidelines. Controls expose properties and methods as is normal for OLE Automation objects. Early-bound access to control properties and methods is provided by defining a primary interface for the control. The primary interface exposes properties as get/set method pairs and object methods as—not surprisingly—methods. Late-bound access to control properties and methods is exposed through **IDispatch**.

A control container determines whether early or late binding is exposed to end users, since the container assigns pointers to embedded objects.

As per normal for an OLE Automation object, a control presents its set of properties and methods through **TypeInfo**. The **TypeInfo** that describes a control's dispatch interface can be retrieved dynamically using the GetTypeInfo method of the control's **IDispatch** implementation. Also, OLE controls introduce a new interface, **IProvideClassInfo**, which should return a **CoClass TypeInfo** describing the control (as opposed to the **DispInterface TypeInfo** returned by **IDispatch::GetTypeInfo**). This interface is described in more detail in "Connection Interfaces."

Controls follow a standard registry convention to give the location of their Type Library and Type Info. Containers which need type information statically can use the registry to locate and load a description of the control. The registry syntax introduced for controls is described in the "Installation and Registration" section.

Events

OLE controls introduces a standard way for OLE compound object model (COM) objects to fire events. The OLE controls architecture, which allows objects to have outgoing interfaces, defines a new connections architecture. The outgoing interfaces complement the normal interfaces an object provides. An object provides normal (or incoming) interfaces by implementing them. Conversely, an object supports outgoing interfaces by calling other objects' implementations of those interfaces.

The set of events fired by a control is modeled as a single outgoing dispatch interface (that is, a single outgoing **IDispatch** interface). This primary event set is the complement for the primary interface exposed by objects. An OLE control collects its set of properties and methods into its primary interface; conversely, it collects its set of events into the primary event set.

Note that just as the control can support other interfaces beyond the primary interface (navigating between the supported interfaces with **QueryInterface**), the control can support other outgoing interfaces beyond the primary event set. The control developer can implement a primary interface to set aside a sub-set of methods, properties, and events that will be commonly used by a beginning programmer. Other interfaces can be created for use by advanced programmers.

Connectable Objects

While OLE 2 COM defines a general mechanism (**IUnknown**) for objects to implement and expose functionality in interfaces, it does not define a general method that allows objects to incorporate external interfaces. That is, COM defines how incoming pointers to objects (pointers to that object's interfaces) are handled, but it does not have an explicit model for outgoing interfaces (pointers the object holds to other objects' interfaces). Instead, ad hoc solutions are invented where needed.

Objects which expose outgoing pointers do so by supporting the interface **IConnectionPointContainer**. As implied by the name, this interface allows the caller to enumerate connection point subobjects, each of which supports the **IConnectionPoint** interface. For each distinct outgoing pointer the object exposes, shown in Figure D.1, a distinct connection point is exposed. For example, a control that fired events through one interface and sent notifications of data changes through another interface would expose two connection points.

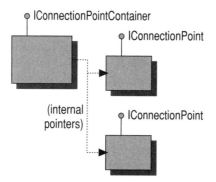

Figure D.1   A Control with Two Exposed Connection Points

To establish a connection, OLE control code finds the right connection point via the **IConnectionPointContainer** interface, then connects by calling a method on that **IConnectionPoint** interface of that connection point. Of course, the code establishing the connection needs to provide an implementation of the interface provided by the connection point. That is, a connection point of the OLE control that exposes an interface **IConnection** is exposing the willingness to call an implementation of the **IConnection** interface. To establish a connection, the caller needs to provide an implementation of the **IConnection** interface to be called. Each connection has two ends—the object calling the interface and the object implementing the interface. The object that calls the interface is called the *source*, while the implementation of the interface is called the *sink*.

For example, Figure D.2 shows what happens if we connected a sink to the event set connection point of the object illustrated previously in Figure D.1.

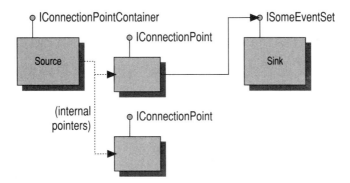

Figure D.2   A Connected Connection Point

Through its subobject, the source object then has a pointer to the sink object's implementation of the event set (in this case, ISomeEventSet). When the source wishes to fire an event, it calls the matching method in the sink's event set implementation.

Many scenarios require multicasting (the ability to broadcast to multiple sinks connected to the same interface), so it is designed into the basic interfaces. Multicasting is implemented by connection points that can hold pointers to multiple implementations of the connection interface and then broadcast outgoing calls to all connected implementations. For example, we might connect another sink to the event set connection point of the example source, as shown in Figure D.3.

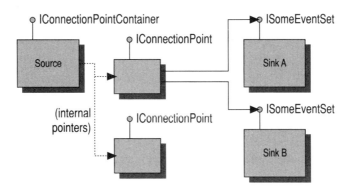

Figure D.3   An Example of Multicasting

The source object then has pointers to both sinks' implementations of the event set. When it fires an event, it calls the matching method on both sinks' implementations. Note that the source object is responsible for implementing the multicasting; rather than calling a single implementation of the outgoing interface, it calls each connected implementation in turn. The source object defines the multicasting semantics—how to reconcile error return codes, how to parse connection point parameters, and so on.

Connection Interfaces

Objects that wish to expose outgoing pointers support the **IConnectionPointContainer** interface and, optionally, the **IProvideClassInfo** interface, as shown in the following example:

```
interface IProvideClassInfo : public IUnknown
{
    GetClassInfo(ITypeInfo ** ppTI);
};

interface IConnectionPointContainer : public IUnknown
{
    EnumConnectionPoints(IEnumConnectionPoints * pEnum);
    FindConnectionPointFromIID(REFIID iid, IConnectionPoint ** ppCP);
};
```

Calling the GetClassInfo method of **IProvideClassInfo** returns a **CoClass TypeInfo** that describes the connectable object. The MKTYPLIB.EXE and TYPELIB.DLL implementations have been revised to describe the outgoing interfaces an object supports via **IConnectionPointerContainer**. Since this information is present in **TypeInfo**, it's available both statically and dynamically.

The EnumConnectionPoints method of **IConnectionPointContainer** enumerates the connection point subobjects contained by the connectable object. Note that these are true subobjects, with independent ref-counts and parallel to the site objects maintained by an OLE container. The FindConnectionPointFromIID method returns the connection point associated with a particular IID; this method fails if there are multiple connection points that exposes the same IID.

As illustrated in the following example, each connection point subobject supports the **IConnectionPoint** interface:

```
interface IConnectionPoint : public IUnknown
{
    GetConnectionInterface(IID * pIID);
    GetConnectionPointContainer(IConnectionPointContainer ** ppCPC);
    Advise(IUnknown * pUnkSink, DWORD * pdwCookie);
    Unadvise(DWORD dwCookie);

    EnumConnections(IEnumConnections * pEnum);
};
```

The GetConnectionInterface method names the interface for which this connection point is able to call implementations. Note that this interface ID also effectively distinguishes this connection point from its siblings; it acts as the "name" of the connection point. It is possible to have more sophisticated naming schemes for connection points (by supporting additional interfaces on the connection point), but in keeping with the goal of keeping things as simple as possible, the base architecture uses only IID's as names. Note that the IID can identify a dispatch interface (as with OLE control-style events) or a normal interface.

The GetConnectionPointContainer method allows code to navigate back to the container object from the subobject.

The Advise and Unadvise methods follow normal OLE conventions, that is, allow connections to be established and broken. The connection point explicitly calls **QueryInterface** for the interface it expects on the sink; Advise does not assume that the pointer passed to it is of the correct type.

Implementations of Advise should never return 0 as a connection cookie value; 0 is not a legal value.

Another method useful for multicasting scenarios is EnumConnections, which enumerates the currently connected sinks along with the connection cookies for them.

OLE control code that is designed to connect to a connectable object can get a **TypeInfo** from the object which describes all its connection points. The code then determines which connection point is appropriate, then iterates through the connection points on the object, checking the interface ID of each until a match is found. Then the Advise method on the connection point is used to establish the connection.

Implementing Events with Connections

OLE controls model events as being the opposite of method invocations. For example, a control method is implemented by the the control and outside code is calling it. However, with a control event, the control does not provide an implementation; rather, by exposing the event the control indicates its ability to call an implementation provided by some other code. Thus the outside code implements the method and the control calls it.

Individual events are gathered into event sets, just as methods are gathered into interfaces. However, a control's primary event set is always implemented using **IDispatch**—so, more specifically, primary event sets are a type of dispatch interface, not a vtable-based interface.

Event sets are described using the same **TypeInfo** constructs as dispatch interfaces as well as the same .ODL file. MKTYPELIB.EXE is extended for OLE controls to identify the outgoing and incoming interfaces for a particular class.

Language Integration

Before events fired by a control can be useful, some object needs to be ready to receive them. Given the different model for events (as compared to the method model), the ability to receive an event requires implementation of the event set in which the event exists. Since event sets are a type of dispatch interface, there must be an object that implements the **IDispatch** for the event set.

The most important recipient for events fired by a control is the control's container. Normally, the container provides its own programming model for controls—containers don't force the developer to explicitly make connections (using the connection point interfaces) between the event sources and the code written by the developer. Instead, the developer writes routines that handle individual events and the container takes care of the details of mapping the control's event set to these invidual routines. OLE controls do not dictate a particular programming paradigm. Instead, a simple standard way of firing events is provided, leaving it up to containers how to expose these events to end users.

A level of isolation is normally present between the control and user-written event handlers. When the control fires an event, it isn't calling user-written event handlers directly. Instead, it calls a language integration piece provided by the container, which in turn calls the user-written event handler. This simplifies many things—for example, the user is not forced to implement completely a full event set just to handle a single event in it.

The container often needs to keep track of some state to perform this event handling properly. For example, the container might need to keep track of what event handlers had been written by the end user so it can route events intended for them appropriately. The container is responsible for generating and saving this state—the control is oblivious to what happens outside it and has no knowledge of what happens inside the event sinks attached to it. This is the main reason why controls are portable between various containers and between different languages.

Containers will often handle only some of the events present in an event interface. The container should return **S_OK** for events that it does not handle and not change any of the event parameters. Controls rely on this behavior when there is some interaction between the event and the control's behavior (for example, a cancellable event, where the event handler can cancel the control's normal processing of the event). The assumed default is that the invocation of the event will succeed and that the parameters will be unaltered. The container is responsible for ensuring this.

At design time, the container enumerates the events a control can fire by looking in the **TypeInfo** for that control's event set. When the control developer chooses to write an event handler, the control container can examine the parameters of the event in the **TypeInfo**, and from them create a stub event handler for the user to fill in.

Note that this connection proposal does not have any explicit support for persistence. Connections between event sources (controls) and event sinks (created by the control container) are implicit. The control always makes a call to **QueryInterface** for its event set on the client site. Any state kept with each event sink is saved by the form as part of its state. In short, the container is responsible for making connections persistent, not the controls.

Event Types

Since events are just methods, they can have arbitrary parameters. (Or, at least arbitrary to the extent that **IDispatch** allows, since the primary event set is implemented with **IDispatch**.) However, if every custom control comes up with its own conventions for what kinds of events are fired and how event parameters are packaged, developers of applications and end users could find this very confusing. Therefore, OLE controls introduce a simple convention for events. This is a convention that individual event sources can move beyond if it is too restrictive, but following it produces a custom control that is easier for developerss and end users to understand.

Again, this is only a suggestion about how to structure control event sets. It is not a required model, nor are there any technical reasons or architecture that force this model or give it an advantage over other possible event models.

In the suggested event set model, there are four basic event types:

Request events
> A control fires a Request event to allow the user to cancel some action. For example, a control container might fire a RequestUnload event, giving a user-written event handler a chance to cancel the close of the control container.
>
> The last parameter of a Request event should be named Cancel and be passed as a by-reference **CancelBoolean**. The type **CancelBoolean** is introduced as a standard OLE controls type (see "Miscellaneous Standard Types"); by using this type for the Cancel parameter, the control allows its container to reliably detect that a given parameter is intended to be a Cancel parameter.
>
> The control should set this parameter to **FALSE** before firing the event, then check the parameter's value after the event has been fired. If the event handler has set the parameter to **TRUE**, the control should cancel the event.

Before events
> Before events are fired before an action occurs to allow the user to complete any actions needed before the event fires. For example, **WM_INITMENUPOPUP** could be considered a Before event since it is fired before the menu is actually displayed. Before events are not cancellable.

After events

> After events are fired after an action occurs to allow the user to respond to the action. For instance, the **WM_SIZE** message could be considered an After event since it is fired after the click happens. After events are not cancellable.

Do events

> Do events are fired to allow the user to override or supplement the control's default handling of the user action. Most window messages fit into this category since a window procedure can defeat Windows' default handling with well-chosen return values or by not calling **DefWindowProc**.
>
> When exposing a Do event, the control often provides default behavior. For example, a smart edit control that can do automatic picture-string formatting might expose a DoFormat event that allows a user-written event handler to supplement or override the control's default formatting behavior. By convention, the last parameter for the DoFormat event will be EnableDefault. The control sets this parameter to **TRUE** before firing the event; after the event has been fired, the control checks the parameter value and does its default processing only if the parameter is still **TRUE**.
>
> This enables two major scenarios. If the user wants to replace the control's default behavior, the event handler should implement the replacement and set EnableDefault to **FALSE**. If thehe user wants to do processing before the control's default behavior occurs, then the event handler should do the processing and leave EnableDefault set to **TRUE**, so the control's default processing will occur after the event handler is done.

Controls allow user-written event handlers to determine whether the default processing takes place through a EnableDefault parameter, passed as a by-reference **EnableDefaultBoolean**. This is another standard type, analogous to **CancelBoolean**. For more information, see "Miscellaneous Standard Types."

Controls should follow a naming convention for their events. If the event is a Request, Before, or Do event, then the event name should begin with the appropriate word, for example, `BeforeMenuDropDown` or `DoFormatting`. Since After events are the most common, they are the default type assumed; event names that do not begin with one of the other type names can be assumed to be After events. For example, `Click`, or `MouseMove`. Control development kits should document and encourage this convention so controls will follow some standardization of naming.

Note that Do events, in some ways, play the same role as virtual functions—they provide a mechanism whereby an object can provide well-controlled ways to specialize it. For example, a list box might expose a DoRenderItem event, which allows its appearance to be customized (similar to Windows owner-draw list boxes).

Interlocking Event Groups

In many cases, a single user action may precipitate the firing of a sequence of related events. For example, the user action may result in a Request event being fired, followed by Before and After events. While the control is in the process of firing this sequence of events, it hands over the thread of execution to event handlers. Those event handlers may in turn attempt to set properties and call methods on the object that sourced the event.

In some cases, it may be necessary for the control to enter a somewhat modal state that disallows some subset of normally permissible activities on the control. Controls are required to expect and be ready to handle reentrancy situations, but they are not required to be arbitrarily functional when reentered. For example, while firing a Request event, it may be illegal to call a method on the object which would itself fire the Request event. This decision is wholly up to the control, but the control should be ready for user-written code that attempts implausible actions.

IConnectionPointContainer and Aggregation

The individual connection points owned by a connection point container each expose a GetConnectionPointContainer method. This may cause problems if the connectable object is also able to be aggregated. If the object were aggregated, its higher level controller might want to expose some new connection points, in addition to the connection points exposed by the aggregated objects. In order to do this, the controller would support **IConnectionPointContainer** and enumerate its own connection points followed by those of the aggregated object.

For this to work, the connection points on the aggregated object must return a pointer to the controlling unknown's **IConnectionPointContainer** implementation, rather than a pointer to the aggregated object (their immediate owner). In general, connection points exposed by objects that can be aggregated should call **QueryInterface** on their controlling unknown for **IConnectionPointContainer**, rather than returning the object's implementation directly.

Property, Method, and Event Standards

For the sake of interoperability and to present a simplified model for end users, OLE controls defines a standard set of properties, methods, and events that controls can support. This section describes the set of defined standards, and specifies the contract for individual properties, methods, and events.

Qualities

Properties, methods, and events are categorized in terms of two qualities: location and variety. Note that the explanations are given in terms of properties, but apply equally to methods and events.

Property Location

Properties that a container exposes to a control through its control site are called "ambient properties." They are used to indicate the state of the form to the control and to communicate information about the environment in which the control is embedded—hence ambient. Ambient properties are implemented by the site.

Note The definition of ambient properties given here supercedes any hints or partial specifications given for ambient properties in earlier OLE specifications.

Properties the container may want to associate with each control it contains are called "extended" properties. For example, a container might want to associate an Enabled property with each control. The container is able to provide, or not provide, this sort of per-control extension. Containers that provide extra per-control properties express them on an object separate from the control itself since the control's implementation is opaque.

Properties implemented by the control itself are called "control properties."

Property Variety

Standard properties have a guaranteed contract for behavior, a negative **DispID**. Controls are not required to implement standard properties but are required to follow the contract if they do implement one. For example, controls are not required to implement a "Caption" property; however, if they do implement a Caption property, it must follow the contract for Caption properties given in the "Control Properties, Methods, and Events" section. Note that the name of the standard property is not an explicit part of this contract. These properties should be accessed only through their **DispID**.

Common properties have a suggested, but not strict, contract for behavior. For example, position properties differ in type for containers with different coordinate models. Despite this, a property named "Left" should always refer to the left edge of the control, no matter what coordinate model the container is using.

Properties that are not standard or common, specific to a particular control or container, are called "Other" properties. Currently this specification does not define any "other" properties.

The Common Ambient category does not contain any definitions; all ambient properties defined in this specification are standard. Of course, containers may implement their own "other" ambients.

Ambient Properties

As mentioned previously, ambient properties are properties that a container exposes to its controls through their control sites. They are used in two ways:

- To give hints to the control on how it should be setting the default value of its properties to appear integrated with its environment. Examples of this are BackColor on a form (that is, the color that the form is using as its background color) or Font in a word processing document (the document might use this to tell a control, "all the text around you is Arial Narrow").

- To convey specific information to the control. For example, **LocaleID** tells a control which locale the container's user interface is using.

Controls need advance knowledge about the ambient properties they might encounter so they can build in behavior that takes these properties into account. There is no general way to handle an arbitrary ambient property. By definition, controls are expected to take some specific action in response to ambient properties, and the control has no way of knowing what specific action is expected without prior knowledge of the set of ambient properties.

The majority of the ambient properties available on any container will be from the list of ambient properties outlined below. The control writer can use this list to decide which ambient properties would help the control behave in a more integrated manner. However, the control writer may choose to add properties that indicate something unique to that container that is not available using a standard ambient property.

Controls can take advantage of application-specific ambient properties in order to make them appear more integrated with a given application, but they should still work reasonably if these properties do not exist. The container will return **DISP_E_MEMBERNOTFOUND** if the control asks for a ambient property that is not implemented; the control should expect this and be able to handle it.

Ambient properties are exposed as the default dispatch interface on the site. The control accesses ambient properties by a call to **QueryInterface** for **IID_IDispatch** on the site. Note that the name of the property is *not* part of the contract; controls should get properties through **DispID**. The control can call **GetIDsOfNames** to access ambient properties by name, but this is discouraged. Standard ambient properties have negative **DispID**'s assigned to them. If an application wants to define application-specific site properties, it should use positive numbers for the ID's, as is normal for dispatch interfaces.

Note also that ambient properties are read-only. Controls are not able to write new values into ambient properties.

Note What determines that a property should be ambient? Ambient properties give information about the state of the container around the control. This will reflect the state of entire container (for example, Backcolor in a control container) or the state in the immediate area of the control. For example, a Word document can contain many different fonts. Depending on where a control is inserted into the document, the Ambient Font property has different values.

Table D.1   Ambient Properties

DispID	Name	Type	Description
-701	BackColor	**OLE_COLOR**	Specifies the color for the interior of a control (in RGB values).
-702	DisplayName	**VT_BSTR**	Specifies the name the control should display for itself in error messages.
-703	Font	**OLE_FONT**	Font information for the control.
-704	ForeColor	**OLE_COLOR**	Specifies the color for the display of text and graphics in a control (in RGB values).
-705	LocaleID	**VT_I4**	Specifies the ID of UI locale.
-706	MessageReflect	**VT_BOOL**	If **TRUE**, the container reflects Windows messages back to the control.
-707	ScaleUnits	**VT_BSTR**	Coordinate unit name being used by container.
-708	TextAlign	**VT_I2**	Specifies how the text should be aligned in a control: 0 is general (numbers to the right, text to the left), 1 is left, 2 is center, 3 is right, 4 fill justify.
-709	UserMode	**VT_BOOL**	Allows the control to determine how it is being used. If it is being used to design a control container (or some other thing), then the value is **FALSE**. If it is being used by an end user interacting with or viewing the control, then the value is **TRUE**. If this property is not present, the control should assume **TRUE**.
			Note that this value may change dynamically, as some containers may not distinguish between designing and using a control container and may switch without destroying (and reloading) the control.

Table D.1   Ambient Properties (*continued*)

DispID	Name	Type	Description
-710	UIDead	**VT_BOOL**	Allows the control to detect situations where the container should not allow the control to interact with user input. The value of this property can change dynamically. If **TRUE**, the control behaves normally. If **FALSE**, the UI is nonresponsive, so the control shouldn't set the cursor and should ignore UI input.

If this ambient property isn't present, the control should assume a value of **FALSE** |
-711	ShowGrabHandles	**VT_BOOL**	If **TRUE**, the control should not display grab handles when UI Active.
-712	ShowHatching	**VT_BOOL**	If **TRUE**, the control should not show the normal UI Active hatching feedback when the UI is activated.
-713	DisplayAsDefaultButton	**VT_BOOL**	Exposed only to button-like controls. If **TRUE**, the button should display itself using default button visuals.
-714	SupportsMnemonics	**VT_BOOL**	If **TRUE**, then the container supports mnemonics.

Control Properties, Methods, and Events

Controls can share many properties, methods, and events with other controls. For example, many controls have a Caption property and many fire a MouseMove event. In some cases, it is useful for containers and other code to know that a particular property (or method or event) has well-understood semantics. For example, if a container knows that a control has a Caption property—not just a property with the name "Caption," but a property that can be relied on to act like other Caption properties—then the container is able to deal with that property with little or no need for special information.

The following sections define a standard set of properties, methods, and events that can (and should) be reused by controls.

Standard properties, methods, and events are identified by a dispatch ID; OLE controls provide a header file that defines **dispID**'s for the standard properties, methods, and events. This implies that a container that has to access a standard property on a control must do so via **IDispatch**. The control may also provide early-bound access to this property in the control's primary interface, but the container has no type-safe way of accessing this property since it will show up in different places in different controls' vtables.

Note that no early-bound mechanism for accessing standard properties is defined. It would be possible to define an interface, **IStandardProperties**, which collects all the properties defined. However, any individual control normally will support only a subset of the large number of standard properties defined, and implementing a wide interface but filling in only a small set of methods is considered too inefficient.

Control Properties

Control properties are named attributes of a control. They define object characteristics (such as caption string, foreground color, background color) or control behaviors. They are managed and implemented by the control itself.

Note What determines that a property should be a control property? These properties specify information needed by the control. If the information is needed by both the control and the container, then it should be a Standard Control property. For example, the Enabled property is used by both the control (to determine its visualization) and the container (to decide whether to stop at the control as the user tabs through the control's form).

Table D.2   Control Properties

DispID	Name	Type	Description
-501	BackColor	**OLE_COLOR**	Specifies the color for the interior of the control (in RGB values).
-504	BorderStyle	**VT_I2**	Determines whether a control is displayed with a border.
-502	BackStyle	**VT_I2**	Determines whether a control is transparent (0) or opaque (1).
-512	Font	**OLEFONT**	Specifics current font for control.
-513	ForeColor	**OLE_COLOR**	Specifies the color for the display of text and graphics in a control (in RGB values).
-514	Enabled	**VT_BOOL**	Indicates whether the control can receive the focus. May also affect the control's appearance.
-515	hWnd	**VT_I4**	Specifies the handle of the control's window.
-517	Text	**VT_BSTR**	Value of a text box, list box, or combo box.
-518	Caption	**VT_BSTR**	Text displayed in or next to control.

Control Methods

A control method is a function that operates on a control. The following methods are Standard or Common for controls.

Table D.3   Control Methods

DispID	Name	Arguments (in order)	Description
-550	Refresh	None	Forces a repaint of the control—synchronously if the control currently has a window; otherwise asynchronously .
-551	DoClick	None	For button-like controls, simulates the button being clicked by the user. This is used to simulate the button being clicked when the user presses ENTER or ESC.
-552	AboutBox	None	Pops up a modal AboutBox dialog for the control.

Control Events

A control event is an action that is fired by a control to a form in response to some user action, such as clicking the mouse or pressing a key, or another action that changes the control. The control user can write code to respond to these events. Events can occur as a result of user action or program code, or they can be triggered by the system. The following table lists those control events that are standard or common.

Table D.4   Standard Control Events

DispID	Name	Arguments (in order)	Description
-600	Click	None	Occurs when the user presses and then releases a mouse button over a control. For some controls, this event is fired when the value of the control is changed.
-601	DblClick	None	Occurs when the user double-clicks in the control.
-602	KeyDown	**KeyCode, Shift**	Occurs when user presses a key when the control has the focus.
			KeyCode Key code for the key pressed.
			Shift Bit mask that details state of the CONTROL, SHIFT, and ALT keys
			KeyCode is passed by reference; changing it sends a different character to the object. Changing **KeyCode** to 0 cancels the keystroke so that the object receives no character.
-604	KeyUp	**KeyCode, Shift**	Occurs when the user releases a key when the control has the focus. See **KeyDown** for argument details.
			KeyCode is passed by reference; changing it sends a different character to the object. Changing **KeyCode** to 0 cancels the keystroke so that the object receives no character.

Table D.4   Standard Control Events (*continued*)

DispID	Name	Arguments (in order)	Description
-605	MouseDown	**Button**, **Shift**, **X**, **Y**	Occurs when the user depresses a mouse button while over a control.
			Button Bit mask that identifies which mouse button is now down (or up, for MouseUp events).
			Shift Bit mask that details state of the CTRL, SHIFT, and ALT keys
			X, Y Current location of mouse over control.
-606	MouseMove	**Button**, **Shift**, **X**, **Y**	Occurs when the mouse moves over the control. See MouseDown for details on arguments; note that for MouseMove events, **Button** identifies the set of buttons currently down.
-607	MouseUp	**Button**, **Shift**, **X**, **Y**	Indicates that the user has released the mouse button over this control. See MouseDown for details on args.

Standard Error Event

In most circumstances, OLE controls will encounter errors when manipulated by the user's code. For example, a list box may run out of memory when its AddString method is called. In this case, the list box will return an error, which is normal for OLE Automation objects.

However, in some cases, a control may encounter an error outside the context of user code. For example, a text box control may run out of memory as the user is typing. No user code is running at this point, therefore the control has no place to which to return an error. Nevertheless, the user should be notified of the error, and the user's code should be allowed to participate in the error handling.

To handle these circumstances, a standard Error event is introduced with a standard dispid of -608. A control fires this event when an error occurs outside of methods or properties being manipulated by user code. The Error event has the following signature:

```
Error(short Number, BSTR* Description, SCODE SCode, BSTR Source,
    BSTR HelpFile, long HelpContext, BOOL* CancelDisplay);
```

The **Number** parameter gives an error number local to the control, while the **SCode** parameter gives an OLE 2 error code. A short description of the error is passed via the **Description** parameter; the description is passed by reference so event handlers can replace the string before the control displays it. The **Source** parameter gives a user-friendly name for the object that raised the error. The **HelpFile** and **HelpContext** parameters point to more detailed information about the error. Normally, after firing this event objects will pop up a message box with the Description string. The **CancelDisplay** parameter allows event handlers to cancel this behavior.

A control does not fire this event unless it has no other means of communicating the error to the user or programmer. If the control is able to return the error through other means—by **HRESULT** for an interface method or **ExcepInfo** for a Dispatch method—it should do so.

Extended Control Properties, Methods, and Events

Extended Control Properties

Extended control properties are those properties that the container associates with each control. Control writers need to be aware of extended control properties for two reasons:

- Containers may, in their end-user programming models, choose to blur the distinction between control properties and extended control properties. Control writers should avoid using the same names that are defined for the standard properties listed in Table D.5.

- Each container can provide its own set of individual control properties. Controls should always refer the user to the container's documentation for more details.

Extended control properties are properties that are managed by the control container itself and only appear to be properties of the control. The control container adds the extended properties to the set of properties that the user sees for the control so that the user is isolated from the actual owner of each property. Control writers need to be aware of standard extended control properties for two reasons:

- Users of a control will see them as an integral part of the control. Control writers should always refer their users to product-specific documentation to find out which extended control properties are added to every control for a given application.

- Control writers should not implement other control properties with the same name as any standard extended control property. If they do, the container's extended object property should override the control's property; the extended object property has precedence over the control's property.

Containers can detect this sort of collision and warn the user, ideally at the point that the end user first adds the control to the container.

Note Why should a property be an extended control property? These properties specify control-specific information that only the container needs to know. This information is available to the control through the GetExtendedControl method in **IOleControlSite** (see below); however, controls that access their extended control object risk becoming specific to a particular container.

In general, controls are not expected to navigate to their extended control object. However, the **IOleControlSite** interface does provide a mechanism for doing this, should it prove necessary. However, a control that relies on the extended control being present and having a certain set of properties is at severe risk of only working in a limited set of containers.

To avoid collisions between the DispIDs assigned to control properties and members (whether standard or control specific) and the container's extended control properties, a range of standard DispIDs are reserved for the container's use. Containers should choose DispIDs for container-specific extended control properties from the range 0x80010000 to 0x8001ffff.

Since these values are negative, the table below gives DispID values that should be bitwise OR'd with 0x80010000 to obtain the true DispID. For example, the standard Cancel extended control property has the value 0x37 listed below; the true DispID for the standard Cancel property is therefore 0x80010037.

Table D.5   Standard Control Properties

DispID	Name	Type	Description
0x00	Name	**VT_BSTR**	This returns the user-defined name of an object.
0x07	Visible	**VT_BOOL**	Indicates if the control is visible on the container.
0x08	Parent	**VT_DISPATCH**	Parent always returns the document that a object is embedded in. A control should be able to use this property to enumerate properties of its container, etc.
0x37	Cancel	**VT_BOOL**	**TRUE** if the control is the default Cancel button for the form.
0x38	Default	**VT_BOOL**	Determines which button on a form is the default button (that is, the default OK button on a dialog).

Note that in some cases a container may purposely elect to override a standard control property in order to modify its semantics. For example, the standard Enabled property applies directly to the control. If it is **FALSE**, the control considers itself disabled and renders itself appropriately. A container which itself had an Enabled property might decide to provide an extended control property Enabled that overrides the control's Enabled property. This version of Enabled might take into account the container's own Enabled property so that the user could tell whether the control was "really" enabled, as opposed to only locally enabled.

Extended Control Methods and Events

Containers may also choose to expose methods and/or events on an individual control basis. Containers should use the same mechanism as properties to do this. OLE controls do not (at this time) define any standard extended control methods or events.

New Interfaces for Controls

In order to support the extended functionality of OLE custom controls several OLE 2 interfaces were created. These interfaces support several abilities and functions unique to OLE controls, such as communication between OLE control and container, special support for button controls, in-place active objects, keyboard interfaces, and many more.

IOleControl and IOleControlSite

OLE controls introduce a pair of interfaces used for communication between the control and its container that goes beyond the normal communication defined by the OLE Compound Documents interfaces. The control implements an interface **IOleControl**, and the container implements an interface **IOleControlSite** on its site objects:

```
interface IOleControl : public IUnknown
{
    GetControlInfo(CONTROLINFO * pCI);
    OnMnemonic(LPMSG pMsg);

    OnAmbientPropertyChange(DISPID dispid);
    FreezeEvents(BOOL fFreeze);
};

interface IOleControlSite : public IUnknown
{
    OnControlInfoChanged(void);
```

```
LockInPlaceActive(BOOL fLock);
GetExtendedControl(IDispatch ** ppDisp);
TransformCoords(
    POINTL * pPtlHiMetric,
    POINTF * pPtfContainer,
    DWORD dwFlags);
TranslateAccelerator(MSG * lpmsg, DWORD grfModifiers);
};
```

The GetControlInfo and OnMnemonic methods of **IOleControl** and the OnControlInfoChanged method of **IOleControlSite** are documented fully in "New Misc Status Bits." They expose control-style keyboard interface support for OLE controls.

The OnAmbientPropertyChange method is called by the container when any of its ambient properties change value. A control that is using ambient properties from the container may need to update its own internal or visual state in response. The container indicates which ambient property changed with the DispID parameter. The container may pass **DISPID_UNKNOWN (= -1)**, in which case the control should assume some unspecified set of ambient properties changed value.

The FreezeEvents method determines whether the control will fire events. When initially created, the control's freeze count is at zero, and the control is free to fire events when appropriate. If the container calls **FreezeEvents(TRUE)**, then the freeze count is incremented and the control should not fire any events until the freeze count returns to zero via the container calling **FreezeEvents(FALSE)**. This mechanism gives the container a way to suppress events being fired until it is fully ready to deal with them.

The control is free to decide whether to discard events which are triggered when the control is frozen, or to queue them up and fire them when the control becomes unfrozen. Normally, a control makes this decision based on how important the event is to the control's contract—if discarding the event is likely to break users' assumptions, and therefore their code, then the control should queue the event.

Controls can call LockInPlaceActive to prevent the container from attempting to demote the control out of the InPlaceActive state. Demoting the control from InPlaceActive (or UIActive) to the Running or Loading state would cause the control to be deactivated and its window destroyed. This avoids potential crashing bugs in Windows 3.1; destroying a Win 3.1 window while (for example) handling a **WM_GETFOCUS** message for that window causes a general protection fault in USER.

Controls often call **LockInPlaceActive(TRUE)** before firing an event, and **LockInPlaceActive(FALSE)** afterwards if destroying the control's window during event processing could cause problems. Note that **LockInPlaceActive** calls should nest; the container needs to keep a "lock count" for each control. Also, a container itself should not go to the Loaded or Running states when one of its embedded controls is locked since that would demote the embedding; locking a control in the InPlaceActive state effectively locks its container in that state as well.

The GetExtendedControl method allows controls to navigate through the site to the Extended Control Object provided for them by the container. The method returns a pointer to the Extended Control Object's default programmability interface, which normally merges the properties and methods of the Extended Control Object with those of the control. With the exception of looking for standard Extended Control properties, there is very little the control can do with the Extended Control that isn't container-dependent.

The TranslateCoordinates method is defined in more detail in "Handling Coordinates."

Normally, a container will fire events as the user moves between controls in the container, changing which control is UI Active. In most cases, the Windows focus will be on the UI Active control; controls normally set the focus to themselves when UI Activated. However, in some circumstances it may be necessary for controls to grab the focus before becoming UI Active; for instance, a control may need to set the focus to itself on mouse down messages, but not UI Activate itself until a mouse up message is received. The OnFocus method allows the control to notify its container that it is doing this.

New MiscStatus Bits

In some cases, containers may need to obtain information about an object's capabilities without creating an instance of that object. The main mechanism for doing this in OLE 2 is MiscStatus bits. Each embeddable class adds a key to the registry which identifies its capabilities. The container (or handler, in its implementation of **GetMiscStatus**) can look in the registry to see if an object supports some particular capability. For example, in OLE 2 the **OLEMISC_INSIDEOUT** bit identifies an object which can be in-place activated without being UI Activated.

OLE controls add some new MiscStatus bits to the set:

- **OLEMISC_INVISIBLEATRUNTIME**

  Used by a container that has a distinction between design-time and run-time, as most control containers do, to only show the object when in design mode. A Timer control that fires a Click event at preset intervals might use this bit; it would be visible at design-time (so the user can set properties on the timer) but not at run-time.

- **OLEMISC_ALWAYSRUN**

  Used by a container to always put objects with this bit set into the Running state, even when not visible. That is, the container should request that it *not* be given the standard handler for this object, but that the server be activated instead. This allows the object to fire events and take other proactive action; again, this is useful for Timer-like objects. This bit is not normally required for in-process servers.

- **OLEMISC_ACTSLIKEBUTTON**

  Used by a container that provides Default/Cancel buttons. Controls that provide this flag are capable of acting like buttons. In particular, the control's primary event can be triggered in its **IOleControl::OnMnemonic** method, and the control is prepared to render itself as the default button based on the ambient DisplayAsDefaultButton.

- **OLEMISC_ACTSLIKELABEL**

  Used by a container that potentially allows OLE controls to replace the container's native label. The container is responsible for determining what to do with this flag (or ignore it). A container that uses this flag will typically intercept mnemonics and/or mouse clicks targeted for the label-like control at run time and reinterpret these messages as attempts to move to the field associated with the label.

- **OLEMISC_NOUIACTIVATE**

  Used by a container to determine if a control doesn't support UI Activation. Under OLE 2 such an object was not very useful since activating it was generally the only way to edit it. With OLE controls, the user can program the control using OLE Automation or set its properties using property pages; therefore, it can use a non-UI activated control. Note that controls can already indicate that they don't support a separate In-Place Active state by not including the **OLEMISC_INSIDEOUT** bit.

- **OLEMISC_ALIGNABLE**

  Used by a container that supports aligned controls. This bit is used by a control that is most useful when aligned on some side of its container. Containers that support such aligned controls can use this bit to decide whether the user should be allowed to align a particular control.

- **OLEMISC_IMEMODE**

  Marks a control that understands IME Mode. This only makes sense for DBCS versions of Windows. Containers will typically add an IMEMode property to the extended control for controls that mark themselves with this bit.

- **OLEMISC_SIMPLEFRAME**

  Used by containers to determine if a control supports the ISimpleFrameSite protocol. Containers that also support this interface will use simple frame controls as parents for other controls in the container. In effect, the simple frame control operates as an OLE compound document container, but the frame control's container does almost all the work.

- **OLEMISC_SETCLIENTSITEFIRST**

  Used by new OLE containers to identify controls that support having **SetClientSite** called first, immediately after being created, and before the control has been completely constructed. Normal OLE compound document containers are written to call **SetClientSite** on embedded objects after calling **IPersistStorage::Load** or **IPersistStorage::InitNew** on the object. Since OLE controls get state through their client site and that state is useful during the load process, they need to have the client site available during Load or InitNew.

Existing OLE Containers ignore these bits, and controls need to be prepared for this. Similarly, existing OLE servers never specify these bits, but containers need to handle such objects.

Container Modality

Many control containers have traditionally changed their behavior according to the mode of their container. For example, many control containers distinguish between design mode (where the author lays out a form) and run mode (where a user uses the form).

This paradigm potentially breaks down with multiple containers that host controls, since the attributes of design mode in one container do not necessarily match the attributes in another container. Hence, suggesting a set of ambient properties such as { DesignMode, TestMode, RunMode } is unlikely to work since the exact characteristics that define these modes is very likely to differ between containers, leading to a set of ambients that are effectively meaningless. A simple set of modes does not allow containers to fully communicate how controls need to modify their behavior.

Instead, the various aspects of control behavior are split out as separate ambients depending on the container's mode. Rather than exposing the reason for a behavioral change (that is, DesignMode), the ambient exposes the intended effect (not showing activation feedback, for example). The ambients exposed for this purpose are:

- **UserMode(BOOL)**

  This property allows the control to determine how it is being used. If it is being used to design a form (or some other thing), then the value is **FALSE** (=Designer). If it is being used by an end user interacting with or viewing the control, then the value is **TRUE** (=EndUser). Note that this value might change dynamically since some containers may not distinguish between designing and using a control container, and might switch user modes without destroying (and reloading) the control.

  Controls may use this property for many purposes. For example, making certain properties read-only to end users in situations where changing the property might be catastrophic; possibly resulting in losing some state that would be inappropriate for end users to deal with. It is recommended, however, that controls should have as few differences as possible between True-EndUser and False-Designer. Different visualization, such as displaying a dotted border around an otherwise totally transparent control is another possibility. Finally, a control could use this property to behave differently when UI Active—allowing visual editing of itself at design time, via mouse clicks, drag and drop, etc.

- **UIDead(BOOL)**

  This property allows the control to detect situations where the container does not want the control to interact with user input, such as in Visual Basic's BreakMode. A well-behaved control can act accordingly, ignoring UI input and not calling **SetCursor**.

  The value of this ambient property can change dynamically as the container changes mode.

Control Activation and Grab Handles

OLE controls follow the normal OLE 2 guidelines about which object is responsible for drawing selection feedback and grab handles: when an object is UI active, it is responsible for drawing activation feedback (the hatched border and grab handles). When an object is inactive, or only in-place active, the container is responsible for drawing any feedback or grab handles.

This makes sense for containers in design mode. However, in run mode for a container like Visual Basic®, the hatched border should not be shown in any case for control-like objects. However, different containers have different concepts of modality so the ability to suppress an active object's border differs between containers. Containers can expose two standard ambient properties, ShowHatching and ShowGrabHandles, to indicate to controls that feedback should be suppressed. Well-behaved controls should look for these ambient properties; if they are present and their values are **FALSE**, the control should suppress drawing a border and grab handles in all circumstances.

If the ShowGrabHandles (with a **BOOL** parameter) ambient property is present and **FALSE**, grab handles should not be displayed for controls on a form in run mode. This ambient allows the container to request that controls not show grab handles when UI Active.

The ShowHatching (with a **BOOL** parameter) ambient property allows the container to tell the control when it is appropriate to display hatching. A well-behaved control should display hatching when UI Active only if ShowHatching is **TRUE** or if the ShowHatching ambient isn't available.

OLE has no provisions in regards to containers communicating to CD objects whether hatching should be displayed when UI Active, since in the relatively heavyweight world of compound documents hatching was always desirable. With controls, some degree of communication is necessary. Hatching should not be displayed around the active control in a run-mode form, for instance.

Although this property may change values dynamically, controls usually only need to inspect it each time they become UI Active. Hence, containers should not change this for a control that is UI Active (or at least not expect the control to immediately respond).

Special Support for Buttons

OLE custom controls offer additional support for button controls. This support includes handling for default buttons and exclusivity for radio buttons.

Default Buttons

The normal command button control can act as the "default" or "cancel" button for a form. If a form has a default button, it is triggered when the user pressed ENTER when the form is active; similarly, the cancel button is triggered when the user types ESC. The default button for a form is normally displayed with a thick border or bold text. However, when the focus is in a control that wants to handle the ENTER key, the form will not trigger the default button on ENTER keystrokes, and will disable any special thick border or bold text displayed by the button.

Providing this behavior requires solving three problems: detecting that a control is "button-like", triggering the button, and communicating to the default button whether to show its special default button rendering.

- Controls indicate they are "button-like" with a new MiscStatus bit, **OLEMISC_ACTSLIKEBUTTON**.

- Containers trigger the button by calling the button's IOleControl::OnMnemonic method. Note the control itself might elect to expose this capability to users via some method.

- Containers let the button know whether to show the default button style with a standard ambient property, DisplayAsDefaultButton.

  This ambient property has different values for the different controls on the form. The control can detect changes in the value of this property through the change notification mechanism for standard ambient properties. The container will update the ambient as the focus moves into and out of controls which themselves process the ENTER key. Containers will normally show this ambient property to all controls, even those that don't act like buttons. Controls that are not button-like should ignore the ambient property, just as they ignore any ambient property they don't expect or recognize.

Containers need to be able to detect which controls process the ENTER key themselves, so that the container can update the DisplayAsDefaultButton ambient property for the container's default button. For example, if the user navigates into a multiline edit control that processes the ENTER key, then the default button should not be highlighted. This information is present in the **CONTROLINFO** struct returned from the **IOleControl** interface.

Exclusive Buttons

Radio buttons and similar controls support exclusivity for their Value property. That is, if one radio button in a group is checked, the other controls in the group should not be checked. Controls indicate that they support exclusivity by using a special type for their Value property. The standard OLE controls Standard TypeLib defines this type:

```
typedef BOOL ExclusiveBool;
```

Containers can then detect which controls are similar to radio buttons by looking for a Value property of this type. However, for containers to take advantage of this property, the control needs to support property binding for its ExclusiveBool Value property. If a control supports property binding for an ExclusiveBool Value property, the container can layer whatever model it wants for radio buttons on top.

In general, controls should not use the ExclusiveBool type for properties other than their Value property. The semantics of this would be too confusing, especially with a heterogeneous group of controls; the only property that all controls are expected to support is Value.

Check boxes and similar controls normally expose a three-state Value, since check boxes support an indeterminate third state, in addition to **TRUE** and **FALSE**:

```
typedef enum
{
    Unchecked = 0,
    Checked = 1,
    Grayed = 2,
} OLE_TRISTATE;
```

This type is also defined in the OLE Controls Standard TypeLib. Containers can provide similar exclusivity functionality for Value properties of type **TRISTATE**.

Handling In-place Active Objects

The released version of OLE 2 includes support for in-place active CD objects; that is, objects that are in-place active (have created a window for themselves) but not UI active (for example, they do not own the menu). Objects are allowed to require that their containers in-place activate them when the container is in-place activated. This implies that containers need to deal with multiple embedded-object windows at a time.

This causes some complications for containers. Suggested ways for containers to deal with these complications are given below. Note, however, that the Controls architecture does not stress having in-place active objects. Most objects are expected to act as normal OLE objects and only be in-place active when UI active.

Z-Order

Many control containers support overlapping embeddings, which were not explicitly supported in OLE 2. For overlapping controls to be useable, the container must be able to implement Z-ordering; a process in Windows where windows are ordered on the screen according to their Z-order. For example, the window at the top of the Z-order appears on top of all other windows in the order.

For inactive controls, implementing Z-ordering is straightforward. The container is rendering the controls so it either renders them from back to front or sets up clipping regions so that the controls' visualizations reflect the proper Z-order.

To have in-place active and UI active controls participate in the Z-order, the container needs cooperation from the in-place active controls. The controls, which have no way to implement Z-order themselves, should cede control of the Z-order of their window to their container. In particular:

- Controls should create their window at the top of the Z-order when in-place activated. This is the default behavior of **CreateWindow**, so this does not mean extra work for the control.

- Controls should not manipulate the Z-order of the window once it has been created. In particular, controls should not attempt to bring their window to the front when they are UI activated.

- Containers manipulate the control's window's Z-order dynamically. Controls should be written to expect this.

A reasonable Z-ordering container is expected to maintain two Z-orders: the logical Z-order and the physical Z-order. The current UI Active object should be maintained on top of the physical Z-order, even though it may not be on top of the logical Z-order. This means that windows can pop to the front as the user moves between fields. The other In-Place Active objects will be next in the physical Z-order, followed by the inactive objects on the bottom. Within the In-Place Active objects or **IViewObject** objects, the relative logical Z-ordering should be maintained.

Containers are notified whenever objects transition between the various states and can obtain the object's **hWnd** when one has been created. Given this, the correct physical Z-order of the objects can be maintained. Since the container does all drawing for the nonactive objects, displaying them in the correct Z-order is straightforward.

Controls Recreating Windows

Some controls may expose properties that map directly to window styles. For example, a control may expose a Border property and implement it with the **WS_BORDER** window style. Changing the window style of an extant window is not well supported in Windows, so the user would normally destroy and re-create a window in order to change its style.

However, in the existing OLE Compound Document architecture, an object is not expected to do this, except when making state transitions between the Running and InPlaceActive states. For compatibility with existing servers, OLE controls should not unilaterally destroy and re-create their window. Destroying and re-creating the window should be done only as part of the transition from the In-Place Active state to the Running state and back again. However, the control can decide to make this transition unilaterally, notifying its container through the appropriate site methods.

Keyboard Interface

Implementing a keyboard interface in the context of OLE presents two basic problems. First, how are the Windows input messages for special keys—TAB, the arrow keys, ENTER—routed to the correct object? Second, how do objects communicate with their container about their specific keyboard interface needs—for example, how does a Label control implement its mnemonic character?

Routing Keyboard Messages with Existing Interfaces

The existing OLE Compound Document interfaces provide enough support to handle some of the work in routing keyboard events to the correct objects. However, to make this work, some existing methods need to be reused in a manner outside their original intent.

The CD interfaces provide the TranslateAccelerators methods used to coordinate accelerator keys, the implementation of which is normally split between the (innermost) UI Active object and the (outermost) Frame object. That is, the UI Active object provides some accelerators, and the Frame provides some. Any object that owns the message loop—which changes with different combinations of EXE- and DLL-implemented servers and containers—is responsible for making sure each of these objects gets a change to translate all keyboard messages.

OLE controls leverage this basic infrastructure for the simpler keyboard event routing cases.

New, Improved OleTranslateAccelerator

The mechanics of accelerator translation is different for a UI active server that is in process and for a server that is out-of-process. The in-process server uses the container's message pump; it relies on the container to feed it input messages. So, the container has the opportunity to filter messages before sending them to the UI active object.

An out-of-process server has its own message pump. In this case, the container is relying on the server to send it messages (since the messages might be accelerator combinations intended for one of the container's menus). The server does this by calling **OleTranslateAccelerator**.

Currently, **OleTranslateAccelerator** only sends messages to the container that match accelerator combinations found in the container's accelerator table. The container does not have an opportunity to change its accelerator table on demand; it must hand its, fully constructed, to objects that it is UI activating. This works for accelerator tables, but doesn't match the requirements for general control keyboard event handling, because the set of key combinations that will be interpreted as mnemonics may change dynamically. For example, the mnemonic for a Label can change as the Label's Caption changes.

OLE controls extend the **OleTranslateAccelerator** API to deal with variable sets of accelerator key combinations. The solution is to allow new-style containers to request that additional keyboard events be sent to it by the UI Active control. This is done by introducing special wildcard entries in the accelerator table. The entries in an acclerator table are structs of the following format (for Win16):

```
struct AccelTableEntry {
    BYTE fFlags;
    WORD wEvent;
    WORD wID;
};
```

The **wEvent** field contains the ASCII character value or virtual-key code of the accelerator key. The **wID** field gives the accelerator identifier that matches it. The following flag values are defined by Windows:

- **0x02**   Top-level menu not highlighted.
- **0x04**   SHIFT
- **0x08**   CONTROL
- **0x10**   Last entry in the accelerator table.

The **wEvent** value 0 is used as a wildcard. **OleTranslateAcclerator** matches any character with the correct set of modifiers when it encounters an entry with **wEvent = 0**. For example, an entry with **wEvent = 0** and **fFlags = 0x08** match any CTRL-key combination. An entry with **wEvent = 0** and **fFlags = 0x14** matches any ALT-SHIFT-key combination.

Some containers want to see all possible keyboard events. The combination of **wEvent = 0** and **(fFlags & 0x1c) = 0** is interpreted as all possible keys, rather than all unmodified keys. Otherwise the container would need to include eight entries in the accelerator table (one for each combination of ALT + SHIFT + CTRL).

Taking this approach lets a container name both a set of specific accelerators as well as a set of wildcards. So, a container could request VK_F3 (for its own internal use) and also ALT-any key (for use as control mnemonics).

Interpreting Special Key Combinations

Some objects want to handle certain keystroke combinations specially. There are two basic examples of this. First, some controls have their own interpretation of keystrokes their container otherwise use in its keyboard interface. For example, a multiline text box control inserts a new line when the ENTER key is pressed, overriding the container, which might instead activate the default button. Second, some controls have mnemonics that are active no matter which of their siblings is currently UI Active (i.e., has the focus). For example, a Label control may change which sibling control is active when the Labels mnemonic is seen.

Objects that need custom interactions with the keyboard interface implement methods in the **IOleControl** interface. Similarly, the container implements keyboard interface methods in its **IOleControlSite** implementation.

```
struct CONTROLINFO
{
    ULONG       cb;         // Structure size
    HACCEL      hAccel;     // Control mnemonics
    USHORT      cAccel;     // Number of entries in mnemonics table
    DWORD       dwFlags;    // Flags chosen from list below...
};

#define CTRLINFO_EATS_RETURN    1    // Control processes VK_RETURN
#define CTRLINFO_EATS_ESCAPE    2    // Control processes VK_ESCAPE

interface IOleControl : public IUnknown
{
    ...

    GetControlInfo(CONTROLINFO * pCI);
    OnMnemonic(LPMSG pMsg, DWORD grfModifiers);
};

interface IOleControlSite : public IUnknown
{
    ...

    OnControlInfoChanged(void);
    TranslateAccelerator(LPMSG pmsg, DWORD grfModifiers);
};
```

At load time, a control container asks each embedded control for **CONTROLINFO** via **GetControlInfo**. The control uses the struct to return an accelerator table containing the mnemonics it wants to expose when not UI active. It also sets the appropriate flags in the structure, telling the container whether the control processes the ENTER and ESC keys when UI Active. This allows the container to properly set the state of the OK and Cancel buttons on the form; the OK button, for example, should have a thick border if typing ENTER will trigger it, but whether this happens changes as the focus moves from control to control.

The form can compare the entries in the accelerator table against the type of key combinations it can intercept. The form decides what key combinations it intercepts ahead of time. Containers may elect to not support arbitrary key combinations as accelerators. For example, a form might decide to intercept only ALT-key combinations; in this case, a control that wants to use CTRL + ENTER as a mnemonic could not.

In any case, when the form receives a key combination that matches a combination in the control's accelerator table, the form calls the control's OnMnemonic method. The control decides what the appropriate response to the mnemonic is; this differs from control to control. Note that OLE controls define special support for handling accelerators on Label-like controls; this support was outlined earlier in this section.

If the mnemonics for a control change while the control is loaded, the control should call **OnControlInfoChanged** on the client site. The container is then responsible for reloading **CONTROLINFO** from the control.

An in-process control should have an **IOleInPlaceActiveObject::TranslateAccelerator** method similar to the following:

```
STDMETHODIMP
CFooControl::TranslateAccelerator(LPMSG pmsg)
{
    // Process any keys that the control wants to "override" its
    // container and frame's accelerators

    hr = m_pOleControlSite->TranslateAccelerator(pmsg, 0);
    if (hr == S_FALSE)
        return hr;

    // Process any keys that the control wants to "override" its
    // frame's accelerators, but not its immediate container's
}
```

The control then processes "normal" keys as OLE compound document objects do, by responding to window messages sent to its window procedure. Note that since the control is in-process, it doesn't delegate messages to the outermost frame.

OK and Cancel Button handling

In OLE controls, a control indicates that it is "button-like" by setting the **OLEMISC_ACTSLIKEBUTTON** MiscStatus bit. Containers can then allow the user to mark such a control as being the default or cancel button for the form. The default button is activated when the user presses ENTER; the cancel button when the user presses ESC.

The container traps the ENTER and ESC keys by including them in its accelerator table. When one of these keys is pressed, the container calls the standard method Click in the appropriate control's primary dispinterface. The standard Click method is described in "Control Methods."

Note that the container's ability to trap the ENTER key will vary as the user moves in and out of controls which themselves trap the ENTER key. The container can detect which controls intercept ENTER by inspecting the **CTRLINFO_EATS_RETURN** bit in **ControlInfo**. To follow the Windows style guide, the container needs to communicate to the default button that it will no longer be triggered when the user presses ENTER ; the container does this through the standard DisplayAsDefaultButton ambient property (described in "Ambient Properties"). Button-like controls should look for this ambient property, track changes to it through the OnAmbientChanged method, and display themselves to match.

Mnemonic Translation

Controls may wish to detect whether their container supports the control-style extended keyboard interface. Containers that do support mnemonic translation should expose the standard ambient property SupportsMnemonics of type **BOOL** with the value **TRUE**. The control can examine this ambient and hide or show its mnemonic feedback (underlining the mnemonic character, for example) appropriately.

Note that during normal usage, a container should not change its SupportsMnemonics value. This includes the container going from the UI Active state to a non-UI Active state. This follows the existing Windows standard, where mnemonic feedback is shown for nonactive windows. This also includes going between design and run mode for modal containers; SupportsMnemonics should be **TRUE** in each mode, even if the container doesn't plan on forwarding accelerators in design mode.

Persistence and Initialization

OLE 2 compound document objects use **IPersistStorage** for persistence. This makes sense for the relatively heavyweight document editor applications OLE 2 focuses on, but makes less sense for controls. Consequently, OLE controls allow controls to support persistence to streams. New containers written for OLE controls can detect this support and save embedded controls to streams rather than storages.

Of course, existing compound document containers only support **IPersistStorage**. Controls will normally want to support being embedded in compound document containers, and should therefore support **IPersistStorage**.

Controls support persistence to streams through the new interface **IPersistStreamInit**:

```
interface IPersistStreamInit : public IPersist
{
    IsDirty(void);
    Load(LPSTREAM pStrm);
    Save(LPSTREAM pStrm, BOOL fClearDirty);
    GetSizeMax(ULARGE_INTEGER * pcbSize);
    InitNew(void);
};
```

The **IPersistStream** interface itself is almost perfect for controls. The major omission is that it doesn't have an analog to the InitNew method in **IPersistStorage**. This method serves two functions for **IPersistStorage** objects: first, it gives the object a pointer to its storage (which the object can hold on to), and second, it notifies the object that it is being newly created (rather than being deserialized).

The first use does not apply to streamed objects—they are not allowed to hold on to the stream pointer passed but rather must load all their state synchronously from the stream and release the pointer—but the second does. Without an InitNew method, a streamed object would be forced to fully construct its state at CreateInstance time, even though that state might be overwritten with a call to **IPersistStream::Load**. With InitNew, the object can avoid performing expensive operations twice during deserialization.

Note that this new interface is not derived from **IPersistStream**. This is because it would imply that the object could be used as a normal **IPersistStream** object, without calling its InitNew method. This would defeat the purpose of having a new contract.

Initialization Order

Normal compound document containers call the **IOleObject::SetClientSite** method after fully loading an instance of the object, either by creating it (**CoCreateInstance** followed by **IPersistStorage::InitNew**) or by loading it from a storage (**CoCreateInstance** followed by **IPersistStorage::Load**). This works fine for normal compound document objects, since their persistent state is self-contained—they have no need to interact with their container through the client site during their creation or deserialization process.

However, OLE controls can get interesting states from their container—specifically, ambient properties—that would be useful during the creation or deserialization process. For example, a control might choose to not serialize those of its properties whose values match ambient properties exposed by the container, choosing instead to copy those properties from the container during deserialization.

For this to happen, the control needs to be given its client site before **Load** or **InitNew** is called (either on **IPersistStorage** or **IPersistStream**), rather than after. A control indicates that it supports this contract by setting the new **MiscStatus** bit **OLEMISC_SETCLIENTSITEFIRST**. New OLE control containers should support controls with this bit set by calling **SetClientSite** before **Load** or **InitNew**.

Controls can detect whether their container supports this new style of initialization by monitoring whether **SetClientSite** or **InitNew/Load** is called first. If the container calls **SetClientSite** first, then it can be counted on to do this in the future.

Interactions Between IPersistStreamInit and IPersistStorage

A control is guaranteed that its parent will follow one of the initialization sequences given above. The container will either use **IPersistStreamInit** or **IPersistStorage**, and will always call **InitNew** or **Load** on the control's interface before using the control. As expected, the container may also make any number of calls to the Save method on the interface, either saving the state of the control to its permanent location or performing a "Save As" to another location to save a new copy of the control.

In some cases, the container may need to save the new copy using either the **IPersistStreamInit** or **IPersistStorage** interface. For example, the container may load and save a control using **IPersistStreamInit**, but need to make a "Save As" copy using **IPersistStorage**. Although the control's **IPersistStream::InitNew** or **IPersistStream::Load** method will have been called in this case, neither its **IPersistStorage::InitNew** or **IPersistStorage::Load** method will have been called. Nevertheless, **IPersistStorage::Save** should normally succeed (as long as an **IStorage** pointer is explicitly passed in, implying a "Save As" operation).

This means that the control's implementations of **IPesistStreamInit** and **IPersistStorage** aren't completely separable. After a legal initialization through either interface, the Save method on the other interface should function correctly.

Control Size Negotiation

Controls can negotiate with their containers for new sizes. When UI Active or In-Place Active, the control calls the **IOleInPlaceSite::OnPosRectChanged** method exposed by its container on the control's site, passing the desired new size. The container in turn calls **IOleInPlaceObject::SetObjectRects** on the control to effect the change. This mechanism functions exactly as it does for normal compound document objects.

When the control is merely Loaded or Running and wants to change its size, it should call the **IOleClientSite::RequestNewObjectLayout** method. This method was introduced as part of OLE Compound Documents, but its semantics were not fully documented. Existing compound document containers will return **E_NOTIMPL** from this method, indicating that they do not support the control's request for a new size.

New OLE Control containers may decide to return **S_OK**, accepting the request. The container should call **IOleObject::GetExtent** to retrieve the control's preferred size. The container does not need to do this synchronously; it may decide to defer the resize until it is convenient. When the container later resizes the control, the control's new size is passed to the control via **IOleObject::SetExtent**.

Standard Types

Since controls share many of the same properties, it isn't surprising that they share many of the same types. For example, many controls have properties that control the colors used for the control. It is useful to be able to identify a particular property as being of a standard **OLE_COLOR** type. Containers and other code can be written to deal specifically with color-valued properties.

This section defines a standard set of types intended for reuse by Controls. These types are defined in a standard Type Library provided as part of OLE controls. Most controls will have references to this type library in their type description.

Handling Coordinates

Different containers provide different coordinate models.

For Extended Control properties and methods, this isn't a problem. Each container implements its own Extended Control, so it exposes whatever coordinate model it likes. Properties are exposed with a data type chosen by the container, as are parameters to methods. The same is true for any Extended Control events—Move or Size, for example—the container chooses the data types and scaling for the event's parameters.

However, controls may also use coordinates—for their own properties, or as parameters on their events and methods. This is common for control events: Click, MouseMove, MouseDown and MouseUp, for example. It is much less common for control properties and methods. A Grid control might have a ColumnWidths property, for example, but examples of this sort of property are relatively rare.

The solution:

- OLE controls provides standard TypeDefs for the different flavors of coordinates:

```
typedef LONG OLE_XPOS_PIXELS;
typedef LONG OLE_YPOS_PIXELS;
typedef LONG OLE_XSIZE_PIXELS;
typedef LONG OLE_YSIZE_PIXELS;
typedef LONG OLE_XPOS_HIMETRIC;
typedef LONG OLE_YPOS_HIMETRIC;
typedef LONG OLE_XSIZE_HIMETRIC;
typedef LONG OLE_YSIZE_HIMETRIC;
```

Since containers may need to provide different mapping of positional and size values into the container's coordinate space, position and size are separated into separate type definitions. For example, a container may apply an offset when mapping a position but not when mapping a size. Similarly, different typedefs are provided for coordinates measured in pixels (the most natural coordinate to use when firing events from window procedures) and those measured in **HIMETRIC** (matching OLE).

- The container can detect event parameters of these standard types. Since the container is interposed between the control and the container's language integration, the container has the opportunity to translate event parameters of these types to the container's preferred coordinate model. Often, the container needs to make this translation in the TypeInfo it provides for the extended control (control + Extended Control), since the container may change the data type of the parameter, along with the other merging work it does in TypeInfo.

- Since the container does not normally interpose itself between user code and the control (at least not for early-bound access to control properties), the container may not be able to provide automatic translation for object properties and method parameters. Instead, the control is responsible for identifying coordinate-valued properties and method parameters and fulfilling a simple contract for them.

To match arbitrary containers, coordinate-valued properties and method parameters should be single-precision floats, and should be defined with standard typedefs provided by the OLE Custom Controls Development Kit (CDK). The control is responsible for translating its own internal coordinate-valued properties into the container's coordinate system when making them visible.

However, since the container owns the coordinate model, the control must delegate to it to perform the translation. The container exposes a method TranslateCoordinates on the control's site to enable this. This method allows coordinates to be converted between **HIMETRIC** and the container's coordinate model and back again, for both positional coordinates and sizes. The flags passed to the method govern the exact manipulation that occurs; note that during the conversion from container coordinates to **HIMETRIC**, the first parameter is the output parameter, a minor deviation from OLE conventions.

```
typedef struct tagPOINTF
{
    float    x;
    float    y;
} POINTF;


interface IOleControlSite
{
    ...

    TranslateCoordinates(
        POINTL * pPtlHiMetric,
        POINTF * pPtfContainer,
        DWORD dwFlags);
};

#define XFORMCOORDS_POSITION            1
#define XFORMCOORDS_SIZE                2
#define XFORMCOORDS_HIMETRICTOCONTAINER 4
#define XFORMCOORDS_CONTAINERTOHIMETRIC 8
```

In addition, the control may show coordinates itself, perhaps in its property pages. In this case, the control should display the property in the container's coordinate model. Using the method described above, it can convert the value. However, it also needs to get the unit name as a string for use as a label for the property. The container provides this string as the standard ambient property ScaleUnits.

In some cases, containers may wish to detect which of a control's properties are container-scaled coordinates. The standard OLE controls Type Library defines standard types for such properties, which the container can then look for by UUID in the control's Type Library.

```
typedef float OLE_XPOS_CONTAINER;
typedef float OLE_YPOS_CONTAINER;
typedef float OLE_XSIZE_CONTAINER;
typedef float OLE_YSIZE_CONTAINER;
```

For most controls, this produces a relatively seamless end-user coordinate model.

Standard Color Type

A helper API is provided to help manage mapping an **OLE_COLOR** value to the matching Windows **COLORREF** value. The helper routines, under Win3.1, return a reasonable default RGB value when asked for those indices.

```
STDAPI OleTranslateColor(OLE_COLOR color, HPALETTE hpal, COLORREF *
pcolorref);
```

This API takes a value of type **OLE_COLOR** and maps it to the corresponding Windows **COLORREF**. The algorithm for doing this is a little complicated. Table D.6 below defines how the conversion happens, based on the input color value, and shows what the output **COLORREF** will be.

Note that **NULL** may be passed for **lpcolorref**, in which case this API is simply verifying that color has a valid value.

Table D.6   Mapping of Colors Using OleTranslateColor

Color	hpal	Resulting COLORREF
invalid	don't care	Error
0x800000xx, xx is not a valid **GetSysColor**() index.	don't care	Error
don't care	invalid	Undefined
0x0100iiii, iiii is not valid for **hpal**	valid palette	Error
0x800000xx, xx is a **GetSysColor**() index	**NULL**	0x00bbggrr
0x0100iiii, iiii is a palette index	**NULL**	0x0100iiii
0x02bbggrr (palette relative)	**NULL**	0x02bbggrr
0x00bbggrr	**NULL**	0x00bbggrr
0x800000xx, xx is a **GetSysColor**() index	valid palette	0x00bbggrr
0x0100iiii, iiii is a valid palette index in **hpal**	valid palette	0x0100iiii
0x02bbggrr (palette relative)	valid palette	0x02bbggrr
0x00bbggrr	valid palette	0x02bbggrr

Standard Font Type

OLE controls define a standard object for fonts, and an implementation of this object is provided as part of OLE controls. With OLE controls, controls are expected to have a single object-valued Font property. Properties of the font itself are accessed through the font object rather than through the control.

The standard font object supports the following interface (described in ODL syntax):

```
dispinterface IFontDisp
{
  properties:
    BSTR     Name;
    CURRENCY Size;
    boolean  Bold;
    boolean  Italic;
    boolean  Underline;
    boolean  Strikethrough;
    short    Weight;
    short    Charset;
};

interface IFont : IUnknown
{

    ...

    HRESULT GetHFont([out]OLE_HANDLE *hFontOut);

    HRESULT IsEqual([in] IFont * lpFontOther);
    HRESULT Clone([out]IFont ** lplpfont);
    HRESULT SetRatio([in]long cyLogical, OLE_YSIZE_HIMETRIC cyHimetric);

    HRESULT AddRefHfont([in]HFONT hfont);
    HRESULT ReleaseHfont([in]HFONT hfont);
};
```

The Name property gives the typeface of the font. The Size property gives the size, measured in points. Note that the type used for the Size property is **VT_CURRENCY**; effectively, this type is used as a generic fixed-point integer type here. The Italic, Underline, and Strikethrough properties give the matching characteristics of the font. The Bold and Weight properties are related; as in Windows, the Weight property ranges from 0 to 1000, and gives the relative weight of the font. A Weight value of 400 is a normal font, while a Weight of 700 is a bold font. The Bold property is **TRUE** if the Weight is greater than the average of these two (that is, 550); setting Bold to **TRUE** sets the Weight to 700, and setting Bold to **FALSE** sets Weight to 400. The Charset property names the character set expressed by the font.

The returns a Windows font handle that matches the other properties. The font object delays realizing this **hFont** object when possible, so consecutively setting two properties on a font won't cause an "intermediate" font to be realized. In addition, as an optimization, the standard font object maintains a cache of font handles. Two font objects (in the same process) that have identical properties will return the same font handle.

Since the font object caches font handles, any particular **hFont** returned has a limited and indeterminate lifetime. If one of the properties of the font object changes, then the **hFont** last returned may be removed from the internal cache and destroyed. Therefore, in normal use, the hFont property should be retrieved from the object, used, then discarded.

In cases where the font handle needs to be kept viable, the user can call the AddRefHfont method. This increments the internal cache reference count kept for the given font, guaranteeing that the font handle remains valid until a matching call to ReleaseHfont is made.

The Clone method creates a copy of a font object from the **hFont** object.

Since the control is not implementing the font object, it doesn't know when the user manipulates the font properties. The control needs to be notified when this happens so that it knows to repaint itself. In the process, the control gets a new font handle by supporting **IConnectionPointContainer** and exposing a connection point for the **IPropNotifySink** interface, which is described in more detail in the "Notifications" section of this chapter.

The font object supports **IPersistStream**. The control normally asks the font object to save itself as part of the process of saving the control. In addition, the font object supports **IDataObject**, following the conventions given in the Save As Text section of this specification. This allows the font object's properties to be saved as a text stream.

OLE controls provides an API to create new instances of the standard font object. This API can be called with a **NULL** description pointer, in which case a default font object is created and returned.

```
typedef struct tagFONTDESC
{
  ULONG cbSizeOfStruct;
  LPOLESTR lpstrName;
  CY    cySize;
  SHORT sWeight;
  SHORT sCharset;              // Used only if lpstrName is ambiguous
  BOOL  fItalic;
  BOOL  fUnderline;
  BOOL  fStrikethrough;
} FONTDESC;

HRESULT OleCreateFontIndirect(
          LPFONTDESC lpfd,
          LPFONT *lpfontObjectOut);
```

Some additional points about the standard Font object:

- The Font object will not actually translate its properties into an actual **hFont** handle until the GetFontHandle method is called. Controls that use the notification connection point should not call this method when they are notified that the font has changed; instead, they should invalidate their contents and set an internal flag. During repaint, they should call GetFontHandle again. The exception to this is OLE controls that are based on existing window procedures, which may need to send **WM_SETFONT** messages in response to the font changing.

- Containers can provide an ambient Font property. Well-behaved controls normally copy this property when created. The user model is that the control has a copy of the container's Font, not an alias to it.

Standard Picture Type

The standard picture type provides a language-neutral abstraction for bitmaps, icons, and metafiles. As with the standard font object, OLE controls provides an implementation of the standard picture object.

```
interface IPicture : IUnknown
{
    ...

    HRESULT GetKeepOriginalFormat([out] BOOL *fKeep);
    HRESULT SetKeepOriginalFormat([in] BOOL fKeep);
    HRESULT Render([in]HDC hdc,
        [in]long x, [in]long y, [in]long cx, [in]long cy,
        [in]OLE_XPOS_HIMETRIC xSrc, [in]OLE_YPOS_HIMETRIC ySrc,
        [in]OLE_XSIZE_HIMETRIC cxSrc, [in]OLE_YSIZE_HIMETRIC cySrc);
    HRESULT PictureChanged();
    HRESULT GetCurDC([out] HDC *lphdcOut);
    HRESULT SaveAsFile(
        [in] IStream *lpstream,
        [in] BOOL fSaveMemCopy,
        [out] LONG *lpcbSize);
    HRESULT SelectPicture(
        [in] HDC hdcIn,
        [out] HDC *phdcOut,
        [out] OLE_HANDLE *phbmpOut);
};

dispinterface Picture
{
properties:
    OLE_HANDLE        Handle;
    OLE_HANDLE        hPal;
    short             Type;
    OLE_XSIZE_HIMETRIC Width;
    OLE_YSIZE_HIMETRIC Height;
};
```

The picture object can contain three kinds of Windows objects: bitmaps, icons, and metafiles. The type of Windows object contained is given by the Type property. The Handle property returns the handle for the Windows object contained by the picture object. The Width and Height properties return the size of the picture, measured in **HIMETRIC** units. The hPal property gives the palette that should be used when rendering the picture.

The Render method draws the picture object's contents into the given device context (DC).

The KeepOriginalFormat property determines how conservative the picture object is about maintaining the complete original source data for the picture across persistences. For example, if a 24-bit RGB bitmap is loaded by a picture object, but the user's display only supports 8-bit color, the bitmap would normally be converted to an 8-bit color bitmap internally. Saving the picture at this point would save the 8-bit color bitmap; the original 24-bit color bitmap would be lost. If the KeepOriginalFormat property is set to **TRUE**, then the picture object keeps a copy of the original data in memory, as well as converting it for the user's display.

Since controls are using a standard implementation of the picture object, they need to be notified when the picture's content changes so that the control can invalidate and redraw itself to match. The picture exposes a connection point for the IPropNotify interface, as with the Font object; when the picture's content (or other properties) changes, notification is sent through this connection point.

Note that since the picture's handle is available, it is possible to directly alter the picture's contents with the Windows API. Code that does this should call the PictureChanged method to notify the picture object that its contents have changed. The picture object then sends notifications of this change through the **IPropNotify** connection point.

The CurDC property and SelectPicture method exist to circumvent limitations in Windows; specifically, the limitation that an object can be selected into exactly one DC at a time. In some cases, a picture object may be permanently selected into a particular device content. For example, a control that exposes its background as a bitmap might expose a Picture property to match. In order to use this picture property elsewhere, it needs to be temporarily deselected from its old DC, selected into the new DC for the operation, then reselected back into the old DC. The CurDC property returns the DC into which the picture is currently selected. The SelectPicture method selects the picture into a new DC, returning the old DC and the picture's Windows object handle. The caller should select the picture back into the old DC when the caller is done with it, as per normal for Windows code.

The standard picture object supports **IPersistStream**. Pictures also support the **IDataObject** interface, as per the Save As Text section of this spec, allowing pictures to be saved into a text stream. However, note that the stream format by definition must be self-describing. The picture may not be the only object in the stream, so it can't rely on using the end of the stream to mark the end of the picture.

Unfortunately, the standard Windows file formats for the picture types rely on this behavior, so the stream format for pictures does not match the file format (the stream format prepends length information). The SaveAsFile method provides a mechanism to save the picture as the appropriate Windows file type—BMP, ICO, WMF.

An API **OleCreatePictureIndirect** is provided for creating new instances of picture objects. This API can be called with a **NULL** description pointer, which creates an uninitialized picture object. The **IPersistStream** methods can be used on the picture to deserialize it; if any other methods are called, the uninitialized picture is converted into an empty (type = None) picture. The **fPictureOwnsHandle** parameter to this API determines whether the picture destroys the Windows handle when the picture object is destroyed.

```
#define PICTYPE_UNKNOWN  -1  // Not valid for OleCreatePicture
#define PICTYPE_NONE      0
#define PICTYPE_BITMAP    1
#define PICTYPE_METAFILE  2
#define PICTYPE_ICON      3

struct PICTDESC
{
    UINT cbSizeOfStruct;
    UINT picType;
    union
    {
        struct
        {
            HBITMAP   hbitmap;        // Bitmap
            HPALETTE  hpal;           // Accompanying palette
        } bmp;
        struct
        {
            HMETAFILE hmeta;          // Metafile
            int       xExt;
            int       yExt;           // Extent
        } wmf;
        struct
        {
            HICON hicon;              // Icon
        } icon;
    };
};
```

```
STDAPI OleCreatePictureIndirect(
        LPPICTDESC lppictdesc,          // Can be NULL
        BOOL fPictureOwnsHandle,
        REFIID riid,
        LPVOID FAR* lplpvObj);
```

The **OleLoadPicture** API can be used to read Windows file formats for bitmaps, metafiles, and icons, returning the matching picture object.

```
STDAPI OleLoadPicture(
        LPSTREAM lpstream,
        LONG lSize,                     // 0 means entire stream
        BOOL fKeepOriginalFormat,       // From container's ambient
        REFIID riid,
        LPVOID FAR* lplpv);
```

The lSize parameter gives the number of bytes that should be read from the stream, or zero if the entire stream should be read. The fKeepOriginalFormat parameter determines whether the picture object maintains the entire original state of the picture in memory, or whether any state not applicable to the user's machine is discarded. The interface pointer matching riid is returned in *lplpv.

Miscellaneous Standard Types

In addition, other types are defined for miscellaneous purposes:

OLE_HANDLE
Used when a Windows handle is being passed. The type is **I2** (or **I4**).

OLE_TRISTATE
Corresponds to the value of a tristate checkbox. The type is enumerated with following available values:

- 0   Unchecked
- 1   Checked
- 2   Gray

OLE_OPTEXCLUSIVE
Identifies controls whose value property can participate in an exclusive group. Containers can support this by detecting controls with a value property of this type, then using the property binding interfaces to detect when the property becomes **TRUE**. At that point, the container can set the value property of the other controls in the group to **FALSE**. The type is **BOOL**. For more information, see the "Special Support for Buttons" section.

OLE_CANCELBOOLEAN
Should be used as the type for Cancel parameters in Request events. The type is **BOOL**.

OLE_ENABLEDEFAULTBOOLEAN
Should be used as the type for EnableDefault parameters in Do events. The type
is **BOOL**.

Save as Text

Some container implementations have the functional requirement that they be able
to save a form definition in a textual stream, such that the text stream can later be
used to recreate the original state of the control container and its controls. OLE
controls define the mechanism by which the text stream corresponding to an
individual control is created and also the mechanism by which that text stream is
later interpreted to recreate the state of that control.

The following are requirements on the textual representation for a control's state:

- The text should be at least somewhat human-readable. That is, properties of the
  control should be identifiable by name, and values should be human
  understandable wherever possible.

- As much information as possible should be represented in such a way that small
  changes to the control's state correspond to small changes to the corresponding
  text. This allows source control systems to manage the files more easily.

- It must be possible to communicate data elements that don't meet these criteria
  (for example, picture values). This can be done by designating an individual
  Stream or Storage in some kind of companion storage.

- The state represented in the text should be semantically equivalent to the state
  created by the Save method in **IPersistStream** or **IPersistStorage**. That is, it
  should represent the complete persistent state of the control.

- From the textual representation, it should be possible to recreate the state in a
  manner semantically equivalent to the Load method in **IPersistStream** or
  IPersistStorage.

The approach taken is to have the control provide an OLE property set consisting of
those properties that make up its persistent representation and put the burden on the
container implementation to emit a stream of text that is coherent and human-
understandable. Later, the text is parsed by the container implementation into an
equivalent property set that is passed to a new control instance to re-create the
previously saved state.

OLE controls define several new field types to complement the set described in the
document on OLE Property Sets, found in this chapter. These field types will be
described in more detail in the next version of the documentation.

Property Set Represenatation

A given object can expose a variety of different property set formats, all within the confines of the OLE 2 property set format. OLE controls define a standard convention for controls using OLE 2 property sets. This canonical format is self-describing. A new standard **FMTID** is introduced that identifies the canonical format, which encapsulates a complete picture of the control's persistent state.

Each property that is part of the persistent state of the control then has a corresponding entry in the property set. Each entry is a { PropertyID (**dword**), Type (**dword**), Value (varies) } triplet.

Note that the property set for an object need not contain values of all properties—only those whose value differs from the value of a newly constructed instance of the object are required. The requirement is that the property set reflect the complete persistent state of the control. A control might choose to only put properties with nondefault values in the property set, and then substitute the default value for any control that does not appear in the property set at load time.

PropertyID

The PropertyID is a 32-bit cookie that, according to the OLE documentation, is supposed to have meaning in the context of a given format. This is a pretty vague definition. In the classic property set example of document summary properties, the OLE documentation lists what properties make up this standard format, with their corresponding PropertyID's.

Typically, a control uses the unique DispID's already defined for its properties as the PropertyID's in the property set. However, this is not required, and containers are not able to rely on it.

Containers must map the PropertyID to a user-readable string. The property set definition addresses this problem by defining a Dictionary property (id = 0) whose value is a table mapping the other PropertyID's to corresponding strings. Containers should look for this Dictionary property (which is required of all controls) and use it to map the control's PropertyID's to strings.

Type

The type element of a property is a 32-bit number that comes from a superset of the variant type enumeration in **IDispatch**.

Notable additions over the **IDispatch** variants are types for Binary Large Object's (**BLOB**), **BLOB**'ed objects (a **BLOB** tagged with a **CLSID**), streams (a **BLOB** in its own substream), streamed objects (a substream tagged with a **CLSID**), storages, storaged objects, and clipboard format/content **BLOB**s. These new types are constants, values for which are defined in a header file provided as part of OLE controls.

The container makes use of this type information to determine the appropriate way to convert the value to a text form. If the container doesn't know how to convert the type to a text form, it will probably elect to shunt those values off into some kind of companion file.

Value

The type for a property determines both how the value is stored and how it is to be interpreted by the container. Simple values and **BLOB**s are stored in situ within the property set stream. Objects can be stored as in-situ **BLOB**s, or as substreams/substorages of the overall storage containing the property set. In these latter two cases, the value designates the name of the substream or substorage, which are presumed to be peers of the contents stream within the property set storage.

Simple Properties

Simple values are stored in situ within the property set stream (or contents stream if the property set is contained within a storage). Because the types of these properties come from the defined **IDispatch VT_** enumeration, most container implementations know how to directly interpret simple property values for text conversion.

Properties for enumerated values present a small problem. Without accessing the **TypeInfo** for the control that created a property set, it's not possible to map the integer value of the enum to its corresponding friendly string. This problem is addressed by adding a new **VT_VERBOSE_ENUM**, which is derived from **VT_BLOB**. The stream format of a **VT_VERBOSE_ENUM** is:

- **I4**   Overall length of **BLOB**
- **I4**   Enumeration value
- Null-terminated string; friendly name for enumeration value

Although strictly speaking the overall length entry is redundant, it follows the convention that new **VT_**'s, which may be unknown to some property set consumers, are derived from **VT_BLOB** and thus can be easily skipped over.

It is possible that on re-creating the property set by reading text, the container may not know the exact type for a given property. For example, the text encoding for an **I2**, **I4**, **R4**, **R8** may be identical. While containers should make their best guesses about the correct type of a property value, the object should be prepared for properties that are not the correct type and attempt to coerce them to the correct type. If the coercion fails, it's an error.

Opaque Binary Properties

These can be represented in one of three ways in the property set—as **BLOB**s stored in situ within the property set stream, as an untagged substream, or as an untagged substorage. Because there is no class or type identification to assist the container in interpreting the bytes, the only way to represent them persistently is to shunt them to a stream/storage in a companion file.

Object-Valued Properties

Object-valued properties can be represented in several ways in the property set. Currently, they can be stored as **CLSID**-tagged **BLOB**s, as tagged substreams, or as tagged substorages. In these representations, the only way the container can interpret the values directly for text conversion is if the container implementation has special knowledge about the stored format of the class. This might be the case for specific types such as Pictures or Fonts, but in general these values need to be shunted to a stream/storage in a companion file.

By introducing new **VT_**'s indicating property-set valued properties, we enable a subobject to present itself as a property set—which means the container could represent (sub)objects in text in the same manner as controls. The object would simply create a property set representation of itself, which would become part of the tree structure of the overall property set for the control. It's then up to the container implementation to determine how to represent this heirarchical structure within the text stream for the form as a whole.

Therefore, we will introduce three new property types:

VT_BLOB_PROPSET   (essentially derived from **VT_BLOB**)

VT_STREAMED_PROPSET   (essentially derived from **VT_STREAMED_OBJECT**)

VT_STORED_PROPSET   (essentially derived from **VT_STORED_OBJECT**)

Note that Streams and **BLOB**s are conceptually interchangeable, and, in fact, an object may put a property set into a **VT_BLOB_PROPSET**, yet be presented with a **VT_STREAMED_PROPSET** on loading, etc.

Subcontrols

One can imagine the situation where the persistent state of a control could include a wholesale representation of the persistent state of a subcontrol within the control. For example, if one were designing a super-flexible combo box, it might be deemed appropriate to save the text box in its entirety as part of the persistent property set. An alternative would be to save individual properties of the text box as part of the combo box's persistent state.

Representing a subcontrol (the text box in this example) actually involves dealing with the X object for the text box, which needs to provide a property set for its own properties and a nested property set for the text box. This nesting is required because, on reloading, we must be able to give a property set back to the text box that describes its persistent state, since the text box knows nothing about the site properties the container associated with it. Mixing up the X object properties with the textbox's properties within a single property set seems like a bad idea.

So the property set for a control which contains a subcontrol, may actually end up being a heirarchy of three levels.

One interesting aspect of subcontrols is that the TypeInfo for the contained subcontrol is not necessarily available to the container responsible for mapping the property sets to text. In the combo box example, the container has the TypeInfo of the combo box, but not necessarily the TypeInfo of the text box. Hence, the use of the Dictionary property to map PropertyID's to strings.

Note that the presence of a dictionary implies that a property set may be locale-specific. The property set format already defines a convention whereby the code page is identified by a predefined property whose ID is 1. Extending on that convention, a predefined property ID of 2 will correspond to a **VT_I4** property containing the **LCID** for the property set. If this **LCID** property is not present, it is presumed to be 0.

The container specifies the desired LCID for the property set it is requesting by specifying **DVASPECT_LOCALE** (= 16 decimal) and putting the **LCID** into the **lindex** field of the **FORMATETC** structure passed to the GetData request.

Nonproperties

A control may want to expose something as part of its persistent state that doesn't correspond directly to an exposed property. For example, a rich text control might save some encoded text stream as its persistent image without wanting to expose that encoding as a property. This could be thought of as a "private property." This is another case where the container does not have adequate information through the TypeInfo for the control to determine how to text-convert the PropertyID to a text name string. Again, the inclusion of a dictionary addresses this problem.

Note that these nonproperties must have names in the dictionary, since that is how they will be identified by the control when the property set is read back later.

Interface Usage

A container gets the property-set representation of a control in a two-step process. First, the container inspects the object's **IDataObject FORMATETC** structures, looking for one that is identifiably of the right format. We will define a new **CF_** that corresponds to the canonical format, by text-converting the **GUID** for our new, canonical **FMTID**.

In the second step, the container calls **IDataObject::GetData** to get the corresponding Stream/Storage property set.

The above two steps are done recursively by the object if it, in turn, contains other controls or objects that are part of its persistent state. Hence the result can be a heirarchy of property sets.

The top-level container then walks through the resulting property-set hierarchy, converting to text all properties it knows about and shunting the rest into appropriate companion storage entries. Specifically, **BLOB**s, substreams, and substorages which are neither property sets nor tagged with a **CLSID** for which the container has special text-conversion knowledge, will be put in the companion storage in binary form and the name of the new stream/storage (invented by the container) will be inserted into the text stream as the "value" for the property.

On reloading, the opposite is done. The top-level container is responsible for parsing the ASCII file—for each control's part of the text, the container creates a property set (which could involve nested property sets, or stream/storage-valued properties), constructs a control object, and passes the property set to the object via **IDataObject::SetData**. The control object is responsible for recursively handling nested property sets.

Nesting (object-valued property or sub property set) can be done via **BLOB**s (which creates a flat stream), or nested **IStream/Storage**. Even if the control has a preferred approach toward nesting, the host won't know what it is when it comes time to later create the property set from text. This implies that the host must be prepared to see property sets that use either nesting approach, and that the control must be prepared to later accept a property set from the host using either nesting approach.

The lifetime of the property set is the duration of the **InitFromData** operation. The one exception to this is that **VT_STORED_OBJECT** typed properties are allowed to AddRef and hold onto the **IStorage** pointer that the control obtained by opening the storage named in the property value. For example, this allows a very large value, such as a video clip or word document, to be read on demand. It is the responsibility of the container implementation to control the **IStorage** implementation in such a way that the lifetime of the **IStorage** pointer can exceed the lifetime of the control itself. This is the case for OLE-implemented Docfiles and memory **IStorage**s.

The object that is holding the **IStorage** may need to be able to write back into it, even if those writes aren't to be committed back to the original source of the data by the host.

Example

Consider the control shown in Figure D.4, named "PictView," which contains a picture box and a text box:

c:\pictures\arch.bmp

Figure D.4   The PictView Control

A user can type the path of a disk file containing a picture, and the picture is displayed in the picture box. Let us suppose that within the set of properties exposed by this control are the picture property and an integer property that contains the size of the picture in bytes. The control writes out these properties as part of its persistent image, plus a private data member, called "Scale," of type Real. In addition, the control has its "PathBox" subcontrol save itself as part of the data.

When the container wishes to save an ASCII representation of the object, it calls **IDataObject::GetData** on the object with the appropriate **FORMATETC**. The object then fills in a data structure in property set format containing all data to be saved. Figure D.5 provides an example:

Property Set Header				
Byte-order Indicator (WORD)	Format Version (WORD)	Originating OS Version (DWORD)	Class Identifier (CLSID (16 bytes))	Count of Sections (1) (DWORD)
Format ID/Offset Pairs				
Format ID for Section 1 (FMTID (16 bytes))		Offset 1 (DWORD) *		
Sections				

Section 1 Header	
Size of section (DWORD)	Count of Properties (5) (DWORD)

Property ID/Offset Pairs	
Property ID 0 (for dictionary) (DWORD)	Offset (DWORD) **
Property ID for "Size" (DWORD)	Offset (DWORD) **
Property ID for "Pict" (DWORD)	Offset (DWORD) **
Property ID for "Scale" (DWORD)	Offset (DWORD) **
Property ID for "PathBox" (DWORD))	Offset (DWORD) **

Properties (Type/Value Pairs)	
# of Entries in Dictionary	Dictionary
Type Indicator for "Size" (DWORD)	Value of "Size"
Type Indicator for "Pict" (DWORD)	Data for "Pict"
Type Indicator for "Scale" (DWORD)	Value of "Scale"
Type Indicator of "PathBox" (DWORD)	Data for "Pathbox" (consists of another property set)

* Offset in bytes from the start of the stream to the start of the section.
** Offset in bytes from the start of the section to the start of the Type/Value pair.

Figure D.5   Stream Containing a Serialized Property Set

Let us suppose that our control is embedded in a control container and the user saves the embedded control container objects as text. The following steps are executed:

1. The container asks PictView for a property set (using the **GetData()** or **GetDataHere()** function).

2. Pictview fills in a property set structure with all of its own persistent data. The following is one example:

```
Offset     Bytes

; Property Set Header
0000    FE FF              ; WORD Byte-order Indicator
0002    00 00              ; WORD Format Version
0004    0A 03 00 00           ; DWORD Originating OS Version
0008    90 31 2B 2B 00 08 60 8A
0010    69 10 F1 0D 01 FD 16 F6        ; CLSID of Pict Browser
0018    01 00 00 00           ; DWORD Count of Sections

; FormatID/Offset pairs
001C    00 00 00 00 00 00 00 00
0024    00 00 00 00 00 00 00 00        ; FMTID of Section 1 - TBD
```

```
002C      30 00 00 00              ; DWORD Offset of Section 1

; Start of section
0030      43 01 00 00              ; DWORD size of section
0034      05 00 00 00              ; DWORD number of properties in section

; PropID/Offset pairs
0038      00 00 00 00              ; DWORD Property ID (0 == dictionary)
003C      30 00 00 00              ; DWORD offset to property ID
0040      03 00 00 00              ; DWORD Property ID (i.e. PID_SIZE)
0044      7F 00 00 00              ; DWORD offset to property ID
0048      08 00 00 00              ; DWORD Property ID (i.e. PID_PICT)
004C      87 00 00 00              ; DWORD offset to property ID
0050      23 01 00 00              ; DWORD Property ID (Generated ID)
0054      15 01 00 00              ; DWORD offset to property ID
0058      34 06 00 00              ; DWORD Property ID (Generated ID)
005C      1D 01 00 00              ; DWORD offset to property ID

; First Property (Type/Value Pair), (which is really the dictionary
; because it has Property ID 0)
0060      05 00 00 00              ; DWORD Number of entries in dictionary
0064      00 00 00 00              ; DWORD dwPropID = 0
0068      0A 00 00 00              ; DWORD cb = 10
006C      "PictView1\0"       ; char sz[10]
0077      03 00 00 00              ; DWORD dwPropID = 3 (PID_SIZE)
007B      05 00 00 00              ; DWORD cb = 5
007F      "Size\0"            ; char sz[5]
0084      08 00 00 00              ; DWORD dwPropID = 8 (PID_PICT)
0088      05 00 00 00              ; DWORD cb = 5
008C      "Pict\0"            ; char sz[5]
0091      7B 00 00 00              ; DWORD dwPropID = 123 (Generated ID)
0095      06 00 00 00              ; DWORD cb = 6
0099      "Scale\0"           ; char sz[6]
009F      7A 02 00 00              ; DWORD dwPropID = 634 (Generated ID)
00A3      08 00 00 00              ; DWORD cb = 8
00A7      "PathBox\0"         ; char sz[8]

; Property (Type/Value Pairs)
00AF      02 00 00 00              ; DWORD type indicator (VT_I2 == 02)
00B3      08 00 00 00              ; INT Frame Number - zero padded to
dword
00B7      65 00 00 00              ; DWORD type indicator (VT_BLOB == 65)
00B9      07 00 00 00              ; DWORD length of Blob data
...            ...      ; BLOB DATA
0145      04 00 00 00              ; DWORD type indicator (VT_R4 == 04)
0149      0D B3 31 87              ; REAL
014D      65 00 00 00          ; DWORD type indicator (perhaps
VT_BLOB_PROPSET?)
0151      00 00 00 00              ; DWORD length of Blob data
0155          ...              ; Property Set data for PathBox
```

3. PictView now asks the subobject "PathBox" to save itself. However, before doing this PictView needs to save site properties relating to the PathBox object (that is, Left, Top, Height, Width). It does this by asking the site object responsible for PathBox to save itself into a sub property set. The site object, in turn, asks the PathBox control to create a property set that is a child of the property set for the site object. What is created is a property set hierarchy, shown in Figure D.6:

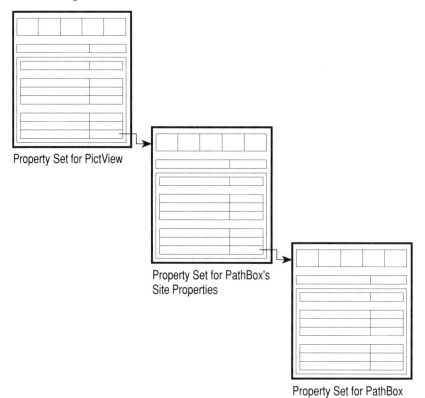

Property Set for PictView

Property Set for PathBox's Site Properties

Property Set for PathBox

Figure D.6   PictView's Property Set Hierarchy

4. PathBox fills in its property set structure with its persistent data in much the same way it did for this object.

5. Depending on which method was used to get PathBox's data, PictView may need to copy data into its own property set and tag it as a **PROPSETBLOB**.

6. The container walks through the property set, looking up each property name in the dictionary. Then, looking at the type indicator, the container decides if the property name can be adequately represented in ASCII and, if so, writes out a line such as `<propname>` = `<value>`. If it cannot be represented in ASCII, the container puts it in a companion Docfile and puts a name in the ASCII stream.

Note the following:

- This scenario assumes that object-valued properties and subcontrols are inserted as **BLOB**s directly into the property set, instead of as separate streams/storages.

- The second **BLOB** (labeled "Property Set data for PathBox") is retrieved from the PathBox subcontrol in the same way that our container is getting its property set data. As an object, we don't have to worry about how many levels down we're embedded, the procedure is the same.

- The dictionary is stored as PropertyID 0. Note that all the saved properties are included in the dictionary. Hence this property set is self-contained, and the container needs no extra knowledge of the object to write out the ASCII stream.

- If the property doesn't have a **DISPID** (that is, it is not exposed), then the object generates an ID for it, such as is the case with "Scale" of type **real**, and with the text box.

The final file, written entirely by the top-level container might look something like this:

```
Begin Form Form1
    Caption = "Form1"
    Begin PictView PictView1
        Height      =      826
        Left        =     1202
        Top         =      120
        Width       =     1424
        .object
        Size        =     3146
        Pict        =     FORM1.FRX:Moniker
        Scale       =      6.23
        Begin TextBox PathBox
            Height      =      372
            Left        =     2400
            Top         =     1080
            Width       =      972
            .object
            Text        =     "c:\pictures\arch.bmp"
        Fnd
    End
End
```

Note the following:

- The picture is stored in a separate Docfile since there is no ASCII representation for it. However, the text box is stored in ASCII representation, since it supplied a property set to our object. If it didn't support the format, it would have been put in the companion file in binary form.

- There are properties attributed to the PictView control (Height = 826, Left = 1202, etc.) that weren't implemented by that control. These are the extended object properties for the control and are supplied by our container. (In this example, the ".object" identifier is used to separate the site properties from the object's properties)

When the user goes to reload the form, the following happens:

1. The container parses the text file and creates a property set heirarchy such as the one in Figure D.6. Note that type indicators are not stored in the ASCII file, so the container has to take its best guess as to what type the value is.

2. The container passes the property set heirarchy to PictView (using SetData()).

3. PictView sets its own properties with the values supplied in the top-level property set. If a value is of the wrong type, PictView coerces it. If it cannot be coerced, it generates an error in the log. When it encounters the property set for PathBox, it first sets the site properties for that subobject from the contained property set. It then passes the property set containing PathBox's properties to that object.

Installation and Registration

One of the design advantages of the OLE Compound Object Model (COM) infrastructure is that it uses the operating system registry. OLE uses the registry for many things, among them enumerating and mapping classes to servers (DLLs and EXEs). As OLE is currently defined, a server DLL is not useful without its registry information, since it is opaque without that information. Consequently, OLE server DLLs and EXEs need an install process.

This is reasonable when the server is a large application like Excel or Word and the existing setup program for the application can be used. However, many control servers carry less overhead and would not otherwise have need of a specific setup process.

Self-Registering DLL's

The registry is the key piece of the puzzle. Without registry information, the DLL is unable to be seen by other OLE applications. There may be other extra files associated with the DLL—help files, for example—but registering with the operating system is unavoidable.

The solution is to have a DLL entry point with a well-known name (using the existing **DllGetClassObject**) that registers the controls in the DLL. A DLL entry point for removing and unregistering a server is defined as follows:

```
HRESULT DllRegisterServer(void);
HRESULT DllUnregisterServer(void);
```

Both of these entry points are required for a DLL to be self-registering. The implementation of the **DllRegisterServer** entry point adds or updates registry information for all the classes implemented by the DLL. The **DllUnregisterServer** entry point removes its information from the registry.

Typical Registry Contents

A control development kit normally supplies a default implementation for these routines. The following sections give typical examples of the registry keys associated with a server.

Registering a Control

```
HKEY_CLASSES_ROOT
    CLSID
      {class id of control}
    ProgID = identifier
    InprocServer = <filename>.DLL
    ToolboxBitmap = <filename>.DLL, resourceID
    Insertable*
    Control*
    verb
        0 = &Edit
        1 = &Properties...
    MiscStatus = 0
        1 = **
    TypeLib = {typelib ID for DLL}
    Version = version number***
```

```
*   If applicable.
**  Value varies, depending on control features.
*** New keys that assist with finding the typelib for a given CLSID.
```

Registering a Property Page

```
HKEY_CLASSES_ROOT
    CLSID
        {class id of property sheet}
        InprocServer = filename.DLL
```

Registering a Type Library

```
HKEY_CLASSES_ROOT
    TYPELIB
      {typelib id for DLL}
    version number
      DIR = name of directory containing .DLL
      lcid = filename.TLB*
```

Identifying Self-Registering Servers

Applications need to check if a given DLL is self-registering without actually
loading the DLL, since loading the DLL executes **LibMain** with possible negative
side-effects. To accomplish this, the DLL (and EXE) modifies the version resource
to hold a self-registration keyword. Since the **VERSIONINFO** section is fixed and
cannot be easily extended, we add the following string to the "StringFileInfo," with
an empty key value:

```
VALUE "OLESelfRegister", ""
```

For example:

```
VS_VERSION_INFO     VERSIONINFO
  FILEVERSION       1,0,0,1
  PRODUCTVERSION    1,0,0,1
  FILEFLAGSMASK     VS_FFI_FILEFLAGSMASK
#ifdef _DEBUG
  FILEFLAGS         VS_FF_DEBUG|VS_FF_PRIVATEBUILD|VS_FF_PRERELEASE
#else
  FILEFLAGS         0 // final version
#endif
  FILEOS            VOS_DOS_WINDOWS16
  FILETYPE          VFT_APP
  FILESUBTYPE       0   // not used
BEGIN
  BLOCK "StringFileInfo"
  BEGIN
    BLOCK "040904E4" // Lang=US English, CharSet=Windows Multilingual
    BEGIN
    VALUE "CompanyName",     "\0"
    VALUE "FileDescription", "BUTTON OLE Control DLL\0"
    VALUE "FileVersion",     "1.0.001\0"
    VALUE "InternalName",    "BUTTON\0"
    VALUE "LegalCopyright",  "\0"
    VALUE "LegalTrademarks", "\0"
    VALUE "OriginalFilename","BUTTON.DLL\0"
    VALUE "ProductName",     "BUTTON\0"
    VALUE "ProductVersion",  "1.0.001\0"
►   VALUE "OLESelfRegister", "" // New keyword
    END
```

```
    END
    BLOCK "VarFileInfo"
    BEGIN
      VALUE "Translation", 0x409, 1252
    END
END
```

To support self-registering DLLs, an application can add a "Browse" button to its Insert Object dialog (or its analog, like Add Control to Toolbox), which pops up a standard File Open dialog. After the user chooses a DLL, the application can check whether it is marked for self-registration and, if so, call its **DllRegisterServer** entry point. The DLL should register itself in this entry point, so the application should refresh the Insert Object dialog to show the newly added classes.

The application can search the registry to find out which classes are implemented by the DLL after it has registered itself. For example, a container with a toolbox might choose to automatically add all the controls implemented by the DLL to the toolbox.

Self-Registering EXE's

There isn't an easy way for EXEs to publish entry points with well-known names, so a direct translation of **DllRegisterServer** isn't possible. Instead, EXEs support self-registration using special command line flags. EXEs that support self-registration must mark their resource fork in the same way as DLLs, so that the EXEs support for the command line flags is detectable. Launching an EXE marked as self-registering with the /REGSERVER command line argument should cause it to do whatever OLE installation is necessary and then exit. The /UNREGSERVER argument is the equivalent to **DllUnregisterServer**.

Other than guaranteeing that it has the correct entry point or implements the correct command line argument, an application that indicates it is self-registering must build its registration logic so that it may be called any number of times on a given system—even if it is already installed. Telling it to register itself more than once should not have any negative side effects. The same is true for unregistering.

On normal startup (without the REGSERVER command line option) EXEs should call the registration code to make sure their registry information is current. EXEs will indicate the failure or success of the self-registration process through their return code by returning 0 for success and non-zero for failure.

Location and Extension Used by Controls

By convention, control DLLs should use the extension OCX. This helps end users locate and identify DLLs that implement control classes. It also helps containers that want to support self-registering control servers by defining a reasonable filename filtering mechanism for the container's browse dialog.

Note that this is only a convention and, in fact, an object may act as a control without being implemented as an OCX-suffixed DLL. In particular, existing OLE compound document servers can easily be retro-fitted to act as controls (that is, as source events, have standard methods and properties, self-register, and so on).

There is no standard location defined for OLE controls. As with other OLE servers, the control's DLL or EXE does not need to be in the user's path; the registry should have the full path to the server. A large or overly complex control or group of controls typically installs itself into its own directory, just as most applications do. A smaller or simpler control may choose to put itself in the Windows system directory.

Toolbar Button Images

OLE 2 defines how classes name a standard-size icon that should be used to represent the class. Classes list the icon in the registry and code that displays the icon extracts its name from the DLL/EXE named in the registry with the **ExtractIcon** Windows API. For example:

```
\Registry\CLASSES\{xxxx-...-xx}\DefaultIcon = myserver.dll, 2
```

Control containers will often have to represent the class on a toolbar button, but a full-size icon is too big. The standard size of bitmaps for toolbar buttons is 16x15 pixels on Win16 and the Macintosh computers. So, the control provides a bitmap of this size and registers it under its class key in the registry:

```
\Registry\CLASSES\{xxxx-...-xx}\ToolboxBitmap = myserver.dll, 301
```

Since there is no analog of **ExtractIcon** for bitmaps, the second argument gives the resource ID of the bitmap. The code that wants to show the bitmap may need to load the EXE or DLL using **LoadModule** to extract the icon, or using the Win 3.1 **GetFileResource** API.

The bitmap should not include beveling around the edges; the container is responsible for drawing this. The bitmap should follow the convention that the bitmap's background color is the lower-left pixel of the bitmap. A container normally uses the DIB routines to substitute the proper background color for this color; for a toolbar button, gray is normally used. Effectively, the lower-left corner of the bitmap identifies a "transparent" color for the bitmap.

Finding OLE Controls

OLE 2 defines how embeddable objects are identified. Each embeddable class adds an "Insertable" key to the registry under its class key:

```
\Registry\CLASSES\{xxxx-...-xx}\Insertable
```

More precisely, containers use this key to determine which classes to list in their "Insert Object" dialog box. Controls that are to appear in Insert Object dialog boxes should register this key.

However, some controls are not supposed to appear in this dialog box, but should still be recognizable as controls. To solve this, our containers introduce another key "Control," parallel to "Insertable," that identifies classes that can act as controls:

```
\Registry\CLASSES\{xxxx-...-xx}\Control
```

This key determines whether the class is listed in an Insert Control dialog box or wherever the container lists controls. Most controls list both keys so that they will be backward compatible with OLE 2 containers. The exception to this is controls that have no usefulness without their events—for example, the Timer control. Such a control would only list the Control key, so it won't be listed in the Insert Object dialog of OLE 2 containers.

New containers that specifically want to disallow control-like objects from the Insert Object dialog can list objects that have the Insertable key but not the Control key.

Licensing

By enabling and promoting a component-oriented approach toward software design, OLE has the potential to significantly expand the marketplace for third-party software vendors. Independent software vendors (ISVs) can create components for integration and use by other applications whose functionality and fit and finish could previously only be accomplished through internal development.

There are benefits to recommending and enabling a common approach to the programmatic enforcement of the license to use components. Third parties inevitably run into questions about how they want to license the use of their components. From the component user's point of view, the way in which this license is structured and enforced is effectively part of the component interface.

Note that OLE components are not limited to reuse by applications, but can also be used to build other reusable components. For brevity, this document often refers to the situation where a component is used by an application. But the intent is that anywhere the word "application" is used, it could be replaced by the word "component."

The notion of distinguishing between situations where a component is being used in designing a consuming application versus being used in running a consuming application is still applicable in the OLE world. However, the current OLE COM interfaces do not make that distinction visible to the component. This deficit must be addressed in order to let component vendors continue to structure and enforce their component licenses in such a way that their components can be freely redistributed for use by a consuming application, without also giving away the ability to design and build other applications with the redistributed component.

This section outlines a set of extensions to COM and the type library interfaces that enable components to enforce their licensing model. This model is flexible in terms of both which behaviors a component can license and how it can detect that the current user (or machine) holds the appropriate license for a behavior.

Requirements

The following requirements must be fulfilled before a control can be licensed.

- No change should be required for the simplest form of license, where the license to use the component is defined by the physical ownership of the component software itself.

- Component license should be able to differentiate between the use of the component by another ISV in designing an application and the use of the component by an end-user of the application. For example, an ISV might charge for the rights to use a component in building an application, but allow unlimited free distribution of the component as part of the application "runtime."

- Differential licensing (different terms for different levels of usage) should be possible without requiring different versions of the licensed component. This avoids potentially major logistical and testing headaches for component providers.

- The enabling COM interface extensions should be designed such that the component provider is in control of how simple or sophisticated their scheme of license enforcement will be. It should be easy to enforce a simple scheme that detects and thwarts casual unauthorized usage. It should also be possible to enforce a more complex scheme that detects and thwarts determined attempts at unauthorized usage.

- License enforcement should be as unobtrusive as possible.

- Client applications that are not "licensing-aware" should still be able to use a user- or machine-licensed component.

- Enforcement scheme should be able to differentiate between the creation of new object instances and loading of instances created under license.

Licensing Design

The core of this design is that the component gates access to some or all of its functionality based on its verification that the current machine or user application is licensed for access to that functionality. This verification can occur in one of two ways.

First, the object can inspect the computer for a known indication of license. For example, a component can require that a particular license key file be present on the machine for the component to run. By verifying the presence of this key file, the component recognizes that the machine has a valid license for the control. This approach can be generalized by components that have more complex needs.

Second, a component can verify its license is to have the client application pass it a cached license key signifying that it is licensed to use the component.

One of the licensing capabilities of a component is its ability to provide a key that can be built into a consuming application. In this way, the key can be presented later on to a machine that may not otherwise be licensed for use of the component. Typically, a component distinguishes between a license valid for creating new applications that use a component (a design-time license) and a license valid to run an application that uses the component (a run-time license).

When the application is being designed, the development environment requests and obtains the key from the component and then bundles the key into the developed application. At run time, the cached key is presented to the component, unlocking its capabilities, even on machines where the physical license key file does not exist. This is regulated by the OLE control, of course.

The following example illustrates the licensing process. Suppose ISV "SampleCorp" is selling an OLE control called "Sample," which is in SAMPLE.DLL. They represent their design-time license with a file called SAMPLE.LIC, which contains a key of some kind. A "Sample developer's kit" includes SAMPLE.DLL, SAMPLE.LIC, and documentation. SAMPLE.DLL can be freely distributed by anyone who buys the Sample developer's kit.

A developer buys the Sample kit and installs it on his or her machine. This amounts to simply copying SAMPLE.DLL and SAMPLE.LIC onto a hard disk. The developer goes to the development environment and attempts to place a Sample control into the control container. This causes SAMPLE.DLL to be first registered (using the self-registration API), then loaded; upon loading, the DLL looks for SAMPLE.LIC to make sure this machine is licensed. It finds SAMPLE.LIC, so a Sample control is successfully created and placed in the form. At this point, the container asks the Sample class factory object for a key that the container can build into the user's application EXE file. Since SAMPLE.DLL earlier verified the presence of SAMPLE.LIC (the design-time license), a license key is returned to the development environment, which puts it into the user's executable, APP.EXE.

Now the developer wants to sell a copy of the application to an end user, "Customer." Money changes hands. The user gives Customer a copy of

APP.EXE and SAMPLE.DLL. Customer goes home and installs the application by copying APP.EXE and SAMPLE.DLL onto the hard disk.

Customer runs the application and the form is loaded. The container gets a pointer to the Sample class factory, which causes SAMPLE.DLL to be loaded. SAMPLE.DLL's LibMain attempts to verify the presence of a design-time license, by looking for SAMPLE.LIC. It is not found, which means that any attempt to create a SampleObject on this machine without passing in a run-time license key will be rejected by Sample's class factory. However, since the container built the key for Sample into APP.EXE, the container is able to pass the key to Sample's class factory along with its request to create a new Sample control. Sample's class factory recognizes the key (thus verifying that APP has a valid run-time license for Sample), and the control is successfully created and placed in APP's control container.

While the example uses a container having an OLE control, it's important to note that the same fundamental interactions would work equally well for any application- or component-creating host, dealing with any COM object. All that is required is that the host detect all class references, request the corresponding keys, and build them into the shippable application or component such that the keys can be presented along with all requests to create and place objects at run-time.

OLE COM Extensions

The currently defined OLE COM interfaces aren't sufficient for the above interactions to take place in a defined manner. Instead, **IClassFactory** is extended to accommodate the necessary interactions

```
typedef struct licinfo
{
    long    cbLicInfo;    // Size of licinfo structure
    bool    fRuntimeKeyAvail;    // True if class offers a runtime key
            // for building into solution
    bool    fLicVerified;    // True if component has already verified
            // machine/user lic
} LICINFO;

interface IClassFactory2 : public IClassFactory
{
    GetLicInfo(LICINFO FAR *plicinfo);
    RequestLicKey(DWORD dwReserved, BSTR FAR *pbstrKey);
    CreateInstanceLic(
        LPUNKNOWN pUnkOuter,
        LPUNKNOWN pUnkReserved,
        REFIID riid,
        BSTR bstrKey,
        LPVOID FAR *ppvObject);
};
```

The GetLicInfo method returns information about the state of licensing for the object. **RequestLicKey** allows the caller to request the licensing key (represented as a BSTR) from the object. **CreateInstanceLic** is analogous to **IClassFactory::CreateInstance**, adding only the license key that allows for the preverification scenarios as outlined earlier.

Using **BSTR** representation of keys in this interface allows them to have self-described length and to contain **NULL**s. These keys are essentially **BLOB**s. The **dwReserved** parameter is included to allow for a future implementation that allows a component to simultaneously offer multiple different keys.

If the consumer passes in a key that connotes functionality that is more restricted than the user or machine license enables, the component should provide the limited functionality for that instance—as if the user or machine license had not been previously verified. This allows the consumer to test its interactions with the component as they occur in an installation that is not machine or user licensed.

The **fLicVerified** flag in the **LICINFO** structure allows the component consumer to detect, prior to the presentation of a key, the situation where the component has already found a valid license for this user or machine. If the container wants the current user or machine license to override the application license corresponding to a key, it can use **fLicVerified** to avoid passing the key unnecessarily.

A new standard **SCODE** is defined,**E_NOTLICENSED**, which should be returned when the control container attempts to construct a licensed object where the license has not been verified or the appropriate key has not been passed.

Many clients currently use OLE-provided cover functions in situations where class instances are created. Because those cover functions are written to **IClassFactory** instead of **IClassFactory2**, clients that want to support retaining or presenting run-time license keys (mainly programming environments) will no longer be able to use those cover functions. For example, this includes **CoCreateInstance**, as well as the many variations of **OleCreate** and **OleLoad**.

Licensing an Object's Capabilities

The example given earlier is fairly straightforward. However, the underlying licensing mechanism is pretty flexible, and it's worth an exploration of what that flexibility enables.

A single executable version of a component can support multiple levels of licensed functionality. For example, the vendor might ship different .LIC files (at different price points) corresponding to different levels of functionality. The contents of the .LIC file determine what behavior was enabled at design time, what key was built into the application, and what functionality was enabled at run time when that key is presented.

While shipping and detecting a .LIC file is a familiar mechanism for verifying a component license, the component vendor is free to choose whatever scheme they wish. For example, the component could use a third-party licensing tool such as Hermes, LSAPI, or some other metered licensing tool to verify that this particular user or machine is appropriately licensed for this component.

A component need not be completely disabled in the absence of a valid license or run time key. For example, a component might allow previously saved object instances to be loaded and viewed, but not edited, even if the current user, machine, or application were not licensed. Or, perhaps the component would allow access to some interfaces, but not others—for example allowing access to simple OLE embedding, but not the object's OLE Automation capabilities. These scenarios imply that the **E_NOTLICENSED** error may be returned from a variety of calls besides **CreateInstance**. This conforms with the guidelines for **HRESULT**s in general; since **E_NOTLICENSED** is a Microsoft-defined error code, it can be returned legally from any entry point.

This error may arise in other situations as well. For example, if a component designer wanted to allow loading of previously saved object instances, but not the creation of new object instances, this would need to be enforced outside of **IClassFactory::CreateInstance**, since that method would be called in either case. If the object were **IStorage** based, this effect would probably be obtained by gating **IPersistStorage::InitNew**. Otherwise it might have to gate all methods except **IPersistStream::Load**.

Licensing with Document Editing Apps

In some cases, the distinction between designing and running an application is not clear. This can make very unclear the decision of when a key should be requested and presented to give the effect of "application licensing." For example, consider a spreadsheet with an embedded licensed control (for example, a workbook). In a sense, the workbook can be thought of as an application for distribution. But anyone with that workbook can modify it arbitrarily to the point where it becomes a very different "application." Unless the original key is automatically discarded, the second user has, in effect, obtained unauthorized application design rights by virtue of the original application license key. Yet many workbook changes—data entry, for example—should not necessarily invalidate the original application license.

It is very important that applications that want to implement "application licensing" be designed to give careful consideration to what differentiates "design-time activity" from "run time activity." Failure to do so erodes the meaning of enforceable application licensing that is key to many third-party licensing and distribution models, which in turn may hamper the market for third-party components.

If the component vendors want their licensed components to be used with applications that are not licensing aware , they need to take this into account when they design their license enforcement schemes. The simplest approach would be to require users of those applications to buy a design-time (machine or user) license for the component. Alternatively, the component vendor might sell a cheaper license for end-users. Or, as outlined above, they might support a restricted set of interfaces such as those required for simple linking and embedding, even in the absence of a valid license.

Versioning

The exising OLE 2 conversion/emulation scheme was devised to make it possible to upgrade a compound document server component in such a way that the new implementation can make use of persistent images saved by the original implementation. This is simplified by the fact that most OLE 2 compound document containers treat OLE 2 compound document servers opaquely. That is, they interact with the server through the generic OLE 2 compound document interfaces rather than through class-specific interfaces.

In that context, the server provides upward compatibility by being able to read existing persistent images. In activating a particular persistent image, the server is tasked with either emulation of the old class or conversion from the old class. Emulation means that the server is to save a changed object back into its original persistent format. Conversion means that the server is to save into the new persistent format.

The server determines which of these two behaviors is desired by inspecting the format, which OLE stores in a special place in the object's **IStorage**. If the format is identified as being an old format, the server knows that either an emulation or conversion is required. The server discriminates between emulation and conversion by inspecting the **fConvert** bit, which OLE also stores in a special place in the object's **IStorage**.

In either case, the server is activated via its new **CLSID**, which is typically accomplished using special forwarding entries in the registry, created by **CoSetTreatAsClass** and **OleSetAutoConvert** calls at the time the upgraded server is registered. The user also has the option of suppressing automatic conversion and emulation, instead applying conversion or emulation on a per-instance basis through container UI.

This scheme leverages and depends on the container's uniform treatment of different object classes. It also depends on the object using an **IStorage** to save itself, so that old instances can be matched up with current implementations, and so that the container can communicate how it wants the new implementation to save a modified instance's data.

OLE controls violate both of these key design points of the current scheme. Containers typically have detailed dependencies on at least two class-specific interface definitions for the control: its primary dispatch interface (and in many cases its interface, as well) and its primary EventSet. Also, for efficiency's sake, controls typically support persistence into streams as well as storages.

A new model is required that enables an upgraded OLE control to correctly satisfy the detailed, class-specific dependencies of containers built against older versions, while also allowing the control to add functional enhancements that new versions of containers can leverage. The remainder of this section describes the OLE controls solution to this problem.

Binary Compatibility

When application A is built against a specific version of a component C, A will have embedded in it detailed assumptions about the set of interfaces that C supports and the definition of those interfaces. Each interface that C supports is contractually specified by an IID, which corresponds to a specific interface definition taken from C's accompanying type library. The collective set of interfaces that C supports is contractually specified by a **CLSID**, which corresponds to a specific CoClass description in C's accompanying type library. Furthermore, the ability to compatibly read and write a persistent image of C is also designated by **CLSID**.

When an upgrade of a component is able to meet the contractual obligations of the original version, as specified by the original **CLSID** and IIDs, it is said to be a "binary compatible" upgrade. The following set of rules define the requirements of binary compatibility:

- The new implementation must support (at least) the original **CLSID**. This means that the implementation is registered under the original **CLSID** in the registry, and that the class factory registered is available via **DllGetClassObject** on the server (or via **CoRegisterClassObject** for local servers).

- The new implementation of a component must support all the interfaces, including connection points, exactly as they were described in the original implementation's type library. This means that the new component's implementation of QueryInterface will be able to return all the interfaces named in the old type library. The component's FindConnectionPointFromIID method, which is supplied to the container, should be able to return a connection point to the container for each outgoing interface named in the old type library. In addition, the component's EnumConnectionPoints enumerator should enumerate a connection point for each as well.

  Following the normal OLE conventions, it's acceptable for the component to return an interface pointer to a new version of IID for the incoming interface, assuming that the new interface is a strict superset of the old interface. This can greatly simplify the task of continuing to support old interfaces. In Dispatch case, doing GetTypeInfo / GetTypeInfoCount may return a description of the new interface if this is done, rather than the old interface.

Similarly, it's acceptable for the component to map connection requests for an old IID connection point onto the connection point for the new version of the outgoing interface. When firing an event via Invoke (for a Dispatch-based connection point), the component may invoke methods that the event sink isn't expecting, corresponding to events that are part of the new version of the outgoing interface. The sink should simply ignore these and return **S_OK**.

With interface-based connection points, supporting multiple versions of the same interface on a single connection point is slightly more complicated. When attempting to Advise to a new event sink, the connection point should first call **QueryInterface** (QI) for the most derived interface (that is, the most recent version). If this QI fails, then the connection point QI's for the next most derived interface, and so on. The connection then keeps track of which version of the interface was supported by each event sink and only calls methods on the event sink that it supports.

- It is acceptable for the new implementation to support additional interfaces and connection points. Furthermore, if the component supports **IProvideClassInfo**, the description returned from a running instance of the component may describe the interfaces for the new version of the component. See notes below on providing simultaneous source and binary compatibility.

- The new implementation must be capable of reading, without loss of information, a persistent image of the component saved by the original implementation. By definition, since an instance of the component was created via its original **CLSID**, any persistent load is an emulation.

- The new implementation must be capable of writing out a persistent image of the component that can be read by the original implementation, where the only loss of information relates to functionality that was not part of the original implementation.

Note **IStream** objects can't use the Read/WriteFmtUserTypeStg or Read/WriteClassStg mechanisms to determine the originating version of a persistent image. It is recommended that some kind of version stamp be included in the stream format for such a class.

Source Compatibility

Typically, a component upgrade provides added functionality that is accessed programmatically. While a previously built application that uses the component in a binary-compatible manner will not know to access this functionality, a new version of that application will most likely want to take advantage of the new behavior. Ideally, this would be accomplished with a minimum of changes to the source code for the application.

Assuming that the source code for application A holds symbolic references to control C's class and interfaces and that A binds these references through an accompanying type library to get binary references, then a source-compatible upgrade to C can be accomplished by making only additive changes and by providing the correct accompanying type library. The following set of rules defines source compatibility:

- If an interface is left intact syntactically and semantically, its corresponding TypeInfo in the type library can remain unchanged and the interface should retain its original name and IID.

- If an interface is extended through the addition of new members and all original members are intact, then the interface should retain its original name but be given a new IID.

- If an interface is modified in other ways, for example, by adding a parameter to an existing method, then the original interface must be described and supported via its original name and the new interface must be given a new name and IID.

- The CoClass description for the component must contain all interfaces and connection points, according to their names, that the original CoClass description for the component contained. It may contain additional interfaces and connection points. The CoClass should retain its original name but be given a new **CLSID**.

- The new type library should be registered under the same **GUID/LCID** as the original type library. It should be given a higher version number.

- The new implementation must support (at least) the new **CLSID**. The requirements are the same as for binary compatibility.

- The new implementation of the component (created from its new **CLSID**) must be capable of reading a persistent image created by the original implementation of the component. It is not strictly required that it be able to write a persistent image that the original component implementation can read.

  If the component supports **IStream** persistence, it should assume that loading a previously saved instance corresponds to a Conversion request. If the component supports **IStorage** persistence, it can distinguish between emulation and conversion requests via the normal OLE 2 **IStorage**-based conventions. See cautions below under "Providing Both Binary and Source Compatibility."

- If the component uses another class, K, such that instances of K are exposed via one of the component's interfaces, and K also has source-compatible changes, then the source-compatible upgrade of the component must include or require a source-compatible upgrade of K so that the application can be correctly rebuilt.

Providing Both Binary and Source Compatibility

Typically, a component upgrade strives to provide both binary and source compatibility. This is accomplished by registering the new implementation under both the old and new **CLSID**s and by providing a source-compatible type library.

This task is greatly simplified if all interface changes are strictly additive in nature. With a little special care, the new implementation can simultaneously support both old and new **CLSID**s. The implementation needs to note the **CLSID** by which a given instance was created so that the implementation can correctly handle any calls with **CLSID**-specific behavior, such as **IPersist::GetClassID**.

Strictly speaking, the new type library need only describe the new, extended interfaces, and a consumer of the old **IID** will not care if it receives a pointer to an interface that happens to support some additional methods. The new implementation could simply map QueryInterfaces for the old **IID** onto the corresponding new interface.

The implementor could also choose to describe the support for both old and new versions of the interface as a derivation in its type library. The old interface is described with its original **IID** in one TypeInfo, while the new version of the interface, with the original name but a new **IID**, is described as being derived from the original interface.

Since a TypeInfo description of the component obtained from a running instance describes the new versions' interfaces, by extension it is reasonable that the registry information for the old **CLSID** be updated to also point at the new type library. It is suggested that the type library contain a "CoClass alias" TypeInfo record that maps the old **CLSID** to the TypeInfo record describing the new CoClass.

If the component vendor also wants to also provide OLE 2-style conversion and emulation support, some significant caveats apply. As described at the beginning of this document, the existing OLE 2 scheme causes the server to be activated via its new **CLSID** in both conversion and emulation scenarios. This raises the following special concerns:

- Instances of **IStream** objects have no OLE-managed stream to carry format and conversion information. Therefore, an instance of an **IStream** object that is identifiably "old" (based on some version stamp within the persistent image stream) can only assume that being invoked via the old **CLSID** is emulation, while being invoked via new **CLSID** is conversion. Because OLE CD containers don't know about **IStream** objects, this situation should only arise in the context of a control-aware container.

- An **IStorage** object instance that is identifiably "old" (based on format info obtained via **ReadFmtUserTypeStg**), invoked via its new **CLSID**, faces a more complex situation. By convention, the server distinguishes between emulation and conversion by calling **GetConvertStg**. If this returns **TRUE**, then a conversion is desired.

Care must be taken such that this situation arises only where the container is prepared for conversion. The server can indicate (with the user's permission at setup time) that it can automatically convert old instances and also enable manual conversion via registry conventions. The container only enables manual conversion through its own UI and enables automatic conversion by deciding whether to call **OleDoAutoConvert**.

- OLE 2-style emulation for OLE controls, where an identifiably "old" **IStorage** instance is invoked via new **CLSID** and **GetConvertStg** returns **FALSE**, is not a well-defined operation, and should be avoided.

The current OLE 2 rules for which behaviors should reflect the old **CLSID** versus which should reflect the new **CLSID** during emulation seem biased toward providing new **CLSID** behavior. The server cannot determine if the container is prepared for this nor can the container determine if the server provides the degree of binary compatibility it may require.

The upgraded server should not be registered as the emulator for an old **CLSID** via **CoTreatAsClass**.

Incompatible Upgrades

A component vendor may wish to ship an upgrade that does not meet the criteria of source or binary compatibility. Assuming they want consumers of the old class to make use of their old application code, they should follow these guidelines:

- Give the accompanying type library a new **GUID**. This requires the consumer to manually change their type library reference to the new type library.

- Reuse previous class, interface, and member names where some reasonable mapping exists. Reusing a name where syntax is the same but semantics are different is dangerous since there would be no compiler warning to cause the user to visit the referencing code.

- Change **CLSID/IID**'s anywhere that the original contractual meaning of the class or interfaces is not fully preserved.

- Ensure that the component is capable of reading a persistent image created with an old implementation.

Consumer Obligations for Ensuring Compatibility

The consuming application or component must also follow rules to enable predictable and convenient upgrade behavior:

- All class or interface references in a consuming application should be held and bound in a similar way to make behavior predictable in the face of an upgrade.

For example, class references in code and the control references on control containers should exhibit the same behavior.

- Built applications should reference classes by **CLSID** and interfaces by **IID**. This ensures that the implementation they connect to will meet the expected contractual obligations.

- Application "source" references should be stored as symbolic class and interface names, as resolved through an accompanying type library.

- A reference to the type library itself must also be held, so that symbolic source references can be bound to actual implementations. The type library reference should consist of a **GUID**, **LCID**, and a major.minor version number

- "Normal" rules for connecting to the correct version of a type library should be followed. If the exact version (major.minor) is available, it should be used. If an exact match cannot be found, then a type library with the same **GUID/LCID** and largest version number (which must be greater than the version number of the reference) should be used. If no such library can be found, then the library reference is "broken" and the user must be alerted.

- Running instances constructed from old **CLSID**, **IDispatch::GetTypeInfo** and **IProvideClassInfo** may return type descriptions of the new version's CoClass and interfaces.

- Version-dependent ProgIDs are equivalent to **CLSID** in terms of being a strong contract. They have the advantage of being moderately user-friendly should a class name ever need to be presented to the user. They have the disadvantage of requiring a registry access in order to be dereferenced to their equivalent **CLSID**.

- Version-independent ProgIDs are a very weak contract since there is no correlation with a type library or a particular set of interfaces.

Property Change Notification

OLE controls introduce support for a simple sort of property change notification. Often, it is useful to have controls reflect values stored in some external data source. For example, the user might construct a form that shows column values of a record in a database. The user might then use this form not only to browse database records but also to enter new records or edit records already in the database.

This sort of property binding is modeled as simply moving data into and out of the control's properties, using the normal property access mechanisms. OLE controls define a new mechanism for the control to send notifications when the values of its properties change.

The actual logic for moving values back and forth between the control and the data source, and for monitoring when the two are out of sync with each other, is done externally. The control supports properties as per normal and sends notifications of property changes, but otherwise has no knowledge of any particular property-binding model. This enables a great deal of flexibility regarding property binding.

Typically, the property binding logic is provided by the control's container. It is also possible that some other entity handles property binding.

This architecture intentionally simplifies, as much as possible, the support required of controls to make property binding work, with the goal of keeping the entry cost low, ensuring that most controls support property binding, thus making it much more useful.

Notifications

An object supports property-binding notifications by exposing a connection point that supports the **IPropNotifySink** interface.

```
interface IPropNotifySink : IUnknown
{
    void    OnChanged(DISPID dispid);
    HRESULT OnRequestEdit(DISPID dispid);
};
```

The object may support property binding for a subset of its properties or may support property binding for nearly all its properties. The object describes its properties in its type library, as with OLE Automation today. It indicates which properties are bindable with some new extensions to Type Libraries, which are outlined in the next section.

For each bindable property, the control should call the OnChanged method on all connected **IPropNotifySink** objects whenever the property changes value. This notification is sent after the property change has occurred and the property whose value changed is identified with the dispid parameter.

Note that this notification should be sent whenever the property changes value, no matter what the cause for the change. The property could change value as a result of some bit of user code running (for example, code setting a property value), through interactions with the control's UI (for example, typing text into a TextBox), or by some internal state change (for example, a property changing value due to a change in some related property).

In addition, the control can call the OnRequestEdit method for properties that are about to change value but have not yet changed. This gives sinks attached to the connection point an opportunity to save the original value (by getting the property value from the object). It also gives sinks a chance to veto the property change. If a sink returns the value **S_FALSE**, then the control should cancel the operation that would have changed the property value. For example, if some bit of user code was attempting to set the property value, then the property set function would return an error.

The control should not fire OnRequestEdit for a property unless it can implement the contract fully. The notification must be cancellable and sent in all circumstances before the property changes value. This may be difficult for some properties; in these cases, the control should support only the OnChanged notification for the property.

In some cases, a large number of control properties may be changing at once. In these cases, the control can pass **DISPID_UNKNOWN (= -1)** as the parameter to OnChanged and OnRequestEdit. This special value indicates that some unspecified subset of the control's properties has changed (or is about to change) value. A sink that is looking for notification about a particular property normally assumes that the property is in the set of properties that have changed (or are about to change).

Finally, controls should not send property change notifications as part of their creation process, nor should they send notifications as part of deserialization. Notifications should be sent only for property changes occurring on fullyconstructed and initialized controls. Implicitly, all the control's properties are assumed to have "changed" as part of the startup sequence, so notifications need not be sent.

Type Library Extensions

OLE controls introduces new functionality and, in some cases, this functionality needs to be described statically. In a limited set of cases, OLE controls uses MiscStatus bits to statically describe a control. When more than a single bit is required, the description is exposed with new entries in a Type Library.

In particular, several attributes are added to the Object Description Language (ODL) and corresponding bits are made available in the Type Library produced. The Bindable, RequestEdit, DefaultBind and DisplayBind attributes relate to data-bound objects, which may have one or more properties that can be bound to a field in a database record. The Licensed, Source, Restricted, and Default attributes have also been added.

Attributes of Data-Bound Objects

The Bindable attribute is allowed on a property and indicates that the property supports property binding. In particular, the object sends notifications through OnChanged when the property changes value, as described earlier. The bindable attribute refers to the property as a whole, so it must be specified wherever the property is defined. This sometimes means specifying the attribute on both the property Get description and on the property Set description. The bindable attribute is represented by **FUNCFLAG_FBINDABLE** or **VARFLAG_FBINDABLE**.

The RequestEdit attribute indicates that the property supports the OnRequestEdit notification. The **OnRequestEdit** notification is raised by an object before the property changes value and gives the notificaton sink an opportunity to cancel the change. The property that has the RequestEdit attribute must also have the Bindable attribute. MkTypLib enforces this restriction. The RequestEdit attribute is represented as **FUNCFLAG_FREQUESTEDIT** or **VARFLAG_FREQUESTEDIT**.

The DisplayBind attribute is set on properties the object determines to be displayed to the user as bindable. It is possible for an object to support property binding but not have this attribute. Controls should specify the DisplayBind attribute for those properties that users would typically want to bind to. A property which has the DisplayBind attribute must also have the Bindable attribute. MkTypLib enforces this restriction. The DisplayBind attribute is represented as **FUNCFLAG_FDISPLAYBIND** or **VARFLAG_FDISPLAYBIND**.

The DefaultBind attribute on a property indicates the single bindable property that best represents the object as a whole; for example, the text property of a textbox object. This is used by containers that have a user model that involves binding to an object rather than binding to a property of an object. Containers that allow binding to any property on the object should suggest the DefaultBind property to users as an default choice. A property that has the DefaultBind attribute must also have the Bindable attribute. It is also illegal to specify DefaultBind on more than one property in a dispatch interface. MkTypLib enforces these restrictions. The DefaultBind attribute is represented as **FUNCFLAG_FDEFAULTBIND** or **VARFLAG_FDEFAULTBIND**.

Examples of Data-Binding Attributes

Properties that have any of these data-binding attributes must be specified in function form, as in:

```
[uuid 00000000-0000-0000-0000-123456789012]
dispinterface MyObject
{
    properties:
    methods:
        [id(1), propget, bindable, defaultbind, displaybind]
        long x();

        [id(1), propput, bindable, defaultbind, displaybind]
        void x(long rhs);
}

[uuid 00000000-0000-0000-0000-123456789013]
dispinterface MyObject
{
    properties:
        [id(1), bindable, defaultbind, displaybind]
        long x;
```

```
        methods:
}

[uuid 00000000-0000-0000-0000-123456789014]
interface IMyOtherObject
{
    [id(1), propget, bindable, defaultbind, displaybind]
    long y();

    [id(1), propput, bindable, defaultbind, displaybind]
    void y(long rhs);
}

[uuid 00000000-0000-0000-0000-123456789015]
dispinterface MyOtherObject
{ interface IMyOtherObject }
```

Other Attributes

The Licensed attribute is specified on a coclass, and indicates that its class is licensed, as per the licensing section given earlier. It is represented as **TYPEFLAG_FLICENSED** on the coclass. The ODL syntax is as the following example:

```
[licensed, 00000000-0000-0000-0000-123456789016] coclass Sample
```

The Source attribute is specified on a member of a coclass that is called rather than implemented. That is, it marks an interface that is available on a connection point. Note that there is no corresponding "sink" attribute; any member of a coclass that is not a source is a sink by default. The Source attribute is represented by the presence or absence of **IMPLTYPEFLAG_FSOURCE**.

For example, a class called Sample that implemented an interface called baz and was able to call an interface bar through a connection point might be described with the following ODL:

```
[uuid 00000000-0000-0000-0000-123456789017]
coclass Sample
{
  [source] interface bar;
  interface baz;
}
```

The Default attribute can be specified on one source coclass member and one sink coclass member. It is represented by the presence of **IMPLTYPEFLAG_FDEFAULT**. If no coclass member has the Default attribute, the Default attribute is assigned automatically by MkTypLib to the first member that does not have the restricted attribute. A control SampleBox, with a primary interface Sample and primary event set SampleEvents, would be described with the following ODL:

```
[uuid 00000000-0000-0000-0000-123456789018]
coclass SampleBox
{
  [source, default] dispinterface SampleEvents;
  [default] interface Sample;
}
```

The Restricted attribute is allowed on a member of a coclass and should be placed on any interface or dispatch interface that is not intended for use by a macro programmer. The Restricted attribute is allowed on a member of a coclass, independent of whether the member is a dispatch or other type interface, and independent of whether the member is a sink or source.

It is illegal for a member of a coclass to have both the Restricted and Default attributes. MkTypLib enforces this restriction.

The Restricted attribute existed in OLE version 2.01 but could not be used on a member of a coclass. In all contexts, the presence of the Restricted attribute means "A macro programmer should never see or be able to access this."

The Restricted attribute is represented by the presence or absence of **IMPLTYPEFLAG_FRESTRICTED** and would appear in an ODL script as follows:

```
[uuid 00000000-0000-0000-0000-123456789019]
coclass Sample
{
  [restricted] interface bar;
  interface baz;
}
```

Example of Source, Default, and Restricted Attributes

```
[uuid 00000000-0000-0000-0000-123456789020]
library MyLibrary
{
    [uuid 00000000-0000-0000-0000-123456789021]
    dispinterface ButtonEvents
    {
        void Click(long X, long Y);
    }

    [uuid 00000000-0000-0000-0000-123456789022]
    dispinterface DButton
```

```
    {
        properties:
            BSTR Caption;
        methods:
    }

    [uuid 00000000-0000-0000-0000-123456789023]
    dispinterface DPlumbing
    {
        void Sample();
    }

    [uuid 00000000-0000-0000-0000-123456789024]
    coclass Button
    {
        [source, default] dispinterface ButtonEvents;
        dispinterface DButton; // Implicitly a "sink"
        [restricted] dispinterface DPlumbing; // Implicitly a "sink"
    }

    [uuid 00000000-0000-0000-0000-123456789025]
    coclass MyButtonHandler
    {
        dispinterface ButtonEvents; // Implicitly a "sink" and "default"
        [restricted, source] dispinterface DPlumbing;
    }
}
```

Summary

Table D.6 summarizes the OLE 2.01 attributes.

Table D.6　OLE 2.01 Attributes

Attribute	Allowed On	Effect	Comments
Bindable	Property	The property supports property binding.	Refers to the property as a whole, so it must be specified wherever the property is defined. This may mean specifying the attribute on both the property Get description and on the property Set description. Representations: **FUNCFLAG_FBINDABLE, VARFLAG_FBINDABLE**
Default	Coclass	Indicates that the interface or dispatch interface represents the default for the source or sink.	Representation: **IMPLTYPEFLAG_FDEFAULT**

Table D.6   OLE 2.01 Attributes (*continued*)

Attribute	Allowed On	Effect	Comments
DefaultBind	Property	Indicates the single bindable property that best represents the object. Used by containers having a user model that involves binding to an object rather than binding to a property of an object.	An object can support property binding but not have this attribute. Property having DefaultBind attribute must also have the Bindable attribute. Cannot specify DefaultBind on more than one property in a dispinterface. Representation: **FUNCFLAG_FDEFAULTBIND**, **VARFLAG_FDEFAULTBIND**
DisplayBind	Property	Set on those properties recommended by the object to be displayed to the user as bindable.	An object can support property binding but not have this attribute. The property which has the DisplayBind attribute must also have the Bindable attribute. Representations: **FUNCFLAG_FDISPLAYBIND**, **VARFLAG_FDISPLAYBIND**
Licensed	Coclass	Indicates that the class is licensed.	Representation: **TYPEFLAG_FLICENSED**
RequestEdit	Property	The property supports the OnRequestEdit notification, raised by a property before it is edited.	An object can support property binding but not have this attribute. Representations: **FUNCFLAG_FREQUESTEDITBIND**, **VARFLAG_FREQUESTEDITBIND**
Restricted	Coclass	Prevents the interface or dispatch interfacefrom being used by a macro programmer.	Allowed on a member of a coclass, independent of whether the member is a dispatch or other type interface, and independent of whether the member is a sink or source. A member of a coclass cannot have both the Restricted and Default attributes.
Source	Coclass	Specified on a member of a coclass that is called rather than implemented.	Representation: **IMPTYPEFLAG_FSOURCE**

Property Browsing

OLE controls introduce a new page-based mechanism for property browsing. This enables the same property browsing UI that will be encouraged for Chicago applications. In short, an object provides property pages, each of which allows the user to edit some related set of properties on the object. The system provides a property frame, which shows the property pages that apply to a particular object (or set of objects).

As with the rest of OLE controls, the interactions among an object, its set of property pages, and the system property frame are all conducted through interfaces. This section describes these interfaces.

Specifying Property Pages

An important issue is how a particular object specifies which set of pages should be used to browse the object's properties. An object specifies pages by supporting the **ISpecifyPropertyPages** interface:

```
struct CAUUID
{
    ULONG cElems;
    GUID FAR* pElems;
};

interface ISpecifyPropertyPages : public IUnknown
{
    GetPages(CAUUID * pPages);
};
```

Property pages are objects. Each type of property page defines a new OLE class and has a **CLSID** assigned to it. Creating an instance of the property page is done with **CoCreateInstance**, just as for any any OLE object.

Asking an object what set of property pages should be used to browse it, then, is equivalent to listing the **CLSID**'s for the object's pages. This is done by calling the GetPages method, which returns a counted array (as per OLE Automation) of the **CLSID**'s for the object's pages. To actually create the pages, **CoCreateInstance** is called for each **CLSID**.

Since **CLSID**'s are unique, this mechanism can be used to determine the set of pages that two or more objects share.

Property Pages

Once the set of property pages is determined, property page objects can be created. Each page is required to support the **IPropertyPage** interface. In turn, the property frame provides a page site to each page; the site supports the **IPropertyPageSite** interface. All interactions between the property frame and its pages occur through these two interfaces.

```
struct tagPROPPAGEINFO
{
    size_t cb;
    LPSTR pszTitle;
    SIZE size;
    LPSTR pszDocString;
```

```
        LPSTR pszHelpFile;
        DWORD dwHelpContext;
    };

    interface IPropertyPage : public IUnknown
    {
        SetPageSite(LPPROPERTYPAGESITE pPageSite);
        Activate(HWND hwndParent, LPCRECT rect, BOOL fModal);
        Deactivate(void);
        GetPageInfo(LPPROPPAGEINFO pPageInfo);
        SetObjects(ULONG cObjects, LPUNKNOWN FAR* ppunk);
        Show(UINT nCmdShow);
        Move(LPCRECT prect);
        IsPageDirty(void);
        Apply(void);
        Help(LPCSTR lpszHelpDir);
        TranslateAccelerator(LPMSG lpMsg);
    };
```

The SetPageSite method is called by the property frame after creating the page and passes in the site object that the page should use to communicate with the frame. The frame calls **SetPageSite(NULL)** as part of closing itself down.

The **PROPPAGEINFO** struct provides enough information about the page for the frame to size itself and list the pages it contains, as well as providing help information. This struct is returned by the GetPageInfo method; the strings are allocated by the control.

The frame calls the Activate method to ask the property page to create a window to display itself. The parent window the page should use and the initial rectangle for the page are passed as parameters. The **fModal** parameter lets the page know whether it is being invoked inside a modal property frame. The window should be created visible. The frame calls **Deactivate** to ask the page to destroy the window created by Activate.

The property frame calls the SetObjects method to pass the set of objects being browsed to the page. Note that the page may be passed multiple objects if the container supports property browsing of a multiple selection. Once the page has the set of objects being browsed, it should be able to load the properties of the browsed object into fields on the property page.

The frame calls Show to show or hide the page's window; the page should pass the **nCmdShow** parameter to **ShowWindow**. Similarly, the frame calls **Move** to reposition or resize the page's window.

The IsPageDirty method is used to determine whether the user has done any editing on the page or, in general, whether the page is out of sync with the known state of the browsed object(s). The page should return **S_FALSE** if it hasn't been changed, or **S_OK** if it has been changed.

The page should apply any changes entered into the page back to the browsed object in response to the Apply method. Note that, in general, property pages should use a delayed commit model. That is, instead of applying changes to the browsed object immediately, or when the user leaves the field, the page should wait until its Apply method is called. This enables the object and its pages to function smoothly in different containers, which may have different property browsing models.

The Help method is used to invoke help for the page.

The frame calls the TranslateAccelerator method for each Windows event it receives. This gives the page a chance to implement a keyboard interface.

```
interface IPropertyPageSite : public IUnknown
{
    OnStatusChange(void);
    GetLocaleID(LCID * pLocaleID);
    GetPageContainer(LPUNKNOWN * ppUnk);
};
```

The page interacts with its frame through the **IPropertyPageSite** interface. The page should call the OnStatusChange method whenever its status changes. This will mainly happen when the page's dirty status changes.

The page can request the locale ID currently in use by the container through the GetLocaleID method. A pointer to the property frame can be obtained with GetPageContainer. Note, however, that no interface has been defined that all property frames can be relied on to support; hence, the type of the pointer returned from this method is unknown.

Property Frame

A standard system property frame implementation is provided as part of OLE. It is invoked with the following API:

```
STDAPI OleCreatePropertyFrame(
        HWND hWndOwner,
        UINT x,
        UINT y,
        LPCSTR lpszCaption,
        ULONG cObjects,
        LPUNKNOWN FAR* ppUnk,
        ULONG cPages,
        LPCLSID pPageClsID,
        LCID lcid,
        DWORD dwReserved,
        LPVOID pvReserved);
```

This creates a modal property frame, with UI details defined by the operating system. The **hWndOwner** parameter names the window that should own the property frame dialog, or **NULL** if it has no owner. The **x** and **y** parameters give the screen position, relative to the owner window (or screen, if there is no owner window). The **lpszCaption** parameter is used as the caption for the property frame dialog.

The **ppUnk** parameter gives the list of objects that should be browsed, with **cObjects** giving the count of objects in the array. The **pPageClsID** parameter names the set of pages that should be used, with **cPages** giving the count of pages. If **pPageClsID** is **NULL**, or **cPages** is 0, then the property frame uses **ISpecifyPropertyPages** on the objects to determine which pages should be used.

The **lcid** parameter determines the locale in which the UI will be displayed.

The **dwReserved** and **pvReserved** parameters are in place for future use; they should be set to 0 and **NULL** (respectively) in all current use of the property frame.

Note that other implementations of the property frame are entirely possible. A container application might choose to provide its own frame, to better match the rest of the container's UI. In the long run, however, applications are expected to converge on the standard property browsing UI style introduced with Chicago.

Per-Property Browsing

The earlier sections define a reasonable mechanism for page-based property browsing. Some containers, though, may need to browse individual property values rather than groups of property values. Some level of per-property browsing is possible using only the information in TypeInfo. For example, a container can clearly allow the user to edit an integer-valued property; at a minimum, the set of built-in OLE Automation types can be browsed. In addition, the container can specially treat the standard types defined for OLE controls and provide reasonable editing for properties of type Font, Picture, and others.

However, this approach does not allow any customization. For example, there isn't a mechanism that allows a string-valued property to indicate that it can only legally contain filenames, other than predefining a standard set of such types and building support for them into all per property browsers.

Control writers are expected to define property pages for their controls, and this support is leveraged in the per property browsing case. The interfaces following allow a per property browser to navigate from any particular property to the property page on which it appears.

```
interface IPerPropertyBrowsing
{
    GetDisplayString(DISPID dispid, BSTR * pbstr);
    MapPropertyToPage(DISPID dispid, CLSID * pclsid);

    GetPredefinedStrings( DISPID dispid, CALPOLESTR * pcaStrings,
        CADWORD * pcaCookies);
    GetPredefinedValue( DISPID dispid, DWORD dwCookie, VARIANT *
        pvaValue);
};
```

A control that wants to support nondefault per-property browsing implements **IPerPropertyBrowsing**. If this interface is not provided by a control, then the property browser does the best it can with the information in TypeInfo.

The control normally provides custom editing for some of its properties and relies on the external property browser to provide default editing for the rest. The GetDisplayString method should return **S_FALSE** for all properties for which the property browser's default string is acceptable. For custom-edited properties, GetDisplayString returns the string that should be displayed in the property browsing grid. For example, for a picture-valued property currently holding a bitmap, GetDisplayString might return the string "(Picture - Bitmap)". A property browser is expected to show a reasonable string for object-valued properties; the string shown might be the name of the CoClass or CoType, or of the primary dispatch interface on the object. Note that the caller can set **pbstr** to **NULL**, if it is only interested on whether a custom string is available, but not in the actual value.

The page that matches a particular property is returned by MapPropertyToPage. If no page is available for a particular property, then this method should return **CTL_E_NOPAGEAVAILABLE**. If a page is available, and should or must be used to edit the property, this method returns **S_FALSE**. If a page is available, but direct editing is also feasible, then **S_OK** is returned. The last two values are distinguished to accommodate properties like filenames, which are of a well-known type (string) but require specialized property editing.

Grids are not expected to allow direct editing of custom display strings; instead, an ellipsis button (or the equivalent) is provided. When the button is pushed, the grid invokes the standard modal property page frame. Note that the grid can explicitly pass in the single matching page **CLSID** to **OleCreatePropertyFrame**. This overrides the normal use of **ISpecifyPropertyPages**, namely to compute the set of pages to show, if it wants to show only the page on which the property appears.

The GetPredefinedStrings and GetPredefinedValues methods allow the object to define a set of legal display strings and values that the caller can use to populate a drop-down list box. These methods should return **CTL_E_NOSTRINGSAVAILABLE** if no list of legal strings is available.

An interface **IPropertyPage2** is defined that allows the frame to navigate to the proper property within a page:

```
interface IPropertyPage2 : public IPropertyPage
{
    EditProperty(DISPID dispid);
};
```

Implementing this interface and method is optional for property pages; pages can return **E_NOTIMPL**, in which case the focus will set to the first control on the page. Otherwise, the page moves the focus to the matching control on the page.

The **OleCreatePropertyFrameIndirect** API allows the initial page and property to to be defined when the property frame is invoked.

```
struct OCPFIPARAMS
{
    ULONG     cbStructSize;
    HWND      hWndOwner;
    int    x;
    int    y;
    LPSTR     szCaption;
    ULONG     cObjects;
    IUnknown **     ppUnk;
    ULONG     cPages;
    CLSID *     pPages;
    LCID    lcid;
    DISPID     dispidInitialProperty;
};

STDAPI OleCreatePropertyFrameIndirect(OCPFIPARAMS * pParams);
```

All members of the **OCPFIPARAMS** struct, except the last, map to parameters in **OleCreatePropertyFrame**. The first member gives the size of the struct. Use the size to mark new versions of the struct, which adds new parameters to the call.

The **dispidInitialProperty** member identifies which property should be browsed initially. The frame first maps the property given to the proper page with MapPropertyToPage, then moves the focus to the matching control with EditProperty. If **DISPID_UNKNOWN** is passed for **dispidInitialProperty**, then defaults are used for the initial page and property. Note that **dispidInitialProperty** = 0 is a legal value. It indicates that the Value property of the control should be edited and is not equivalent to **DISPID_UNKNOWN**.

Miscellaneous

Controls can be embedded in old-style OLE 2 compound document containers that were written long before OLE controls were introduced and which know nothing about property browsing. However, for many controls, the interesting capabilities of the control are provided solely through properties. Not allowing the user to set properties severely restricts the usefulness of controls in old-style containers.

To address this scenario, a new standard OLE Verb is introduced that invokes the modal system property browser on the control. Controls should name this verb "Properties...," and list it with their other verbs. Well-behaved OLE 2 containers list the verb with the other verbs exposed by the control, so the user can access the properties dialog for a control even when the control is embedded in an old-style container.

```
#define OLEIVERB_PROPERTIES    (-7L)
```

Summary of OLE Controls Architecture

OLE Custom Controls is a set of extensions to the existing OLE 2 compound document specifications. It builds on the concepts of embedded objects, in-place activation, and OLE Automation to meet the specific interaction requirements between controls and control container. Controls are more than just editable embedded objects. They transform end-user events, like mouse clicks and keystrokes, into programmatic notifications to the container, which can use those transformed events to execute other code.

A control is a standard embedded object capable of in-place activation with several interfaces implemented in an in-process server DLL. In addition to the standard interfaces, **IOleObject**, **IDataObject**, **IViewObject**, **IPersistStorage**, and **IOleInPlaceActiveObject** (**IOleCache** is optional), the control also implements **IPersistStream** and **IDispatch** interfaces to handle the control's properties and methods, and the new interfaces **IOleControl**, **IConnectionPointContainer**, and **IConnectionPoint**, which handle control mnemonics and events. All of these interfaces combined meet all the needs of any control, even those that currently exist in Windows as simple window classes.

A control container is a standard in-place capable embedded object container with the **IOleClientSite**, **IOleIn-PlaceSite**, and **IAdviseSink** interfaces on its site objects, **IOleInPlaceUIWindow** on its document objects, and **IOleInPlaceFrame** on its frame object. To work properly with controls, the container also implements an **IDispatch** for ambient properties and an **IDispatch** for control events on its sites, along with the new **IControlSite** interface that serves as a notification sink for changes in a control's mnemonics.

All these interfaces create the necessary standard mechanisms through which an arbitrary control container can use any arbitrary control to create any type of Windows application. Obviously, there is a lot of work involved in implementing all these interfaces, so the Microsoft Foundation Class Library includes a Control Wizard to simplify the process of writing a control, by automatically giving you all the compound document code you need. All you have to do is add a few customizations where necessary, and you have a great new control that will serve you now and well into the future.

Index

H

Handle property 366
HeadingFont property
    adding 162
    modification to control code 162
Height property 366
Help
    method 407
    option for generating files 105
hFont property 363
Hit testing, usage in FlashColor property 50
hPal property 366

I

IClassFactory, interface extension 388
IClassFactory2, licensing functions 171
IConnectionPointContainer
    Advise/Unadvise methods 329
    aggregation controls 333
    EnumConnectionPoints method 328
    GetConnectionContainer method 329
    GetConnectionInterface method 328
    usage 326
IDispatch
    additional variant types 370
    exposing methods 325
    GetLicInfo method 388
    GetTypeInfo method 325
IFontDisp 363
IFontNotification 164
IgnoreApply member function
    COlePropertyPage class 244
IMPLEMENT_OLECREATE_EX macro 283
IMPLEMENT_OLETYPELIB macro 283
Implementing read- and write-only properties 141
In-place active objects 350
Inactive controls, z-ordering by control container 351
Inactive state 101, 117
InCircle function 50–51
Incompatible upgrades, guidelines 396
InitializeFont member function
    CFontHolder class 189
InitializeIIDs member function
    COleControl class 215
InitNew method 357
InPlaceActive method, called by control 344
Insert Object dialog box, list contents 385
Insertable key, usage of in a control 384
Interfaces
    incoming 325
    outgoing 325
    primary 325

Interlocking events, firing 333
InternalGetFont member function
    COleControl class 159, 215
InternalGetText member function
    accessing Caption property 65
    COleControl class 215
InvalidateControl member function
    COleControl class 215
Invisible at runtime option 106
IOleControl
    described 343
    FreezeEvents method 344
    interface described 343
    OnAmbientChanged method 344
IOleControlSite
    described 343
    GetExtendedControl method 345
    InPlaceActive method 344
    OnFocus method 345
IOleDispatch, accessing control properties 324
IPerPropertyBrowsing
    GetDisplayString method 409
    GetPreDefinedStrings method 409
    GetPreDefinedValues method 409
    interface description 409
    MapPropertyToPage method 409
IPersistStorage
    interaction with IPersistStreamInit 358
    usage 356
IPersistStreamInit
    analog for InitNew method 357
    interaction with IPersistStorage 358
    interface description 357
    usage by control 357
IPicture
    CurDC property 366
    interface description 365
    SelectPicture method 366
IPropertyNotifySink, implementation 165
IPropertyPage
    Activate method 406
    Apply method 407
    described 405
    Help method 407
    interface description 405
    IsPageDirty method 406
    SetObjects method 406
    SetPageSite method 406
    Show method 406
    TranslateAccelerator method 407
IPropertyPage2
    EditProperty method 410
    interface description 410
IPropertyPageSite 405

R

S

T

Contributors to the
Microsoft OLE Control Developer's Kit

Jim Bolland, Writer
Frank Crockett, Writer
Mike Eddy, Production
Steve Murray, Editor
Bill Nolan, Writer